The Nuremberg S   , 1945-1958

Atrocity, Law, and History

Based on extensive archival research, this book offers the first historical examination of the arrest, trial, and punishment of the leaders of the SS-Einsatzgruppen – the mobile security and killing units employed by the Nazis in their racial war on the eastern front. Sent to the Soviet Union in the summer of 1941, four units of Einsatzgruppen, along with reinforcements, murdered approximately 1 million Soviet civilians in open air shootings and in gas vans and, in 1947, twenty-four leaders of these units were indicted for crimes against humanity and war crimes for their part in the murders. In addition to describing the legal proceedings that held these men accountable, this book also examines recent historiographical trends and perpetrator paradigms and expounds on such contested issues as the timing and genesis of the Final Solution, the perpetrators' route to crime, and their motivation for killing, as well as discussing the tensions between law and history.

Hilary Earl is Assistant Professor of History at Nipissing University, North Bay, Ontario, Canada. Her research has been featured in several collections, including *Lessons and Legacies IV* (2004), *Secret Intelligence and the Holocaust* (2006), and *Biography between Structure and Agency: Central European Lives in International Historiography* (2008). Her most recent project, *The Genocide Paradox: Prosecuting Genocide from Nuremberg to The Hague,* is a historical examination of the legal outcomes of war crimes trials from the post–World War II period through the trials conducted by the International Criminal Tribunals for the former Yugoslavia. She has received fellowships from the Holocaust Educational Foundation, the Center for Advanced Holocaust Studies at the United States Holocaust Memorial Museum, the Leonard and Kathleen O'Brien Humanitarian Trust, and the Joint Initiative for German and European Studies.

"Earl has written a highly readable, impeccably researched, and richly informative book about an important and insufficiently studied trial. A timely and valuable contribution."

– Lawrence Douglas, Amherst College, and author of *The Memory of Judgment: Making Law and History in the Trials of the Holocaust*

"This is a compelling, well-written, and well-researched book. In this imaginative and important study, Hilary Earl both tells the story of the Nuremberg Einsatzgruppen Trial, the 'biggest murder trial in history,' and paints a fascinating collective portrait of some of history's biggest killers. In the Einsatzgruppen Trial, the Americans prosecuted twenty-four members of the leadership corps of the SS-Einsatzgruppen, the mobile killing squads that initiated the Final Solution in the Soviet Union. In a world where the concept of genocide was as yet ill defined, prosecuting racialized mass murder proved a daunting challenge. Earl provides a compelling account of how both the prosecution and the defense responded to this challenge in the course of the trial. At the same time, she tells us a great deal about the men who perpetrated some of the most brutal crimes of the Holocaust: who they were, what their backgrounds were, and what their motives might have been. Along the way, she sheds new light on the question of whether and when Hitler might have issued a formal order to initiate the Final Solution."

– Devin O. Pendas, Boston College

"Scholars in Holocaust studies have long understood more about the broad mechanics of mass murder than about the men who carried it out. Hilary Earl's groundbreaking work is a corrective to that understanding in directly focusing our attention on the actions of the leaders of the SS-Einsatzgruppen and thoroughly tracing their subsequent arrest, trial, and punishment. Moreover, she does so in a uniquely interdisciplinary way, drawing – accurately and insightfully – on perspectives from a wide range of historical, social scientific, legal, and humanistic sources to offer a mature and nuanced comprehension of what all too often is passed off as incomprehensible."

– James Waller, Auschwitz Institute for Peace and Reconciliation

The Nuremberg SS-Einsatzgruppen Trial, 1945–1958

Atrocity, Law, and History

HILARY EARL

Nipissing University

CAMBRIDGE
UNIVERSITY PRESS

CAMBRIDGE UNIVERSITY PRESS
Cambridge, New York, Melbourne, Madrid, Cape Town, Singapore,
São Paulo, Delhi, Dubai, Tokyo, Mexico City

Cambridge University Press
32 Avenue of the Americas, New York, NY 10013-2473, USA

www.cambridge.org
Information on this title: www.cambridge.org/9780521178686

First published 2009
Reprinted 2010 (twice)
First paperback edition 2010

A catalog record for this publication is available from the British Library.

Library of Congress Cataloging in Publication Data

Earl, Hilary Camille, 1963–
The Nuremberg SS-Einsatzgruppen trial, 1945–1958 : atrocity, law, and history / Hilary Earl.
p.   cm.
Includes bibliographical references and index.
ISBN 978-0-521-45608-1 (hardback)
1. Einsatzgruppen Trial, Nuremberg, Germany, 1947–1948. 2. War crime trials—Germany.
3. World War, 1939–1945—Atrocities. 4. Nationalsozialistische Deutsche Arbeiter-Partei.
Schutzstaffel. Sicherheitsdienst. 5. Holocaust, Jewish (1939–1945)—Soviet Union.
6. Holocaust, Jewish (1939–1945)—Poland. 7. Germany—History—1933–1945. I. Title.
KZ1179.E36E37   2009
341.6'090268 – dc22   2008044211

ISBN 978-0-521-45608-1 Hardback
ISBN 978-0-521-17868-6 Paperback

For my parents, John and Barbara Earl

Contents

Illustrations and Tables

Illustrations

Tables

Abbreviations

CCL10	Control Council Law No. 10
CIC	Counter Intelligence Corps
HICOG	The Office of the American High Commissioner for Germany
IMT	International Military Tribunal
JA	Judge Advocate
JAD	Judge Advocate Division
JAG	Judge Advocate General
JCS	Joint Chiefs of Staff
Kripo	*Kriminalpolizei* or Criminal Police
NMT	Nuremberg Military Tribunals
NO	Nazi Organizations
OCCPAC	Office of the Chief of Counsel for the Prosecution of Axis Criminality
OCCWC	Office of the Chief of Counsel for War Crimes
OKW	Oberkommando der Wehrmacht
OMGUS	The Office of the Military Government, United States
RSHA	*Reichssicherheitspolitzei*
RuSHA	*Rasse- und Siedlungshauptamt*
SD	*Sicherheitsdienst*
Sipo	*Sicherheitspolizei*
USHMM	United States Holocaust Memorial Museum
WCB	War Crimes Branch
WCR	War Crimes Records

Acknowledgments

Scholarly work is always the result of more than the efforts of the author; my work is no exception. I am profoundly grateful to my family, friends, and colleagues, for their support and encouragement of this project.

This book began as a dissertation at the University of Toronto, under the supervision of Michael Marrus. His guidance and supervision during the early phase of the project was invaluable. My doctoral committee members, Jacques Kornberg, Jim Retallack, and Ron Pruessen, offered useful and timely counsel, and Peter Black, the Chief Historian of the Center for Advanced Holocaust Studies at the USHMM, acted as the outside examiner and continues to offer his expertise and friendship.

The research for this project took me to thirteen different archives in the United States and Germany. I am indebted to each and every staff member, librarian, and archivist who helped in my endeavors. I am particularly grateful to Benjamin Ferencz, who shared his recollections about his experiences at Nuremberg and whose insight added flavor to the narrative, and to Henry Lea, a Nuremberg translator and Professor Emeritus at University of Massachusetts, Amherst, who read the manuscript from cover to cover and then met with me to discuss his recollections of the trial. Mr. Spinelli, the archivist at the Gumberg Library at Duquesne University gave me unlimited access to Michael Musmanno's papers, and, with Al Lawson's help, I filled in some of the gaps of Musmanno's early career.

The research and writing of this book was made possible with the financial assistance of a number of organizations and institutions. Foremost among these was the University of Toronto, the O'Brien Humanitarian Trust, and the Visiting Scholars Program of the Center for Advanced Holocaust Studies at the United States Holocaust Memorial Museum in Washington, DC. I must also thank the Holocaust Educational Foundation, especially Zev Weiss, who has liberally supported my research over the years and allowed me to test my ideas in a variety of settings. The Province of New Brunswick, the Joint Initiative for German/European Studies, and York University have also contributed. Finally, my home institution, Nipissing University, has been exceptionally generous in their support and funding of this project.

I am grateful to my many friends and colleagues for their assistance during the various stages of writing this book. I am especially indebted to Gerhard Weinberg, whose daily talks while I was a Fellow at the CAHS were particularly helpful, for his continuing support of my work. He is a true mentor. I would also like to thank Simone Gigliotti and Alex Rossino for their constant encouragement, critical assessments, and patience, and Richard Steigmann-Gall and Carla Shapiro, who, for more than a decade, have been faithful friends and colleagues. Special thanks go to the organizers and participants of the USHMM workshop on the Subsequent Nuremberg Trials I attended in July 2008, in particular to Robert Ehrenreich and Suzanne Brown-Fleming of the University Programs of the CAHS for funding the workshop and especially to Alexa Stiller and Kim Priemel for organizing and leading it. The expertise of Valerie Hébert, Lawrence Douglas, Jan Schulte, Dirk Poppmann, Jonathan Bush, and Paul Weindling helped me to finalize my ideas for this book. Finally, I must thank Stephen Tyas for freely sharing his knowledge of the Einsatzgruppen and for his willingness to engage in endless transatlantic discussions about Otto Ohlendorf.

Many friends have been unfailingly kind and supportive, especially Mitchell Webster, whose passion for this subject sometimes outweighs my own. Eva Plach, Blaine Chiasson, and Ronda Ward have been with me from the beginning of graduate school, and my friends Joe Savoie, Paul Salsman, Maureen Allain, Niole Vytas, and Alasdair Scott helped make Toronto a great place to live and work. At York University, Myra Rutherdale and Carolyn Podruchny befriended me immediately, as did George Urbaniak, Steve Connor, and Erich Haberer at Wilfrid Laurier. Various other scholars have helped me along the way by answering questions I couldn't answer on my own, including Doris Bergen, Christopher Browning, Jürgen Förster, Jeffrey Herf, Michael Kater, Konrad Kweit, Jürgen Matthäus, Devin Pendas, Dan Rogers, Phil Rutherford, Jim Waller, and Herb Ziegler. Special thanks to my family in the United States: Mary Wray and Tony and Pat Kostreba, who always ensured I had a roof over my head. Last, but not at all least, I owe special thanks to my colleagues at Nipissing University: Katrina Srigley, Gordon Morrell, Derek Neal, Gillian McCann, and Anne Clendinning especially are the most supportive friends a person could have.

Most of all, I extend special gratitude and love to my family: to my brother Jack and his family, who have always encouraged me, and to my sister Sarah, who shared her own expertise by reading and commenting on much of this book. She, my brother, and my parents, John and Barbara Earl, have always been my biggest cheerleaders and supported me in ways only a family can. I especially want to thank my father, John Earl, without whose generosity of spirit and time I might never have started this project, let alone finished it. He has always been my inspiration.

Selections from Chapters Two and Four are reprinted in significantly revised form with permission from Northwestern University Press, Enigma Books, and Berghahn Books.

Introduction

Just after midnight on the night of June 7, 1951, five men – Otto Ohlendorf, Paul Blobel, Werner Braune, Erich Naumann, and Oswald Pohl – were executed for crimes against humanity at Landsberg war crimes prison in Landsberg-am-Lech, Bavaria, southern Germany. The five executions took a little less than two hours and marked the conclusion of an international legal process begun by the Americans in the summer of 1945. In the 6 years since the end of the war, the Palace of Justice at Nuremberg had housed a number of high-profile war crimes trials; the most renowned was the International Military Tribunal (IMT) in which twenty-two major Nazi war criminals, including Hermann Göring and Albert Speer, were tried by the Allies in the first international court.[1] Albeit the most well-known, the IMT was but the first of thirteen so-called Nuremberg war crimes trials that covered an array of crimes not limited to either soldiers or the conduct of the war. Following the IMT, between 1946 and 1949, there were 12 additional Nuremberg trials or NMT, prosecuted by the Americans alone. The subject of this book is one of these trials, Case 9 against Otto Ohlendorf and the SS-*Einsatzgruppen* leaders, officially titled: "The United States of America v. Otto Ohlendorf et al.," more commonly known as the *Einsatzgruppen* case.[2] The reference to "military" is confusing and somewhat of a misnomer

---

[1] Important works on the IMT include: Whitney Harris, *Tyranny on Trial: The Evidence at Nuremberg* (New York, 1954); Wilbourn E. Benton and Georg Grimm (eds.), *German Views of the War Crimes Trials* (Dallas, 1955); Joe Heydecker and Johannes Leeb, *Der Nürnberger Prozeß* (Cologne, 1958); Robert Kempner, *Das Dritte Reich im Kreuzverhör. Aus den unveröffentlichten Vernehmungsprotokollen des Anklägers Robert M.W. Kempner* (Munich, 1969); Bradley F. Smith, *Reaching Judgment at Nuremberg* (New York, 1977); Robert Conot, *Justice at Nuremberg* (New York, 1983); Ann Tusa and John Tusa, *The Nuremberg Trial* (London, 1983); and Telford Taylor, *Anatomy of the Nuremberg Trials: A Personal Memoir* (Boston, 1992).

[2] The trial was referred to as the Ohlendorf case because Ohlendorf was the primary defendant. The trial transcript is available from the U.S. National Archives Records and Administration,

as this trial and the eleven other NMT were conducted in civilian, not military courts. Confusion derives from the fact that the governing body in Germany between October 1946 and April 1949 was the United States military government (OMGUS), and, hence, they were responsible for overseeing the trials. Even though the tribunals were composed of civilian judges, the Americans preferred to call the tribunals "military" rather than "occupational." The NMT should not be confused with the proceedings conducted by the United States Military, which were bona fide military trials, held in military courts, against military personnel.[3] The NMT were part of the American plan to punish members of the Nazi hierarchy and educate Germans about the criminal and inhumane behavior of their leadership, as well as to assist in the denazification and democratization of Germany. It was believed that if Germans witnessed liberal democratic justice in action – the underpinning of a functioning and healthy democracy – they would eschew their authoritarian tendencies and embrace democracy, its principles, and practice. Nuremberg, it could be argued, was the first example of transitional justice. The American trials were held after the major German war criminals had been tried before the IMT at Nuremberg and, hence, became known as the "Subsequent Nuremberg proceedings."[4]

In the NMT, the Americans used legal precedents set during the IMT proceedings to try a variety of high- and mid-ranking Nazi civilian and military war criminals. Under these laws, the United States indicted 185 individuals in 12 cases. Four of the defendants committed suicide before they could be tried, and an additional four were judged too sick to stand trial. Thus, only 177 individuals were brought before the courts. Of these, thirty-five defendants were acquitted, twenty-four were sentenced to death, and twenty were sentenced to life in prison, whereas the majority, ninety-eight, were sentenced to prison terms ranging from eighteen months to twenty years. The average sentence for those convicted was 10 years.[5]

At war's end, historians estimate that 8 million Germans were members of the Nazi party; needless to say, it was impossible to investigate all of these people, let alone prosecute them in individual trials. How then did the

Microfilm Publication M895, *The United States of America v. Otto Ohlendorf et al.*, 38 rolls (from here forward simply *Trial*, roll, page, or frame). An abridged version of the trial is published as *Trials of War Criminals before the Nuernberg Military Tribunals under Control Council Law No. 10*, vol. 4 (Washington, 1951; hereafter *TWC*). Also published by NARA is a comprehensive finding aid to the trial, referred to as "Special List No. 42," John Mendelsohn (ed.), *Nuernberg. War Crimes Trial Records of Case 9: United States of America v. Otto Ohlendorf et al.* (Washington, 1978).
[3] See n. 129. For a complete history of the twelve Subsequent trials see the American Chief of Counsel, Telford Taylor, *Final Report to the Secretary of the Army on the Nuernberg War Crimes Trials under Control Council Law No. 10* (Washington, 1949).
[4] In addition to being called the Subsequent Nuremberg proceedings, these trials are also referred to as the Subsequent Nuremberg trials or simply the Subsequent trials or proceedings or the NMT. All of these variations are used throughout.
[5] Taylor, *Final Report*, 90–93.

Americans decide which individuals to indict? Telford Taylor, the American lawyer in charge of organizing the NMT, decided that each trial should comprise individuals who represented a particular aspect of the Nazi system. In essence, he wanted to select representative samples from the worst-offending Nazi groups.[6] Within these broadly defined groups, defendants were selected for prosecution based on evidence American researchers had unearthed accidentally or in targeted investigations. The groups investigated and tried included: Nazi doctors who had conducted medical experiments on the inmates of death and concentration camps and who had participated in the murder of the mentally ill in the so-called euthanasia program (Case 1); Field Marshal Erhard Milch, who was involved in the slave labor program (Case 2); leading judicial figures from Nazi Germany (Case 3); those involved in the administration of the concentration camp system, such as *Waffen SS* General Oswald Pohl (Case 4); representatives of three of the major industrial combines – Flick, IG Farben, and Krupp – whose companies helped advance the war through the criminal utilization of slave labor (Cases 5, 6, and 10); representatives of the *Wehrmacht* involved in the murder of civilians (Case 7); representatives of the *Rasse- und Siedlungshauptamt* or Race and Resettlement Main Office (RuSHA) who had been involved in the deportation and murder of Jews from Poland and Western Europe (Case 8); the leaders of the *Einsatzgruppen* responsible for the mass murder of Soviet Jewry (Case 9); a catch-all trial of government officials involved in the design and implementation of the racial laws, aryanization of Jewish agriculture, and the confiscation of Jewish property (Case 11); and finally, officers of the German High Command who violated the military laws of war, especially with regard to the war on the eastern front (Case 12).[7] The charges were far from limited to wartime transgressions; in fact, most of the charges dealt with crimes that spanned the entire life of the regime. The Americans tried fewer than 200 individuals in these 12 trials, but, because of their scope, the Subsequent Nuremberg trials remain, as one historian has observed, "the single most concerted prosecution effort" against Nazi criminals in the postwar period.[8]

The Subsequent trials involve the prosecution of captured Nazi war criminals, who in the historiography of the Holocaust and the Third Reich are referred to as "perpetrators." This book deals specifically with one group of

---

[6] Taylor, *ibid.*, 106–161 identified five groups for trial: doctors and lawyers; the SS and police; industrialists and financiers; leading military personnel; and government ministers.

[7] The transcripts of the 12 NMT are available on microfilm RG 238, from the National Archives of the United States. The proceedings of the trials are published in abridged form as *Trials of War Criminals before the Nuernberg Military Tribunals under Control Council Law No. 10*, 15 volumes (Washington, 1951, hereafter *TWC*), sometimes referred to as "the green series."

[8] Dick de Mildt, *In the Name of the People: Perpetrators of Genocide in the Reflection of their Post-War Prosecution in West Germany. The 'Euthanasia' and 'Aktion Reinhard' Trial Cases* (The Hague, 1996), 19.

perpetrators, elite members of the SS known as the *Einsatzgruppen*. Translated, *Einsatzgruppen* literally means "special groups," but, in the context of the Third Reich, it means "mobile security and killing units." The *Einsatzgruppen* were special paramilitary task forces (not trained military men) of the SS and police, originally formed in 1938 to operate as the vanguard of a security-police presence in the annexed territories of Austria and Bohemia-Moravia. Further units were then created one year later for action in the Polish campaign, during which *Einsatzgruppen* personnel initiated the first large-scale killing operation of the war directed against Poland's educated elite and leading social and political classes.[9] Although the focus of *Einsatzgruppen* activities changed over time to incorporate mass murder in ever greater measure, their security and intelligence-gathering functions remained constant throughout the period from 1938 to their deployment in the Soviet Union in 1941, when German policy makers expanded their activities to include the wholesale murder of Soviet Jews.[10] At the beginning of Operation Barbarossa, in June 1941, these motorized units of the SS were formed into four groups designated A, B, C, and D, and were officially assigned the task of providing security for German troops in areas behind the front line.[11] Neither the leadership cadre nor regular members of the mobile security units received much in the way of formal military training, highlighting the more political nature of their assignment. Whereas the *Einsatzgruppen* of the Security Police and Security Service operated under the tactical command of the German army in Russia, in reality they were mobile field offices of the *Reichssicherheitspolitzei* or RSHA and, therefore, their leaders took their orders from Heydrich, the organization's chief.[12] In practice, their principal

---

[9] For a discussion of the early activities of the *Einsatzgruppen* in Austria and Czechoslovakia, see Helmut Krausnick, *Hitlers Einsatzgruppen: Die Truppe des Weltanschauungskrieges, 1938–1942* (Frankfurt, 1993). For a discussion of the *Einsatzgruppen*'s activities in Poland, see Alexander Rossino, *Hitler Strikes Poland: Blitzkrieg, Ideology, and Atrocity* (Lawrence, 2003).

[10] The literature on the role of the *Einsatzgruppen* in the Final Solution is vast. Examples include: Raul Hilberg, *The Destruction of the European Jews*, 3 vols. (1961); Ralf Ogorreck, *Die Einsatzgruppen und die Genesis der Endlösung* (Berlin, 1996); Peter Longerich, *Politik der Vernichtung: Eine Gesamtdarstellung der nationalsozialistischen Judenverfolgung* (Munich, 1998); Peter Klein (ed.), *Die Einsatzgruppen in der besetzten Sowjetunion 1941/42. Die Tätigkeits-und Langeberichte des Chefs der Sicherheitspolizei und des SD* (Berlin, 1997); Helmut Krausnick and Hans-Heinrich Wilhelm, *Die Truppe des Weltanschauungskrieges: die Einsatzgruppen der Sicherheitspolizei und des SD, 1938–1942* (1981); and Andrej Angrick, *Besatzungspolitik und Massenmord. Die Einsatzgruppe D in der südlichen Sowjetunion 1941–1943* (Hamburg, 2003).

[11] For a discussion of the cooperation between the Wehrmacht and the *Einsatzgruppen*, see Christian Streit, *Keine Kameraden. Die Wehrmacht und die sowjeischen Kriegsgefangenen 1941–1945* (Bonn, 1991).

[12] For instance, 10 defendants from the *Einsatzgruppen* trial came from the various agencies of the RSHA including: Ohlendorf, Jost, Sandberger, Seibert, Schulz, Six, Braune, Hausmann, Schubert, and Haensch.

task was security, which in the context of Operation Barbarossa meant not only intelligence-gathering and protection from partisan attacks, but also the elimination of perceived political and racial enemies of the Reich, particularly Soviet Jews and communists, the mentally ill, the infirm, and Gypsies. To cover a larger geographic area, the *Einsatzgruppen* were divided into formations called *Sonderkommandos* and *Einsatzkommandos*. These subcommands then frequently divided into smaller units called *Teilkommandos* and *Vorkommandos*. What did these groups do?

One month before they were deployed, the *Einsatzgruppen* were assembled at Pretzsch, a small German town on the Elbe River bordering Soviet territory where a training school for police was located. Here, the men were briefed about their assignments (what they were told is a matter of debate among historians of the Third Reich and Holocaust and will be dealt with later in the book) and given some rudimentary training.[13] The men were then allocated to one of the four mobile security units and each one of these was assigned to work with an army group. Each army group was responsible for conquering a particular geographic region of the western Soviet Union. *Einsatzgruppe* A, led by Franz Walter Stahlecker and, later, Heinz Jost, was assigned to Army Group North and operated in and around Lithuania, Latvia and Estonia. *Einsatzgruppe* B, led by Arthur Nebe and, later, Erich Naumann, was assigned to Army Group Centre and it operated in and around the area of Minsk. *Einsatzgruppe* C, led by Otto Rasch, was attached to Army Group South that operated in Ukraine. Finally, *Einsatzgruppe* D, led by Otto Ohlendorf, was assigned to the Eleventh Army that operated in and around the Crimea. The *Einsatzgruppen* joined the invasion of the Soviet Union on June 22, 1941, and almost immediately began to murder civilians.[14] For the first six to eight weeks of the campaign, the mobile units, with a few exceptions, limited their killing to communist functionaries, Jewish men, Gypsies, and, occasionally, the infirm. Beginning in August, however, their targeted killing escalated into a full-scale genocidal campaign against Soviet Jewry. Their role as killers of civilians, particularly Soviet Jews, has led many to refer to the *Einsatzgruppen* as "mobile killing units."[15]

[13] The debate revolves around the issue of whether or not the *Einsatzgruppen* were briefed on their extra-military task and whom they would target and when. The issue is dealt with at length in Chapter 5.
[14] For first-hand accounts of the atrocities, see, Joshua Rubenstein and Ilya Altman (eds.), *The Unknown Black Book: The Holocaust in the German-Occupied Soviet Territories* (Bloomington, 2008).
[15] Nuremberg helped to create the impression that the sole task of the *Einsatzgruppen* was killing. Although it is true that one of the main functions of these groups was killing, killing was part of the larger intelligence and security work that was at the heart of the original *Einsatzgruppen* formations. For the purpose of this work the terms "mobile killing unit," "mobile security unit," and "mobile security and killing unit" will be used.

After August 1941, when killing operations had expanded and civilians were being shot in large numbers, the *modus operandi* of all four *Einsatzgruppen* was remarkably consistent. Once the German army had cleared an area, one of the mobile killing units would immediately enter the sector, round up the Jews and other civilians targeted for murder, rob them of their belongings, and, finally, kill them in open-air shootings. Initially the murders were carried out in public, but because this endangered security, the murder sites were soon moved to more secluded areas, usually outside of towns. The victims would be led to a collection point from where they were then taken in groups of between ten and fifty (more in the case of the Babi Yar massacre) to a grave where they were told to strip off their clothing. One of three methods of execution was then employed. Some group leaders preferred to have the Jewish victims line up on the edge of the grave and have "specialists" shoot them in the back of the neck.[16] Ohlendorf disliked this method of execution and, instead, had his men shoot as a group from a distance, more like a military firing squad, which helped minimize individual responsibility. Still other commanders had victims lie face down at the bottom of the grave where the victims would be shot from above. Once the victims were dead, another group would be forced to lie on top of them. They, too, were then shot. Because many Jews escaped the initial roundups, especially if they received prior warning that the Germans were advancing, the mobile units would frequently return to an area more than once to ensure that they captured and killed all of a community's Jews. Raul Hilberg estimates that of the 5 million Jews living in Soviet territory in June 1941, as many as 1.5 million either escaped from the advancing German forces or were evacuated further east.[17] Despite such evasions, the four units of the *Einsatzgruppen*, along with reinforcements, rounded up and murdered on average 100,000 people per month from July 1941 to July 1942.[18]

Although the massacre of Jews by shooting proved highly effective in terms of the large numbers killed, it had distinct disadvantages as a method of mass murder. For the perpetrators, such massacres caused considerable psychological stress, which could not always be overcome. Some of the men could only cope with their job by consuming large quantities of alcohol and others had nervous breakdowns. It was not that they had any great moral objection to what they were doing in theory, but, in practice, shooting women and children at close range took its toll on the shooters. Himmler was well aware of this situation. He had visited the site of a mass shooting

---

[16] These shooters were not specialists in the sense that they were trained to shoot civilians in the back of the neck. They were "specialists" in the sense that killing individuals was their singular job.

[17] Hilberg, *Destruction*, 291–295. Hilberg's figure of 5 million includes nearly 1.5 million Jews residing in former Polish territory annexed by the Soviet Union in 1939.

[18] *Ibid.*, 317.

in Minsk in the late summer of 1941 and had allegedly fainted when blood landed on his face during one execution. Shaken by the incident, he later was to have remarked that shooting was not the most "humane" and "rational" method of mass killing. Of course, he was not thinking of the victims, but rather the perpetrators. In Himmler's view, an alternate method of mass murder was needed that could still liquidate large numbers of people quickly, but would also be psychologically easier on the men of the killing units.

One solution was the gas van. The use of poison gas had already been tested in the autumn of 1941 on Soviet prisoners of war in Sachsenhausen, and even earlier, in 1940, it had been used as part of the euthanasia program against the mentally ill in Germany. The first gas van was deployed in the Soviet Union in December 1941 and over the next 3 years the *Einsatzgruppen* used some 15.[19] Although many thousands of Jews were killed in this way, the gas vans were not popular with SS personnel because they proved just as unpleasant as shooting victims at close range; sometimes gassing required more effort and contact with the victims than shooting. Despite the ability of the gas vans to kill large numbers of people at once, they were not always as efficient as Himmler had hoped. Over time, the doors of the vans lost their seal allowing fresh air to mix with the noxious fumes. As a result, it often took more time for those inside to die.

It has been estimated that in their ideological campaign, the *Einsatzgruppen* were responsible for the murder – by shooting and gassing – of approximately 1 million Jews.[20] The four units of *Einsatzgruppen* consisted of approximately 3,000 men, mostly taken from the offices of the SS-*Sicherheitsdienst* or Security Service (SD), the *Sicherheitspolizei* or Security Police (Sipo), and the *Geheimstaatspolizei* or Secret State Police (Gestapo). Historians used to believe that the *Einsatzgruppen* alone were responsible for all 1 million murders. Research has shown, however, that they had help killing. Himmler sent thousands of reinforcements from the *Kriminalpolizei* or Criminal Police (Kripo), the *Ordnungspolizei* or Order Police (Orpo), the *Waffen*-SS (armed SS), and the *Wehrmacht* (military) to ensure his ideological soldiers could carry out their orders to the fullest. The activities of

---

[19] Longerich, *Politik der Vernichtung*, 441–448 and Shmuel Spektor, "Killings in the Gas Vans behind the Front," in Eugen Kogon, Hermann Langbein and Adalbert Rückerl (eds.), *Nazi Mass Murder: A Documentary History of the Use of Poison Gas* (New Haven, 1993), 52–63.

[20] Whereas the *Einsatzgruppen* were at the center of the killing process, the situation in the east was far more complex than this. Research into the activities of the Orpo has shown that the *Einsatzgruppen* constituted a fraction of the German paramilitary organizations involved in the murder process in the east. Our enhanced understanding of the front-line perpetrators is the result of a number of factors, not the least of which was the opening of the archives in the former Soviet Union, which led to an upsurge in research on local auxiliary police units and their role in the Final Solution. Although narrowly focussed on one battalion, Christopher Browning's seminal study *Ordinary Men: Reserve Police Battalion 101 and the Final Solution in Poland* (New York, 1992) also unwittingly contributed to this shift.

the *Einsatzgruppen* and their helpers in Russia during the summer of 1941 represented a watershed in Nazi racial policy toward the Jews, a policy that, in 1942, proliferated into a European-wide program of murder. In the summer of 1947, the Americans decided to hold these men accountable for their acts and indicted twenty-four leaders of the *Einsatzgruppen* units for the murder of 1 million Soviet-Jewish civilians, a crime that the international community later identified as genocide, but which, in 1947, was still considered a crime against humanity.[21] The indictment against Otto Ohlendorf and the *Einsatzgruppen* leaders was based largely on the evidence gathered from their own Operational Situation Reports that thoroughly chronicled the part they played in the initial phase of the Final Solution.[22]

The *Einsatzgruppen* trial was the ninth of 12 trials held at the Palace of Justice, Nuremberg, Germany, beginning with the so-called Doctor's Trial in December 1946. In many respects, the NMT are a landmark in international law. Never before had an international criminal court combined the adversarial system of law in which decisions are reached by a judge who acts as an impartial arbitrator for the prosecution and defense, with the continental system of law where the judge plays a much more active role in the presentation and evaluation of evidence and in questioning witnesses.[23] In the adversarial system, facts emerge from the process of prosecution and defense whereas in the continental system, truth is established by an inquiry into the facts by the judge. Because international criminal law was in its infancy in 1945, the NMT also had jurisdiction to apply and interpret the newly written laws that governed the trials. The NMT derived its authority from international agreement, in particular from the *London Agreement* of August 8, 1945 (the law that formalized the IMT) and Allied Control Council Law No. 10 of December 20, 1945 (the law that allowed the Allies to hold trials independent of one another). Representatives of the United States, Britain, France, and the Soviet Union signed these laws. The Subsequent trials were also governed by zonal law, especially American Military Ordinance No. 7 of October 18, 1946, which laid out the rules under which the tribunals would function in the American zone.

In an attempt to ensure a fair process, the organizers of the NMT permitted full access to selected members of the German public and to the

---

[21] According to Taylor, *Anatomy*, 103, the term "genocide" was first used in August 1945 during the London negotiations to describe the "the extermination of racial and national groups."

[22] For a thorough discussion of the Operational Situational Reports, see Ronald Headland, *Messages of Murder: A Study of the Reports of the Einsatzgruppen of the Security Police and Security Service 1941–1943* (London and Toronto, 1992).

[23] Stephan Landsman, *The Adversary System: A Description and Defense* (Washington and London, 1984) and *Readings on Adversarial Justice: The American Approach to Adjudication* (St. Paul, 1988).

international press. The trials themselves were bilingual, carried out simultaneously in German and English, and after they were completed, the transcripts were published in abridged form, but only in English. Defense attorneys fluent in both languages frequently corrected the official record when they detected mistakes in translation, but not all mistakes were caught. Each defendant also had the right to counsel of his own choosing. The Americans believed that Germans were best able to represent German defendants, not just linguistically, but culturally and politically too. Whereas defense attorneys outnumbered prosecution staff by more than two to one, the prosecution had an army of researchers not available to the Germans. The American Military Government paid the defense salary of 3,500 marks per month, provided them with three meals per day (with a caloric content calculated at 3,900, more than American soldiers received at the time), and supplied them with a much-coveted carton of cigarettes per week.[24] Defense counsel was given office space and furniture, and a "Defendant's Information Center" was established where defense attorneys could procure documents and witnesses. This office acted ostensibly as the liaison between the defense, prosecution, and the tribunal. Under the uniform rules of procedure outlined in Control Council Law No. 10 (CCL10), each defendant had to be supplied with an indictment, in German, at least thirty days before trial began and all were given the right to be present at trial, testify in his own behalf, and to present evidence in support of his defense. With rules and procedures in place to ensure due process, one would assume Nuremberg was procedurally fair. As will be shown, however, criminal law was not always applied evenly nor as it would have been in the United States, and, in addition, structural issues had an impact on elements of the process.

On July 29, 1947, the American Office of Chief of Counsel for War Crimes (OCCWC), the legal organization that administered the NMT and headed by Brigadier General Telford Taylor, indicted twenty-four *Einsatzgruppen* leaders on 3 counts of criminality: crimes against humanity, war crimes, and membership in organizations declared criminal by the IMT.[25] Prior to their recruitment to the *Einsatzgruppen*, all twenty-four defendants had been members of the SS, SD, or Gestapo, organizations declared criminal in the judgment of the IMT. Twenty-four defendants were indicted, yet, only twenty-two were tried. One of the defendants, Emil Hausmann, an officer in *Einsatzkommando* 12, committed suicide in his prison cell immediately after receiving his indictment. Otto Rasch, considered one of the "most vicious killers in the dock," was excluded from the case after the trial had begun

[24] Interim Report in Taylor, *Final Report*, 156 and 173–175 and Ferencz, "Nürnberg Trial Procedure and the Rights of the Accused," *Journal of Criminal Law and Criminology* 39 (July–August, 1948), 146–147.
[25] The original indictment was filed July 3, but was amended.

because of a severe and advanced case of Parkinson's disease that limited his ability to participate in his own defense.[26] Rasch died in prison nine months after the conclusion of the trial. Each defendant entered a plea of "not guilty," and many added the statement: "in the sense of the indictment," with no objection from the court.[27] Few denied participating in the murderous campaign in the Soviet Union; rather, their defense hinged on the argument that under the circumstances of total war and a state of emergency, they had acted legally, as soldiers, and merely had been following orders.

The defendants were arraigned between September 15 and 22, 1947, at the Palace of Justice before Military Tribunal II-A (later renamed Military Tribunal II). The tribunal consisted of three judges, two of whom were culled from American state courts because federal judges were prohibited from working at the NMT. Michael Angelo Musmanno was a reserve naval captain and judge from the Court of Common Pleas, Allegheny County, Pennsylvania, and was named presiding judge. John Joshua Speight, a member of the Alabama bar had no experience as a judge before coming to Nuremberg, and Richard Dillard Dixon, a judge from the Superior Court of North Carolina was the final member of Tribunal II. Each defendant was permitted to choose his own advocate and the vast majority of indictees opted for an additional defense attorney. All defendants testified on their own behalf. Under German criminal law, the right to testify before the court is determined by the judge, who decides if defendant testimony is reliable enough to be heard. At Nuremberg, the defendants were automatically granted the right to testify under oath and were permitted to address the court after closing statements were made, which they did, but not under oath.[28] Along with the defendants, the defense called only eighteen witnesses to the stand. This was unusual, but, given the time constraints, the tribunal ruled that the defense could submit any and all evidence (including hearsay evidence) that might exonerate the defendants.[29] The ruling led to the submission of 549 affidavits (mostly statements about the defendants' characters from school teachers, ministers, family, friends, and colleagues) on behalf of the defense and in lieu of direct testimony. The tribunal calculated that the submission of affidavits in lieu of direct testimony saved more than five months of court time; of course, it also meant that witnesses could not be cross-examined in open court, something that never would have been permitted in an American criminal proceeding where affiants must be available

---

[26] Press release, September 1947, 5-1-4-62, NMT, OCCWC Press releases, 1947, TTP.

[27] Only one defendant ever pled guilty, SS officer Ernst Wilhelm Bohle, who was tried in the Ministries case. Press release, March 28, 1948, 5-1-4-63, NMT, OCCWC Press releases, 1948, TTP.

[28] "Oral Testimony by Defendants," in *TWC*, vol. 15, 714–715.

[29] Because the rules of evidence were flexible and because the charges were so grave, Musmanno claimed he wanted to ensure the defendants had every opportunity to prove their innocence, see *Trial*, roll 4, 2841.

in person for cross-examination.[30] Finally, under the rules that governed the trial, each defendant had the right to make a final statement to the court. All the defendants except Rasch did so.

After 138 court sessions beginning September 29, 1947, the trial came to a close on April 10, 1948, when sentences were pronounced in open court. In all, fourteen of the defendants received the death penalty. Ernst Biberstein, Paul Blobel, Walter Blume, Werner Braune, Walter Haensch, Waldemar Klingelhöfer, Erich Naumann, Otto Ohlendorf, Adolf Ott, Martin Sandberger, Heinz Schubert, Willy Seibert, Eugen Steimle, and Eduard Strauch were sentenced to death by hanging. Heinz Jost and Gustav Nosske were sentenced to life in prison. Waldemar von Radetzky, Erwin Schulz, and Franz Six received twenty-year sentences and Lothar Fendler and Felix Rühl were sentenced to ten years each. Matthias Graf, the lowest-ranking SS officer indicted, was released based on time served.

The Americans provided no process or structure for appeals, forcing the convicted men to apply directly to the American Military Governor Lucius Clay, and, later, to the American High Commissioner John McCloy, for clemency. In March 1949, Clay affirmed all fourteen-death sentences in the *Einsatzgruppen* case, but U.S. officials nevertheless granted a stay of execution when irregularities were detected in other, non-Nuremberg (army) trials. During this period, Clay also introduced a system whereby convicted war criminals received a credit of five days per month for time served in pretrial confinement and for good behavior. This decision reduced the sentences of all convicted war criminals – including the *Einsatzgruppen* leaders – by one quarter.

Those sentenced to death by hanging had their executions postponed until officials in Washington reviewed their cases. The U.S. Senate investigated accusations of unfair trial practices and declared in the spring of 1949, that although there had been some irregularities, trials had generally been carried out in a just fashion. In June 1949, the convicted war criminals, fearful that they would be executed imminently, flooded the American military government with further requests for clemency. In 1950, John McCloy replaced Clay as U.S. High Commissioner for Germany and established an Advisory Board to investigate the issue. On January 31, 1951, the Advisory Board recommended that only four of the original fourteen death sentences be carried out, the other ten, they thought, should be converted to life in prison. The High Commissioner largely agreed with the Board's recommendations. The clemency process came to an end on June 7, 1951, when Ohlendorf, Blobel, Braune, Naumann, and Oswald Pohl were hanged at Landsberg war crimes prison. Between 1951 and 1958, all but three of the remaining convicted *Einsatzgruppen* defendants were released from prison either through an act of clemency or parole. And, on May 9, 1958, only ten years

[30] See *TWC*, vol. 15, which is devoted to explaining the rules of procedure.

after they had been originally sentenced for mass murder, the three remaining *Einsatzgruppen* leaders still in prison were released back into German society where they lived out the remainder of their lives in relative obscurity.

The study of war crimes trials is not new. Almost as soon as the IMT convened in 1945, the utility and legal value of war crimes trials was the subject of intense scrutiny, mostly from legal scholars and those in the legal profession, and from those who participated in the trials. They also generated a great deal of controversy at the time, especially between 1949 and 1951 – a period when German opposition to the prosecution and execution of war criminals was most pronounced. Although legal scholars were debating issues of law, historical interpretations of Nuremberg were not as plentiful and what scholarship did exist revolved around the issue of whether or not Nuremberg was an act of justice or vengeance, especially whether or not Nuremberg was victor's justice. Even though Nuremberg was a place where historical narratives of the Third Reich and the Holocaust took shape, generally speaking, historians have tended to avoid narrative histories of the postwar trials. This should not be surprising given the mammoth amount of documentation the trials produced and the inherently difficult and time-consuming task of analyzing such material. Besides, criminal trials are not inherently interesting as narratives and, contrary to the *Law and Order* franchise, extracting a compelling story can be challenging. Contemporary accounts of Nuremberg attest to this as they almost always describe it with few exceptions as "boring," even "tedious." Instead of recreating the narrative, scholars have availed themselves of the opportunity to use documentation from the trials to construct historical interpretations of the Third Reich and its policies such as Raul Hilberg did so masterfully in *The Destruction of the European Jews* and as Helmut Krausnick and Martin Brozat did in their ground-breaking book, *The Anatomy of the SS State*. The focus of historical inquiry regarding war crimes trials has changed recently. In the last 15 years or so, historians have begun to ask new questions of trial material. This shift has led to a revolution in scholarship, beginning with Christopher Browning's path-breaking book *Ordinary Men*, in which he uses trial testimony to help determine perpetrator motivation. Postwar trials have also been examined to assess the ability of law to confront and contend with traumatic history such as the Nazi Holocaust against the Jews. And, most recently, legal scholars such as Lawrence Douglas, *The Memory of Judgment: Making Law and History in the Trials of the Holocaust*, and historians such as Donald Bloxham, *Genocide on Trial: War Crimes Trials and the Formation of Holocaust History and Memory*, have asked whether or not law and history are compatible mediums and what impact the law has had on history and historical memory. *The Nuremberg SS-Einsatzgruppen Trial* fits into this new and evolving body of literature on postwar trials; its genesis comes from a series of current historical (and historiographical) questions on the history of the Third Reich, the Nazi genocide against European Jews, and the postwar international context in which this trial was conducted.

The book is organized chronologically, following the *Einsatzgruppen* trial from its ideological, political, and historical origins through to the final judgment against the defendants and their fate after the trial. Along with providing a chronology of this trial, the book is also organized thematically. The first theme is the origins of the Subsequent Nuremberg trials. The book asks how the Americans came to decide on judicial proceedings against high-ranking, albeit lesser-known Nazis; in short, what factors impelled the Americans to hold additional war crimes trials subsequent to the IMT? In his book on the American war crimes trial program in Germany, Frank Buscher argues that the NMT were part of the American plan to "reeducate the German people" to demonstrate the virtues of democracy and the "evils of totalitarianism."[31] Whereas Buscher's assessment of the didactic aims of Nuremberg is essentially borne out, the evidence also suggests that the United States pursued further trials for political reasons and especially because of the emerging cold war with the Soviet Union. If the cold war was the impetus for the Subsequent trials generally, what led specifically to the trial of Ohlendorf and the other *Einsatzgruppen* leaders?

Like many criminal trials, it was accidental in the sense that it was in response to new and damning evidence unearthed during a routine investigation of documents. Evidence of wrongdoing was so strong in this case that it simply could not be ignored. Unlike the IMT trial, which was planned by the highest officials, political factors did not play such a significant role in the selection of defendants of the NMT because the Americans were determined to bring indictments against leading Nazis based only on evidence unearthed during the course of the IMT case. This, coupled with the fact that one of the major purposes of holding further trials was to expose the criminal scope of the Nazi regime, made certain members of the SS very likely candidates for prosecution. In 1945–1946, when the Americans were planning the NMT, they already had SS-General Otto Ohlendorf in custody, and, fortunately for them, he had publicly confessed to his crimes. His admission to supervising mass murder almost certainly assured Ohlendorf a place in the dock. When the Operational Situation Reports of the *Einsatzgruppen* that chronicled in meticulous detail the mass murder of Jews and other civilians in occupied Soviet territory were discovered, American authorities responded to the evidence and turned their attention to the atrocities committed by the *Einsatzgruppen*, indicting two dozen former members for crimes against humanity.[32]

---

[31] Frank Buscher, *The U.S. War Crimes Trial Program in Germany*, (New York, 1989), 8–9.

[32] Determining exactly how many civilians were murdered by the mobile units is a difficult, if not impossible, task given the inaccuracy of the reports, the possibility of duplications and omissions in the reporting process, and because of the complexity of the killing operations

Along with answering conventional questions about origins, this book is also about war crimes trials as sites of testimony and what trial testimony reveals about the perpetrators of genocide. I am most especially interested in the perpetrator's own narratives about their behavior and whether their explanations reinforce perpetrator behavior types as they have been elucidated in the historiography thus far. When I first began research for this project, I assumed that every explanation the defendants offered was a lie. These men were mass murderers after all, why should I believe anything they had to say and why especially should I believe what they say in a courtroom, where it was in their best interest to construct false images of themselves and lie about their behavior?[33] This is not a fruitful way of examining testimony. Historians need to take individual explanations for killing seriously. It is not that defendants did not lie about the motives for their actions, because they surely did; but, rather, because the courtroom is often the only venue where perpetrators themselves have accounted for their crimes. Only by listening to what they have to say, and then critically assessing the veracity of the statement and comparing it to the historical record, will scholars be able to approach a more informed answer to "why men kill."[34] Using perpetrator testimony to reconstruct the historical narrative has always been suspect, yet using it to understand human experience and motivation has proved quite fruitful.[35] This book builds on that trend. Added to this evidence base are other perceptions and views of the perpetrators and their behavior gleaned from the recently declassified intelligence documents of the United States and Britain, which have proved to be a valuable source for reassessing perpetrator paradigms. One of the aims of this book is to better understand the role of elite members of German society in the genocidal campaign on the eastern front. This analysis is especially relevant to the *Einsatzgruppen*

---

and the involvement of non-*Einsatzgruppen* personnel in murder. Estimates of Jews murdered range from a low of 700,000 according to Hilberg, *Destruction*, 1201–1220, to a maximum of 1,152,731 by Headland, *Messages of Murder*, 96–106. For the purposes of this work the figure of 1 million is accepted.

[33] Browning talks about the dangers of perpetrator testimony in the courtroom in *Collected Memories. Holocaust History and Postwar Testimony* (Madison, 2003), 3–36.

[34] To determine the veracity of Adolf Eichmann's testimony, Browning employs a series of questions. He asks whether the testimony was self-interested and how vividly Eichmann recalled a particular event. He compares Eichmann's testimony with all available contemporary documentation and checks veracity through pattern behavior, *Collected Memories*, 11–12.

[35] Browning has written extensively on perpetrator testimony, most recently in *Collected Memories*. Christian Gerlach, "The Eichmann Interrogations in Holocaust Historiography," *Holocaust and Genocide Studies* 15, no. 3 (winter 2001), 428–452, and Karin Orth, "Rudolf Höss und die 'Endlösung der Judenfrage,'" *Werkstattgeschichte* 18 (1997), 45–57, have also written about perpetrator testimony. From the victim's perspective, Annette Wieviorka, *The Era of the Witness* (Ithaca and London, 2006) explores the history of victim testimony from the postwar period through today.

leaders who, in another time and place, would have been leading members of society, yet, in the context of the Third Reich, became the vanguard of genocide. Contrary to Daniel Goldhagen's assertion, this book will show that these men were not born to kill, but, rather, were groomed to do so.

The biographical method employed throughout is used to understand how and why these men willingly participated in the crimes of the Third Reich and ultimately how they became genocidal killers. Although biographical methods always run the risk of enhancing the role of the individual whereas sacrificing the role of structure, if done properly, it can augment our historical understanding of the Nazi period by bringing to life the history of the individual and especially their personal journeys to Nazism. The biographies conveyed here are not conventional heroic accounts of individual lives. Rather, biographical method is employed to explain the individual perpetrator's path to murder, and, in the process of elucidating this, it tests the reliability of perpetrator narrative as expressed in the courtroom during trial.[36] Put another way, biographical method offers the opportunity to critically re-examine established perpetrator narratives like Ulrich Herbert and Karin Orth have done in their biographies of Werner Best and Rudolf Höss.[37] What results here is a reinterpretation of one of the most notorious Nazi perpetrators, Otto Ohlendorf.

While using traditional biographical methods to tell the life stories of individual defendants, the methods of collective biography are used to examine the defendants as a group. Michael Wildt and others have employed this method with aplomb.[38] To highlight the generational dimensions of the group he studies, and to determine their particular group characteristics, Wildt analyzes the biographies of individual members of the RSHA. He comes to the conclusion that there were significant generational similarities among this group of men. Although nowhere near as comprehensive as Wildt's study, I employ the methods of collective biography, albeit for a much smaller sample: the twenty-four defendants of the *Einsatzgruppen* trial. The result is a biography of the *Einsatzgruppen* leadership, which is startling in its uniformity. The twenty-four defendants in the dock, by all definitions, formed a group not only in their ideology and membership in various Nazi organizations, but also generationally in their shared social, political, and economic experiences. The various features of this group are

[36] de Mildt, *In the Name of the People*, 15–16.

[37] Ulrich Herbert, *Best: biographische studien uber Radikalismus* (Bonn, 1996) and Orth, "Rudolf Höss und die 'Endlösung der Judenfrage,'" (1997), 45–57.

[38] Michael Wildt, *Generation des Unbedingten. Das Führungskorps des Reichssicherheitshauptamtes* (Hamburg, 2003) and Orth, "The Concentration Camp SS as a Functional Elite," in Ulrich Herbert (ed.), *National Socialist Extermination Policies: Contemporary German Perspectives and Controversies* (New York and Oxford, 2000), 306–336. See also Andrew Donson, "Why did German youth become fascists? Nationalist males born 1900 to 1908 in war and revolution," *Social History* 31: 3 (August, 2006), 337–358.

unremarkable on their own, but together they help to define this cohort of young men and their particular attraction to Nazism.

Much of the story of this trial is told through the lens of biography and it is not limited to the defendants. The lives of the other participants and how they came to Nuremberg and helped to shape the trial are also a central feature of this research. Of course, a trial of such magnitude required the participation of hundreds of people, all of whom I could not include here. I was especially fortunate, however, that there exists a rich documentary record of the *Einsatzgruppen* trial and several of the leading figures of the trial left accounts of their experiences. In particular, Michael Musmanno, the presiding judge, left an extensive private archive including all of his Nuremberg records. He is a contentious historical and legal figure whose role in the trial is significant. He was so dominant, he set the trial's course and tone. As a seasoned jurist with a penchant for the dramatic, he virtually usurped the role of the prosecution, at times taking over much of the direct examination of the defendants during the trial. This was highly controversial and unusual behavior for an American judge, but given Musmanno's past, may not be surprising. From his days as a defense attorney for the notorious Sacco and Vanzetti, to his reprehensible redbaiting during the McCarthy era, Musmanno's legacy is nothing if not controversial. In the courtroom, he was a bully, but he still may very well have been the right man for this job.[39] Along with examining the role of the presiding judge, I also had the good fortune to interview several of the participants of the trial. Benjamin Ferencz, the Chief Prosecutor of the trial spoke to me at length about his experiences, as did Henry Lea, one of the *Einsatzgruppen* trial's most prominent translators. Both helped me enormously in understanding their experiences at trial. As with all evidence-based disciplines, the documentary record is uneven and this trial is no exception. Unfortunately, not all participants left behind accounts of their experiences, thus, not everyone is portrayed as vividly as the principal characters who did leave archives behind of their experiences.

No story of a criminal trial would be complete without an epilogue because seldom do trials end when sentences are passed. The *Einsatzgruppen* trial is no exception. What happens to the twenty-four men tried for crimes against humanity after sentences were rendered is the final theme of the book. More death sentences were imposed in the *Einsatzgruppen* trial than in all of the other Subsequent trials, yet only four of the sentences were carried out. Why? For two reasons: law and politics. Unable to appeal their sentences, those who were condemned to death in the IMT proceedings were executed almost immediately. This was not the case with

---

[39] For example see Stephan Landsman, *Crimes of the Holocaust: the Law Confronts Hard Cases* (Philadelphia, 2005) who raises the issue of Musmanno's peculiar interpretation of evidence during his testimony at the Eichmann trial in Jerusalem in 1961. Musmanno is the subject of chapter 6.

the Subsequent proceedings where nearly all of the defendants filed appeals almost as soon as their sentences were passed. In lieu of an appellate court, the *Einsatzgruppen* defendants appealed for mercy directly to the Military Governor Lucius Clay and, later, to John McCloy, Clay's replacement as U.S. High Commissioner. Most defendants were successful and only four of the original fourteen death sentences were carried out. All others had their sentences reduced with the last defendant released from prison in 1958, a mere ten years after the original judgment. We should not be surprised by such sentence reductions, given that by 1949 domestic and international political considerations were taking precedence over American punishment policy. Cold war stresses coupled with mounting pressure from the German public forced the United States to overturn the convictions of as many as one half of all those tried for war crimes and even those convicted of crimes against humanity.[40]

More than sixty years after the conclusion of World War II and the birth of international justice, genocides continue unabated and so do war crimes trials. Nuremberg established a precedent. From the trial of Adolf Eichmann in Israel to the special ad hoc tribunals set up to try war criminals from the former Yugoslavia and Rwanda, for better or worse, Nuremberg was the legal template for everything that followed. Because the history of the *Einsatzgruppen* trial has not been told, this inquiry constitutes a significant addition to the history of the prosecution of war criminals in general, and, specifically, those tried after the Second World War. The trial of the *Einsatzgruppen* leaders was an important historical event. As part of a series of trials designed to punish Nazi perpetrators, it is a noteworthy addendum to the criminal Nazi regime, yet, the trial is also important for our understanding of the history and development of international criminal law. It was the first and perhaps only trial to prosecute a group of men whose sole job it was to execute Nazi genocidal policy against the Jews: what today we refer to as the Holocaust. Although all the Nuremberg trials had an element of this in it (how could they not when everything the Nazis did was in the furtherance of ideology), the *Einsatzgruppen* trial was exclusively about the murder of Russia's civilian (mainly Jewish) population in 1941–1942. A punitive success, ultimately the trial gives us a surprisingly lucid picture of the process of the Final Solution in Russia, but fails to employ the appropriate terms and paradigms with which to name these crimes. As imperfect as the prosecution of this trial was, it laid the groundwork for future trials of this type and we can see its legacy at the current trials of war criminals from the former Yugoslavia. However, the Nuremberg legacy is not just legal. The *Einsatzgruppen* trial, as part of the larger Nuremberg project, is also important historically. These thirteen trials, collectively referred to as

[40] Thomas Alan Schwartz, "John J. McCloy and the Landsberg Cases," *American Policy and the Reconstruction of West Germany, 1945–1955* (Washington, 1995), 435–440.

Nuremberg, were instrumental in shaping our historical understanding of Nazi criminality and, in the *Einsatzgruppen* trial specifically, in shaping the historiography of the Final Solution. In the aftermath of the most destructive war in European history, it was amazing that such a process took place at all. The following chapters recount the story of the fate of twenty-four high-ranking members of the Nazi regime who helped perpetrate genocide and provides a detailed analysis of how the perpetrators of genocide accounted for their actions and how a group of three American judges and a tenacious prosecution team weighed the evidence, determined the guilt, and ordered their punishment.

I

The United States and the Origins of the Subsequent Nuremberg Trials

It is generally acknowledged, among symphony conductors and trial lawyers alike, that the vital work is done before the show begins. Gesticulate and exhort as the conductor may during a concert, the quality of the performance will be largely determined by the caliber of the players he has selected, and the sensitivity and unity of purpose that he has imparted to them in rehearsal.

Telford Taylor[1]

When exactly did the Americans decide to punish Germans for the atrocities they committed during the war? It was not until after the death of wartime President Franklin Roosevelt that the United States decided on a legal solution to the German problem. Punishment was not a new idea, however. As early as November 1, 1943, in what became known as "The Moscow Declaration on German Atrocities," the allied leaders Winston Churchill, Franklin Roosevelt, and Joseph Stalin explicitly warned the German government that at war's end, "all those who have taken a consenting part in atrocities, massacres and executions" of innocent people will be pursued "to the uttermost ends of the earth and will [be] delivered to [their] accusers in order that justice may be done."[2] Despite such strongly stated intentions, the Allies did very little during the remainder of the war to prepare for such an eventuality, supporting one historian's assertion that "there never was a fixed or well-defined Nuremberg plan or policy."[3] This

[1] Taylor, *Final Report*, 86.
[2] The complete text of the Moscow Declaration can be found in *TWC*, vol. 4, x.
[3] Smith, *Judgment at Nuremberg*, xvii and William Frachter, "American Organization for Prosecution of German War Criminals," *Missouri Law Review* 13 (1948), 70. Arieh Kochavi, *Prelude to Nuremberg*, has argued that the war criminals issue was discussed in London and Washington from 1941 on, but it was not given serious consideration until 1944. Michael Marrus, "The Nuremberg Doctors' Trial in Historical Context," *Bulletin of the History of Medicine* 73 (1999), 110, argues the Subsequent trials "had a haphazard, improvised character" as well.

will come as no surprise to students of American history especially as it is well known that Roosevelt kept a tight rein on foreign policy and was loathe to reveal his plans for the postwar world, particularly with respect to Germany.[4] American planning for the punishment of war criminals was thus deferred and, in the interim, the Allies grappled with the "German question": should they strip Germany of its war-making potential or should they attempt rehabilitation by purging German society of Nazism and punish the surviving officials of the regime?

The Allies could not decide until the conclusion of the war. In the meantime, they met in February 1945, at Yalta, and agreed that along with unconditional surrender, Germany would be occupied and divided into four zones. The Soviets would occupy the eastern portion of the country, the British the northwest, the Americans the south, and the French a small portion of southwest Germany that bordered their country. As for the war criminals question, they could not agree.[5] The British favored summary execution; as did the Russians; American opinion was divided.[6] Some officials in Washington supported the now-infamous proposal of the Secretary of the Treasury, Henry Morgenthau, Jr., who believed Germany should be dismembered, demilitarized, denazified, and de-industrialized.[7] Faced with political pressure from Stalin who believed the Morgenthau plan was too soft on the Germans, the Americans looked for other ways to deal with Germany. Secretary of War Henry Stimson, Assistant Secretary of War John McCloy, and others in the War Department responded with an alternative plan that included the recovery and reintegration of Germany into the European community and the adoption of a judicial solution to the war criminals problem.[8] That Roosevelt refused to commit to any plan before the war was over highlights the difficulty the Americans had in planning for the transition from war

---

[4] Prior to the Yalta Conference, Roosevelt refused to settle political issues with his allies, preferring instead to concentrate his energies on winning the war. For an overview of American foreign policy during the war, see Robert D. Schulzinger, "The Politics of Coalition Warfare, 1939–1945," in *idem* (ed.), *American Diplomacy in the Twentieth Century* (New York, 1990), 167–200. One of the best discussions of FDR's foreign policy remains Robert Dallek, *Franklin D. Roosevelt and American Foreign Policy, 1932–1945* (New York, 1979).

[5] For a good discussion of the level of disagreement between the British and Americans, see Kochavi, *Prelude*, 201–217.

[6] Schulzinger, "The Politics of Coalition Warfare," 186. For a discussion of Russian attitudes toward the question of punishment, see Kochavi, *Prelude*, 217–222.

[7] Peter Maguire, "A Cold War Conflict of Interest," PhD dissertation, Columbia University, 1995, 150–151 published as *Law and War: An American Story* (New York, 2000), 87.

[8] On the genesis of American policy and the differences between the Stimson and Morgenthau plans, see Jeffrey K. Olick, *In the House of the Hangman: The Agonies of German Defeat, 1943–1949* (Chicago, 2005), 25–94; Kochavi, *Prelude*, 80–87; and, Robert Wolfe, "Flaws in the Nuremberg Legacy: An Impediment to International War Crimes Tribunals' Prosecution of Crimes against Humanity," *Holocaust and Genocide Studies* vol. 3, no. 2 (Winter, 1998), 435–438.

to peace. It was not until after Roosevelt died on April 12, 1945, when Harry Truman took office, that an official decision was made concerning the war criminals issue.

Samuel Rosenman, a judge on the bench of the New York Supreme Court and a former advisor to Roosevelt, easily persuaded the new president that a judicial solution was the best course of action for the United States.[9] Truman agreed: the rehabilitation of German society could be accomplished using the law.[10] German society would be denazified by eradicating all Nazi institutions, leadership, and political culture.[11] This, coupled with the trial and punishment of the highest-ranking Nazi war criminals, the Americans hoped, would go some way toward re-educating Germans and remaking German society. On April 26, 1945, exactly two weeks after Roosevelt's death, Truman approved the first occupation statute for Germany: Joint Chiefs of Staff (JCS) 1067.[12] The directive was designed to govern the initial phase of the American occupation of Germany and closely mirrored the War Department's proposal.[13] JCS 1067 is historiographically controversial.[14] For this story, what is important is that the directive had a significant impact on war crimes policy because it called for the apprehension and arrest of thousands of war criminals including all Nazi party officials, members of the *Gestapo*, the SD, the *Allgemeine*, and *Waffen SS*, as well as all other Nazis and Nazi sympathizers, an enormous number of individuals by western legal standards.[15] As a result of this far-reaching directive, literally hundreds of

[9] Biographical information, War Crimes File, Samuel I. Rosenman Papers, HST.

[10] For discussions of Truman's policies, see Barton Bernstein (ed.), *The Politics and Policies of the Truman Administration* (Chicago, 1970); Schulzinger, "The Early Cold War, 1945–1952," in *American Diplomacy in the Twentieth Century*, 201–231; David McCullough, *Truman* (New York, 1992); and Robert J. Donovan, *Conflict and Crisis. The Presidency of Harry S Truman, 1945–1948* (New York, 1977). For the War Department's plan, see Henry Stimson and McGeorge Bundy, *On Active Service in Peace and War* (New York, 1948).

[11] Elmer Plischke, "Denazification in Germany. A Policy Analysis," in Robert Wolfe (ed.), *Americans as Proconsuls: United States Military Government in Germany and Japan, 1944–1952* (Carbondale, IL, 1984), 198–200. The most recent scholarship on denazification focuses on regional analyses. For example, see Jorg D. Kramer, *Das Verhältnis der politischen Parteien zur Entnazifizierung in Nordhein-Westfalen* (Frankfurt, 2001) and, Damien van Melis, *Entnazifizierung in Mecklenberg – Vorpommern: Herrschaft und Verwaltung 1945–1948* (Munich, 1999).

[12] Plischke, "Denazification in Germany," 207.

[13] Much has been written about American occupation policy in Germany. For example, see Olick, *House of the Hangman* (2005); John Willoughby, *Remaking the Conquering Hero: The Social and Geopolitical Impact of the Post-War American Occupation of Germany* (New York, 2000); Richard Merritt, *Democracy Imposed: US Occupation Policy and the German Public, 1945–1949* (New Haven, 1995); Rebecca Boehling, *A Question of Priorities: Democratic Reform and Economic Recovery in Postwar Germany* (Providence, RI, 1996); and, Jeffry Diefendorf (ed.), *American Policy and the Reconstruction of West Germany, 1945–1955* (Cambridge, MA, 1993).

[14] Olick, *House of the Hangman*, 29–33.

[15] JCS 1067/6 to Commander in Chief of U.S. Forces of Occupation Regarding the Military Government of Germany, April 26, 1945, in Alvin J. Rockwell Papers, OMGUS file, HST.

thousands of Germans were arrested and interned until it could be decided exactly how to determine their culpability and punishment. Truman needed someone to undertake this task immediately. He asked Supreme Court Justice Robert H. Jackson to take on the responsibility. Jackson agreed and was immediately appointed Chief of Counsel for the Prosecution of Axis Criminality (CCPAC), a position that included developing American war crimes policy.[16]

Jackson firmly believed in his task. As an early proponent of transitional justice, he advocated the creation of a legal framework to try and punish Nazi perpetrators, especially if the Allies wanted to avoid vigilante justice and re-educate Germans on the principles of democracy.[17] He worked fast, outlining his proposals for American war crimes policy in his first report to Truman, who he answered to directly, stressing America's moral and legal responsibility to investigate Nazi criminality.[18]

Convinced of his mission, Jackson set out to persuade America's allies that transitional justice was in their best interest too. He did this when the four powers met in San Francisco in early May 1945. The Soviets immediately embraced the American proposal believing that a public trial "would serve positive political goals" as well as punishing those responsible for the war of aggression that had left 27 million Soviet citizens dead.[19] The British were not so enthusiastic;[20] however, without an alternative plan for the treatment of major war criminals, they were forced to submit to the American initiative.[21] Besides, given the deaths of the most important Nazi leaders, including Hitler, Himmler, Goebbels, and, possibly, Bormann (many were convinced that Bormann was still alive despite rumors to the contrary) the British plan for summary execution had lost much of its appeal.[22] Ultimately,

---

[16] Truman, Executive Order No. 9547, "Providing for Representation of the United States in Preparing and Prosecuting Charges of Atrocities and War Crimes against the Leaders of the European Axis Powers and their Principal Agents and Accessories," May 2, 1945, in NARA RG 260, OMGUS, Executive Office, The Office of the Adjutant General box 640, Ordinance No. 7 folder.

[17] Smith, *Road to Nuremberg*, 247–248.

[18] Report, Jackson to Truman, June 7, 1945, WHO File 325A, OCCAC, HST.

[19] Francine Hirsch, "The Soviets at Nuremberg: International Law, Propaganda, and the Making of the Postwar Order," *American Historical Review*, vol. 113 (June, 2008), 713–714.

[20] Oral History, Samuel Rosenman, 41–42, HST.

[21] Kochavi, *Prelude*, 220.

[22] Marrus, *Nuremberg War Crimes Trial*, 38. The origins of the IMT have been the subject of numerous studies, some of these include: Sidney Alderman, "Negotiating the Nuremberg Trial Agreement, 1945," in Raymond Dennett and Joseph E. Johnson (eds.), *Negotiating with the Russians* (Boston, 1951); Bradley F. Smith, *The Road to Nuremberg* (New York, 1981); George Ginsburgs, "the Nuremberg Trial: Background," in George Ginsburgs and V.N. Kudriavstev (eds.), *The Nuremberg Trial and International Law* (Dordrecht, 1990); and, Anthony Glees, "The Making of British Policy on War Crimes: History as Politics in the UK," *Contemporary European History*, vol. 1, no. 2 (July, 1992), 171–197.

the wartime Allies agreed that the solution to the problem of punishment of major Nazi war criminals would be judicial, and that these individuals would be tried before an international military tribunal to be composed of representatives of the wartime alliance, including France.

Once a judicial solution had been accepted, American, British, Soviet, and French jurists met in London in July and August 1945, to negotiate an agreement for the unprecedented international trial that was to take place, and to decide whom to indict. Negotiations for the establishment of the IMT took the better part of a month. The task of reconciling discrepancies that arose because of substantive differences in the legal systems of the four countries proved to be exceedingly challenging and, at times, almost impossible for the jurists. For instance, the Soviets never could understand the appeal of the adversary system.[23] Nonetheless, the parties came to an agreement, deciding the trial would be held in Nuremberg – a symbolic and practical venue for the Allies because of that city's former importance to the Nazi party and because its Palace of Justice was still relatively intact. The main charge against the Nazi leadership was the common plan or conspiracy to commit aggressive war, more commonly known as crimes against peace. This created serious problems for the French and Soviet representatives, because their national laws included no provision for the crime of "conspiracy." Finally, the Americans insisted that particular Nazi organizations such as the SS, SA, German High Command, and the Reich Cabinet be prosecuted in the expectation that conviction of these organizations would facilitate the conviction of individual members in later proceedings. The result of these negotiations was the London Agreement and its Charter of August 8, 1945, a compromise agreement signed by the British, Americans, Soviets, and French, which, although flawed, provided the Allies with a legal foundation to try and punish the highest-ranking Nazi war criminals.[24]

The IMT was convened at the Palace of Justice in Nuremberg in November 1945. On trial were twenty-two of the highest-ranking political and military leaders of the former regime.[25] The trial was the longest in U.S. history and the second longest in British, lasting a full year and producing eleven death sentences. The conduct of the IMT and the outcome of the trial would have a significant impact on later American and British war crimes policy. Almost as soon as the trial began, difficulties arose among the prosecutors from the four allied nations. These conflicts prompted the

[23] M. Cherif Bassiouni, *Crimes against Humanity in International Criminal Law* (The Hague, 1999), 20.

[24] Charter of the IMT, August 8, 1945 in *TWC*, vol. 4, xii–xviii. See also Wolfe, "Flaws in the Nuremberg Legacy," 441–442 & Bassiouni, *Crimes against Humanity*, 21.

[25] Only twenty-one defendants appeared in the dock at Nuremberg. Gustav Krupp von Bohlen und Hallbach was indicted, but too sick to stand trial. Martin Bormann was tried in absentia, and Robert Ley hanged himself before the trial began.

Americans to promulgate new legislation that would allow for a continuation of judicial proceedings against additional Nazi war criminals, but on a zonal (national) rather than international level. What resulted were twelve Subsequent Nuremberg proceedings, one of which was the *Einsatzgruppen* trial.

Many historians have written on the subject of the origins of the original IMT trial in 1945. But very little has been written about the additional twelve Subsequent Nuremberg proceedings, and there is scarcely a reference anywhere in the literature to their origins.[26] In what follows, I attempt to go some way toward filling this gap by explaining why and how the Americans decided to hold war crimes trials subsequent to the IMT. This is no easy task. Documentation is scattered between many different record groups and private collections and, even then, it is a challenge to figure out the genesis of the decision. In some ways, this is not surprising given that America's German policy was not fixed in the early postwar period. The emphasis here is on the transitional period between the beginning of the IMT in 1945 and the beginning of the NMT in 1946. This chapter shows that Robert Jackson, the U.S. Supreme Court Justice appointed by President Truman in May 1945 to prosecute the most prominent Nazi war criminals, was not only instrumental in the planning and preparation of the original IMT, but he also played a significant role in the origins of the NMT as well. It was his negative experiences during the IMT that led him to conclude that the United States should not participate in a second internationally prosecuted trial, if at all possible. Jackson believed the United States would be better off prosecuting war criminals without their allies, or at least without the Soviets. Cold war attitudes quickly made their way into the courtrooms of Nuremberg. Far from being the last great act of allied cooperation then, Nuremberg was the first battleground of the cold war. What resulted was the abandonment of further legal cooperation with the Soviets and the adoption of laws and rules that would enable the Americans to initiate and develop their own trial program involving 185 individuals in twelve separate cases, all prosecuted at Nuremberg, but by the Americans alone.

[26] This trend is changing. Paul Weindling has written about the origins of the Doctors' trial, "From International to Zonal Trials: The Origins of the Nuremberg Medical Trial," *Holocaust and Genocide Studies* 3: 14 (Winter, 2000), 367–389 and *Nazi Medicine and the Nuremberg Trials: From Medical War Crimes to Informed Consent* (New York, 2004). Peter Maguire published his PhD dissertation on the Ministries trial (Case 12 of the NMT) as *Law and War: An American Story* (New York, 2000) and Valerie Hébert's book on the trial of the German High Command will be published by University Press of Kansas as *Hitler's Soldiers on Trial: The Nuremberg High Command Case and the Politics of Punishment, 1947–1958* in 2009. In addition, Donald Bloxham, *Genocide on Trial: War Crimes Trials and the Formation of Holocaust History and Memory* (Oxford, 2001) and "'The Trial that Never Was': Why there was no Second International Trial of Major War Criminals at Nuremberg," *History* 87 (2002), 41–60, discusses the origins of the trials.

American War Crimes Policy

When Robert Jackson became Chief of Counsel for the Prosecution of Axis Criminality in May 1945, the United States had no definite plan to try war criminals other than those indicted by the IMT. Rather, the Americans formulated their war crimes policy for Germany between June 1945, and November 1946, during which time trials were ongoing. Planning was ad hoc, but began seriously in the summer of 1945, while Robert Jackson was in London negotiating with America's allies to establish an international tribunal (what became the IMT) to try war criminals. During this time a legal team was assembled in the United States to work with Jackson on the unprecedented international trial. Jackson's interim report of June 7, 1945, laid the foundation for a basic war crimes policy for occupied Germany and it was subsequently codified in Joint Chiefs of Staff 1023/10, titled "The Identification and Apprehension of Persons Suspected of War Crimes." JCS 1023 was broad; it called for the punishment of all individuals who committed crimes from January 30, 1933, onward. Given that 8 million Germans were members of the Nazi party in May 1945, the number of potential war criminals was staggering.[27] The expectation was that acts committed prior to the war would be prosecuted and first-hand participants of crime, as well as those who aided them, were indictable. Significantly, for later trials, the directive stated that those who were "members of groups or organizations connected with the commission of such crimes" were also considered potential war criminals.[28] Because of its vast scope, JCS 1023 posed enormous challenges for those planning war crimes trials; nonetheless, it became the basis of American war crimes policy until 1949, when the Americans ceased prosecuting war criminals altogether.[29]

The 1023 directive replaced JCS 1067 as a statement of policy on the issue of war criminals.[30] Whereas JCS 1067 was ambiguous in its aims, JCS 1023 was pointed. It specifically instructed American military authorities to "investigate, apprehend and detain all persons" suspected of war crimes and it "urged" the other occupying powers to adopt policies for their zones of occupation similar to the ones the Americans applied to theirs.[31]

---

[27] Memorandum, "Organization for further Proceedings against Axis War Criminals and Certain Other Offenders," December 5, 1945, in NARA RG 153, War Crimes Branch (WCB) Nuremberg Administration Files 1944–1949, box 2, I 84–1 folder. On the number of Germans who were members of the Nazi party see Jeffrey Herf, *Divided Memory: The Nazi Past in the Two Germanys* (Cambridge, MA, 1997), 202–203.

[28] Taylor, *Final Report*, 4–5.

[29] *Ibid.*, 6.

[30] Maguire, *Law and War*, 145–146.

[31] JCS 1023/10 was approved by the Joint Chiefs of Staff on July 15, 1945, Taylor, *Final Report*, 4 and 242–249. In July 1947, Americans replaced its punitive policy with one that encouraged German recovery. Bloxham, *Genocide on Trial*, 27 and Maguire, *Law and War*,

General Eisenhower charged Brigadier General Edward C. Betts, the Theater Judge Advocate and former Professor of Law at the United States Military Academy, with the task of implementing and administering JCS 1023.[32] One hundred thousand Germans were immediately arrested and imprisoned for future trial. Many of these men were considered minor criminals, to be dealt with by the denazification courts then being set up, but several hundred were considered major war criminals, at least as important as those being tried by the IMT, and Betts wanted to deal with them immediately.[33] Thus, he ordered the U.S. Legal Division of the Control Council (the quadripartite organizational authority formed in June 1945 to deal with occupation issues of which the OMGUS was the American component) to develop a new legal strategy for the punishment of war criminals zonally. Charles Fahy, an important legal advisor to the Military Governor and the Department of State, was to head the committee.[34] There is no question that the Americans needed to develop a new legal framework to deal with the ever-growing number of detained war criminals, yet, they were also looking for a way to extricate themselves from the Soviets, who they found difficult to work with. Cold war tensions reinforced American views that zonal trials were a more expeditious way of prosecuting war criminals than international tribunals. Recent research has shown that the Soviets may have been even more disappointed with the course of the IMT than the Americans. The Soviets had gone to Nuremberg with the expectation that they would have a lot of control over the proceedings, but were sorely disappointed when they perceived the Americans to have "highjacked" the proceedings as their own.[35] Ironically, the Americans felt the same way. For them, the Soviets had too much presence, clear evidence that even at this early date the two superpowers ideologically clashed. Under these trying circumstances, who better to promote zonal trials than someone who had experienced quadripartite prosecution first hand – the American Chief Prosecutor.

145–147. Also, Memorandum, "Law Providing for the Punishment of War Criminals and Similar Offenders," September 28, 1945, in NARA RG 260, OMGUS, Executive Office, the Office of the Adjutant General, box 642, CCL10 folder.

[32] Betts was made Deputy Director for War Crimes in the Legal Division of the American element of the Control Council. Betts died in May 1946. Fratcher, "American Organization for Prosecution of German War Criminals," 53–54 and 70.

[33] Memorandum, "Further Trials," January 30, 1946 in NARA RG 260, OMGUS, Functional Offices and Divisions, OCCWC, box 2, Subsequent Proceedings Division folder. See also, Taylor, *Final Report*, 16 and Weindling, "From International to Zonal Trials," 366.

[34] Under the Potsdam Agreement supreme authority in Germany was to be the Control Council, which consisted of the United States, Great Britain, the Soviet Union, and France. The Legal Division was the American component of the Legal Directorate that was the quadripartite legal body of the Control Council. See Charles Fahy, "Legal Problems of German Occupation," *Michigan Law Review* 47 (1948), 15 and 17.

[35] Hirsch, "Soviets at Nuremberg," 701–703, 714–715.

When problems among the prosecution teams at Nuremberg surfaced early on in the IMT, Jackson made his opposition to a second international trial known. He insisted that the most effective and least costly way to punish major war criminals (here he was thinking about the German financiers and industrialists who had escaped indictment) was to ensure the continuation of trials on a zonal basis, not by quadripartite prosecution, as was the case with the IMT. However, if the Americans were to proceed alone, as Jackson favored, they needed an alternative legal structure to the *London Charter*, which was due to expire on August 8, 1946.[36]

The Americans acted quickly and drafted a law permitting for the punishment of war criminals on a zonal basis.[37] After much rewriting, a draft of new legislation was approved by the Coordinating Committee of the Control Council on November 1, 1945, and was promulgated on December 20 as Control Council Law No. 10 (CCL10). All four occupation governments approved the law, which was patterned on the *London Charter*. The promulgation of CCL10 satisfied the demands of JCS 1023, which called for the adoption of uniform legal policies for Germany, and provided the Americans an escape valve if they decided it was desirable to extricate themselves from further international legal cooperation, yet still pursue additional prosecutions.[38]

Although CCL10 was not everything the Americans hoped it would be, it did give each occupying government the authority to arrest, indict, and prosecute anyone considered to have committed a crime under Article 2 of the law, which was similar to the *London Charter's* Article 6 that specified four acts as criminal: crimes against peace, war crimes, crimes against humanity, and membership in organizations declared criminal by the IMT.[39] In the indictment filed with the IMT, the charge of conspiracy was used as the unifying element for all of the other charges before the court.[40] Although conspiracy was included in CCL10, it never held the same sway as it had at the IMT trial; in fact, the judges convened for the Subsequent proceedings dismissed the charge in the Medical, Justice, and Pohl cases.[41]

---

[36] Letter, Jackson to Robert Patterson, Secretary of War, February 7, 1946 in NARA RG 466, Prisons Division, Security Segregated Records, box 10, War Crimes Trials (WCT) 1949 folder.

[37] Minutes of the Twelfth Meeting of the Coordinating Committee, October 6, 1945 in NARA RG 260, U.S. Element of Inter-Allied Organizations, Allied Control Authority, Coordinating Committee 1945–1948, box 135, Minutes 1945 folder.

[38] Allied Control Authority Control Council CONL/P(45)53(Final), December 20, 1945 in NARA RG 260, U.S. Element of inter-Allied Organizations, U.S. Element Allied Control Authority, Control Council, box 125, master file CONL/P(45)51–64 folder.

[39] Indictment, *Trial*, roll 1, 3. See also "Control Council Law No. 10," in *TWC*, vol. 4, xviii–xxi and Letter, Jackson to Taylor, July 28, 1949, TTP 5-3-2-16.

[40] Taylor, *Final Report*, 70–71.

[41] *Ibid.*

Article 1 of the new law was intended to incorporate the substance of the *London Charter* although it eventually ended up replacing it.[42] Article 1 gave official sanction to the Moscow Declaration of 1943, which had promised that those Germans responsible for atrocities in specific geographic areas would "be sent back to the countries in which their abominable deeds were done," so that they could be punished accordingly and by local authorities. To facilitate this possibility, rules of extradition had to be written.[43] Thus, Articles 4 and 5 of CCL10 provided for the exchange and extradition of suspected war criminals. Article 2 replicated in large part the crimes outlined in the *London Charter*: crimes against peace, war crimes, and crimes against humanity with one major exception. In the new law, the connection between crimes against humanity and war crimes was severed from crimes against peace representing a paradigmatic and legal shift away from the crime of aggressive war that the Americans had focused on at the IMT.[44] The fourth crime, membership in organizations declared criminal by the IMT was new and was written in response to the need for a provision in the law that would permit the courts to try and punish individual members of the organizations then being prosecuted at Nuremberg.[45]

Articles 2, 3, and 4 of the law were also designed to provide a uniform legal foundation to try war criminals in the four zones of occupation authorizing zonal commanders to arrest and indict suspects as well as establish zonal tribunals to try them. Although the intention of these articles was to provide uniformity, like virtually all elements of the occupation, their application was anything but uniform. Ultimately, only the Americans and French made use of the provisions. The British were to handle war crimes in military courts and under Royal Warrant.[46] The Soviets, on the other hand, had been trying war criminals since 1943, but under CCL10 they established no tribunals whatsoever.[47] CCL10 made no provision for rules of procedure

[42] "Comparison between the *London Charter* and Control Council Law No. 10," undated in NARA RG 238, OCCWC, Executive Office, Publications Division, box 5, folder 6.

[43] "Declaration of German Atrocities," November 1, 1943 in *TWC*, vol. 4, x.

[44] Lawrence Douglas made this argument orally at the United States Holocaust Memorial Museum (USHMM) summer workshop, "From Prosecution to Historiography: American, German and Jewish Perspectives of the Subsequent Nuremberg Trials," July 21–August 1, 2008.

[45] Control Council Law No 10, "Punishment of Persons Guilty of War Crimes, Crimes against Peace and Against Humanity," December 20, 1945, quoted in Taylor, *Final Report*, 250.

[46] On the limitations of the Royal Warrant, see Bloxham, *Genocide on Trial*.

[47] Robert K. Woetzel, *The Nuremberg Trials in International Law* (New York, 1962), 220 and Taylor, *Final Report*, 136–137. On the Soviet trials, see Andreas Hilger, *Deutsche Kriegsgefangene in der Sowjetunion 1941–1956. Kriegsgefangenenpolitik, Lageralltag und Erinnerung* (Essen, 2000); Andreas Hilger, Ute Schmidt, and Günther Wagenlehner (eds.), *Sowjetische Militärtribunale. Band 1: Die Verurteilung Deutscher Kriegsgefangener 1941–1953* (Köln, 2001); and, Gerd R. Überschär (ed.) *Der Nationalsozialismus vor Gericht: Die alliierten Prozesse gegen Kriegsverbrecher und Soldaten 1943–1952* (Frankfurt, 1999).

nor did it establish any tribunals. These issues were left to the zonal commanders to set up later, and at their own discretion.[48] The promulgation of CCL10 provided the Americans with a basic administrative and legal framework for the Subsequent Nuremberg proceedings and gave them the opportunity to prosecute war criminals on their own.[49] Ultimately the new law offered a much broader scope for prosecution than the *London Charter* had, suggesting that the Allies wanted a broader program of punishment.

While Fahy's legal team was writing CCL10, General Betts was grappling with the logistics of implementing JCS 1023. The task was daunting. How were the Americans to avoid the problems of quadripartite prosecution? Who would direct and administer the new American war crimes program? Who would prosecute the seemingly endless numbers of German war criminals? Betts believed he had some answers and the first order of business was to ask Jackson to head a new American-only war crimes program, whether the Justice would accept remained to be seen.[50]

As it turned out Jackson supported Bett's initiative. He felt strongly that the American war crimes program would be discredited if U.S. authorities failed to follow through with the prosecution of members of criminal organizations and other war criminals currently in American custody. Thus, Jackson encouraged Betts to pursue additional war crimes trials in the American zone, but he warned him that a new war crimes program was no small undertaking; Washington would have to ensure that there was adequate staffing and funding to do the work properly. This never happened. As Telford Taylor (Jackson's successor) would discover, the staffing problem at Nuremberg plagued the Office of Chief of Counsel for its entire existence.[51]

How to organize and prosecute additional war criminals was the subject of intense discussion for months. At issue was who would take over Jackson's job as Chief of Counsel when he retired. Jackson would help with the planning of the future trials, he promised Betts, but he preferred to return to his job on the Supreme Court in Washington rather than stay in Germany.[52] Also unresolved was which U.S. agency would be in charge of supervising

[48] Taylor, *Final Report*, 7–10.
[49] It also enabled zonal commanders to grant jurisdiction to German courts for crimes against humanity, which each zone handled differently.
[50] Letter, Betts to Jackson, October 19, 1945 in the Papers of Robert H. Jackson, Library of Congress Manuscript Division, box 110, Nuremberg War Crimes Trial Office File, Subsequent Trials folder 1 (from here forward simply RHJ Papers, box number, file, folder) and Letter, Betts to Jackson, October 19, 1945 in Telford Taylor Papers (from here forward TTP), 20-1-2-16, IMT-Biddle.
[51] Letter, Jackson to Betts, October 24, 1945 in RHJ Papers, box 110, Nuremberg War Crimes Trial Office File, Subsequent Trials folder (1).
[52] Jackson was in Europe for nearly eighteen months. During that time, twenty Supreme Court cases were delayed. Jeffrey D. Hockett, "Justice Robert H. Jackson, the Supreme Court, and

prosecutions, and finally, the logistics and feasibility of trying hundreds of thousands of war criminals as dictated by the JCS 1023 directive.[53] Jackson, Betts, and Bedell Smith, the Chief of Staff of the United States Forces, agreed that time was of the essence; they should begin preparing immediately for further proceedings rather than wait until the completion of the IMT. Even at this early date, there is evidence to suggest that American officials felt constrained for time, and many expressed the view that they wanted an expeditious end to programs that had not yet been implemented, such as zonal war crimes trials. By 1947, virtually every nation in Europe wanted to see an end to war crimes trials. By then, the world was ready to move on. But, in December 1945, Betts decided that Jackson's Office of the Chief of Counsel would extend its work "beyond the present trial," and take on the work of "all further war crimes proceedings."[54]

If Jackson would not run the office though, who would? Finding a replacement was a pressing issue. Many officials believed that Telford Taylor, one of Jackson's most able assistants at Nuremberg, should become the new Chief of Counsel.[55] Taylor was a good choice. He was a Harvard-trained lawyer and "New Dealer" who had worked as an intelligence officer during the war for the American military in London.[56] At the IMT, he had been responsible for prosecuting the case against the General Staff and High Command of the German Armed forces.[57] Taylor admitted he was not an expert on European affairs, but in some ways his military training and experience during the war made him better qualified for the job of Chief Prosecutor than Jackson, even though he did not carry the same clout as the latter in Washington nor was his name as widely recognized in legal circles.[58] Taylor was appointed Jackson's successor in December 1945, although he did not officially accept the position until March of the following year.[59] By that time, the legal, political, and administrative foundations for the subsequent trials had been laid and the Americans were committed to prosecuting them.

the Nuremberg Trial," Gerard Casper, Dennis J. Hutchinson, and David A. Strauss (eds.), *The Supreme Court Review: 1990* (Chicago, 1990), 257 and 274.

53 Memorandum, "Organization for Further Proceedings against Axis War Criminals and certain Other Offenders," December 5, 1945 in NARA RG 153 (JAG), WCB, NA Files 1944–1949, box 2 I 84-1 folder.

54 Taylor quoted in Weindling, "From International to Zonal Trials," 366.

55 Fahy and Betts recommended Francis Shea (Associate Counsel at IMT) for the position. See Diary of Francis M. Shea, October 19 and 20, 1945 in TTP, 20-1-3-35.

56 Maguire, *Law and War*, 148.

57 Taylor, *Anatomy*, 236.

58 Biographical Data Telford Taylor, May 1946 in RHJ Papers, box 110, Nuremberg War Crimes Trial Office File, U.S. Chief of Counsel Subsequent Trials folder.

59 The delay in acceptance revolved around Taylor's wife and securing her passage to Germany. Jackson informed Truman about his decision to appoint Taylor his successor in January. Telegram, Jackson to War Department and Charles Fahy, March 14, 1946 in *ibid*.

Taylor's new job would be "to organize and plan for further prosecutions – before another international military tribunal, or in zonal courts, or in both, as developments may dictate."[60]

The IMT, many historians would argue, was the last great act of international cooperation by the wartime Allies. If true, then the NMT marks a shift away from wartime cooperation. Evidence suggests that tensions between the superpowers were gestating well before the conclusion of the IMT.[61] Certainly, part of the transition from war to peace was to regularize American policy under the authority of the military government. As Chief of Council, Jackson had only to answer to the president; after all, American participation in the IMT was an executive decision. To normalize the system for the future prosecution of war criminals, the system had to be restructured.[62] In practice, this meant the separation of military and civilian crimes. Betts divided jurisdictional responsibilities between the Office of the Theater Judge Advocate and Taylor's new organization. The Judge Advocate would be responsible for overseeing all military crimes, particularly crimes committed against U.S. nationals and prisoners of war, and atrocities committed in concentration camps that the U.S. forces liberated. Taylor's organization would handle the most important and high-profile trials of war criminals. Civilian, not military, courts would prosecute the high-profile cases, although they would be under the jurisdiction of the American Military Government. Rather than remove war crimes trials from the political arena, dividing up jurisdiction reinforced the political nature of the civilian trials.[63]

Taylor's new responsibilities could be likened to those of a district attorney under American state law. To handle the planning of future trials, Jackson created a "Subsequent Proceedings Division" within his own office. Again, very much like an office of a district attorney, where the DA decides against whom indictments are filed. On January 16, 1946, President Truman agreed to these proposals issuing Executive Order 9679, which officially sanctioned the new course American war crimes policy would take.[64]

[60] Letter, Jackson to Truman, December 4, 1945 in NARA RG 466, HICOG Board, War Criminals, box 15, folder 43.
[61] Hirsch, "Soviets at Nuremberg," 726–727, argues that the role of the IMT in the postwar world needs reconceptualization. Far from being the last act of allied cooperation, it was in fact one of the first battlegrounds of the Cold War.
[62] Letter, W.B. Smith to Jackson, December 1, 1945 in NARA RG 466, HICOG Board, War Criminals, box 15, Subsequent Proceedings folder.
[63] Letter, Jackson to Truman, December 4, 1945 in WHO File 325A, Office of the US CCPAC, HST.
[64] Executive Order No. 9679, January 16, 1946 in NARA RG 260, OMGUS, Executive Office of the Adjutant General, Military Government Ordinances 1945–1949, box 640, Ordinance No. 7 folder.

A Second International Trial?

Having put the wheels in motion for the future prosecution of war criminals in the American zone, there was one major question left to answer: should the Americans also participate in a second international trial? A second international trial would not have been an issue at all had it not been for a legal blunder regarding the prosecution of the German industrialist Gustav Krupp von Bohlen und Halbach. The issue was intimately connected with the prosecution of German financiers and industrialists who escaped prosecution in the IMT trial and who Americans hoped to try in a subsequent trial.

From the outset of negotiations in London, in the summer of 1945, the Allies quarreled over who should be indicted at Nuremberg. Ultimately, cross-sections of leading Nazis were selected, not because the evidence against them was conclusive, but rather because the planners of the trial wanted to try the highest-ranking and most recognizable of the leading Nazi personalities still alive.[65] From the very beginning of negotiations, the Allies had considered German industrialists and financiers major war criminals, responsible in large part for the planning and perpetration of aggressive war that was at the heart of the legal case. The defendants, the Allies reasoned, should be tried for crimes against peace and crimes against humanity and should be held as responsible as the German military leadership and high-ranking party officials for the planning and waging of aggressive war.[66]

In the summer of 1945, during the negotiations that led to the IMT indictment, Jackson and his colleagues decided that Gustav Krupp (the patriarch of the industrialist Krupp empire) should be indicted. Unfortunately, no one bothered to check whether the elderly Krupp was capable of withstanding a trial, nor did anyone realize that Gustav's son, Alfried, had taken over sole control of the family business during the war. As it turned out, in 1945, the senior Krupp was both senile and bedridden and, therefore, incompetent to stand trial, but none of the prosecutors knew this. Had they known, they would have included Krupp's son Alfried in the original indictment. Once the indictment was filed, however, there was little the chief prosecutors could do to have Alfried, who was just as guilty as his father, added to the roster of defendants. They appealed to the court for an indictment against Alfried, but it was rejected. Carelessness of planning meant that neither Krupp would appear in the dock at Nuremberg; more importantly for the origins of the Subsequent proceedings, this meant that no representative of German industry would be tried in 1945.[67]

---

[65] Harris, *Tyranny on Trial*, 28–30.
[66] Taylor, *Anatomy*, 81.
[67] *Ibid.*, 87–94.

The French were unhappiest about this situation. The German industrialists had employed large numbers of Frenchmen as slave-laborers during the war and the French wanted the industrialists to account for their crimes. In their view, something had to be done to rectify this situation. To placate its citizens and bring justice to the victims of slave labor, the French enlisted the support of the British, whose chief prosecutor, Sir Hartley Shawcross, promised them support in a second international trial of industrialists.[68] On November 20, 1945, the day the IMT began, the French and British publicly declared that they were contemplating a further international trial of leading German industrialists, including Alfried Krupp.[69] Whereas Jackson never disagreed that German industrialists and financiers should be held accountable for their crimes, he consistently refused to commit the U.S. to a second international trial, and certainly not before the conclusion of the IMT.[70]

From the very beginning of the Nuremberg process, Jackson had deeply distrusted the motives of the Soviets. As early as the summer of 1945, he had felt frustrated by the Russian view of the trial as "formality."[71] He feared the Soviets were using the Nuremberg trial for political reasons rather than justice. Although Americans were not beneath politics themselves, one of their stated aims for Nuremberg was to demonstrate to the German people the benefits of democratic justice, and Soviet-style show trials were clearly not what Jackson had in mind.[72] Jackson was also not beneath personal ambition and he naturally worried that Nuremberg could potentially harm his own legal standing on the Supreme Court. As he saw it, Russian behavior compromised the IMT's integrity and, therefore, his own. He feared that if the Soviets were not checked, Nuremberg would be viewed negatively, a political show trial staged for the sole purpose of conviction.[73] Jackson worried about Nuremberg's credibility and feared the landmark judicial process he helped to establish would be tainted by Soviet actions. He was especially anxious now that a second four-power trial was being considered and the Soviets desired control over it.[74] The Soviets felt, perhaps rightly so, that the first IMT trial was too much an "American show."[75] Even if the Russians agreed to American or British leadership, there was no guarantee they would in any way help pay the costs of a second four-power trial. Everyone except

---

[68] Bloxham, "'The Trial that Never Was,'" 46.

[69] Taylor, *Final Report*, 23.

[70] *Ibid*, and Taylor, *Anatomy*, 72.

[71] Memorandum, Brabner-Smith to Jackson, July 22, 1946 in NARA RG 153 (JAG), WCB, NA Files 1944–1949, box 2, I84–1 folder.

[72] Letter, Jackson to Truman, April 24, 1946, President's Secretary's Files, HST.

[73] Jackson quoted in Hockett, "Justice Robert H. Jackson," 259 and 278.

[74] Letter, Jackson to Howard Peterson, May 22, 1946 in *ibid.*, box 1, Second International Trial folder and memorandum, Jackson to Taylor, February 5, 1946 in *ibid.*

[75] Memorandum, Brabner-Smith to Jackson, July 22, 1946 in NARA RG 153 (JAG), WCB, NA Files 1944–1949, box 2, I84-1 folder.

the United States was broke, and, as a result, none could make good on their commitments to provide adequate staffing for the IMT. The burden of staffing and, ultimately, most of the costs of the original Nuremberg trial thus fell to the United States.[76]

Taylor was not as fearful of the Soviets as Jackson. In fact, he tentatively supported the idea of a second international trial as long as it was not in the Soviet zone and it prosecuted industrialists and financiers who had escaped justice the first time round.[77] For Taylor, it was not an either/or situation; rather, he envisioned a second international trial and a series of zonal trials.[78] Although Jackson had sway in Washington, he also had to be careful. He did not want a public confrontation with the Soviets or with Taylor, most especially, however, he did not want a second four-power trial. How could he prevent both? By appealing to policy makers in Washington. Thus, he telegrammed the War Department emphasizing his concerns.[79] He and Patterson discussed the issue at length, yet no consensus was reached.

The issue of a second international trial was like an open wound for Jackson, it would not go away. In the spring of 1946, it reared its ugly head again when the British Chief Prosecutor, Hartley Shawcross, raised the issue at a meeting of the chief prosecutors. When asked directly if the United State would participate, Jackson was noncommittal. The French and Soviets both favored a second international trial, although the Soviets tended to agree with Jackson that before they could fully support the idea they would have to wait for the conclusion of the trial in progress. In solidarity with the French, the British publicly supported a future four-power trial of Nazi industrialists; in private, however, they were much more reticent.[80] They had fewer resources at their disposal than the Americans, who were the only nation to come through the war financially unscathed, and they also worried that a second trial might turn into an ideological sparring match.[81] As a compromise, all parties agreed they would begin to collect evidence for

---

[76] Telegram, Jackson to War Department, February 7, 1946 in RHJ Papers, box 110, Nuremberg War Crimes Trial Office File, U.S. Chief of Counsel, Subsequent Trials folder. On the cost of the trial, see Letter, Truman to Musmanno, October 15, 1958, file 1470, President Truman folder, Michael Musmanno papers, Gumberg Library, Duquesne University, Pittsburgh, PA (hereafter MMP).

[77] Memoranda, Taylor to Jackson, January 30, 1946 and February 5, 1946 in NARA RG 153 (JAG), WCB, Nuremberg Administration File, box 1, Second International Trial folder.

[78] *Ibid.*

[79] Telegram, Jackson to War Department, February 7, 1946 in RHJ Papers, box 110, Nuremberg War Crimes Trial, Office File, U.S. Chief of Counsel, Subsequent Trials folder.

[80] Memorandum, Jackson to the Secretaries of State and War, April 8, 1946, in *ibid* and "Minutes of Chief Prosecutors held in room 117, April 5, 1946," in Taylor, *Final Report*, 269–270. Compare with Weindling, "From International to Zonal Trials," 368–369 who argues that Shawcross initially supported a second international trial.

[81] *Ibid.*, 48–49.

a future trial of "a dozen" or so industrialists, but with the understanding that this evidence did not have to be used in a four-power trial.[82] Jackson relayed the news to Washington. Word came back on April 24, 1946, when Secretary of War Patterson, informed Jackson that a second international trial was "highly undesirable," but not entirely unthinkable. Patterson thus directed Taylor to prepare for a second trial just in case the U.S. changed its mind.[83] Whereas Patterson and Jackson agreed, their views were not without detractors. One of those who had helped to persuade Truman to hold war crimes trials in the first place, Samuel Rosenman, was perhaps the most vociferous, believing it was America's moral duty to work with its wartime allies and prosecute as many war criminals as possible.[84]

Jackson and Rosenman's disagreement about American participation in a future international trial probably reflected their cold war attitudes, but whether or not Jackson had the upper hand is debatable. What is certain was that both men were outspoken, actively lobbying the president on their respective positions.[85] For instance, in a rather lengthy letter to Truman, Jackson set out the reasons he believed a second international trial would be a political mistake. Cold war attitudes clouded his judgment. He argued that the proposed trial of Nazi industrialists and financiers was legally weak under Soviet leadership because their ideology prohibited them from an objective prosecutorial position. He also feared the public might perceive a trial that dealt only with financiers and industrialists as political.[86] A trial that dealt solely with industrialists would expose the role of the Soviet Union in the early years of the war, particularly vis-à-vis Poland, which would embarrass all of the IMT participants, not just the Soviets. Given Jackson's personal stake in the IMT, and its potential contribution to international law, it is not surprising that he would shudder at the thought of publicly exposing the aggressive actions of the Soviets in the early part of the war.[87] During a period when the United States was growing increasingly wary of Soviet

[82] Memorandum, Jackson to the Secretaries of State and War, April 8, 1946, in RHJ Papers, box 110, Nuremberg War Crimes Trial, Office File, U.S. Chief of Counsel, Subsequent trials folder.

[83] Taylor, *Final Report*, 24.

[84] Letter, Samuel I. Rosenman to Truman, May 27, 1946 in Subject File (Foreign Affairs, Germany), Nuremberg War Crimes folder, HST.

[85] Letter, Fahy to Jackson, February 20, 1946, RHJ Papers, box 110, Nuremberg War Crimes trial office file, Subsequent trials folder and telegram from Clay to War Department, February 19, 1946, NARA RG 153 (JAG), WCB, NA Files 1944–1949, box 3, Bk4 85-2 folder.

[86] Letter, Jackson to Truman, May 13, 1946, in President's Secretary File, box 179, Subject file (Foreign Affairs), HST. See also memorandum, Jackson to Truman, May 13, 1946, quoted in Taylor, *Final Report*, 276–279.

[87] Hockett, "Justice Robert H. Jackson, the Supreme Court, and the Nuremberg Trial," 257–263.

actions, Jackson recommended that the United States "shed responsibility [for additional trials] rather than assume more [responsibility.]"[88] Telford Taylor was more ambivalent.

Well before the Truman administration made a decision about a second international trial, Taylor was kept busy preparing as if the there would be one. Between May 15 and July 2, 1946, he consulted the delegates of the other powers concerning the logistics of a future international trial, particularly where the trial would be held and who would preside over it, but also who to indict. As the U.S. representative, Taylor put forward the names of two of the managing directors of the IG Farben chemical combine, Hermann Schmitz and Georg von Schnitzler. U.S. authorities had investigated the chemical giant and discovered the company had participated in the elaborate slave labor program. Should there be a second IMT, the British wanted the Cologne banker Kurt von Schröder to be included and the French proposed Hermann Röchling, an important figure in the Saarland's coal and steel industry. All agreed that Alfried Krupp, the man who had escaped punishment the first time around, would head the roster of indictees. Oddly, the Soviets did not put forward any names for consideration, although they did reserve the right to add names to the list.[89]

Although Taylor reserved judgment on the location of a second trial, the British and French agreed that Nuremberg should be the site, arguing that it would preserve continuity of staffing and facilities, although the British privately shared Jackson's fears about holding a second international trial in the Soviet zone.[90] Understandably, the Soviets preferred Berlin, especially as they had only reluctantly agreed to hold the first international trial in the American zone.[91] Whatever its new locale, the delegates agreed that the judges would select the new tribunal's president as had been done for the IMT. Following the final meeting of July 2, 1946, the committee broke up and the delegates took the proposals back to their governments for consideration.[92]

Taylor's findings confirmed Jackson's worst fears and prompted high-level discussions in Washington. During the summer and fall of 1946, Secretary of State James Byrnes, Assistant Secretary of War Howard C. Petersen (Petersen was officially in charge of all matters involving war crimes), Jackson, and Taylor discussed – at length – the issue of a second

[88] Letter, Jackson to Truman, May 13, 1946 in President's Secretary File, box 179, Subject file (Foreign Affairs), HST.

[89] Taylor, *Final Report*, 24–25.

[90] Bloxham, "'The Trial that Never Was,'" 52.

[91] Hirsch, "Soviets at Nuremberg," 717.

[92] Minutes, Meeting of Committee, June 6, 1946 in RHJ Papers, box 110, Nuremberg War Crimes Trial Office File, U.S. Chief of Counsel, Subsequent trials folder and Minutes of Meeting of Committee, May 15, 1946 in NARA RG 260, Functional Offices and Divisions, OCCWC, box 1, Support of OCCWC.

internationally prosecuted trial. Jackson felt so strongly that he met with Byrnes to discuss the issue in person.[93] Jackson's arguments may have induced the already predisposed cold warriors in Washington to err on the side of caution as it was decided that the unofficial American position was "to avoid a second international trial," if at all possible. But Rosenman's concerns were also taken seriously: if avoiding a second internationally prosecuted trial would cause embarrassment or political problems, the U.S. would participate rather than give the appearance of abandoning their moral position.[94] Petersen and Byrnes decided that if there were to be no second international trial, the evidence that Taylor and the Subsequent Proceedings Division had amassed against the industrialists and financiers would be used to try these individuals in American courts in Germany. To this end, on September 16, 1946, the Americans secretly requested the extradition of six industrialists from the British.[95] The British decision to comply with the American request not only "signalled the end of British contemplation of a further international trial," but it also helped to shape the American war crimes program in that many of those tried in the NMT came from the British zone.[96] Under these circumstances, it was felt all efforts should be made to discourage Truman from opting for American participation in a second four-power trial.[97] Byrnes and Petersen had reached consensus, it was now up to Jackson to persuade the president that the United States should, at all costs, avoid a second international trial.[98]

Jackson had his chance at the conclusion of the IMT, in the autumn of 1946, when he sent his final report to Truman. Reiterating his earlier arguments, he suggested that each occupation authority pursue justice in their own zones against prisoners in their custody. "A four-power...trial" he wrote, "is inevitably the slowest and most costly... there is neither moral nor legal obligation on the United States to undertake another trial of this character. The quickest and most satisfactory results will be obtained... from immediate commencement of our own case."[99] Although Jackson did not make his feelings about the Soviets explicit in this report, he and others in the State and War Departments were clearly wary. Many feared that the Soviets wanted to use a second internationally prosecuted trial as a vehicle for

---

[93] Taylor, *Final Report*, 25–27 and 272–284.

[94] Memorandum, Byrnes to the Secretary of War and Truman, May 29, 1946 in NARA RG 153 (JAG), WCB, NA Files 1944–1949, box 1, Second International Trial folder and Letter, Howard Petersen to Taylor, June 17, 1946 in *ibid.*

[95] Bloxham, "'The Trial that Never Was,'" 53.

[96] *Ibid.*, 54–55.

[97] Memoranda, Jackson to Taylor, August 16, 1946 and August 21, 1946, in RHJ Papers, box 110, Nuremberg WCT File, United States Chief of Counsel Subsequent trials folder.

[98] Memorandum, Jackson to Byrnes, August 21, 1946 in *ibid.*

[99] Jackson, "Final Report on the Nuremberg War Crimes Trial," October 7, 1946 in WHO File 325A, Office of the US CCPAC, HST.

propaganda at home, and what better case to do so than one against "business, finance, and capital," which, given the emerging icy climate, could be
used as an "indirect attack on the American free enterprise philosophy."[100]
Research suggests that Jackson was right in one way: the Soviets did see the
courtroom as a vehicle for domestic propaganda, only their propaganda was
not intended to embarrass their western allies, but rather it was intended to
promote their own heroic role in the war against the Nazis.[101] The tensions
between east and west were exacerbated by Churchill's cold war rhetoric
and, by the autumn of 1946, most cold warriors in Washington were so
worried about the Soviets they did not want to give them any platform
whatsoever to embarrass the United States. The war had begun. Jackson's
arguments were persuasive with the cold war president, who finally decided
that the United States would not participate in a second four-power trial.
Instead, war criminals would be tried zonally and international cooperation
was superseded by national initiatives. The path to the NMT was now firmly
established.

The Americans kept quiet about their decision, however, hoping that
with time the issue of a second international trial would simply disappear.
Perhaps it would have had it not been for the French government who,
in January 1947, sent official notes to the Americans, Soviets, and British
requesting that a committee of prosecutors convene "as soon as possible"
to prepare for a second international trial.[102] The Americans were horrified, and realized they had to make their decision public, which Truman
did shortly thereafter, politely declining the French request. The American
decision to abandon a second four-power prosecution had repercussions.
The British, for example, abandoned their earlier support of the French and
planned instead to develop a trial program that corresponded to the American one. They never carried through with the elaborate plan, however,
opting instead to cooperate with American requests for extradition of prisoners from their zone.[103] By this time, the Americans had already enacted
Military Ordinance No. 7, authorizing the establishment and organization
of tribunals in its zone of occupation and Taylor's organization was well
on its way to prosecuting former Nazi doctors in the first of the NMT that
had already been in session since December.[104] Taylor's organization was
also busy gathering evidence to indict additional members of the National
Socialist hierarchy. In all, eighteen trials including several of Nazi financiers

---

[100] Letter, Col. Andrus to Father Edmund Walsh, May 1946 in RHJ Papers, box 110, NG
    WCT OF, U.S. Chief of Counsel, Subsequent trials, folder 2.
[101] Hirsch, "Soviets at Nuremberg," 717 & 719–720.
[102] "Substance of note Addressed by Embassies London, Moscow, and Paris to British, French
    and Soviet Governments," January 22, 1947, in Taylor, *Final Report*, 285.
[103] Bloxham, "'The Trial that Never Was,'" 54–55.
[104] Ordinance No. 7, in *TWC*, vol. 4, xxiii–xxvii.

and industrialists were being planned. Given the magnitude of this program the last thing the Americans needed or wanted was further entanglements with a former partner they could not trust. The Cold War, as luck would have it, ensured the continuation of war crimes trials.

Planning the Subsequent Nuremberg Proceedings

Just as the IMT trial was hastily planned in the summer of 1945, so too were the NMT. As one scholar has commented of the Subsequent proceedings, they had a "haphazard, improvised charter."[105] Indeed, it took but one year – May 1946 to May 1947 – for Taylor and his office to gather evidence, interrogate suspects, and form a plan of action to indict war criminals, a remarkably short time given the magnitude of the task at hand.[106] Preparations for their program of zonal trials took place during the same period the Americans were debating the wisdom of participating in a second international trial, and many of those involved in planning the Subsequent proceedings were also working with Jackson on the IMT. With chronic staff shortages and an enormous volume of work, it is no wonder that the planning of the trials was hurried.

The first concrete step was a change in the administrative structure for dealing with war crimes. It had been decided in the spring of 1946, that once Jackson resigned, full responsibility for the prosecution of war crimes, including responsibility overseeing the Office of Chief of Counsel, would devolve to the American Military Government. As the American authority in Germany, the OMGUS was put in charge of overseeing the entire American zonal trial program. General Lucius Clay, the Deputy Military Governor from 1945 to 1947 and Military Governor from 1947 until 1949, was in charge of implementing American policy including the administration of war crimes trials held subsequent to the IMT. A number of other American agencies also became involved in the organizational process. In Washington, the War Department's War Crimes Branch, under the direction of Colonel David "Mickey" Marcus, was responsible for recruiting staff, whereas Assistant Secretary of War Howard Petersen, oversaw all policy decisions.[107] In January 1946, the Subsequent Proceedings Division of the OCCPAC was formed and, in March, Taylor became its head, not officially replacing Jackson as Chief of Counsel until October 24, 1946, three weeks after the judgment had been rendered in the IMT case and one week after Jackson resigned. Taylor would not have as much control over the NMT as Jackson had over the IMT, but as Chief of Counsel, he was

---

[105] Marrus, "The Nuremberg Doctors' Trial in Historical Context," 110.
[106] Taylor, *Final Report*, 57.
[107] *Ibid.*, 13–14.

responsible for deciding which individuals would be indicted and tried.[108]
This proved to be a challenging and onerous task.

Concerns about whom to indict came to the fore in January 1946, when
Taylor received an alarming memorandum from Charles Fahy, Director
of the Legal Division of OMGUS. Fahy warned that under Article 2 of
CCL10, which stated that membership in organizations declared criminal
by the IMT was an indictable offense, close to 2 million Nazis would be
considered war criminals. Would they all have to be tried? The problem was
that the IMT was not willing to "make a blanket and categorical finding of
criminality" as to the members of the indicted organizations; instead, it had
to be shown that the individual members knew that the organizations they
joined were criminal or that they participated in the criminal activities of
the organization.[109] To try 2 million members of former Nazi organizations
was not only impossible, but completely unrealistic. To address this issue
Taylor prepared a plan for how the United States might best deal with a
problem of this magnitude. He thought the majority of these individuals
would have to be dealt with by the denazification courts, as it would be
simply impossible to arrange trials for so many. Besides, Taylor thought the
most important part of the new American program would be the trial of
major war criminals, those whose crimes were so serious the death penalty
would be warranted, not those low-ranking individuals who had little or no
power in the Reich and who posed no serious threat to the reconstruction of
Germany.[110] Although Taylor could not give an exact number, he estimated
that there were approximately 100 (when he became more familiar with
the operation of the Third Reich he revised this figure to between 200 and
500) individuals in the *major* war criminal category.[111] Given that the IMT
had taken a full year to prosecute twenty-two individuals, the prospect of
trying 500 more was an unrealistic and daunting task. Anxious to expedite
the process and eliminate as many low-ranking war criminals as they could
from the docket, Petersen told Taylor that no individual should be indicted
and tried on the basis of membership alone. This eliminated thousands,
perhaps hundreds of thousands, of individuals as suspects.[112]

---

[108] General memorandum No. 15, from Jackson, March 29, 1946 in RHJ Papers, box 110,
Nuremberg War Crimes trial Office File, U.S. Chief of Counsel, Subsequent trials folder.

[109] Taylor, *Final Report*, 16–17.

[110] Memorandum, Taylor to Jackson, January 30, 1946 in NARA RG 153 (JAG), WCB, NA
Files 1944–1949, box 1, Second International Trial folder; and, "Denazification," *Monthly
Report of the Military Governor, US Zone*, December 20, 1945, No. 5, 4, HST.

[111] Memorandum, Taylor to Jackson, re: Further Trials (No. 2), February 5, 1946 in NARA
RG 153 (JAG), WCB, NA Files 1944–1949, box 1, Second International Trial folder. See
also memorandum, Fahy to Jackson, 6 February 1946 in *ibid*.

[112] Telegram, Jackson to War Department, February 7, 1946 in RHJ Papers, box 110, Nuremberg WCT Office File, U.S. Chief of Counsel, Subsequent trials folder.

Taylor began the task of deciding whom to indict immediately. By this time, the Subsequent Proceedings Division of the Office of Chief of Counsel was well on its way to amassing a large amount of evidence against Nazi industrialists and financiers. Drexel Sprecher, a U.S. prosecutor at Nuremberg and an employee of OCCWC, had set up a section of the Subsequent Proceedings Division to deal specifically with the case against Nazi financiers and industrialists in the event that they would be prosecuted in a second four-power trial, and, if not, by the Americans alone. Recently, one historian has claimed that the "SS was at the centre of Allied perceptions of Nazi criminality."[113] This is not entirely true, however. In April 1946, at least, it was German financiers and industrialists who the Americans were planning to prosecute. The question of how extensive the American program of war crimes trials should be and how far down the scale of Nazi criminality they should go was left to Taylor to decide.

Taylor decided that the OCCWC would not indict anyone because of his political leadership in the Nazi enterprise. As Taylor phrased it, "it was not the purpose of Nuremberg to try *Nazis* who might or might not also be criminals, but to try suspected *criminals* who might or might not also be Nazis."[114] In his opinion, membership in the Nazi party, per se, was not sufficient cause to indict a person as there were millions of such individuals and they could be processed through the denazification courts; rather, "substantial evidence of criminal conduct" had to be demonstrated before a prosecution at Nuremberg was warranted.[115] Moreover, Taylor thought that only those who were *most* responsible for the planning and execution of mass atrocities and who were in American custody should be tried. But, who were these individuals and how could they be identified? It was impossible and unrealistic for Taylor's small organization (initially twenty-five lawyers in May 1946, which grew to 113 by July) to examine the case of every individual within the Third Reich.[116] Instead, he decided to grapple with this problem by coming to a greater understanding of how the regime functioned and who was responsible for the crimes it committed.[117] Understanding the Third Reich and how it functioned was no small undertaking

[113] Bloxham, *Genocide on Trial*, 195–196.
[114] Taylor, *Final Report*, 84.
[115] Taylor, "Nuremberg Trials, War Crimes and International Law," in *ibid.*, 160.
[116] By October 31, 1947, the number of people employed by the OCCWC had peaked at 1,746 of which 904 were German, 539 were American, 192 were Allied personnel, and 111 were military personnel. Memorandum, the Public Information Office, OCCWC, "Background Information for Correspondents," February 1, 1949 in NARA RG 238, OCCWC, Executive Office, Publications Division, Correspondence 1948–1949, War Crimes Data, box 2, E196 folder (II). See also Taylor, *Final Report*, 14 and 43–44, who states that numbers peaked on October 17 at 1,774 with 919 German employees.
[117] Taylor, *Final Report*, 54.

so he formed an "over-all study section" within the Subsequent Proceed-ings Division whose job it was to narrow the scope of possible defendants through a greater understanding of the regime. The group, headed by Werner Peiser and assisted by Paul Gantt and Barton Watson, had to act quickly because OMGUS was coming under increasing pressure to release internees and Clay felt that it was "impossible" to stabilize Germany as long as so many people were left waiting to find out their fate.[118]

In addition to the "over-all study section," several other groups were formed within the Subsequent Proceedings Division. Two groups were put in charge of investigating the case against German industrialists and financiers, another was to prepare evidence against Nazi organizations such as the military and navy, and a fourth group was in charge of investigating the crimes of the SS and leaders of the German medical profession. The fifth group concerned itself with evidence against leading officials in the German foreign office.[119] Taylor instructed each group to familiarize itself with the structure and operations of the Third Reich; this made their job significantly less complicated when they began to sort out the evidence and compile lists of the most culpable individuals.[120] Those documents that pertained to Nazi organizations such as the SS or Hitler Youth were designated "NO," those dealing with the Nazi industrialists were given the designation "NI," and documents relating to the German government were labeled "NG." A final category of documents relating to the German army were labeled "NOKW" – "N" for Nuremberg and "OKW" for *Oberkommando der Wehrmacht* – to distinguish them from the military documents used dur-ing the IMT. In addition to the documentary evidence, interrogations of internees such as Ohlendorf (an economics expert and former leader of *Ein-satzgruppe* D) were a valuable source of information for the Division.[121] By August 1946, the group had amassed enough evidence to form a basic picture of the guiltiest Nazis. They then compiled a list of just under 5,000 individuals identified as suspected major war criminals, which Taylor next distributed to the commanders of the various prisoner-of-war camps asking them not to release these individuals because they were wanted for possible trial in Nuremberg.[122]

The process of whittling down the list of 5,000 took the better part of a year, until the summer of 1947. Determining who was to be indicted was the exclusive domain of Taylor, who likened this part of his job to

---

[118] Letter, Clay to Oliver P. Echols, War Department, June 28, 1946 in NARA RG 466, OMGUS, War Criminals, box 22, War Crimes and War Criminals folder.

[119] Memorandum, Taylor to the Subsequent Proceedings Division, May 17, 1946 in NARA RG 260, OMGUS, Functional Offices and Divisions, OCCWC, box 2, Subsequent Proceedings Division folder.

[120] Taylor, *Final Report*, 75.

[121] Ibid., 17–18.

[122] Ibid., 54.

that of an American district attorney. Taylor knew from the beginning of the planning process that his office would indict – in a four-power or zonal trial, whatever the case might be – certain Nazi industrialists and financiers, including Alfried Krupp, several of the managing directors of the IG Farben chemical combine, and Friedrich Flick, owner of one of the Ruhr's largest industrial combines.[123] This had been clear since the first Nuremberg trial. Beyond these men, however, there were so many other possible candidates for indictment.[124] Realistically, he knew he could never exhaust the list of the truly guilty even if he were to indict several thousand individuals, and, thus, he had to content himself with what he decided was a representative sample from each of the four categories: government officials, party officials, including the SS and police, military leaders; and bankers and industrialists.[125] Next, he made a list of the most important individuals in each category and he analyzed the evidence his office had. Finally, his organization attempted to locate each person. The locator branch of the Military Government was largely responsible for finding the defendants. This proved to be a difficult and lengthy process. Administrative considerations – "time, staff, and money" as Taylor referred to it – also influenced who was to be indicted, just as did such mundane things as the court room and the size of the dock.

Military Government officials felt that the war crimes trials were important politically and that it was vital that the public remain interested in them; therefore, they should begin as soon as possible.[126] Unlike the IMT, defendants would not be tried in one comprehensive trial, but rather in separate trials focussing on the areas of the Third Reich in which the defendants worked.[127] Taylor decided in November 1946 that the first group to be tried would be medical professionals who had carried out experiments on human beings and had been involved in the medical euthanasia program. His organization had enough evidence on them to begin prosecution immediately and he did not feel that the case was particularly complicated.[128]

At the time Taylor was busy organizing the Subsequent trials, he and Clay had to decide when it would be appropriate to issue an ordinance authorizing the Military Governor to officially appoint a successor to Jackson and set up the required military tribunals to try war criminals not charged with

---

[123] Summary of points covered in an OCC-OMGUS Meeting, May 28, 1946, in NARA RG 238, OCCWC, box 1 NM-70, entry 159, Subsequent Proceedings Basic Policies folder.

[124] Memorandum, organization of the Subsequent Proceedings, undated in TTP 20-1-3-34, IMT – Origins of Subsequent Proceedings NMT.

[125] Memorandum, Taylor to Jackson, October 30, 1946 in RHJ Papers, Nuremberg WCT, Final Report to the President folder.

[126] Taylor, *Final Report*, 73–77.

[127] Memorandum, Taylor to Clay, November 1, 1946 in NARA RG 466, Security Segregated Records 1945–1947, Prisons Division, box 10, WCT Correspondence, 1946–1947 folder.

[128] Memorandum, Taylor to Clay, November 1, 1946 in *ibid*.

offenses under the authority of the Theatre Judge Advocate.[129] Of course, the Americans had not yet decided whether they would be participating in a second four-power trial, thus the timing of their announcement was important for political reasons. They decided against releasing news of the ordinance immediately, preferring to wait until after the completion of the IMT.[130] On October 24, the day Military Ordinance No. 7 was announced, the Military Governor ordered the dissolution of Jackson's organization, OCCPAC, and the creation of the successor organization, the OCCWC, as a division of the Military Government, making the office part of the occupational government and, thus, answerable to Clay.

Ordinance No. 7 proscribed that each tribunal should comprise three judges and one alternate, none of whom were to have less than five years judicial experience. All had to be from state benches, and the tribunals would select their own presiding judge.[131] Given the staffing problems that the OCCWC faced, these requirements were not always adhered to in practice, as was the case in the *Einsatzgruppen* trial, where one of the tribunal members had not been a judge. In an attempt to keep some vestige of the international character of the trials, Ordinance No. 7 adopted the same rules of procedure as those under the London Charter of August 8, 1945. Although the trials were to be held in the American zone, Ordinance No. 7 also provided for the possibility of joint prosecutions and, hence, they *could be* international in their prosecution. In practice, no such case arose even though the Americans invited the French to participate in the prosecution of the German diplomat and former State Secretary of the Foreign Office Ernst von Weizsäcker. The French, however, declined the offer.[132] Under Article 3 of Ordinance No. 7, the Chief of Counsel was authorized to determine who should be indicted.[133] By October 1946, Taylor and his organization had

---

[129] Taylor insisted on civilian rather than military judges because he wanted to ensure that judicial opinions were written. Normally, military courts do not write legal judgments. Taylor, *Final Report*, 28–29. The War Department had decided that even though the tribunals were to be composed of civilian judges, they preferred to call them "military" rather than "occupational" tribunals. Memorandum, War Department to Clay, OMGUS, October 24, 1946, in NARA RG 260, OMGUS, Executive Office, the Office of the Adjutant General, Military Government Ordinances 1945–1949, box 640, Nos. 1–18, Ordinance No. 7 folder.

[130] Military Ordinance No.7-Legal and Judicial Affairs, in *Monthly Report of the Military Governor, US Zone*, October 1–31, 1946, No. 16, 7, HST.

[131] Establishment of Tribunals for Trials of War Criminals Pursuant to Allied Control Council Law No. 10, by command of General Joseph T. McNarney, Headquarters, US Forces European Theater, APO 757, in the Papers of Eleanor Bontecou, WWII file, F-Sh, box 13, Authority for IMT folder, HST.

[132] Taylor, *Final Report*, 29.

[133] Press release, Department of the Army, Public Information Division, Press Section, May 17, 1948, quoted in Taylor, *Final Report*, 114 and 155–156.

largely settled on the scope of the Subsequent proceedings, but still the final decision on individual defendants was often left to the very last minute, as in the case against the *Einsatzgruppen* leaders, when the particulars were not finalized or an indictment filed until July 1947.

Between the autumn of 1946 and 1947, Taylor refined his program. Initially he decided on eighteen trials, but, by May, the number had dwindled to sixteen and by mid-September 1947 to twelve – the actual number of cases tried by the NMT.[134] Twenty-three physicians were the first to be indicted, followed by a group of leading Nazi jurists that was slated to begin in December.[135] Also scheduled were trials against Field Marshal Erhard Milch and Oswald Pohl of the Main Economic and Administrative Department of the SS. There was a substantial amount of evidence against members of the RuSHA and those involved in the planning and destruction of the Warsaw ghetto. The OCCWC was gathering evidence against government officials and Generals Warlimont, Reinecke, and Rendulic were scheduled to appear in the dock.[136] Finally, Taylor planned a trial of leading officials of the SS, Gestapo, and the RSHA; the principal defendant was to be Ohlendorf who had confessed to supervising the murder of 90,000 people in the Soviet Union while testifying as a prosecution witness before the IMT. The other defendants in this case were to be selected from a grab bag of leading SS and police personnel.[137] Initially, six tribunals were to operate simultaneously, but, because of the enormous difficulties Taylor had attracting respected and reliable jurists from the United States, several judges heard multiple cases. At its peak, six trials were being heard at the same time. By the spring of 1947, the OCCWC was well on the way to prosecuting a number of leading Nazis.

[134] In September 1947, six of the sixteen scheduled trials had yet to begin and Taylor was told by OMGUS to file all indictments by December 1947. He thus merged some of the trials as well as dropping the case against the members of the Economics and Agriculture Ministries and the press and propaganda case. Telegram, Clay to Royall, September 8, 1947, in NARA RG 153 (JAG), WCB, NA Files, box 1, File III folder. Less than a week later, Secretary of War Kenneth Royall recommended to Clay that the trial against the German banks (the Dresdner bank case) be terminated. Memorandum, Royall to Clay, September 12, 1947, in *ibid.*

[135] Memorandum, Ferencz to Section Chiefs of the OCCWC, October 2, 1946, in NARA RG 238, OCCWC, BB, GR, Correspondence 1946–1948, box 2, Correspondence 1946, August 46–January 47 folder. The Justice case was the third of the 12 trials. Ingo Müller, *Hitler's Justice: the Courts of the Third Reich*, trans. Deborah Lucas Schneider (Cambridge, MA, 1991), 270–271.

[136] These trials were cancelled due to difficulty obtaining the requisite number of judges.

[137] Taylor outlined his program in two memoranda, one in March and the other in May 1947. See memoranda, Taylor to Clay, March 14, 1947 and May 20, 1947, both in NARA RG 338, WCB, General Administration Records, box 1, Organization 1947 folder.

2

Otto Ohlendorf and the Origins
of the Einsatzgruppen Trial

> In Ohlendorf's case I am completely convinced that he believed in the necessity
> and rightness of what he was doing... Ohlendorf did not picture himself as
> a ruthless killer. Nor should he be made to appear as an ordinary felon or
> madman. He was a man of great intellect and dedication. He was one of the
> very few men tried at Nuremberg who appeared to be telling the truth.
>
> Benjamin Ferencz[1]

At the conclusion of the IMT in the autumn of 1946, the Americans knew
they wanted to bring to justice a broad range of the Nazi leadership. Chief
of Counsel for War Crimes Telford Taylor, thus turned his attention to
planning eighteen trials against leading figures of the Nazi regime. Among
the individuals targeted were some of the highest-ranking members of the
SS, an organization the IMT declared criminal.[2] One of the principal defendants was to be SS-*Brigadeführer* Otto Ohlendorf, the former head of *Einsatzgruppe* D, a mobile security unit that had operated behind German
lines in the occupied Soviet Union. Following his arrest in 1945, Ohlendorf had admitted to authorities that he and his unit were responsible for
the deaths of approximately 90,000 people, the overwhelming majority of
whom were Soviet Jews. Under Taylor's original plan, Ohlendorf and several other high-ranking (and identifiable) officials of the security, intelligence,
and police branches of the SS were to stand trial as representatives of the

---

[1] Letter, Ferencz to Michael G. Shanahan, July 7, 1972, RG 12.000 BBF Collection 1919–1994,
drawer 24 WCT, box 2, folder C Nuremberg Supplementary Material, USHMM (from here
forward simply BBF).

[2] IMT, *Trial of the Major War Criminals before the International Military Tribunal*, Nuremberg, November 14, 1945–October 1, 1946, vol. 22 (Nuremberg, 1947), 498–518, and memorandum, Taylor to Chief of Staff OMGUS, APO 742, May 20, 1947, in NARA, RG 260,
OMGUS, Functional Offices and Divisions, OCCWC, box 2, Program WCT per. General
Taylor folder.

SS offices where they had worked.[3] Over the next several months, however, Taylor's legal approach changed, because of, in large part, the personality and behavior of Ohlendorf. Taylor had not intended to try other members or leaders of the *Einsatzgruppen* in a separate or exclusive trial, but he could not ignore the fact that Ohlendorf's confession seriously implicated all of the mobile security units in mass murder.[4] Taylor's resolve to try Ohlendorf and other former members of the *Einsatzgruppen* was further strengthened by the accidental discovery and subsequent analysis of the *Einsatzgruppen* reports.[5] Taken together, the convergence of Ohlendorf's confession and the sudden appearance of new evidence provided the basis for a strong case against all of the *Einsatzgruppen* leaders. It was all simply too damning to ignore.

Selecting defendants for the NMT differed considerably from the methods used at the IMT, where political considerations played a significant role. By the time Taylor's attention shifted to the Subsequent trials, he had decided

---

[3] Taylor, *Final Report*, 79–80.

[4] For instance, Franz Six, former leader of *Vorkommando* Moscow, was originally scheduled to be tried in the case against government officials for his work on cultural issues for the Foreign Office. Memorandum to Deputy Military Governor, OMGUS, APO 742, March 14, 1947, NARA RG 338, JAD, WCB, General Administrative Records, box 1, Organization 1947 folder.

[5] No one has written a biography of Ohlendorf. Most of what has been written about him pertains to his role as an economics expert, as *Amtchef* in the RSHA, and as leader of *Einsatzgruppe* D. The most comprehensive attempts to come to terms with Ohlendorf's life and career is Hanno Sowade, "Otto Ohlendorf: Non-conformist, SS Leader and Economic Functionary," in Ronald Smelser and Rainer Zitelmann (eds.), *The Nazi Elite*, trans. Mary Fischer (New York, 1993), 155–164, and David Kitterman, "Otto Ohlendorf: Gralshüter des Nationalsozialismus," in R. Smelser and E. Syring (eds.), *Die SS: Elite unter dem Totenkopf* (Schöningh, 2000), 379–393. Angrick, *Einsatzgruppe D in der südlichen Sowjetunion 1941–1943* (2003) is the first thorough history of *Einsatzgruppe* D published. Angrick offers a biographical and social profile of Ohlendorf and his role in the murder process. See also, Angrick, "Die Einsatzgruppe D," in Peter Klein (ed.), *Die Einsatzgruppen in der besetzten Sowjetunion 1941/42: Die Tätigkeits – und Lageberichte des Chefs der Sicherheitspolizei und des SD* (Berlin, 1997), 88–110, and "Otto Ohlendorf und die SD Tätigkeit der Einsatzgruppe D," in Michael Wildt (ed.), *Nachrichtendienst, politische Elite, und Mordeinheit: der Sicherheitsdienst Reichsführers SS* (Hamburg 2003), 267–302. Alexander Stollhof, has written an important study of Ohlendorf and his career, but his dissertation, "SS-Gruppenführer und Generalleutnant der Polizei Otto Ohlendorf – eine biographische Skizze" from the University of Vienna in 1993 is not yet published. Others who have looked at some aspect of Ohlendorf's career include Shlomo Aronson, *Reinhard Heydrich und die Frühgeschichte von Gestapo und SD* (Stuttgart, 1971), who examines Ohlendorf's position within the SD; Ludolf Herbst, *Der totale Krieg und die Ordnung der Wirtschaft: Die Kriegswirtschaft im Spannungsfeld von Politik, Ideologie und Propaganda 1939–1945* (Stuttgart, 1982) who examines Ohlendorf's role as an economic functionary; and, most recently, Peter Longerich, *Politik der Vernichtung* who examines Ohlendorf's leadership role in *Einsatzgruppe* D and his testimony on the existence and timing of the Führerbefehl. Many others have raised the issue of Ohlendorf's testimony at the IMT proceedings, but seldom does the literature go beyond mentioning that Ohlendorf supervised the killing of 90,000 people in the Soviet Union in 1941–1942.

that indictments would be based strictly on documented evidence of criminal wrong-doing, that is to say on evidence unearthed by his researchers and not for political reasons.[6] As head of the Berlin Branch of the OCCWC remembered, "we were not necessarily looking for evidence against particular individuals," but rather, "we were fishing for evidence of crime."[7] Taylor insisted that compelling documentary evidence had to be available to prove guilt beyond a reasonable doubt, and that the individuals targeted were in American custody or at least accessible through extradition. Certainly, Ohlendorf met all of these prerequisites.

In practice, most of Taylor's staff was immersed in sifting through mountains of captured documents during the preparatory phase of the NMT. Their search for incriminating evidence against individuals judged to be "major criminals" took them to repositories located in Germany and throughout Europe. At the same time, the Locator Branch of the OCCWC was doing its best to find out whether these individuals were in allied custody and, if so, where. If they were in occupation zones other than the American, they had to arrange to have them extradited to Nuremberg.[8] As it turned out, few of the top-ranking SS officials Taylor's office had identified as criminals could be located. Many had escaped to neutral countries or were in hiding, and several others had turned up dead or were presumed to have committed suicide. The fact that U.S. intelligence was not always accurate also hampered the search, as happened, for example, when the Counter Intelligence Corps (CIC) determined that Adolf Eichmann had committed suicide and called off the search for him.[9] Despite the obstacles, numerous commanders and subordinate officers of the *Einsatzgruppen* were identified, located, and apprehended. Sheer good luck also played a part, as had been the case when the Berlin Branch of the OCCWC, at the time under Benjamin Ferencz's direction, accidentally located and analyzed one of the only surviving copies of the *Einsatzgruppen* reports. The impact of these reports, which explicitly detailed the criminal activities of the *Einsatzgruppen* in the Nazi-occupied east, cannot be underestimated.[10] When coupled with Ohlendorf's admission that he had supervised mass murder as ordered by his superiors, these reports convinced Taylor to scrap the plans for a general trial of the SS in favor of one dealing exclusively with the activities

---

[6] Taylor, *Anatomy*, 47–48.

[7] Interview with Ferencz, April 24, 1997, who stated "we didn't have specific lists of defendants at that time."

[8] Taylor, *Final Report*, 15.

[9] Peter Walton wrote, "the C.I.C. appears reasonably satisfied from the information available that this man [Adolf Eichmann] committed suicide in late April or early May 1945." Memorandum, Walton to Edmund Schwenk, OCCWC, September 30, 1946, in NARA RG 238, OCCWC, BB, General Records (GR), Correspondence 1946–1948, box 2, Correspondence 1946 E202, Correspondence August 1946–January 1947 folder.

[10] Apparently the Soviets had also acquired some of the reports. Translations from German to Russian are available on microfilm at the USHMM.

of the *Einsatzgruppen*. By July 1947, therefore, Taylor's trial strategy had undergone a significant transformation and Ohlendorf and twenty-three other SS officers and former members of the *Einsatzgruppen* were to be indicted in their own criminal trial. The reports proved that these men had participated in the murder of more than 1 million people, all of whom came from identifiable groups. Theirs' was an atrocity of such magnitude that the principle charge in the case would be crimes against humanity. Although the formal charge was not unprecedented – the defendants at the IMT had been charged with crimes against humanity as well – this crime and the genocide associated with it were in the process of being singled out for definition by the international community. From the beginning, the *Einsatzgruppen* trial thus had the potential to contribute to the development of international law as well as to historical understanding of crimes against humanity and genocide. The "biggest murder trial in history," an extraordinary investigation into the genocidal activities of the Third Reich in the occupied east, was set to begin; it would remain to be seen whether or not the prosecution and judges would understand the magnitude of it.[11]

The Surrender of Otto Ohlendorf, Early Interrogations, and Confessions of Mass Murder

On May 8, 1945, the day Germany surrendered to the Allies, Otto Ohlendorf was in his office in Flensburg, a town near the Danish border where Hitler's successor Admiral Karl Dönitz had set up his headquarters and was later arrested. At the time, Ohlendorf was drafting an outline for a plan to create a "public opinion service" for Germany's new occupation authorities. Like others in the SS during the final days of the war, Ohlendorf believed he had something useful to offer Germany's new rulers.[12] He was, therefore, hopeful, perhaps even confident, that the Allies would accept his proposal. Given the experience Ohlendorf had acquired conducting opinion research on economic matters (he fancied himself an expert in economics), he expected to head the new organization.[13] In hindsight, ambitions like Ohlendorf's seem clearly misguided, but, at the time, his self-assurance was not entirely unfounded.

---

[11] USHMM, RG 50.030*269, Oral History, BBF, August 26, 1994, tape 2.

[12] Ohlendorf was not the only high-ranking SS man to believe he had something to offer the Allies. For instance, see the "Preliminary Interrogation Report of Martin Sandberger," June 23, 1945, in NARA RG 319, Office of the Assistant Chief of Staff, G3 Intelligence Records, IRR, box 191, Sandberger folder.

[13] British interrogators found that Ohlendorf was "opposed to German resistance movements and was anxious to maintain the organisation of *Amt* III intact, in order to place it at the disposal of the Western Allies as soon as possible." See, "Proposed Collaboration with the Allies #99," in CSDIC (UK) Report of Ohlendorf, September 30, 1945, in NARA RG 319, G-2 Security Classified Intelligence and Investigative Dossiers, box 165A, Ohlendorf file.

As head of *Amt* III (Office of Domestic Intelligence) in the RSHA, Ohlendorf had been instrumental in shaping and refining Nazi intelligence-gathering practices. His area of expertise was economics, an important issue in any political structure, but, in the newly forming postwar world, his plan to work for the Allies was clearly delusional; besides, Ohlendorf was far too high profile to be any use whatsoever to the Allies.[14] This did not seem to occur to him and he surrendered, optimistic that the Anglo-Americans would utilize his expertise and experience once they came to realize his natural intellectual strengths. In May 1945, while other SS men were planning their escape or preparing for a Fourth Reich, the arrogant and delusional Ohlendorf believed he could help the Allies, and, in return, they might give him a job in the new postwar world order.[15]

It was with this belief firmly in mind that on May 21, at 3 o'clock in the afternoon, as a member of the Dönitz government, Ohlendorf and hundreds of others surrendered to British forces. Ohlendorf was not afraid; rather, he was convinced that he could easily demonstrate his value and that British authorities would single him out to utilize it. This attitude helped to seal his fate.[16] In the chaos of May 1945, instead of turning himself in as he did, he could have just as easily attempted to escape or even committed suicide, as did many leading Nazis. Ohlendorf had no intention of becoming a martyr for the Nazi cause though, nor did he want to hide; rather, he had decided to give himself up, and to "explain in detail what the SD meant and what it had done."[17] This was not such unusual behavior, as many high-ranking Nazis put themselves in the same position. What was so odd was his subsequent willingness to implicate himself. The evidence suggests that Ohlendorf had a peculiar sense of his own character and never once imagined that the British might consider him a war criminal. Contrary to his expectations, however, the British did not immediately embrace Ohlendorf, regardless of his skill as an opinion researcher or his economic expertise. Rather, they treated

[14] Analysis of Ohlendorf's interrogations suggests that the British thought his hopes of working for the Allies were exceedingly misplaced. For example, see Foreword to CSDIC (UK) Notes on Corruption and Corrupted Personalities in Germany, PW Paper 133, August 11, 1945 in NARA RG 319, box 165A, Ohlendorf folder.

[15] CSDIC (UK) Report on Information Obtained from PW CS/2262 SS Gruf Ohlendorf, September 30, 1945 in *ibid*; Arthur L. Smith, Jr., "Life in Wartime Germany: Colonel Ohlendorf's Opinion Service," *The Public Opinion Quarterly* 36 (Spring, 1972), 7 and Herbst, *Totale Krieg*, 187.

[16] NA Microfilm Collection M1270, "Interrogation Records Prepared for War Crimes Proceedings at Nuernberg, 1945–1947, OCCPAC Interrogations," roll 13 and CSDIC (UK) Report on Information Obtained from PW CS/2262 SS Gruf Ohlendorf, #150, September 30, 1945, in NARA RG 319, box 156A, Ohlendorf folder.

[17] NA Microfilm Collection M1270, "Interrogation Records Prepared for War Crimes Proceedings at Nuernberg, 1945–1947, OCCPAC Interrogations," roll 13, See also CSDIC (UK) Report on Information Obtained from PW CS/2262 SS Gruf Ohlendorf, #150, September 30, 1945, in NARA RG 319, box 156A, Ohlendorf folder.

him with suspicion and disdain, just as they treated all other suspected war criminals. Upon arrest, he was summarily imprisoned and interrogated for information about the upper echelons of the Nazi regime. He was then assessed and transported to London for further interrogation.

This in itself is curious. At this early date, the British transported few prisoners directly to Britain, yet they brought Ohlendorf there immediately, why? Unless the British MI5 declassifies documents, the reasons will likely remain a mystery. What we do know is that during his first interrogation in London on May 31, 1945, Ohlendorf quickly became a collaborator, providing the British with written and oral information about the Hitler regime, although not yet divulging his personal role in it. Intelligence reports suggest that from the very start, however, the British viewed parts of his confession with suspicion. They considered him an opportunist in spite of efforts he made to portray himself as an opponent of National Socialism. What did Ohlendorf tell the British about his involvement in the Third Reich? Did he immediately confess to being involved with the *Einsatzgruppen* or did he try and conceal his incriminating past from them? He admitted his rank and position in the SS largely because British intelligence agents already knew he had been head of *Amt* III in the RSHA. He also repeatedly insisted that his primary role within the Reich had been in the Economics ministry (*Wirtschaftsministerium*), working as a deputy for Walther Funk, but he did not tell them about his position in the *Einsatzgruppen*. By early summer 1945, the British were cognizant of Ohlendorf's intelligence work and economics background, yet they remained ignorant of his role in *Einsatzgruppe* D.[18]

Not everyone was in the dark about the existence of mobile security units such as the *Einsatzgruppen*, because British officials did have some wartime intelligence, but whether or not the information was available to his interrogators is unknown.[19] What we can say with certainty is that the *Ereignismeldungen* (the field reports of the *Einsatzgruppen* detailing their activities) had not yet been discovered. Until records surfaced describing the *Einsatzgruppen* and their activities, the only way the British could have obtained comprehensive information was if Ohlendorf disclosed it himself. Shockingly, he did precisely that in late summer 1945. British intelligence reports reveal that during his May 31 interrogation in London, he was silent

---

[18] Stephen Tyas, an expert on the activities of the *Einsatzgruppen*, notes that although the British did have decodes from January 1942 referring to Ohlendorf's leadership with *Einsatzgruppe* D, the information they had did not mention what the *Einsatzgruppen* did.

[19] For example, there are a series of CSDIC (UK) reports from 1943, detailing some of the activities of the *Einsatzgruppen* from a former member of *Einsatzgruppe* D. See CSDIC (UK), SIR 101, January 8, 1944; CSDIC (UK), SIR 179, March 27, 1944; and CSDIC (UK), SIR 295, June 9, 1944 in NARA RG 332, USFET, G-2, boxes 1 & 2. See also, Richard Breitman, *Official Secrets: What the Nazis Planned, What the British and Americans Knew* (New York, 1998), 190–191 and "Intelligence and the Holocaust," in David Bankier (ed.), *Secret Intelligence and the Holocaust* (Jerusalem, 2006), 17–47.

about his activities on the eastern front stating only that during the crucial years 1941 and 1942, he was an *Oberführer* in the SS and only later was he promoted to *Brigadeführer*. Ohlendorf gave no reason for the promotion, nor does the report indicate that anyone asked him to clarify the nature of his duties in the SS. Not surprisingly at the time, British interrogators seemed more interested in his knowledge of other leading Nazis than they were in Ohlendorf himself, and he was more than willing to oblige them in this task.[20] Without being pressed by his interrogators, Ohlendorf was successfully able to limit incriminating information to a history of his political career and his experiences during the demise of the regime in the closing months of the war; about his crimes on the Eastern front, he told them nothing. When, and under what circumstances, then, did the British first learn about Ohlendorf's activities as leader of *Einsatzgruppe* D?

The precise circumstances are difficult to determine, although the record intimates that Ohlendorf's reticence remained intact throughout most of the summer of 1945. For instance, during the first two interrogations in May and June there was no mention whatsoever of Jews, the *Einsatzgruppen*, or the Eastern front. Then, suddenly, in an interrogation report dated August 11, 1945, Ohlendorf is mentioned for the first time as having participated in *Einsatzgruppen* operations in the occupied USSR and with the new information, the tenor of the analysis changed. The report asserts that Ohlendorf was "violently anti-Semitic" and while "in charge of Einsatzgruppe D of the SS in the CRIMEA was responsible for the mass execution of 80,000 Jews, including women and children."[21] Undoubtedly, Ohlendorf was an antisemite, but the characterization of him as "violently anti-Semitic" seems out of character and probably better reflects the deductive view of the interrogator who believed that the act of killing is an accurate and self-evident reflection of ideology. In other words, Ohlendorf killed Jews because he was a violent antisemite and he was a violent antisemite because he killed Jews.[22] More curious is why, after two and a half months of captivity (and silence), did the British learn of his activities with the *Einsatzgruppen* on August 11? Under what circumstances was this information obtained? Did Ohlendorf make this disclosure, and, if so, did he do so voluntarily? Did he ask for a deal in exchange for the information or did he even recognize the criminal nature of his acts? Did the British threaten to try him in a war crimes case or did they ask him to participate in their prosecution of major war criminals at the IMT? A comprehensive understanding of Ohlendorf's early captivity

[20] Preliminary Interrogation Report of G-2, Special Section SHAEF on Otto Ohlendorf, May 31, 1945 in NARA RG 319, G-2 Security Classified Intelligence and Investigative Dossiers, box 165A, Ohlendorf folder.
[21] PW Paper 133, Notes on Corruption and Corrupted Personalities in Germany, August 11, 1945, NARA RG 319, box 165A, Ohlendorf folder.
[22] This is Goldhagen's argument in *Hitler's Willing Executioners*. The Chief prosecutor in the case has also characterized Ohlendorf as an "eager" executioner.

is impossible given the unavailability of the records, but certainly the stunning revelation appears to have come from Ohlendorf entirely on his own initiative. Why he admitted to having taken part in such horrendous crimes remains a mystery, but, whatever the reason, on August 11, the floodgates opened and information about the murder of the Jews continued to flow from Ohlendorf thereafter.

Once he had told of the murders, there was no stopping him. In a fourth intelligence report dated September 30, Ohlendorf provided the first evidence linking Reinhard Heydrich, the former head of the RSHA, and his superior SS chief Heinrich Himmler, to the implementation of the so-called Final Solution to the Jewish Question. The report states,

[b]etween Jun 41 and Jun 42 PW went as an RSHA delegate attached to the staff of the 11th Army at SIMFEROPOL to deal with security tasks in 11th Army area. He was the Comd of Sipo and SS Einsatzgruppe D. He was also responsible for the voluntary recruiting of Tartars. His Einsatz Kdos were directly responsible, under his comd, on orders received from HEYDRICH and HIMMLER, for liquidating a total of approx 7,000 Jews at NIKOLAJEV (Jul 41' to Nov 41) and SIMFEROPOL (Dec 41).[23]

After this report, the British intelligence record provides little information on what happened next, although the later record shows that the British shared their intelligence with the Americans, who were preparing for the upcoming IMT trial. American prosecutors had learned from the British that Ohlendorf was a long-standing National Socialist and an SS commander responsible for "mass atrocities" in the Crimea, having told the British as early as August 11 – perhaps earlier – that he was responsible for supervising the mass execution of tens of thousands of Jews while working for the RSHA.[24] The British had no immediate plans to prosecute Ohlendorf.[25] Given his important position in the RSHA, and his apparent willingness to talk, the Americans hoped to use him in their case against Ernst Kaltenbrunner (Heydrich's successor and leader of the RSHA) at the upcoming IMT proceedings. The Americans had intelligence that suggested that Kaltenbrunner and Ohlendorf were close; perhaps, this is the genesis of the transfer.[26]

---

[23] CSDIC (UK) Report, September 30, 1945, RG 319, Intelligence and Investigative dossiers, box 165A, Ohlendorf folder.

[24] Ohlendorf told the British his unit killed 80,000 people. This may be a typographical error. CSDIC (UK), Notes on Corruption and Corrupted Personalities in Germany, PW Paper 133, August 11, 1945 in NARA RG 319, box 165A, Ohlendorf folder.

[25] Bloxham, "'The Trial that Never Was,'" 55, claims that the transfer of Ohlendorf to the Americans was the result of the British decision not to hold zonal trials, yet, the intelligence reports suggest that the Americans requested Ohlendorf's extradition well before the British had made up their minds about subsequent trials.

[26] Final Interrogation Report No. 7, SS Ostubaf ARTHUR SCHEIDLER, July 11, 1945, in the British National Archives, formerly known as the Public Record Office (London), WO 208-4478. I want to thank Steve Tyas for bringing this document to my attention.

In any case, Ohlendorf remained in British custody for several months, until October 18, 1945, when the Americans requested his extradition to Landsberg prison.[27] The British obliged and there the former head of *Einsatzgruppe* D remained until his execution on the night of June 7, 1951.[28]

At Landsberg, Ohlendorf attempted to achieve with the Americans what he had been unable to with the British: to secure his freedom. To this end, rather than negotiate a deal for his release, he instead collaborated with the Americans, volunteering information to his new captors without reservation. Through disclosure he seems to have hoped to make himself indispensable to the Americans and their legal efforts – a pattern of behavior begun with the British and one that he continued throughout his entire incarceration. Again, not such unusual behavior among captured war criminals, but disclosing his personal involvement was exceptional. Because of his value as an informant, American officials formulated no immediate plans to prosecute Ohlendorf for his own crimes. During his prolonged captivity, he was interrogated more than any other war criminal, at least forty-two times.[29] Not only did they ask him about his activities as head of *Einsatzgruppe* D, but also about the functioning of the RSHA, the structure of the SS, Nazi economic policy, and about his knowledge of many individuals particularly Ernst Kaltenbrunner, and those responsible for economic matters.[30]

On the morning of October 24, the Americans interrogated Ohlendorf for the first time. They knew immediately he was a "dynamic [and] committed" Nazi idealist and, to their surprise and delight, and without any inducement at all, Ohlendorf spoke freely of his experiences. Just as he had with the British earlier, he did not display or express any shame or regret about his personal behavior; rather, he projected self-confidence, and was perhaps even boastful when he assured his American interrogators – particularly Lieutenant Colonel Smith W. Brookhart, Jr. – that he had done nothing wrong. Killing noncombatants, he repeatedly insisted to Brookhart, had been a legal and humane act because it was carried out under the authority of Himmler and Hitler and not on individual initiative.

Ohlendorf's cooperation with American interrogators was absolutely critical to the evolution of a criminal case against members of the *Einsatzgruppen*. He told the Americans virtually everything and anything they wanted to

[27] Summary of PW CS/2262 SS-Gruf Ohlendorf, CSDIC (UK), August 19, 1945, NARA RG 238, USCPAC, box 12, NM 70 CSDIC PW Reports folder 53.
[28] American prosecutor Whitney Harris maintains that he requested that the British turn over Ohlendorf to the U.S. for questioning to further their case against the Gestapo and SD. "Interview with Whitney Harris," Harry James Cargas (ed.), *Voices from the Holocaust* (Lexington, 1993), 110.
[29] IMT Interrogation Report, March 29, 1949, NMT-OCCWC Interrogation Branch, IMT Interrogations – Amen, 5-1-4-58, TTP.
[30] For a complete record of American interrogations of Ohlendorf see NA Microfilm Publications, M1019 and M1270.

know. As one intelligence report noted, "in two brief conversations [Ohlendorf] has sold to us Hitler, Rust, Schellenberg, Kranefuss [sic.], Six [sic.], Osenberg, [and] Bütefische [sic.]. Himmler himself, obviously much nearer to him than all others, does not escape criticism."[31] The reports indicate that although Ohlendorf was initially reticent to talk freely, it was not long before he got used to his new circumstances and then became remarkably candid about his actions.[32] He was most frank, surprisingly, about the inner workings of the RSHA and his role as leader of *Einsatzgruppe* D.[33] Unlike the British, who were more interested in the upper echelons of the Nazi regime, the Americans focused almost exclusively on the activities of the RSHA. Over time, they questioned Ohlendorf less and less about his intelligence and economics work and more and more about the ideological war against civilians in the occupied USSR, in 1941 and 1942. When asked by his captors about his activities, Ohlendorf was never evasive. Like the British, the Americans were naturally suspicious of Ohlendorf, believing he had other motives, and, thus, they were reluctant to accept everything he disclosed at face value.[34] As one intelligence analyst observed, "Everything [Ohlendorf] has ever done, including his surrender to the Allies, appears to have been carried out with the sole object of gaining an influential position."[35] Ohlendorf was divulging everything he knew to curry favor with his captors, yet, he never realized until it was too late that he had nothing to gain and everything to lose from admitting his role in the *Einsatzgruppen*. For, without his confessions, the Allies never would have indicted him for the crimes he had committed. For a smart man, he proved foolish at this juncture.

The acts that Ohlendorf described were so uniquely and utterly horrifying that skeptical U.S. intelligence officers often had difficulty believing their prisoner was in full possession of his sanity. In Ohlendorf's first interrogation, the former SS officer described when and how the order to murder the Jews of the occupied Soviet territories was given to the leaders of the *Einsatzgruppen*. He stated the *Einsatzgruppen* were given two orders, both of which "pertained to the execution of Jews."[36] He implied that both orders were oral, not written, reinforcing Michael Wildt's conclusion that the *Einsatzgruppen*'s orders had a practical character and were more in the

---

[31] Preliminary Interrogation Report of G-2, Special Section, SHAEF on Ohlendorf, May 31, 1945, in NARA RG 319, box 156A, Ohlendorf folder.

[32] *Ibid.*

[33] A summary of Ohlendorf's discussion with British authorities includes detailed information about the formation, function, and dissolution of Office III. See CSDIC (UK) Report, September 30, 1945, in *ibid.*

[34] "Preamble," in *ibid.* See also, Counter Intelligence War Room, London, The Development of Amt III (SD), August 6, 1945.

[35] *Ibid.*

[36] Interrogation, Ohlendorf, October 24, 1945, M1270, roll 13.

form of an authorization to act at their own discretion rather than a direct command to murder.[37] As Ohlendorf explained the process, the first order was "given by Hitler directly" in May 1941, before the invasion of the Soviet Union, to the leaders of the *Einsatzgruppen*.[38] We know that the leaders of the *Einsatzgruppen* were given a written order before the invasion of the Soviet Union, but it did not call for the wholesale murder of Soviet Jews. Whether this is the order Ohlendorf is referring to is difficult to assess because Brookhart, never asked for clarification. It is unlikely that Hitler directly transmitted the order, this was not his method of ruling; to the untrained eye of Brookhart however, that Hitler issued the order was undoubtedly not a far-fetched idea. What about the second order to murder? According to Ohlendorf, it came from Himmler, who orally repeated Hitler's initial order to a group of *Einsatzgruppen* leaders in October 1941, during a visit by the *Reichsführer-SS* to Nikolayev (a city on the Black Sea).[39] Ohlendorf told Brookhart that the legal sanction given to the murder of Jews by Hitler and Himmler absolved him and his men of any legal or moral responsibility for the killings.[40] Apparently, Ohlendorf took Himmler's assurance of absolution to heart. His belief that the Allies would use his particular expertise in their occupation government, coupled with his admission to mass murder, attests to this and says much about his skewed worldview in which he seemed to genuinely believe that supervising the murder of civilians was not wrong. His matter-of-factness, indeed, the rather blasé portrayal of his job in the Soviet Union that Ohlendorf offered, baffled his American captors. Lacking any documented studies or analyses of ideologically committed murders perpetrated in the past, they had absolutely no frame of reference by which to evaluate his attitude and actions. One prison psychologist in particular, Major Leon Goldensohn, found Ohlendorf difficult, if not impossible to understand. A man who was at once intelligent *and* a mass murderer, and who appeared to have no remorse for his actions was anomalous to his understanding of human behavior.[41] Ohlendorf's comportment mystified Goldensohn, who could only conclude that this SS man must have been

[37] Michael Wildt, "The Spirit of the Reich Security Main Office (RSHA)," *Totalitarian Movements and Political Religions*, vol. 6, no. 3 (December 2005), 345.

[38] Interrogation, Ohlendorf, October 25, 1945, M1270, roll 13.

[39] *Ibid.* Ohlendorf told his interrogator that Himmler's visit was in September. He was wrong. It was in October. This is not to suggest Ohlendorf was lying, just that he got the dates wrong.

[40] Interrogation, Ohlendorf, October 24–25, 1945, M1270, roll 13.

[41] I have argued elsewhere that Ohlendorf's confessions were a strategy to avoid execution. See Earl, "Confessions of Wrong-doing or How to Save Yourself from the Hangman? An Analysis of British and American Intelligence Reports of the Activities of Otto Ohlendorf, May–December 1945," in David Bankier (ed.), *Secret Intelligence and the Holocaust* (New York and Jerusalem, 2006).

"a sadist, a pervert or a lunatic" to have carried out such monstrous orders; only these mental defects could explain the complete lack of a conscience.[42] Goldensohn's response to Ohlendorf was fairly typical of many of those involved in the investigation and prosecution of war criminals. Even today, many still believe that genocide is a psychotic behavior in spite of research by social psychologists such as James Waller who debunk this as myth.[43]

Surprisingly, Ohlendorf was not unique in his frankness. Many captured Nazi war criminals spoke openly to American authorities. Telford Taylor recalls that during pretrial interviews many perpetrators talked freely of the jobs they had held and the tasks they had performed during the Nazi period. Of course, not all had participated in mass murder. Their bravado was most likely the result of their false assumptions about the way the American system operated – many assumed they would simply tell their stories and then be released. Some, undoubtedly, were opportunists who attempted to gain reprieve from prosecution themselves while emphasizing the actions of others whose crimes were worse. This suggests that most typical perpetrators knew that what they had done was wrong. Ohlendorf's behavior, on the other hand, suggests something different. He was willing to talk freely of his crimes and expressed no remorse because, it would seem, he did not feel any. Whatever wrong Ohlendorf had done, he seemed truly to believe it was right.[44]

Unable to reconcile the seeming contradictions of Ohlendorf's personality, many American officials simply concluded that he was psychologically disturbed. Even Ohlendorf's friend and colleague in the economics ministry, Walther Funk, felt there was something at odds inside Ohlendorf telling Nuremberg personnel that although Ohlendorf was essentially "a decent man" who loved his family, he also "had something in his soul which bothered him."[45] But, Ohlendorf was not crazy; far from it. He was bright

[42] Memorandum, Sander Jaari to Brookhart, "Conversation with Otto Ohlendorf, March 7, 1946," M1270, roll 13. Gustav M. Gilbert, *Nuremberg Diary* (New York, 1947 and 1995), 3. Leon Goldensohn, "Otto Ohlendorf," in Robert Gellately (ed.), *Nuremberg Interviews: An American Psychiatrist's Conversations with the Defendants and Witnesses* (New York, 2004), 390. Goldensohn was the prison psychologist at Nuremberg for most of the IMT trial. His response was not unusual. Many people, including other Nuremberg psychiatrists, concluded that the Nazis were psychologically "abnormal." This assessment gained currency after an autopsy was performed by American doctors on Robert Ley's brain following his suicide and it was discovered that he had "neuropathology," (i.e brain damage). For a full accounting of this episode, see: Eric A. Zillmer, Molly Harrower, Barry A. Ritzler, and Robert P. Archer, *The Quest for the Nazi Personality: A Psychological Investigation of Nazi War Criminals* (Hillsdale, NJ; 1995), 20–35.

[43] James Waller, *Becoming Evil. How Ordinary People Commit Genocide and Mass Killing*, 2nd ed. (New York, 2007).

[44] Goldensohn, *Nuremberg Interviews*, 390.

[45] Funk quoted in *ibid.*, 82–83.

and well-educated, *and* a committed National Socialist. In the truest sense, Ohlendorf was a dedicated ideological soldier of Nazism.[46] Evidence of this can be found in his SS record that shows he was a model party member. He is recorded as holding the Gold Party Badge (*Goldenes Ehrenzeichen der NSDAP*), and the War Service Cross first class with Swords (*Kriegsver-dienstkreuz I. Klasse mit Schwertern*). He also held the civilian rank of Under Secretary of State or *Unterstaatssekretär*, as well as being a Major General of the Police (*Generalleutnant der Polizei*).[47] He was, as his British interrogators discovered early on, a man who believed unwaveringly in the Nazi revolutionary mission and his role in it. Put another way, Ohlendorf's actions had not been motivated or enabled by a lack of conscience; rather, they were governed by the distorted sense of right and wrong that character-ized a Nazified conscience.[48] Add to this Ohlendorf's arrogance and sense of mission and one begins to see why he never tried to hide his actions. Until the end of his life, he was convinced of the rightness of his acts, telling those present at his execution on June 7, 1951, that one day the world would see that he was right after all.

That Ohlendorf, an intelligent, highly trained, and well-spoken man could simultaneously be a mass murderer presents an apparent inconsistency. The picture of him that emerges from allied interrogation reports is of a man who is fully cognizant of what he had done. It is certainly not that of a man with a violent disposition or severe personality disorder that would have explained or kept him from understanding the gravity of his crimes. Ohlendorf seemed perfectly comfortable with his horrific actions, discussing them within a framework of rational thought, as if they were simply the duties of a profes-sional man who had carried on with his daily work schedule. The question then is how such a well-educated man, who by all accounts interrogators actually liked, became a perpetrator of genocide. To borrow a phrase from scholar Dick de Mildt, what was Ohlendorf's "route to crime?"[49]

Ohlendorf's Route to Crime

Ohlendorf was born on February 4, 1907, in Hoheneggelsen near Hannover. The youngest of four children, including two brothers and a sister, he was not close to any of his siblings, although his brother William worked for

---

[46] Aronson, *Frühgeschichte von Gestapo und SD*, 211–212 and 229 argues that, unlike other leaders of the SD, Ohlendorf came to the organization in its infancy and out of conviction rather than for opportunistic reasons.

[47] SS-Dienstaltersliste, November 9, 1944 for SS-Oberst-Gruppenführer – SS-Standartenführer Otto Ohlendorf in RG 242, The collection of Foreign Records Seized, BDC, A3343 SSO-356A, F862.

[48] This is the argument put forward recently by Claudia Koonz, *The Nazi Conscience* (Cambridge, MA, 2003).

[49] de Mildt's, *In the Name of the People* explores this question in-depth.

the regime as well.[50] His middle-class, Protestant (Evangelical) family was typical for the time and nothing in his childhood presaged his later role in the activities of the mobile killing units. Ohlendorf's father Heinrich owned a farm and his mother Martha (nee Loges) kept house.[51] The political beliefs of Heinrich Ohlendorf (he was a member of the German Nationalist People's Party or DNVP) may well have influenced the evolution of his son's political philosophy, although this is at best a theory.[52] Perhaps the best indicator that he would assume a leadership role in the Third Reich was his admission after the war that he had been interested in politics from a young age, and, like many young men of his generation, he was a German nationalist.[53] His interest in politics and dream of socially and politically uniting Germans made him a likely candidate for an extreme nationalist political movement, particularly because his political beliefs were also stridently anti-Marxist.[54] Living at a time when traditional institutions seemed utterly incapable of solving Germany's problems; Ohlendorf also "despise[d] bourgeois values."[55] Because Ohlendorf believed in none of Germany's established political parties, he joined the NSDAP and its paramilitary wing, the *Sturmabteilung* – SA in 1925, at the age of eighteen, and was assigned membership number 6531.[56]

There is no question that Ohlendorf was a natural leader. In 1926, he founded the first Hitler Youth organization in his town and a year later he joined the SS with membership number 880.[57] Whereas these issues may seem unimportant, they are not insignificant indicators of his future or his commitment to National Socialism. The fact that he took a leadership role at such a young age and in support of extremist views suggests a predisposition toward far right-wing politics. According to Wildt, Ohlendorf's proclivity toward the political right was typical of a generation of young men that was born between 1900 and 1910 in Germany. This particular age-cohort, Wildt

[50] For basic information on Ohlendorf's life and career, see "Case Record Otto Ohlendorf," April 27, 1948, in NARA RG 338, JAD, WCB, Executed Prisoners 1946–1951, box 9, Ohlendorf folder; Testimony, Ohlendorf, October 8, 1947, *Trial*, roll 2, 476–478; Questionnaire of Ohlendorf, undated, M1270, roll 13; and Angrick, "Einsatzgruppe D," (PhD), 273–276.

[51] Angrick, "Einsatzgruppe D," (PhD), 273; Aronson, *Frühgeschichte von Gestapo und SD*, 210; and, Herbst, *Totale Krieg*, 182.

[52] Angrick, "Einsatzgruppe D," (PhD), 273 and Sowade, "Otto Ohlendorf," 155.

[53] Testimony, Ohlendorf, October 8, 1947, *Trial*, roll 2, 477.

[54] *Ibid.*

[55] Wildt, "Spirit of the RSHA," 338.

[56] Personal Bericht, Otto Ohlendorf, RG 242, BDC, A3343-SSO-356A, F865 and Angrick, "Einsatzgruppe D," (PhD), 273.

[57] Case Record, Ohlendorf, April 27, 1948 in NARA RG 338, JAD, WCB, Executed Prisoners 1946–1951, box 9, Ohlendorf folder; and, Testimony, Ohlendorf, October 8, 1947, *Trial*, roll 2, 476–478; Sowade, "Otto Ohlendorf," 155; Angrick, "Einsatzgruppe D," 273; and, Peter D. Stachura, *Nazi Youth in the Weimar Republic* (Santa Barbara, 1975), 30–31.

argues, were unduly influenced by the Great War; the war was their defining moment. Or perhaps more accurately, the loss of the war and their inability to participate in it was so devastating and traumatic that it pushed Ohlendorf and his cohort toward institutions and behaviors that would strengthen Germany, especially nationalist paramilitary and youth organizations. Ohlendorf was not as unique as it would seem; he was part of what Wildt calls the "generation without limits," by which he means a generation of young men whose lives had been so ruptured by the tumult of their youth that they broke with the traditions and values of the past and became actors in the future. They joined nationalist and ultra-nationalist political organizations in their youth and as adults they formed the leadership corps of Heydrich's RSHA. They embraced a worldview that was characterized by action and not fixed ideologies; they understood politics as a revolutionary impulse, not a theoretical concept to be debated. They were not fettered by the constraints of bourgeois Europe, they were rather free to promote the German nation and advance their new political ideology of action.[58] Ohlendorf's life trajectory was, in fact, emblematic of the larger generation without limits.

In 1928, when Ohlendorf was twenty-one, he entered university to study law and political economy.[59] During his university days he remained politically active. For instance, while at the University of Göttingen, he worked tirelessly and was instrumental in assisting the Nazis to win their first electoral victory at the *Gau* (district) level in Hannover-South.[60] Youthful political activity was not unique to Ohlendorf; it conforms to Wildt's findings, where Ohlendorf's cohort of young, university-educated men was able and eager to change German society.[61] Action was a dominant element of Ohlendorf's worldview, and what better place to begin than within the university, where so many young men of his generation were primed to accept the promises of a rabid nationalism. He graduated from university in 1931 and that year received a scholarship to study fascist economics at the University of Pavia, Italy.[62] It was during this time that he claims he developed his worldview.[63] Anyone who has read Ohlendorf's intellectual musings, his interrogation reports, or his testimony to the court knows that he was not a straight-forward thinker, or at least he did not articulate his ideas in a lucid fashion. His postwar statements on economics illustrate this. Apparently, he objected to many aspects of Italian Fascism, including its statism and corporatism, preferring instead the more collective (i.e. nationalist) nature

---

[58] Wildt, *Generation des Unbedingten*, 11–14 and 23–29 and "Spirit of the RSHA," 339–340.

[59] Herbst, *Totale Krieg*, 182, argues that Ohlendorf "was little suited for a career as a lawyer," because his interests revolved around resolving problems dealing with the state and economics.

[60] Testimony, Ohlendorf, October 8, 1947, Trial, roll 2, 478.

[61] Wildt, *Generation des Unbedingten*, 72–143.

[62] Sowade, "Otto Ohlendorf," 155 and Herbst, *Totale Krieg*, 181–183.

[63] Herbst, *Totale Krieg*, 183.

of Nazism. He also believed in Hitler's view of the *Volksgemeinschaft*, the building of a German "community of the people." This is what he claims distinguished National Socialism from its Italian counterpart: a community of blood and race.[64] Corrupt business practices irked Ohlendorf, particularly if they benefited individuals more than the national community, and he disliked any attempt to expand enterprises owned by the Party. Instead, he preferred a planned, centralized economic system for Germany.[65] Throughout his career, according to Ohlendorf's own narrative, his political philosophy coupled with his unwillingness to tow the official party line earned him a reputation as an "intellectual know all," frequently bringing him into conflict with high-ranking members of the Party, particularly Heinrich Himmler, who Ohlendorf claimed resented his "superior attitude."[66] Ohlendorf's disagreements with Himmler never reached the breaking point; in fact, the opposite is true despite his insistence otherwise. His hard work eventually earned him the respect of his colleagues and he steadily rose through the ranks of the SS; he won medals, became an SS Major General in 1942, and eventually in 1944, a Lieutenant General.[67]

Ohlendorf was intelligent, but he was not the intellectual he fancied himself to be nor the zealous opponent of National Socialism he repeatedly claimed he was to American and British authorities after the war. Rather, both of these characterizations were carefully manufactured fabrications; images he took every opportunity to project during his captivity in an attempt to curry favor with the Allies.[68] Ohlendorf was incarcerated from May 1945, until his execution on June 7, 1951. During this time, he tried to win over his captors and secure release from prison. One of the ways he attempted to do this was by portraying himself as an intellectual opponent of Nazism, which he thought would be a compelling reason to release him. Neither the British nor the Americans agreed. They did not believe Ohlendorf's claims to opposition. Although it is true that he began a doctoral degree in economics and he did want an academic career, it is also true that he never completed his studies. Instead of finishing his Ph.D. in economics, Ohlendorf began training for a career in law.[69] Just because

---

[64] Testimony, Ohlendorf, October 8, 1947, *Trial*, roll 2, 480.

[65] Interrogation, Ohlendorf, November 9, 1945, M1270, roll 13. See also Felix Kersten, *The Kersten Memoirs, 1940–1945*, trans. Constantine Fitzgibbon and James Oliver (London, 1956), 206–208 and Robert Koehl, *The Black Corps: The Structure and Power Struggles of the Nazi SS* (Madison, WI; 1983), 231.

[66] Sowade, "Otto Ohlendorf," 156. See also Heinz Höhne, *The Order of the Death's Head: the Story of Hitler's SS*, trans. Richard Barry (London, 1970), 234 and Kersten, *Memoirs*, 209–210.

[67] Sowade, "Otto Ohlendorf," 158.

[68] For example, "Opposition" and "Reasons for Opposition," in CSDIC (UK) Report, September 30, 1945, NARA RG 319, box 156A, Ohlendorf folder.

[69] Ohlendorf began his doctoral studies in economics in 1932, after he returned from a year of study in Italy. He abandoned his academic career in 1933, when Jessen hired him. See "Appendix 1," CSDIC (UK), September 30, 1945 in *ibid*.

he did not formally finish his studies, however, does not automatically make him an anti-intellectual. But, Ohlendorf was not an intellectual in the liberal sense (a person characterized by his ability and willingness to think critically and independently); he was a man of action, neither capable nor desirous of reflecting on his own actions and behaviors. Even at this early age, he was an arrogant ideologue, trapped by Nazi parameters and not at all open to contrary perspectives. He was, after all, an early member of the Nazi party in 1925 and an ideological National Socialist – anything but the free thinker he pretended to be. As one British analyst astutely observed after interviewing Ohlendorf in 1945, "he has a host of ideas on every subject, be they on education, religion, politics, economics, or finance. He has, however, studied none of these subjects more than superficially."[70] Ohlendorf was as Himmler had characterized him, an arrogant know-it-all.

When the Nazis came to power in 1933, Ohlendorf seemed to have a change of heart about his intellectual pursuits, illustrating a more careerist sensibility. He gave up his legal studies fairly early on when he was offered a job by his former supervisor, Professor Jens Peter Jessen, as "assistant director" of the *Institut für Weltwirtschaft* (Institute for World Economics) in Kiel.[71] Combining theory with action appealed to Ohlendorf and he happily accepted the position. It was while under Jessen's supervision that Ohlendorf developed what can only be described as an independent and highly personal theory of economics, what Hanno Sowade calls a "middle-class oriented economic ideology."[72] Ohlendorf worked in Kiel until 1934, when he and his mentor had a severe falling out with local Nazi Party officials over the content of their economic theories and teaching.[73] Their criticism of National Socialist economic policy finally resulted in their expulsion from the Institute in December 1934.[74] Tutor and student went to Berlin where an incident similar to the one in Kiel again led to conflicts with local Party officials. Realizing his economics career was probably over, Ohlendorf, on the suggestion of Jessen, joined the *Sicherheitsdienst* (Security Service or SD) in 1936, a decision that ended all hopes of an academic career and one that would alter the course of his life permanently by drawing him into the activities of the criminal Nazi police state when the SD became the feeder organization of the *Einsatzgruppen*.[75]

Ohlendorf had a large ego and he was flattered when he first encountered Professor Reinhard Höhn, the individual in charge of recruiting for

---

[70] CSDIC (UK) Notes on Corruption and Corrupted Personalities in Germany, PW Paper 133, August 11, 1945 in NARA RG 319, box 165A, Ohlendorf folder.

[71] Angrick, "Die Einsatzgruppe D," (Ph.D.), 274.

[72] Sowade, Otto Ohlendorf," 157.

[73] Testimony, Ohlendorf, October 8, 1947, *Trial*, roll 2, 484–488. See also Sowade, "Otto Ohlendorf,"156.

[74] Questionnaire, Ohlendorf, undated, M1270, roll 13.

[75] Testimony, Ohlendorf, October 8, 1947, *Trial*, roll 2, 489.

the offices of the SD, who told him that the SD "needed critical intellects like his."[76] Ohlendorf had always been an ambitious individual, and thus was intrigued by the possibility that he might be able to put his academic training to practical use in the SD.[77] Under Höhn's supervision, Ohlendorf became director of *Abteilung* II (Domestic Economics) and later he was promoted to leader of the entire Central Division of the office.[78] The job seemed ready made for him because his main task was to develop an economics information office. Ohlendorf had always preferred economics to law, spending his earlier years developing his own economic philosophy, which he hoped would be taken seriously by the Party.[79] As head of *Abteilung* II, he gathered all information about economic matters, analyzed it, and wrote reports designed to guide National Socialist economic policy.[80] At a time when Germany was fighting its way out of the Depression, Party officials appreciated Ohlendorf's unorthodox style. In the SD, he thought he had finally found a role for himself within the Party; a place where he could freely discuss his ideas about economics and their application to National Socialism. This is a common theme among the *Einsatzgruppen* leaders tried at Nuremberg. Many of them had been lured into the offices of the SD with the expectation that they could contribute to changes in German society. Ohlendorf became disillusioned, however, when he first discovered that the offices of the SD were not as independent as Professor Höhn had promised him they would be. This seems somewhat surprising in light of the collective nature of Nazism. Certainly after the war, American prosecutors had great difficulty believing Ohlendorf when he told them about his disappointment with the SD and his discovery that "there was no such thing as an [independent] SD information organization."[81] Like all other Nazi organizations, the offices of the SD were carefully scrutinized by Party bosses, the process of which proved to be very limiting for an arrogant, "free thinker" like Ohlendorf. Ohlendorf was not alone, but rather was typical of the type of young intellectuals attracted to the SD; an organization Heydrich was attempting to build as a base for his personal power, with many of his recruits being young, idealistic university students.[82] What young man would not jump at the chance to influence the Party? By using the offices of the SD as a vehicle to expose and correct what Ohlendorf referred to as "mistaken developments in the National

---

[76] Höhne, *Death's Head*, 212–213.

[77] Sowade, "Otto Ohlendorf," 156.

[78] *Ibid.*, 156–157.

[79] *Ibid.*, 155–156.

[80] Aronson, *Frühgeschichte von Gestapo und SD*, 213.

[81] Testimony, Ohlendorf, October 8, 1947, *Trial*, roll 2, 489.

[82] Höhne, *Death's Head* and Wildt, *Generation des Unbedingten*, 163–189. Lutz Hachmeister, *Der Gegnerforscher: Die Karriere des SS-Führers Franz Alfred Six* (Munich, 1998), 7 has argued that Franz Six, like Ohlendorf, represented the ideal type of SS-intellectual in the Third Reich.

Socialist philosophy," the young men of Germany hoped to shape their own futures.[83] Conveniently, after the war Ohlendorf used his role in the SD as a way to bolster his contention that he was not a passive follower of Nazism, but rather a free thinker, even a critic of the regime. In the SD, Ohlendorf felt he had at last found a place within the National Socialist movement where he could freely express himself and put his intellect to practical use to further the true National Socialist cause.[84] Perhaps, under these circumstances then, Ohlendorf had all the more reason to feel disappointed when his idealistic hopes were dashed upon the rocks of hard, bureaucratic reality.

For nearly two years while working in the SD, Ohlendorf and a team of economists investigated and reported on National Socialist economic policy. His reports were, more often than not, both critical of Nazi economic policy and extremely pessimistic about the future; they were particularly critical of policymakers' insistence on deficit spending, state control of business, and the Four Year Plan.[85] He believed the future of Germany would be threatened if the state were allowed, as in Italy, to spend beyond its means and control big business. He foresaw an end to entrepreneurship and free enterprise in Germany if corrupt men like Hermann Göring and Robert Ley (leader of the Labor Front) were allowed to use big business as a means of power and wealth for themselves.[86] Of course, because of Ohlendorf's training in Italy, he believed himself to be an expert in fascist economics, a fact that when coupled with his arrogance, led him to be very critical of Party policy. After the war, Ohlendorf claimed this type of criticism was not well received and resulted in a severe reprimand by Himmler, who felt Ohlendorf's egotistical and defeatist attitude was an unbearable combination, and by Heydrich, who, in September 1937, forbade him from engaging in any critical analysis of the regime whatsoever.[87] Unhappy with the prospect of merely rubber-stamping the regime, Ohlendorf says he attempted to resign from the SD, but was denied permission to do so by Heydrich who, despite Ohlendorf's critique of the Party, felt his skills as an economist could still be valuable to the organization. According to Ohlendorf, in 1938, Heydrich finally acquiesced and allowed him to transfer to the Reich Group Commerce on the condition that he continue to work part-time for *Abteilung* II.[88] Apparently,

[83] Testimony, Ohlendorf, October 8, 1947, *Trial*, roll 2, 489.
[84] Herbst, *Totale Krieg*, 183.
[85] Testimony, Ohlendorf, October 8, 1947, *Trial*, roll 2, 490–493.
[86] Interrogation, Ohlendorf, November 9, 1945, Nuremberg in M1270, roll 12; and, Testimony, Ohlendorf, October 8, 1947, *Trial*, roll 2, 498–499. See also Kersten, *Memoirs*, 207–208.
[87] Testimony, Ohlendorf, October 8, 1947, *Trial*, roll 2, 498–499 and Kersten, *Memoirs*, 209–210. Herbst, Totale Krieg, 271 argues that "although the relationship between Ohlendorf and Himmler was at times personally difficult, they possessed a high measure of agreement in substantial points of economic policy."
[88] Testimony, Ohlendorf, October 8, 1947, *Trial*, roll 2, 490–493. See also Höhne, *Death's Head*, 235–236 and Herbst, *Totale Krieg*, 186.

Ohlendorf maintained his position in the SD, on an honorary basis, working two hours a day, but he preferred his new position with the Reich Group Commerce where he worked until June 1939.[89] At this time, Heydrich was in the process of integrating the SD and SIPO into the larger RSHA organization, and, thus, he recalled Ohlendorf to the SD to work full-time. For someone who had supposedly lost favor with the two most powerful figures of the terror state, Ohlendorf seemed to have had no difficulty advancing his career. He was like many in the SD, "flexible, mobile, [and] eager," characteristics that enabled him to "perform his duties" anywhere.[90] Less than three months after Heydrich recalled him to the SD (in September), he was made head of *Amt* III (Office of Domestic Intelligence) and was subsequently put in charge of compiling national research on German public opinion.[91] This was a major career advancement for Ohlendorf and I believe quite telling of his real power in the regime. He was not the marginal figure he claimed he was after the war, but rather a significant and critical voice for the regime.

That Ohlendorf was a tried and true Nazi is borne out by the facts, yet why select him for such an important task when there were undoubtedly others who were just as qualified and more compliant? Ohlendorf was selected to head *Amt* III because he was loyal to the Party. During the initial phase of the war, Heydrich wanted individuals in charge of the offices of the SD who would help strengthen support for the regime by honestly assessing German attitudes to Party policy and making adjustments where necessary. As Hanno Sowade has noted, this job was tailor-made for Ohlendorf, who was more than willing to express views contrary to official Party lines, but, yet, was also fiercely loyal to the Third Reich and Hitler.[92] After the war, Ohlendorf wanted the Americans and British to believe he was an outspoken critic of the Reich and a marginal figure in the regime. His persistent criticism of Nazi economic policy, coupled with the hundreds of affidavits that spoke of his human qualities and that were entered into evidence at Nuremberg, seem to attest to this. In casting himself as an "ardent anti-Nazi" and taking every opportunity to "condemn" his colleagues and superiors, Ohlendorf undoubtedly hoped to win the trust of his captors.[93] He even went so far as to claim he had several "violent altercations" with Hitler over the implementation of National Socialist policy and while in captivity he deliberately ostracized himself from the other war criminals and inmates.[94] The record indicates that all aspects of Ohlendorf's behavior

[89] Sowade, "Otto Ohlendorf," 157.

[90] Wildt, "Spirit of the RSHA," 343.

[91] Angrick, "Einsatzgruppe D," (Ph.D.), 275; Herbst, *Totale Krieg*, 185; and, Sowade, "Otto Ohlendorf," 157.

[92] Sowade, "Otto Ohlendorf," 158.

[93] Preliminary Interrogation Report of G-2, Special Section, SHAEF on Otto Ohlendorf, May 31, 1945 in NARA RG 319, box 165A, Ohlendorf folder.

[94] *Ibid.*

or story did not so easily fool the Allies. Although they acknowledged his power and knowledge in economic circles and they believed much of the content of what he told them, they also recognized that his "difference[s] of opinion with other leading Nazis were nothing else than the constant struggles for power within the Nazi state."[95] The Allies were more astute than Ohlendorf gave them credit and thus his intellectual opposition to Nazi policy should not be overstated. Although Ohlendorf's motivations for these statements were fairly transparent, one intelligence report noted, "he is a coward who tries to save himself by betraying most of his erstwhile friends and collaborators and all of his rivals and enemies." Nonetheless, the British and Americans considered him to be "personally honest," an ironic and disturbing characterization of a man responsible for supervising the murder of tens of thousands of individuals.[96]

The fact is that by the summer of 1941, Ohlendorf was irreversibly drawn into the horrors of the Nazi regime; it was almost as if he had been groomed from an early age to assume this role. He was the type of individual whom the regime trusted: he had supported National Socialism since he was a teenager – he and National Socialism had grown-up together – and he was a man of action willing to do just about anything to ensure its success. This Nazi ideologue was now asked to put his theories into practice, and, in the process, his loyalty to the state and its ideology was tested.[97] Unfortunately, Ohlendorf, like many men of his generation and education, would pass the test with honors. His transformation from intellectual critic of National Socialist economic policy to head of one of the mobile security and killing units in the Soviet Union is a good example of how the Nazis were able to involve even the most free-thinking members of the Party into mass murder and how men like Ohlendorf would prove to be some of the most effective instruments of Nazi racial (genocidal) policy. In fact, Ohlendorf's transformation was indicative of how amenable the intellectual elite of the new German society was to Nazi racial plans in the east. In 1941, Ohlendorf was recruited for a leadership role in the *Einsatzgruppen*, the mobile security and killing units Himmler wanted to deploy alongside the German army when Operation Barbarossa was launched.

None of the commanders of the *Einsatzgruppen*, including Ohlendorf, volunteered for leadership roles in these security and killing units, except perhaps, as legend has it, Arthur Nebe, the head of the *Kriminalpolizei* who supposedly volunteered. Nor, I am certain, did any of them grow up dreaming they would become heads of murderous police battalions. If

[95] CSDIC (UK) Notes on Corruption and Corrupted Personalities in Germany, PW Paper 133, August 11, 1945, in NARA RG 319, box 165A, Ohlendorf folder. Virtually, every historical and legal account of Ohlendorf's postwar confessions highlights his level of truthfulness.
[96] *Ibid.*
[97] Herbst, *Totale Krieg*, 182 and 185.

neither sadism nor volunteerism were his motive, what circumstances led to Ohlendorf's job in the *Einsatzgruppen?* This is difficult to say with certainty, because there is no official record of the recruitment process. Perhaps selection of personnel for Operation Barbarossa was similar to the Polish campaign in 1939, where the leaders of the *Einsatzgruppen* were carefully chosen from the ranks of the various police and security organizations of the state based on their rank and loyalty to the Party.[98] In the case of the highest-ranking SS-Police officers who served on the eastern front, we also know that Himmler selected them himself. There is no reason to suspect Ohlendorf's recruitment was significantly different.[99] According to Käthe, Ohlendorf's wife, her husband had accepted the assignment in the Soviet Union because he felt the need to redeem himself with Himmler, with whom he had conflict.[100] The *Reichsführer*-SS was Ohlendorf's direct superior and the two apparently did not share the same outlook; reportedly, Himmler sarcastically characterized the ambitious and arrogant young Ohlendorf as a *Gralshüter* or knight of the Holy Grail. Himmler felt, according to Käthe, that Ohlendorf was too much a man of theory and, thus, he needed to get his hands dirty to learn what sacrifice for National Socialism really entailed.[101] Thus, when Himmler was looking to staff his SS army, he recruited Ohlendorf.[102] This may well be true as Wildt suggests it would be in keeping with the flexible and action-oriented nature of members of the SD, RSHA, and *Einsatzgruppen.* More than likely, Ohlendorf was also recruited because he was loyal to the regime and a careerist. To avoid the label of coward, and perhaps to lessen some of the tensions between him and his superiors, Ohlendorf claimed at trial that he reluctantly accepted the position as head of *Einsatzgruppe* D in the spring of 1941.[103] Actions speak louder than words, however. Although he may have been hesitant at

---

[98] On selection for the Polish campaign, see Rossino, *Hitler Strikes Poland,* 29–57.

[99] On the recruitment of the Higher-SS and police leaders see Ruth Bettina Birn, *Die Höheren SS- und Polizeiführer: Himmlers vertreter im Reich und den besetzten Gebietenr* (Düsseldorf, 1986).

[100] Höhne, *Death's Head,* 356–357. Ohlendorf married Käthe sometime in the 1930s and they had 5 children, two boys (Henning, born February 11, 1938, and Behrend born September 18, 1943) and 3 girls (Irmtraut born March 25, 1936, Meinhard born October 30, 1940 and Ulrike born May 11, 1945) see B305/147 deutsch Kriegsverurteilte im Landsberg-Einzelfälle (1949–1950), Ohlendorf folder, Bundesarchiv (BA), Koblenz.

[101] Herbst, *Totale Krieg,* 185 and Richard Breitman, *The Architect of Genocide: Himmler and the Final Solution* (Hanover, NH; 1991) 43–44. George Browder, *Hitler's Enforcers: the Gestapo and the SS Security Service in the Nazi Revolution* (New York, 1996), 157–158, does not entirely agree with this conclusion. He writes, "Although men like Otto Ohlendorf claimed that Heydrich assigned them to lead Einsatzgruppen as a policy of Blutkitt, that may be the rationalization of a brutalized executioner trying to explain his own failure [to resist being drawn into the killing process]."

[102] Testimony, Ohlendorf, October 8, 1947, *Trial,* roll 2, 513–514.

[103] Herbst, *Totale Krieg,* 182 and Sowade, "Otto Ohlendorf," 158.

first, once given the task of leading an SS battalion, Ohlendorf performed his duties with military efficiency, later boasting about the strict regimen he established with his men, even admitting to sending those too weak of heart to carry out their bloody task back to Berlin for reassignment.[104] His behavior in the east, coupled with a strong ideological commitment to Nazism and long history with the Party, suggests that perhaps he was not as averse to accepting the job as he maintained after the war. After all, he had a vested interest in stressing the involuntary nature of the assignment in court – his life depended on it. Moreover, Ohlendorf's commitment to National Socialist ideology was so strong that he told the court and all of his interrogators after the war and during his incarceration that he carried out his duties in the Soviet Union "to the best of his ability and with a clear conscience." In practice, this meant his unit killed 90,000 people. Michael Wildt's findings seem to support the conclusion that Ohlendorf, like most of the leaders of the *Einsatzgruppen,* was both a man of theory and of action, willing and able to assist the aims of the regime at his desk in Berlin or in the killing fields of Russia.[105] We also know that when given the opportunity, he refused an early discharge from his duties in the east, staying longer than all other *Einsatzgruppe* leaders who had begun working there the same time as he.[106] Just as he applied himself to his work in the SD, it seemed, he also worked hard in the occupied east. He remained in the Soviet Union for a full year, convinced of the necessity of his task and of his ability to do more for the National Socialist cause in the field rather than in Germany proper.[107]

If Ohlendorf was sent to the eastern front as a test, he passed with honors, yet, the rogue National Socialist was not tamed by his experience. When he returned to Germany in the summer of 1942, he immediately resumed his career as *Amtchef* RSHA III (Domestic Intelligence). For the remainder of the war, Ohlendorf spent his time collecting opinions and documenting German opposition to National Socialist policy. He highlighted areas in which Germans were unhappy with the regime, and noted ways in which the Party could improve policy. Later in the war, even when his reports were ignored by Hitler, rather than give up his efforts, he diligently recorded public attitudes toward National Socialist policy. As a Nazi theorist, he assumed it was his duty to do so.[108] But, as Sowade has aptly pointed out, Ohlendorf's willingness to criticize the regime should in no way be construed

---

[104] Testimony, Ohlendorf, October 14, 1947, *Trial,* roll 2, 592. Stephen Tyas believes this is overstated. Whereas he acknowledges that Ohlendorf does mention sending "weak" officials back to Germany, he notes that there is only one proved case, that of Martin Mündschutz. Outside of his return to Berlin, he has not found a single other incident. Correspondence with Tyas, January 23, 2007.

[105] Wildt, *Generation des Unbedingten,* 679–701.

[106] Sowade, "Otto Ohlendorf," 159–160.

[107] *Ibid.*

[108] Smith, Jr., "Life in Wartime Germany," 6; Kersten, *Memoirs,* 210–211 and 218–219; Herbst, *Totale Krieg,* 187; and, Sowade, "Otto Ohlendorf," 160–163.

as "opposition to Hitler." Rather, it was Ohlendorf's way of attempting to improve the regime by emphasizing areas where Germans were unhappy and eliminating them, or perhaps even a way to leverage change through "legitimate" means.[109]

Was Ohlendorf a typical SD man as Michael Wildt has suggested he was?[110] Certainly this is not the way he characterized himself to the Allies. He told authorities repeatedly that throughout his career in the Third Reich, he refused to pay lip service to National Socialist ideas with which he disagreed, even at the expense of his academic career, which was, apparently, his first calling. At the same time, like so many of his cohort, this burgeoning intellectual was willing to do the dirty work of the regime in the Soviet Union. Because of these seemingly contradictory positions, Ohlendorf claimed his reputation as an uncompromising and unselfish idealist was justified.[111] He spent his time in captivity trying to convince the Allies that he differed from other Nazi criminals, and there is some evidence to suggest that the Americans, at least, believed he was. After the war, Ohlendorf's behavior certainly could be characterized as unusual. He was one of the few, high-ranking Nazis (Albert Speer is another), who actually admitted his actions, albeit with none of Speer's questionable remorse.[112] His willingness to cooperate and his sincerity about his crimes perplexed his captors, leading one judge to lament that he wished all defendants were as forthcoming.[113] What is not in doubt, is that this so-called Dr. Jekyll and Mr. Hyde (so named by Musmanno, the presiding judge in the *Einsatzgruppen* trial, who believed that there was a good and a bad Ohlendorf) remained a committed National Socialist until the end, never disagreeing with the Reich's racial policies and never demonstrating unease at the path he had chosen.[114] Indeed until he was hanged in 1951, he seems to have believed in the rightness of his tasks, something his captors could never reconcile with the refined man who sat before them in the dock.

In spite of Ohlendorf's crimes, his comportment had a seductive effect on his captors. During his numerous meetings with American authorities, he and his interrogators seemed to have developed a relationship of mutual respect.[115] According to Robert Conot, Ohlendorf and his principal

[109] Sowade, "Otto Ohlendorf," 160.
[110] Wildt, *Generation des Unbedingten*, 41–208 has argued that Ohlendorf was typical of the young, educated, and idealistic youth who were attracted to the Nazi party and who were born between 1900 and 1910.
[111] Letter, Käthe Ohlendorf to Nikolaus Ehlen, October 26, 1950, KLE 66, NL Ohlendorf, B2, BA.
[112] Whether or not Speer was genuinely remorseful is a matter of debate.
[113] Judgment, April 8, 1948, *Trial*, roll 7, 132.
[114] *Ibid.*, 131.
[115] Ohlendorf's good relationship with his captors was not unusual. Even the notorious Hermann Göring developed a very strong bond with prison psychiatrist Douglas M. Kelley, M.D., who returned the admiration. Frequently, the prison officials were the prisoners'

interrogator Lieutenant Colonel Smith W. Brookhart grew very fond of one another, so much so that Brookhart promised that he would help Ohlendorf write his memoirs.[116] Brookhart and Ohlendorf spoke to one another almost daily, and his trust in Brookhart grew during the course of his incarceration as evidenced by his increasing willingness to reveal important information about the Third Reich. For instance, Ohlendorf told Brookhart about the secret agreement between the German High Command and the RSHA that enabled Hitler's plan for a war of extermination to be carried out in the east. He also explained in detail how the *Einsatzgruppen* operated, and he described their relationship to the army, their tasks, and how and when they received their orders. Ohlendorf seemed to trust Brookhart so much that he was unable to keep silent; and, to his later detriment, he gave Brookhart all the information he requested and even some he did not solicit.

Well aware that he might offend some of his imprisoned colleagues, Ohlendorf nonetheless detailed all of their activities in the Soviet Union, including the process of mass murder. During one interrogation he helped the American prosecution team construct a chart outlining the structure of the Security Police and Security Service (SD) explaining precisely the role and position of all officials.[117] This was later used in court as prosecution evidence and, ultimately, helped indict several of his colleagues. Ohlendorf kept little to himself. He was so forthcoming that when reading the interrogation record one gets the impression that he was not a hostile prisoner of the American authorities at all, but perhaps a confidant or even a friend. Of course, Brookhart masterfully exploited Ohlendorf's attachment to him, which undoubtedly encouraged the imprisoned war criminal to be more open and frank than he might otherwise have been.

On only one occasion did Ohlendorf ever appear worried or shaken. This happened in March 1946, when he was told that at the conclusion of the IMT proceedings he would be extradited to the Soviet Union to stand trial for crimes he had committed there in 1941 and 1942. Upon hearing this news he admitted to needing "moral support" and "begged" Sander Jaari, one of the Nuremberg interrogators, to visit him from "time to time"[118] This is the only time Ohlendorf ever openly expressed fear about his fate, either before he was indicted, or after, suggesting he assumed that eventually he would be released. At one point, American authorities raised the issue of the safety of his loved ones, pointing out that his family might be in jeopardy because of his public testimony at Nuremberg against the

---

only contact, and, as such, they developed strong attachments to their captors. For a full recounting of the issue, see Zillmer et al., *The Quest for the Nazi Personality*, 78–88.

[116] Conot, *Justice at Nuremberg*, 233.

[117] *Ibid.*

[118] Memorandum, Jaari to Brookhart, "Conversation with Otto Ohlendorf, March 7, 1946," M1270, roll 13.

German High Command in 1949 when he was labeled a traitor (*Verräter*) by German nationalists.[119] Ohlendorf seemed genuinely surprised by the suggestion. Whatever his relationship with his captors, his verbosity made him a remarkably effective witness for the prosecution at the IMT and ultimately led to his indictment for crimes against humanity in 1947.

Because of Ohlendorf's willingness to discuss the criminal activities of the Nazi regime the Americans immediately recognized his potential as a witness for their prosecution of the major war criminals being tried by the IMT. On January 3, 1946, the day after the court heard an affidavit by Hermann Gräbe describing in excruciating detail an execution he had witnessed by an *Einsatzkommando* in the Soviet Union, Ohlendorf was called to the stand as a prosecution witness in the case against Ernst Kaltenbrunner, the sole member of the security branch of the SS then on trial.[120] Ohlendorf proved to be a star witness and his sensational testimony captivated the court. Here was an extremely cultivated, well-educated SS officer who had joined the Nazi Party as a young man, rose through the ranks, who during the war had held important positions within the intelligence and security service of the SS, and who spoke unreservedly about Kaltenbrunner and the criminal activities of the SS. Ohlendorf's testimony in court confirmed an earlier declaration he had made to Brookhart in which he stated that "every individual will have to stand for what he has done and be held responsible for what he has done, and also make a complete statement of what he has done."[121]

Ohlendorf was neither an imposing nor brutish figure, as was Kaltenbrunner, yet when he spoke people listened. There are conflicting views of Ohlendorf's character and personality. Felix Kersten, Himmler's masseur, remembered him as a dominant man who appeared quite authoritative and "who always spoke the truth regardless of the consequences."[122] Unquestionably, he was young and handsome, speaking with precision and frankness. Even though this appears true, Goldensohn believes "his manner is of a man who is expected to be insulted at any moment and is being defensive about it."[123] This was in private, however. In public, he behaved differently. Unlike other defendants and witnesses at Nuremberg, he appeared very calm during his

[119] Interrogation, Ohlendorf, January 10, 1946, *ibid* and Letter, Rudolf Aschenauer to Landesbishof D. Hauck, February 26, 1949 in Bestand D1 Nachlass D. Theophil Wurm, Band 310 Kriegsverbrechen, Landeskirchliches Archiv, Stuttgart (from here forward simply BD1, NL Wurm, file, LKA); and, Letter, Aschenauer to Neuhäusler, February 26, 1949, KLE 66, NL Ohlendorf, B2, BA.
[120] FBI Case Record, Ohlendorf, US Department of Justice, Civil Fingerprint Card, April 27, 1948, in NARA RG 338, JAD, WCB, Executed Prisoners 1946–1951, box 9, Ohlendorf file.
[121] Ohlendorf quoted in Conot, *Justice at Nuremberg*, 233.
[122] Kersten, *Memoirs*, 206–207.
[123] Goldensohn, "Otto Ohlendorf," 386.

testimony.[124] One reporter even compared Ohlendorf's comportment to Göring's, noting that both men were stage directors (and actors) and both performed for the court.[125] Henry Lea, an interpreter at Nuremberg, believes that Ohlendorf was no more or less charismatic than any of the other defendants. He was simply "more clean-cut, articulate and smooth than the other [defendants]" and nothing more.[126] What is not open to debate is that in court Ohlendorf dispassionately repeated what he had said to his interrogators the previous October: that at least some of the German High Command had intimate knowledge of the role the *Einsatzgruppen* played in liquidating Soviet commissars and Jews; that the *Einsatzgruppen* leaders were given their orders in Pretzsch, east Prussia, three or four days before they were mobilized for Operation Barbarossa in June 1941; and that *Einsatzgruppe* D, the mobile security unit he commanded in the Crimea between June 1941 and 1942, was responsible for the "liquidation" of approximately 90,000 men, women, and children. The men were shot, he told the court, and the women and children were asphyxiated by carbon monoxide in the so-called gas vans.[127] When asked how he could be so precise about the number of victims, Ohlendorf explained to the court that the numbers of those killed were compiled in reports that were sent back to Berlin. Naturally, he knew the figures for his own group, and because he had access to other group leader's reports, he was able to come up with an educated estimate of the total number of victims. He stated that in his opinion, their figures, which incidentally exceeded his, were exaggerated. His numbers, he was certain, were accurate.[128]

Ohlendorf's testimony horrified the court. Telford Taylor noted in his memoir of the IMT trial that he recalled "the stunned silence of the audience that followed" Ohlendorf's "cold, impassive statement."[129] Dr. Gustav M. Gilbert, the German-born prison psychologist, recorded in his diary that Ohlendorf's testimony had had a "depressing" effect on the defendants because it laid bare "the inescapable reality and shame of mass murder . . . by the unquestionable reliability of a German official."[130] Indeed, there is scarcely an account of the IMT proceedings that does not include at least one reference to Ohlendorf's testimony, a reminder that his comments had a profound impact on both participants and spectators alike, and it was the shocking content of his testimony perhaps more so than his comportment that people recalled.

[124] Taylor, *Anatomy*, 246–249.
[125] Tom Reedy, undated and untitled article, 1948 in MMP, Gumberg Library, NG Correspondence, 1445.
[126] Letter, Henry Lea to Hilary Earl, July 3, 2006.
[127] Testimony, Ohlendorf, January 3, 1946, *Trial of the Major War Criminals before the International Military Tribunal, Nuremberg*, vol. 4, 308–355.
[128] Testimony, Ohlendorf, January 3, 1946, *ibid.*, 318–319.
[129] Taylor, *Anatomy*, 5.
[130] Gilbert, *Nuremberg Diary*, 101.

FIGURE 1. Mass shooting by an unidentified unit of the EGN in the Soviet Union
USHMM photo archive (#89063)

Ohlendorf's compulsion to explain and justify his actions in the Soviet
Union sealed his fate. Because of his incriminating testimony and his willingness to give information freely to his American interrogators, the OCCWC
had a growing body of evidence to use against him if they decided to put
him on trial. Early on in the planning phase for the Subsequent proceedings,
American investigators were divided in their opinion about what to do with
Ohlendorf.[131] As it was, some of the investigators wanted to hold off trying
the former SS man precisely because such a large proportion of the evidence
they had against him dealt "only with his activities as Group leader of *Einsatzgruppe* D," a crime they did not fully understand at the time. Moreover
they argued, his crimes were committed on Russian soil and under article
4(c) of the *Nuremberg Charter*, the Russians had the right to try anyone who
committed crimes against humanity or war crimes on their territory, and so
there was the possibility that the Soviets might want to extradite Ohlendorf and try him themselves.[132] Some attorneys believed that the Americans
should hold off trying Ohlendorf because thus far he had proved to be such
a valuable source of information against many leading Nazis and, therefore, they should, "as a matter of expediency . . . postpone" his prosecution

[131] Whitney Harris maintains that Ohlendorf's testimony is what broke the *Einsatzgruppen*
case wide open. The evidence seems to indicate that Ohlendorf's testimony and interrogations sealed his own fate, but not that of the other leaders of the mobile units. See "Interview
with Whitney Harris," Cargas (ed.), *Voices from the Holocaust*, 110–111.

[132] M. Cherif Bassiouni, "The History of Universal Jurisdiction and Its Place in International
Law," in Stephen Macedo, ed., *Universal Jurisdiction. National Courts and the Prosecution
of Serious Crimes under International Law* (Philadelphia, 2004), 52.

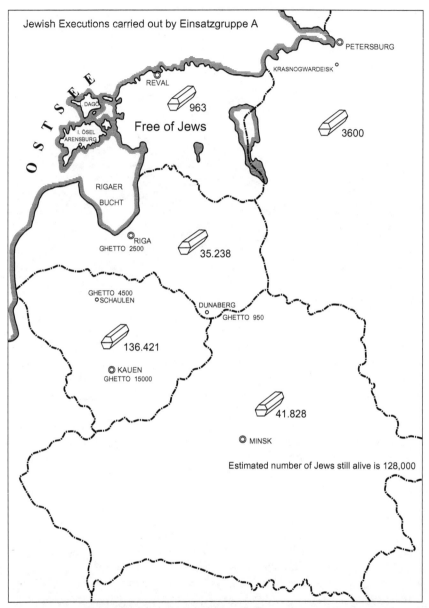

FIGURE 2. A map that accompanied a secret undated report on the mass murder of Jews by EG A, used as evidence in the trial, USHMM photo archive (#03550)

until they had obtained all possible information from him.[133] The fact that Taylor's organization already had Ohlendorf's confession together with the discovery of the *Einsatzgruppen* reports late in 1946 or early 1947, and the projected scope of the trials virtually assured Ohlendorf a well-deserved place in the dock at some point. For the time being, however, his case was put on the back burner while Taylor's researchers scoured the archives for additional evidence against other members of the SS, Gestapo, and SD.

Benjamin Ferencz and the Discovery of the *Einsatzgruppen* Reports

The chief prosecutor in the trial of the *Einsatzgruppen* leaders, Benjamin Ferencz, was an important and dynamic member of Taylor's staff. In fact, it was his team in Berlin that uncovered and analyzed the *Einsatzgruppen* reports while searching for evidence to use against the SS. When the twenty-six-year-old Ferencz arrived in Nuremberg in May 1946, he was one of the youngest attorneys present. He was also already an experienced war crimes investigator, having served nearly a year in Europe in the Theater Judge Advocate's Division as a field investigator for war crimes at Dachau and other camps as well as investigating the deaths of downed American fliers.

Ferencz was the child of Romanian-Jewish parents who immigrated to the United States when he was an infant. While growing up in New York City he wanted to be a lawyer and after college he won a scholarship to Harvard Law School where he worked with Sheldon Gleuck, a noted professor of criminal law who helped draft the *Nuremberg Charter*.[134] While he was at Harvard, the war broke out. Ferencz recalls that he attempted to enlist in the Air Force, but for some reason he was disqualified. After graduating from Harvard in May 1943, he again tried to enlist, this time he was successful. He was assigned to an anti-aircraft artillery battalion preparing for the invasion of France and was almost immediately promoted from Private to Corporal. Although his unit was involved in five major battles, Ferencz never killed a single person. Despite his good fortune, he intensely disliked the "military experience" finding it a humiliating and dehumanizing ordeal.[135] In February 1945, while Ferencz's unit was stationed in Luxembourg and because he could speak French, he was transferred to the Judge Advocate's

---

[133] Memorandum, Walton to Edmund Schwank, September 30, 1946, in NARA RG 238, OCCWC, BB, GR, Correspondence 1946–1948, box 2, Correspondence 1946 E202, Correspondence August 1946 folder.

[134] Letter, Ferencz to Eugene Kaufman, Executive Director Hias, Baltimore, January 8, 1958, RG 12.000, Drawer 11, Biographical Material, folder A, Personal Correspondence 1957–1962, BBF, USHMM. Glueck was one of the American representatives of the UN War Crimes Commission.

[135] Interview with Ferencz, April 24, 1997, 3.

Section of the Army to investigate war crimes.[136] Ferencz was an investigator of war crimes in general, and crimes against allied soldiers in particular. As the war drew to a close and more and more atrocities came to light, much of his work involved frantically traveling from concentration camp to concentration camp gathering evidence before it was destroyed. Fieldwork of this type was gruesome, and there were times, Ferencz claimed, when he was forced to dig up corpses with his bare hands.[137] He stayed with the Judge Advocate's Division until December 26, 1945, when he received an honorable discharge from the military with the rank of Sergeant.[138] Ferencz returned to the United States. He had not been home very long before he received a call from Colonel Marcus who wanted to recruit Ferencz to come back to work for the Theater Judge Advocate. Because of his intense dislike of the Army, Ferencz declined Marcus' offer. At about the same time though, Taylor was in Washington recruiting staff for the Subsequent proceedings. Sheldon Gleuck, Ferencz's mentor at Harvard, called Taylor and recommended Ferencz for a job. On March 20, 1946, Ferencz accepted a position as a civilian war crimes investigator for the OCCWC and left for Germany almost immediately.[139]

When Ferencz arrived in Germany in mid–1946, Taylor's staff was busy searching for the evidence needed to indict those individuals his office had already decided to prosecute. Only with great difficulty had Taylor been able to recruit personnel to work on the Subsequent proceedings, and his office was chronically short staffed. So when an experienced field investigator such as Ferencz arrived on the scene, he was immediately put to work. Taylor sent him to Berlin to set up a team of analysts to sort through the seized Nazi documents housed there.[140] A month after Ferencz's arrival in Berlin, Taylor appointed him Chief of the Berlin Branch of the OCCWC.[141]

---

[136] Letter, Ferencz to Gertrude Ferencz, February 20, 1945, USHMM, RG 12.000, Drawer 31 *Einsatzgruppen* Trial, box 1, folder J, Letters from Benjamin Ferencz to Gertrude 1944–1945, BBF, USHMM.

[137] USHMM, RG 50.030*269, Oral History, BBF, August 26, 1994, tape 1.

[138] "Biographical Information and Material regarding Gertrude Ferencz," RG 12.000, Drawer 11, Biographical Material, box 1, folder A, Gertrude Ferencz Biographical Material, BBF, USHMM.

[139] USHMM, RG 50.030*269 Oral History, BBF, August 26, 1994, tape 2. See also "Biographical Information and Material Regarding Gertrude Ferencz," RG 12.000, Drawer 11, Biographical Material, box 1, folder A, Gertrude Ferencz Biographical Material, BBF, USHMM. On Taylor's trip back to the United States for recruiting purposes, see Taylor, *Anatomy*, 289–290.

[140] Letter, Taylor to Ferencz, July 18, 1946 in NARA RG 238, OCCWC 1933–1949, Chief of Counsel GR, Correspondence 1945–1949, Correspondence file, box 4, NM70, entry 159, Mr. Ferencz folder.

[141] Memorandum, OCCWC to Ferencz, APO 124A US Army, August 16, 1946 in NARA RG 238, OCCWC 1933–1949, Chief of Counsel GR, Correspondence 1945–1949, Correspondence file, box 4, NM70, entry 159, Mr. Ferencz folder. See also RG 12.000, Drawer 11, Biographical Material, File C, Job Related Biographical Material, BBF, USHMM.

As head of the Berlin office, Ferencz's job description was broad enough to permit him to respond quickly to the needs of the prosecutors who were attempting to assemble cases against Nazi industrialists, doctors, military men, and SS officers. It was a demanding task. He had to be familiar with all the analyzed material so he could help buttress further prosecution cases. He also had to assess the researchers' findings so that he could make recommendations to Taylor about the "possibility [of] prosecution or further lines of development."[142] One of the most important discoveries made by the researchers of the Berlin Branch of the OCCWC was the *Einsatzgruppen* reports.

Ronald Headland, an authority on the *Einsatzgruppen* reports, has traced the story of their seizure back to September 3, 1945. He notes that the reports were received as part of a massive two-ton collection of documents that the Berlin Document Center (BDC) team had recovered from the fourth floor of the *Gestapo* headquarters in Berlin.[143] Because of the enormous volume of documents (Ferencz estimated that the BDC alone had between 8 and 9 million documents) and the limited number of investigators in Ferencz's office, it is not surprising that it took a long time before any of his staff discovered the reports. Even though Ohlendorf had referred to the reports during his testimony at the IMT in January 1946, Ferencz's researchers were not looking for them specifically.[144]

Ferencz does not recall exactly when his unit found the reports, but both he and Headland believe it was sometime in late 1946 or early 1947. There is some OCCWC correspondence referring to the *Einsatzgruppen* reports as early as January 15, 1947, but there is also correspondence from later in January and early February that seems to indicate that the reports had not yet been discovered, or at least that those responsible for decision-making did not know of their existence or content. Much of the later correspondence is in the form of requests from attorneys in Nuremberg to the Berlin Document Centre asking researchers to locate more evidence against Ohlendorf and other leaders of the Gestapo and the RSHA, which suggests that Taylor still had not decided to limit the scope of the SS trial.[145] Also, the analysis of the

---

[142] "Standard Job Description Sheet, European Theater," June 9, 1947 and "Office Memorandum," undated, RG 12.000, Drawer 11, Biographical Material, box 1, folder Job Related Personal File, BBF, USHMM.

[143] Headland, *Messages of Murder*, 13–14.

[144] Interview with Ferencz, April 24, 1997, 1; USHMM, RG 50.030*269 Oral History, Ferencz, August 26, 1994, tape 2; and, Taylor, *Anatomy*, 258.

[145] For example, see memorandum, Rolf Wartenberg to Henry Sachs, January 15, 1947, who writes: "For the preparation of the case against Einsatzgruppen the following documents are essential . . . " followed by a list of the *Einsatzgruppen* reports. In NARA RG 238, OCCWC, BB, GR, Correspondence 1946–1948, box 2, E202, Correspondence 1947, Correspondence January 20, 1947–end folder. See also memorandum, Walton to all Section Chiefs, February 5, 1947 in *ibid.*, box 3, Correspondence E202, Incoming Correspondence folder; and, memorandum, Ferencz to Section Chiefs, OCCWC, February 5, 1947 in *ibid.*

Einsatzgruppen reports was not undertaken until March and April 1947.[146] At this time, it was discovered that certain individuals later indicted in the case against the *Einsatzgruppen* leaders, such as Heinz Schubert, had been released from custody because at that time there was no evidence against "them as perpetrators of, or as witnesses to, any alleged war crime."[147] Most important, perhaps, is a memorandum dated March 14, 1947, from Taylor to the Deputy Military Governor outlining his plan for the Subsequent trials. In this memo, Taylor explains that the proposed trial of Ohlendorf and "other principal officials of the *Sicherheitsdienst,* the Gestapo, and the Main Security Office (RSHA) of the SS" might not be necessary. Taylor was under time and monetary constraints, and felt that in the event he was forced to reduce the size of his program, three of the eighteen trials proposed were "less necessary" than the others. He believed that these three trials, one of which was Ohlendorf's, overlapped some of the other SS cases and that if he were forced to cancel some of them doing so would not compromise the American program of trying a representative sample of Nazis.[148] This suggests that at this late date Taylor and his office of researchers were not yet aware of the scope of criminality of the mobile security units.

Whether the reports were found in late 1946 or early 1947 remains a matter of speculation. Ferencz does recall, however, his excitement when one of the German researchers who worked in his office accidentally discovered twelve binders (*Leitz Ordners*) filled with top secret daily reports from the eastern front itemizing the carnage of the mobile security and killing units.[149] These reports were a gold mine of information for the prosecution because they were written by the perpetrators themselves and listed dates, places, and times, as well as some of the identities of the participants (not individual perpetrators, but the commanders of the groups). Once discovered, they were brought directly to Ferencz's attention.[150] The reports were not the originals, but rather duplicates (the originals had been mimeographed and about 100 copies had been distributed to various offices of the Third Reich – the copy discovered by Ferencz's researcher was one of these). They are one of the only known surviving sets and have been a tremendous resource

[146] The vast majority of the Operational Situation Reports were analyzed between March 27, 1947, and April 11, 1947, in *ibid.,* Evidence Division, Document Center, SS Series 1934–1945, SS 2636–2991, box 11, E211, NM to SS 2717-2726, SEA's only folder.

[147] Memoranda, Howard Bresee to Commanding Officer, War Crimes Control Suspect and Witness Enclosure, Dachau, January 18, 1947, and January 29, 1947, "Clearance of War Criminals" in *ibid.,* Executive Office, 201 files, box 24, Schubert, Heinz folder.

[148] Memorandum, Taylor to Clay, March 14, 1947, in NARA RG 338, JAD, WCB, General Administration Records, box 1, Organization 1947 folder.

[149] Interview with Ferencz, April 24, 1997, 1. See also memorandum, "Request for Original Documents from the Berlin Document Center," August 11, 1947, in NARA RG 238, OCCWC, BB, GR, Correspondence 1946–1948, box 3, Correspondence 1947, Correspondence January 20, 1947-end folder.

[150] Interview with Ferencz, April 24, 1997, 1.

for historians ever since.[151] According to Ferencz, he realized their importance immediately and flew to Nuremberg where he showed them to Taylor. Taylor acknowledged their value but informed the young attorney that, unfortunately, there simply was not enough staff, time or money to conduct trials other than those already planned. It is unclear what changed Taylor's mind, perhaps it was Ferencz's urging or the certainty of the evidence, what ever it was the case against a catch-all group of SS leaders in which Ohlendorf was to be the main defendant was transformed into a trial specifically of *Einsatzgruppen* leaders. Taylor appointed Ferencz chief prosecutor of the case.[152] With Ferencz's new assignment settled, Taylor agreed that a few lawyers (John Glancy, Peter Walton, James Heath, and Arnost Horlik-Hochwald) could be culled from some of the other cases still pending to assist Ferencz. At twenty-seven, Ferencz liked to tease that he was the youngest prosecutor at Nuremberg, and "his first case" appeared to be, as the press later dubbed it, "the biggest murder trial in history."[153]

Planning the *Einsatzgruppen* Trial: Interrogations, Law, and the Indictment

Taylor's decision to transform the general trial of the SS into a trial expressly of *Einsatzgruppen* leaders meant there would be delays getting the process started. It took several months to build the case. The Soviets had to be consulted, the defendants located, and the indictment written. CCL10 provided for the extradition of prisoners from one zone of occupation to another, and for the joint prosecution of war criminals by the former allies. Several of the defendants were extradited from the British and French zones. No one was extradited from the Soviet zone perhaps because they did not have anyone in custody worth trying or, maybe, because they simply chose to ignore the American's request. In any case, it was not for want of trying. Under the terms of the Moscow agreement, the Allies had

---

[151] Letter, Ferencz to Henry Lea, November 27, 1989, RG 12.000, Drawer 24, WCT, box 2, Nuremberg Supplementary Materials folder, BBF, USHMM. Stephen Tyas notes that the USHMM has Individual Operational Situational Reports on microfilm as part of their collection from the Soviet archives. He does not believe these are part of those discovered by Ferencz's team. See RG-11.00 1m.01 reel 1, RSHA Berlin, Osoby; fond #500 (Fond 500-1-25), "Activities of Einsatzgruppen (E65), Einsatzkommandos, and Sipo/So in Occupied Eastern Territories. Includes orders, activity reports (Tätigkeits – und Lagebericht), and events reports (Ereignismeldung). Includes Jaege/Taeger Reports. Guidelines for SuSD (sic.) Kommandos in Pow Stulags V Dulags for "Cleansing the Camps...465 pp." Correspondence with Tyas December 7, 2008.

[152] Memorandum, Walton to Henry Sachs, March 22, 1947 in NARA RG 238, OCCWC, BB, GR, Correspondence 1946–1948, box 3, Correspondence 1947, Correspondence January 20, 1947-end folder.

[153] Letter, Ferencz to Hilary Earl, February 27, 1997. See also Ferencz, "Needed: An International Criminal Court," *Constitution* (Fall, 1993), 79.

FIGURE 3. American army staffers organize stacks of German documents collected by war crimes investigators USHMM photo archive (#03549)

agreed that perpetrators would be returned to the location of their crimes and Taylor's office wanted to ensure that the Soviets would not object to the American prosecution of individuals whose crimes had been perpetrated on Russian soil.[154] To this end, the Soviets were contacted. In his initial memorandum to the Soviets, Ferencz explained that he needed their help. Even with the *Einsatzgruppen* reports in hand, Ferencz apparently had doubts about the evidence to convict these men; he worried it was "inadequate," not enough to convict them beyond a reasonable doubt. Part of the problem was that although the reports were clear evidence of the crime, they were not clear evidence that the defendants were personally responsible. Moreover, he wanted help locating members and leaders of the units, as well as witnesses who might help identify the killers.[155] Many years after the trial was over, Ferencz would state that the reason no witnesses were called by the prosecution was because of the existence and strength of the *Einsatzgruppen* reports; this evidence of criminality was so strong that no witnesses were necessary. This may be true. Ferencz's memorandum to the Soviets might

[154] The Moscow Agreement was codified in Control Council Law No. 10.
[155] Memorandum, Ferencz to Colonel General Serov, Soviet Deputy Commander in Chief, Civil Administration in Germany, March 12, 1947 in NARA RG 238, OCCWC, BB, GR, Correspondence 1946–1948, box 3, Correspondence 1947, January 20, 1947, end folder.

have been entirely perfunctory, designed so as not to offend the Soviet's right to try individuals who had perpetrated crimes on their soil. Frederic S. Burin, a member of the liaison team at the OCCWC and a civilian researcher in Berlin working on the SS case, was sent out in early March 1947 to discuss the issue of evidence-gathering and possible witnesses with the Soviet Military Administration in Berlin. Initially the Soviets were intrigued with the suggestion that the U.S. and Soviets cooperate in the prosecution of the *Einsatzgruppen* leaders: as Soviet representative Prishchepenko rightly pointed out, the United States and Soviet Union had not cooperated on any war crimes issue for quite some time. Toward the end of their meeting, Major Prishchepenko seemed to have had second thoughts, and told Burin that in all likelihood the Soviets would want to prosecute these men on their own.[156] As it turned out, nothing came of the American suggestion that the *Einsatzgruppen* leaders be prosecuted jointly; in fact, after the initial contact, the Soviets never responded to the American initiative. Fortunately, quite a number of *Einsatzgruppen* leaders were in American and British custody and a trial could be scheduled without the cooperation of the Soviets or the extradition of war criminals from their zone.[157]

After the feelers to the Soviets came to naught, it took only four months to put the case against the *Einsatzgruppen* leaders together. Between March and July 1947, Ferencz's team worked fanatically preparing for the trial. A group of lawyers, researchers, and interrogators attempted to uncover more evidence, located those to be charged, interrogated witnesses and possible defendants, procured judges, and, finally, prepared the indictment. By mid-June, it had been decided that of the 2 to 3 thousand *Einsatzgruppen* members they knew of, only twenty-four of the highest-ranking leaders would be indicted because, as Ferencz duly noted, that was all the room there was in the dock.[158]

Which defendants were selected for the dock depended largely on the contents of the *Einsatzgruppen* reports. Because these were the primary source of evidence against the defendants (other than their own affidavits) the prosecution team had to dissect the reports to ascertain who was responsible and for what crime. Ferencz's team compiled lists of the numbers of murders, by category of victim (Jews, Gypsies, the mentally ill, and partisans), and the regions in which the murders were committed. This method of deduction is precisely how the number of 1 million people killed

---

[156] Memorandum, Frederic Burin to Henry Sachs, March 5, 1947 in *ibid.*

[157] Memorandum, Walton to Sachs, March 22, 1947 in NARA RG 238, OCCWC, BB, GR, Correspondence 1946–1948, box 3, Correspondence 1947, January 20, 1947–end folder.

[158] Memorandum, Taylor to Chief of Staff, OMGUS, May 20, 1947 amended June 18, 1947, in NARA RG 260, Functional Offices and Divisions, OCCWC, box 2, WCT Program, Taylor folder. See also Ferencz, "Speech delivered to the McGill Conference on Human Rights," November 3–4, 1987, RG 12.000, Biographical Information, Speeches, Conferences, etc., box 1, File D McGill Conference folder, BBF, USHMM.

TABLE I. *Defendants and their Rank**

Name	Rank at Time of Arrest	Unit of Command
Jost, Heinz	SS Brigadeführer	Commander Einsatzgruppe A
Naumann, Erich	SS Brigadeführer	Commander Einsatzgruppe B
Ohlendorf, Otto	SS Brigadeführer	Commander Einsatzgruppe D
Rasch, Otto	SS Brigadeführer	Commander Einsatzgruppe C
Biberstein, Ernst	SS Standartenführer	Einsatzkommando 6
Blobel, Paul	SS Standartenführer	Sonderkommando 4a
Braune, Werner	SS Obersturmbannführer	Einsatzkommando 11b
Blume, Walter	SS Standartenführer	Sonderkommando 7a
Fendler, Lothar	SS Sturmbannführer	Deputy Chief Sonderkommando 4b
Graf, Matthias	Oberscharführer	Officer Einsatzkommando 6
Haensch, Walter	SS Obersturmbannführer	Sonderkommando 4b
Hausmann, Emil	SS Sturmbannführer	Einsatzkommando 12
Klingelhöfer, Waldemar	SS Sturmbannführer	Vorkommando Moscow
Nosske, Gustav	SS Obersturmbannführer	Einsatzkommando 12
Ott, Adolf	SS Obersturmbannführer	Einsatzkommando 7b
Radetzky, Waldemar von	SS Sturmbannführer	Deputy Chief Sonderkommando 4a
Rühl, Felix	SS Hauptsturmführer	Officer Sonderkommando 10b
Sandberger, Martin	SS Standartenführer	Sonderkommando 1a
Schulz, Erwin	SS Brigadeführer	Einsatzkommando 5
Seibert, Willy	SS Standartenführer	Deputy Chief of Einsatzgruppe D
Six, Franz	SS Brigadeführer	Vorkommando Moscow
Steimle, Eugen	SS Standartenführer	Sonderkommando 7a & 4a
Strauch, Eduard	SS Obersturmbannführer	Einsatzkommando 2

* Indictment, The United States of America v. Otto Ohlendorf et al., in *TWC*, vol. 4, 13–15.

by the *Einsatzgruppen* was established and recorded in the indictment.[159] Whoever was in charge of the group that had committed the murders and the various officers associated with the crime were also identified. Once Ferencz's team had determined the number of victims, the location of the murder, and the person or persons in charge of the *Kommando*, the difficult and time-consuming process of locating individuals began.[160] If the perpetrator was in U.S. custody, it was not difficult to have him transferred to the prison at Nuremberg for further questioning. If, however, the individual was not in U.S. custody, a search had to be undertaken. Once Ferencz and his team had located a reasonable number of potential candidates, they interrogated them.

---

[159] "I counted over a million people deliberately murdered by these special action groups." Ferencz, *Less than Slaves: Jewish Forced Labor and the Quest for* Compensation (Cambridge, MA; 1979), xv.

[160] For example see "Staff Evidence Analysis" of the Operational Situation Reports of the Einsatzgruppen USSR Nos. 1–8, 10–12, 14–15, 17, 19–21, 24–25, 28, 30–32, 34, 36–37, 40, 43, 45, 47–48, 50–51, 54, 56, 58–61, 66–68, 74, 76, 78, 80–81, 85–89, 91–92, 94–97, 101, 105–108, 110–111, 116–117, 119–120, 123–125, 128–132, 135–143, 147–150, 153, 155–157, 163–165, 170, 172–173, 177–178, 180, 182–184, 186–187, 189–191, and 193–195, which still contain the original OCCWC markings. Analysis took place between March 27 and April 11, 1947 in NARA RG 238, OCCWC 1933–1949, BB Evidence Division, Document Center, SS Series 1939–1945, box 10 SS 2391-SS 2635, SS 2552 folder.

Much of the evidence these individuals gave during their interrogations was used against them during the trial and ultimately helped to convict them.

This raises some important legal and philosophical questions that the Nuremberg historiography does not address; namely, whether the way evidence was gathered and used against the defendants and the way the interrogations were conducted was consistent with the American canon of justice. The record of Ohlendorf's interrogation suggests a number of shortcomings. As mentioned earlier, during his incarceration between 1945 and 1947, Ohlendorf was interrogated on numerous occasions; it was not until he was indicted in July 1947, however, that he was provided with legal counsel. The record suggests that Ohlendorf was never told that he might be charged with criminal offenses, rather interrogations seem to have been conducted with the sole aim of information gathering for the IMT trial where he was to be one of the prosecution's star witnesses.[161] Quick to offer his version of events, Ohlendorf incriminated himself in a vast array of crimes. Under American criminal law as it existed at the time an individual only has a right to an attorney when they are arraigned, but arraignment must be expeditious, usually within a few days of arrest. It was not until after 1966, post *Miranda*, that it extends to any custodial interrogation situation. Ohlendorf was in custody for more than two years before he was officially charged. Had he been represented by counsel during his detention, or had he known that he was a possible candidate for trial, it is doubtful that he would have been quite so willing to supply what proved to be self-incriminating evidence. Of course, Ohlendorf's case was not unique; there were hundreds of incidents of voluntary admissions of guilt in the course of assembling evidence for the war crimes trials. These admissions led to the defense argument, at least in the case of the *Einsatzgruppen* leaders, that defendants had not been warned that the information they volunteered might be used against them. It is worth keeping in mind that in the U.S. the right against self-incrimination is fundamental, enshrined in the Fifth Amendment to the constitution that states: "no man is bound to accuse himself or be a witness against himself," whereas at Nuremberg no such right was afforded defendants and no attorneys were present to advise them to keep silent.[162] It should also be stressed that, in 1945, *Miranda* rights did not exist in the United States. *Miranda* prevents American courts from using self-incriminating statements made by individuals when they are arrested and questioned by police, without that individual first being informed of his Fifth Amendment right to remain silent and his right to consult with an attorney before and during questioning. In 1966, the U.S. Supreme Court made *Miranda* law. When a suspect is first arrested, the arresting officer has an obligation to inform him that if he chooses to speak, what he says may be used against him later, in a court

---

[161] Taylor, *Final Report*, 60 & 345.

[162] For the full text of the Fifth Amendment see *Findlaw*, "US Constitution," http://caselaw.lp. findlaw.com/data/constitution/amendment05/

of law. The prevention of self-incrimination had always been a basic right
of the accused and a fundamental tenet of American justice because of the
Constitution. *Miranda* ensured that a suspected criminal knew this from the
time of his arrest.[163]

As problematic was Taylor's admission that many of those interrogated
in 1945–1946, were far more voluble than they should have been. In many
cases, informers were simply attempting to deflect guilt by pointing "the fin-
ger of suspicion at others if such behavior seemed advantageous to them."[164]
In any case, Taylor noted, it would not have occurred to most interrogators
to warn a suspect that anything "he said might be used against him" because
the interrogations were not conducted in the same manner as pre-trial interrogations in American criminal investigations, where coerced or involuntary
confessions would have been inadmissible.[165] This is not to suggest that confessions were gained through coercion, only that potential suspects had no
Fifth Amendment to protect them from themselves. From the hundreds of
interrogation reports I have read, there is no evidence of mistreatment of the
suspect, fear, or coercion to confess, but of course it is unlikely this would
have been recorded had it occurred. Even so, after the trials were over there
was a general impression among Germans that the Americans had coerced
statements from suspected war criminals. For example, in a 1948 forum for
German youth to discuss the conduct and process of the NMT, one of the
central questions posed by the Germans was the way that confessions were
obtained by the Americans. All suggestions of impropriety were denied, but
again whether or not this is true is impossible to determine.[166]

Exactly how interrogations took place or what instructions interrogators were given is not entirely clear. What we do know is that Jackson's
OCCPAC established an interrogation division in August 1945, headed by
Colonel John Harlan Amen. Under Amen's leadership, interrogations were
carried out by attorneys and usually through an interpreter, because few of
the attorneys were bilingual.[167] Taylor found this method wanting. He thus
employed native German speakers, few of whom were attorneys, but all

---

[163] See *Miranda v. Arizona* 384 US 436, Certiorari to the Supreme Court of Arizona, No.
759 and in New York to the Court of Appeal, No. 760, *Vignera v. New York*, argued
February 28–March 1, 1966, decided June 13, 1966. See *Findlaw. Laws, Cases, Codes,
and Regulations* at http://laws.findlaw.com/us/384/436.html. Coincidently, and not at all
linked to Nuremberg, Taylor was the attorney who argued against *Miranda* rights in the
New York Court of Appeal.
[164] Taylor, *Final Report*, 59.
[165] For example see *Lisenba v. People of the State of California* 314 U.S. 219 (1941), in
which the Supreme Court of the United States ruled that statements garnered through
coercion were inadmissible as evidence. *Justia*, U.S. Supreme Court Center. http://supreme.
justia.com/us/314/219/.
[166] Forum, "Are the Nuremberg Trials Just and Fair?" German-American Youth Club, May
19, 1948, TTP 5-1-7-111.
[167] Taylor, *Final Report*, 58–59.

of whom had experience. Rolf Wartenberg, a German émigré and the most important interrogator in the *Einsatzgruppen* case, for instance, had worked for the Seventh Army Interrogation Center before going to Nuremberg.[168] Interrogators such as Wartenberg worked closely with the trial teams who mimeographed and recorded all such meetings.[169] Although the OCCWC had clear guidelines of how to carryout interrogations, the rules were flexible.[170] The OCCWC interrogations seemed to be, more or less fishing expeditions, aimed at eliciting information about the structure and operation of the Third Reich often to identify suspects, explaining why detainees were never told they could remain silent and not self-incriminate.[171] Although the right against self-incrimination and the right to counsel in the U.S. were not coupled until the *Miranda* decision in 1966, many criticized the OCCWC for offering neither of these rights to detainees.

In his *Final Report* in 1949, Taylor attempted to deflect criticism of his office's actions regarding the detention and interrogation of war crimes suspects by citing the extraordinary nature of the situation. It would have been impossible in 1945, Taylor argued, to provide counsel for each and every suspected war criminal. The OCCWC had had a great deal of trouble staffing its own trial teams with qualified American lawyers. Finding enough impartial (non-Nazified) German attorneys to represent all indictees (185) at Nuremberg was an even more formidable task. Given recruitment problems, it was absolutely unthinkable that hundreds of thousands of interned Germans could be supplied with counsel. In 1945, the idea of hiring any significant number of German attorneys was also totally out of the question given that most of them, the Americans felt, were of questionable reliability because of their past affiliation with the Nazi Party and because of the corrupt nature of the Nazi judicial system. As Taylor explained, "in an ideal world" no one would have been incarcerated without first being arraigned and those incarcerated would have had access to counsel; both are fundamental tenets of American criminal justice. But, as Taylor rightly points out, the situation in postwar Germany was far from ideal. Under the circumstances, expediting justice was seen as vital to ensuring due process, highlighting the structural limitations of liberal-democratic justice to adequately contend with war crimes on such a large scale.[172]

Just because the *Miranda* decision was not in effect in 1945 does not mean all Americans supported the custodial interrogation of unrepresented

---

[168] Rolf Wartenberg, Introduction, *In Their Words*, October 1, 1986, box 1, folder 2, 2005-347, Rolf and Hannah Wartenberg Collection, USHMM.

[169] Taylor, *Final Report*, 61 and Memorandum Walter Rapp to Ferencz, December 19, 1946, RG 238, OCCWC, BB, General Records, Correspondence 1946–1948, box 2, August 46–January 47 folder.

[170] Taylor, *Final Report*, 345.

[171] *Ibid.*, 50–59.

[172] *Ibid.*, 54–57.

suspects; there were many American jurists who in fact did not agree with the processes employed at Nuremberg. For example, Alvin Rockwell, the Associate Director of the Legal Division of OMGUS and a good friend of Taylor's, was very concerned about the issue of legal representation for detained war criminals, complaining in March 1947 that suspects were neither appointed legal counsel nor allowed to consult with a lawyer while they were in detention and being interrogated. Taylor rationalized this procedure, insisting that interrogations were a necessary step in determining who should be tried and who should be released. In the absence of documentation, often the only way to gain knowledge of a crime was through interrogation and, in any case, his organization was "taking all possible steps to insure that no one who is tried by us is in any way prejudiced by having been confined without counsel prior to the time that he is indicted."[173] How Taylor ensured this is not at all clear. Although defendants did get to select their own defense counsel once they had been indicted, ultimately, they were at a distinct legal disadvantage because indictment depended on a confession. This practice was a holdover from Jackson who had decided that the IMT was not going to follow the same rules of procedure as American criminal courts, particularly "where defense is a matter of constitutional right." Jackson loathed the obstructionism practiced by criminal attorneys in the U.S. and felt it was possible to avoid such pitfalls at Nuremberg by simply denying suspects this right.[174] Certainly not all legal systems require suspects to have legal representation during questioning and the NMT were not based exclusively on American criminal law, but the U.S. Constitution does protect the rights of the accused and Jackson's decision to omit this for German suspects may have inadvertently left the Nuremberg procedure open to criticism.

Whereas hindsight is 20/20, in the context of the postwar period, the rights of the accused were unquestionably limited. Taylor knew full well that suspects might have been less forthcoming had they had lawyers to advise them not to make incriminating statements. In the absence of legal advice, interrogators found it relatively easy to obtain the necessary evidence of criminal responsibility – especially when a suspect had no understanding of the judicial process or intimation that he might be indicted. The fact that the prosecution team was part of the occupation government meant that they were at an advantage. At the very least, they had structural benefits because they had at their disposal organizations created and supported by the occupation government. That said, some defense attorneys gained considerable experience during the life of Nuremberg such as Dr. Freidrich Bergold–Bormann's attorney at the IMT – but, in a system that promised

---

[173] Letter, Taylor to Alvin Rockwell, March 12, 1947 in NARA RG 466, Security Segregated Records, box 9, WCT, Military Tribunals 1947-Erhard Milch, 1946–1947, War Crimes Military Tribunals folder.

[174] Letter, Jackson to Truman, June 7, 1945, HST, WHO File, 324–325 (1945–1949), 3.

equal Justice under the law, the defense was disadvantaged and without exception. During the course of the trial, every defense attorney raised the issue of fairness and representation during their client's interrogation.[175] The judges in the *Einsatzgruppen* trial did not think the rights of the accused had been infringed, and the court found no evidence of mistreatment or coercion by the interrogators (unlike the Malmédy trials by the U.S. Army where the evidence of mistreatment was quite apparent). The judges also found the documentary evidence against the defendants so weighty that even without the self-incriminating statements they might have found some defendants guilty.

In spite of these major shortcomings, the Americans believed they had implemented important safeguards to assure procedurally fair trials.[176] For instance, the indictments and trials were bilingual, in German and English, and the courtroom was open to the public. So sure the trials would be fair, the entire trial was a matter for the public record.[177] The Americans were also very concerned that defendants be adequately represented at trial, and there was some debate about whether German lawyers with Nazi pasts should be allowed to act as defense counsel. Ultimately, the defendants had the last word about who would represent them, yet, former Nazis and those deemed to be followers by the courts were prohibited from representing defendants. The truth was, however, that the defense was at a legal disadvantage. Not only did the Americans control the structural nature of the legal process as well as its evidentiary basis, in terms of actual legal practice in court, they also had the upper hand. Even defense attorneys who were deemed to be worthy had spent the past twelve years under Nazi rule during which time they could not hone their skills.[178] To make up for their lack of practical experience, American attorneys were made available to German defense counsel for consultation during trial, although this was often not enough to make up for their lack of experience with adversarial trial procedure.[179] Defense counsel was given the prosecution's evidence before the trial, but they did not have the means to assess it the way the Americans did. That would have required a team of analysts not at their disposal. The numerous shortcomings of the NMT, of course, do not render the entire process "victor's justice"

---

[175] Bergold, the attorney for Biberstein, had served as a defense attorney at the IMT and then as Erhard Milch's attorney. Henry King recalled that he was an outstanding lawyer. King quoted in *Witnesses to Nuremberg. An Oral History of American Participants at the War Crimes Trials* (New York, 1998), 169.

[176] Development of Uniform Rules of Procedure, *TWC*, vol. 15, 58–78.

[177] USHMM, RG 50.030*269 Oral History, BBF, August 26, 1994, tape 5, 51–52. See also Ferencz, "Nürnberg Trial Procedure," 144–151.

[178] Landsman, *Crimes of the Holocaust*, 51–52.

[179] Memo Ernest McClendon to Rockwell, October 28, 1946 in RG 466, Security Segregated Records 1945–1947, Prisons Division, box 10, WCT Correspondence folder. And, "Defense Memorandum No. 1," undated, RG 260, OMGUS, OCCWC, Administration Records, Defense Counsel, box 161, miscellaneous folder.

as some critics would argue.[180] Rather, under the circumstances, American authorities believed they did much to make the Subsequent trials as fair as possible. As Ferencz bluntly noted some years later, "if we [had] wanted an injustice, we [simply] would have killed them to begin with."[181] Even the presiding judge at the trial thought that the charges against the defendants were so grave that he should bend the rules of evidence in favor of the defense. Because of his willingness to be very flexible about legal procedures, at the conclusion of the trial, the Nuremberg defense attorneys presented him with a three foot bronze statue of a penguin. The statue symbolized their appreciation of his famous *Penguin Rule*, which allowed defendants to submit any and all evidence that might establish their innocence including the evidence of the social life of the Antarctic penguin if that would help their case. Naturally, this did not sit well with the prosecutors who objected that such bias resulted in the submission of thousands of questionable affidavits on behalf of the defendants, what they mockingly referred to as "affidavits by the bushel."[182] Ferencz, in particular, felt that the tribunal had given the defense too much latitude. In the end, as imperfect as some of the Nuremberg procedures may appear to us in hindsight, in the context of the day they were mostly reasonable, perhaps, even fair.[183]

Once all the interrogations had been conducted and the defendants chosen, the indictment for the *Einsatzgruppen* trial was written, which differed in both scope and focus from the indictment in the IMT. The IMT had been carried out under the legal framework of the *London Charter* of August 8, 1945, that had defined three acts as criminal: war crimes, crimes against humanity, and crimes against peace. The first and most straight forward of these was war crimes, or violations of the laws and customs of war, laid out in agreements such as the *Hague Convention*, which included such acts as the unrestrained murder of prisoners of war and the use of excessively violent weapons such as poisonous gas. The second and more controversial crime specified in the *London Charter* was crimes against humanity.[184] Robert Jackson had introduced this charge during the London conference as

[180] Michael Marrus, "Nuremberg: Fifty Years After," *International Law* 66 (Autumn, 1997): 563–570, has addressed some of the revisionist tendencies in the Nuremberg historiography.
[181] Interview with Ferencz, April 24, 1997, 19.
[182] *Ibid.*, 6.
[183] USHMM, RG 50.030*269 Oral History, BBF, August 26, 1994, tape 5, 51–52.
[184] The notion of crimes against humanity dates back to 1915, when the British, French, and Russians declared the massacre of the Armenians by the Turks to be "crimes against humanity and civilization." For an analysis of the development of the concept of crimes against humanity, see Roger S. Clark, "Crimes Against Humanity," in George Ginsburgs and V.N. Kudriavtsev (eds.), *The Nuremberg Trial and International Law* (Dordrecht, Netherlands; 1990), 177–199 and Iu.A. Reshetov, "Development of Norms of International Law on Crimes against Humanity," in *ibid.*, 199–212. See also, Jacob Robinson who discusses the legal implications of crimes against humanity as interpreted by the IMT in, "The International Military Tribunal and the Holocaust: Some Legal Reflections," *Israel Law Review* 1:7 (January 1972), 1–13, and Robert Wolfe, "Flaws in the Nuremberg

FIGURE 4. Defendants receive their indictments from Col. C.W. Mays, Marshal of the Military Tribunal USHMM photo archive (#81980)

a way to ensure that stateless civilians who had been persecuted by the Nazis would have their crimes vindicated at trial.[185] The Americans were hesitant to make foreign nationals their concern, yet were also under a great deal of pressure from victim groups to punish Germans. To tackle this problem and to avoid charges themselves, they decided to link crimes against humanity to the planning, preparation, and conduct of aggressive war.[186] It was not until much later that crimes against humanity came to symbolize the mass murder of civilian populations by the Nazis during the war, particularly atrocities committed against racial, religious, political, and ethnic groups. Finally, and most problematic legally, was the charge of crimes against peace, which included the planning and preparation for aggressive war – war carried out in violation of established treaties – as well as its initiation and waging.[187] For the Americans, the most important focus of the trial was proving that

---

Legacy: An Impediment to International War Crimes Tribunals' Prosecution of Crimes Against Humanity," *Holocaust and Genocide Studies* 3:12 (Winter 1998), 434–453.

[185] Marrus, *Nuremberg War Crimes Trial*, 185–187.

[186] William A. Schabas, *Genocide in International Law. The Crime of Crimes* (Cambridge, 2000), 34–35.

[187] Taylor, *Final Report*, 64–65.

planning, initiating, and waging aggressive war was illegal.[188] As Jackson put it, an aggressive war was "an illegal attack on the international peace and order" the consequences of which extended beyond the belligerent parties to the "whole world."[189]

Central to the American prosecution strategy was the notion of conspiracy.[190] It was employed to prove criminal responsibility beyond first-hand participants, to "those who were not 'major' war criminals yet who had contributed in important ways to the Nazi enterprise."[191] And second, it was used to illustrate the Nazi "grand design" for the control and reordering of Europe. In other words, the conspiracy charge was designed to prove that individual Nazis who had not physically committed the deliberate acts of destruction, plunder, and murder, were still legally responsible for them and conversely as Jackson phrased it to Truman in the summer of 1945, to prove that "individual barbarities and perversions" did not occur "independently" of "the Nazi master plan."[192] Ultimately the charge was used to illustrate that Nazi criminality was a group enterprise, symbiotically carried out by those who formulated policy and by those who implemented it. The conspiracy charge was not nearly so important in the Subsequent trials and was omitted entirely in the *Einsatzgruppen* case.[193]

Instead, the indictment against the *Einsatzgruppen* leaders filed on July 29, 1947, charged the defendants with war crimes, membership in criminal organizations, and crimes against humanity.[194] As in the IMT indictment, war crimes, was the most straightforward legally. Specifically, the *Einsatzgruppen* leaders were charged with "wilfully (sic.) and knowingly" violating Articles 43 and 46 of the *Hague Convention* and the "Prisoner of War Agreement" of the 1929 *Geneva Convention*. War crimes included atrocities committed against military persons and property in territories controlled by Germany. This included the unrestrained murder of prisoners of war and the theft and destruction of property.[195] The prosecutions' evidence for these crimes came entirely from the *Einsatzgruppen* reports, which detailed the transgressions.

Membership in criminal organizations proved to be the least significant of the three charges in the *Einsatzgruppen* case because Article 10 of the *London Charter* provided that the criminal nature of the organization did not need to be proved repeatedly in the Subsequent trials. Once the SS and

---

[188] Marrus, *Nuremberg War Crimes Trial*, 122–123.

[189] Jackson quoted in ibid., and IMT, *Trial of the Major War Criminals before the International Military Tribunal*, vol. 22, 427.

[190] Smith, *Reaching Judgment*, 19.

[191] Marrus, *Nuremberg War Crimes Trial*, 122–123.

[192] Report, Jackson to Truman, June 6, 1945, quoted in *ibid.*, 42.

[193] Taylor, *Final Report*, 70–71.

[194] Steimle, Braune, Haensch, Strauch, Klingelhöfer, and von Radetzky were not included in the original July 3 indictment.

[195] Count Two–War Crimes, paragraphs 11–12, Amended Indictment, July 29, 1947, *TWC*, vol. 4, 21–22.

SD had been deemed criminal by the IMT, their criminal nature was taken as established fact in all the Subsequent trials. However, the tribunal in the IMT had ruled that membership in a criminal organization alone was not sufficient grounds to convict an individual if he could demonstrate that he was unaware of the criminal nature of the organization, even though he was a member.[196] Further, if a defendant could prove that he left the criminal organization before the start of the war on September 1, 1939, he could not be found guilty of membership. If a defendant was found guilty of membership alone, the tribunals were instructed to impose a sentence no harsher than those imposed by the denazification courts. In some cases, there would be no punishment at all. For example, Matthias Graf, the lowest-ranking officer in the *Einsatzgruppen* trial escaped punishment entirely because he was convicted only of membership. The aim of the policy was to preclude disparities in punishment in membership cases within the American zone.[197] If membership and war crimes were not central to the *Einsatzgruppen* case, what was? As Taylor noted in his 1949 *Final Report*, it was the defendants' participation in the "Final Solution of the Jewish question" that formed the heart of the case against the *Einsatzgruppen* leadership.[198] The trial thus focused overwhelmingly on count one of the indictment – crimes against humanity.

The definitions of crimes against humanity and genocide have evolved over time and today are quite intricate and distinct legal concepts, but during the life of the Subsequent trials international law was in its infancy, and genocide had yet to be defined legally. To be sure, the term had been brought to world attention in 1944 with the publication of Raphael Lemkin's book *Axis Rule in Occupied Europe*, where he defined it so broadly that it included nonlethal forms of racial persecution as well.[199] When the United Nations formalized the definition in its convention on December 9, 1948, as "the intention to destroy, in whole or in part, a national, ethnical, racial, or religious group,"[200] they removed this component from

---

[196] Matthew Lippman, "The Other Nuremberg: American Prosecutions of Nazi War Criminals in Occupied Germany," *Indiana International and Comparative Law Review* 1:3 (Fall 1992), 9.

[197] The British believed it was up to the prosecution to prove an individual had knowledge of the criminal nature of the group, whereas the Americans believed membership in the criminal organization presumed knowledge. See memorandum, Ferencz to British Liaison Officer, June 3, 1947, in NARA RG 260, OMGUS, Functional Offices and Divisions, OCCWC, box 101, Organizational Memos, Special Projects Division folder.

[198] Taylor, *Final Report*, 69.

[199] Dirk Moses, "The Holocaust and Genocide," in Dan Stone, ed., *The Historiography of the Holocaust* (New York, 2004), 535.

[200] Raphael Lemkin, *Axis Rule in Occupied Europe: Laws of Occupation, Analysis of Government, Proposals for Redress* (Washington, 1944), 79–95. Ferencz remembers that Lemkin was at Nuremberg during the time in which he was writing the indictment. Interview with Ferencz, April 24, 1997, 9. And, UN Convention on the Prevention and Punishment of the Crime of Genocide, December 9, 1948, http://www.hrweb.org/legal/genocide.html.

the official definition.[201] They also did not view mass murder as the only way to destroy a group: preventing births, transferring children from the group, and inflicting untenable life conditions were also considered genocidal "techniques."[202] Although the definition was not yet formalized, the framers of the *Nuremberg Charter* were well aware of the atrocious and systematic crimes the Nazis perpetrated against various civilian groups; in fact, it was the need to hold them accountable for these atrocities that formed the impetus to distinguish crimes against humanity from the more traditional charge of war crimes. With the exception of the murder of their political enemies, today the activities of the *Einsatzgruppen* and other Nazi agencies unquestionably would be deemed genocidal, but between 1945 and 1948, they were defined quite differently.[203]

As Taylor noted, the *Einsatzgruppen* trial dealt almost exclusively with the murder of civilians. As such, the principal charge in the case was crimes against humanity. Although crimes against humanity had a long pedigree in practice, in international criminal law it was only first identified and defined in article 6 (c) of the *Nuremberg Charter* as "murder, extermination, enslavement, deportation, and other inhumane acts committed against any civilian population, before or during the war," and was the result of the need to expand the definition of war crimes.[204] Although atrocities committed against civilian populations were clearly at the heart of this definition, the IMT construed it very narrowly to include acts committed only in connection with crimes against peace and war crimes and as such crimes committed against civilians prior to 1939 were not punished.[205] CCL10, the law that governed the NMT, was patterned after the *London Charter*. Notwithstanding the removal of a semicolon from the text, CCL10 defined crimes against humanity similarly, and for that reason according to one legal scholar, the same legal issues apply to it.[206] Count one of the indictment in the *Einsatzgruppen* trial charged the defendants with crimes against humanity. It read,

Paragraph 1
between May 1941 and July 1943 all of the defendants herein committed crimes against humanity... in that they were principals in, accessories to, ordered, abetted, took a consenting part in, were connected with plans and enterprises involving, and were members of organizations or groups connected with, atrocities and offenses, including but not limited to, persecutions on political, racial, and religious grounds, murder, extermination, imprisonment, and other inhumane acts committed against civilian populations, including German nationals and nationals of other countries....

[201] Moses, "Holocaust and Genocide," 541.
[202] *Ibid.*, 542.
[203] Mark A. Drumbl, *Atrocity, Punishment, and International Law* (New York, 2007), 4 and 35.
[204] Bassiouni, *Crimes against Humanity*, 1–18 & Bloxham, *Genocide on Trial*, 18.
[205] *Ibid.*, 24–25 and Telford Taylor, "The Meaning of the Nuremberg Trials," April 25, 1947, RHJ, Nuremberg War Crimes Trial, Office File, USCC, box 110, Subsequent trials folder.
[206] Bassiouni, *Crimes against Humanity*, 1–2 & 24–25.

Paragraph 2
[and that] the acts, conduct, plans, and enterprises charged in paragraph 1 of this
count were carried out as *part of a systematic program of genocide*, aimed at the
destruction of foreign nations and ethnic groups by murderous extermination.[207]

Not wanting to limit themselves to crimes committed against any one particular group, paragraph 1 of the charge was exceptionally inclusive and
included groups that would later be excluded from the UN's definition of
genocide. The techniques used to carryout crimes against humanity were also
not circumscribed as they were in the later UN convention. Completely at
odds with the later UN definition of genocide, however, is that crimes against
humanity as defined in paragraph 1 of count 1 of the indictment, are not limited to the group. A crime against humanity can be as simple as murder. As
Telford Taylor explained this to a group of French jurists in 1947, however,
the charge was not aimed at the "occasional murders" that "unfortunately
occur" in "most orderly and democratic nations;" rather, murder here refers
to the kind of "wholesale campaigns" designed by states "to make life intolerable for . . . or to exterminate large groups of the civilian population."[208]
Hence, paragraph two of the definition limits the acts to very specific situations. The charge gets more complicated, however, as the indictment seems
to invoke the notion of conspiracy. Although conspiracy was not a formal
part of the indictment against the *Einsatzgruppen* leaders, it was implied in
Paragraph 2, which held that the individual crimes of the *Einsatzgruppen*
were carried out as part of a larger conspiracy – the intention of which was
to destroy various ethnic, national, political, or religious groups. There is
a noticeable tension here. Although crimes against humanity are unquestionably the main charge, the way the count is written makes it appears as
if murder and all the other techniques to kill or harm people are part of
something larger – namely a *systematic program of genocide*. The question
is: why was the indictment written this way?

It seems that Nuremberg may well have been a testing ground for
the new legal concept. Although genocide had yet to be legally codified as a crime, the term had already been employed in the IMT trial
as well as in the trial of Nazi Doctors – case 1 of the NMT – and
against members of RuSHA or case 8 of the NMT.[209] At the Medical
trial, prosecutors endeavored to employ the term genocide according to
Lemkin's definition and in Taylor's opening statement, he made reference to a program against the Jews that linked the doctors' crimes to it.

---

[207] Crimes against Humanity, amended Indictment, July 3, 1947, *TWC*, vol. 4, 15.

[208] Telford Taylor, "The Meaning of the Nuremberg Trials," April 25, 1947, RHJ, Nuremberg
War Crimes Trial, Office File, USCC, box 110, Subsequent trials folder.

[209] I want to thank the participants of the workshop, "From Prosecution to Historiography:
American, German and Jewish Perspectives on the US War Crimes Trials at Nuremberg,
1946–1949," at the USHMM July 21–August 1, 2008, for their stimulating discussion
about the crime of genocide at the NMT.

Medical experiments were described as pilot studies for the gas chambers and the so-called "wild euthanasia" program targeting Jewish concentration camp victims was interpreted as a critical stepping-stone toward the Final Solution.[210] The RuSHA trial also invoked genocide, but they interpreted it much more broadly than did the prosecutors at the Medical trial.[211] The RuSHA case focused on Nazi race and resettlement policy, which had an impact on different population groups including Slavs and other east Europeans, whereas the extermination of Jews was seen as one crime amid many. Although the prosecution interpreted racial policy as part of a larger program of genocide, the crimes associated with the Holocaust were not seen as unique. In the prosecutors' view, Poles and Jews suffered equally.[212] This case could not act as a precedent, however, as it was running concurrently to the *Einsatzgruppen* trial. In terms of the IMT, genocide was only dealt with incidentally although the judgment did view the persecution of the Jews as "systematic" and the aim of Nazi policy as the total eradication of Jews from German life.[213] Although most of the Subsequent trials were not about the Final Solution per se, even at this early date, the Nuremberg prosecutors had some sense of what constitutes genocide. As John Glancy, Associate Counsel for the prosecution at the *Einsatzgruppen* trial clearly declared in opening statements, "the Einsatzgruppen trial deals mainly with the crime of genocide."[214] Even so, the prosecution in the *Einsatzgruppen* trial did not pursue a line of questioning that would lead to the development of the definition for international law. In fact, the opposite occurred. Because of the way crimes against humanity was described, the prosecutors were content to prove that an individual defendant had ordered or participated in individual and seemingly disconnected incidents of mass murder and sometimes not even that. Not only did the prosecutors fail to prove that the defendants were party to, or even knew about Hitler's Final Solution, but there was also no attempt to show that the murders they did participate in constituted a systematic Russian or European-wide program of murdering Jews. Perhaps unsure of how to formulate a case around the collective crime of the defendants and the group they killed or perhaps because crimes against humanity were liberally defined to include individual murder, they relied on tried and

---

[210] Paul Weindling, "Victims and Witnesses of Medical War Crimes: Uncovering Nazi Medicine at the Nuremberg Trials," paper presented to CAHS/USHMM workshop, "From Prosecution to Historiography," July 24, 2008.

[211] The prosecution introduced Lemkin's definition of genocide to the official record as well as an extract from a newspaper article discussing the first draft of the UN convention for the punishment of genocide. "Selection from the Arguments and Evidence of the Defense in the RuSHA Case," *TWC*, vol. 5, 3–5.

[212] Alexa Stiller, "The First Genocide Trial and Why it Failed: Perspectives, Strategies, and Dynamics of Prosecution and Defense in the RuSHA Case," paper presented to CAHS/USHMM workshop, "From Prosecution to Historiography," July 24, 2008.

[213] IMT, *The Judgement of Nuremberg, 1946*, uncovered and abridged edition (London, 1999), 123 & 125.

[214] John Glancy, Opening Statement, *Trial*, roll 1, 3.

true methods of criminal prosecution that enabled them to secure convictions on an individual basis. This may have been a wise course of action; after all, prosecutors in international criminal tribunals today have great difficulty securing convictions for genocide, the burden of proof is so high it is next to impossible to illustrate a perpetrator's intention to destroy the group, which has come to distinguish crimes against humanity from genocide. By opting to prosecute defendants along more traditional lines, the Nuremberg attorneys ensured an extremely high conviction rate. Even though the *Einsatzgruppen* trial introduced the world to the crime of genocide, in the end, the issue was largely avoided at trial and the prosecutors thereby missed an early opportunity to develop the legal concept into positive law.[215]

In most of the twelve cases under CCL10, the defendants were not charged with direct participation in atrocities because, more often than not, they held more important positions within the Nazi regime and were not required to carry out the actual policy. Instead, these men were charged with the formulation and/or dissemination of orders. In the case against the *Einsatzgruppen* leaders, however, the defendants were held directly responsible for both; they were accused of disseminating the order to kill the Jews and Gypsies as well as taking a "consenting part" in their murder.[216] Paragraphs 6 through 9 of crimes against humanity laid out, in eighty-six separate incidents, the murder of between 723,661 and 1 million persons between June 1941 and July 1943, a crime of such staggering proportions that case 9 warranted the moniker of "biggest murder trial in history."[217] That the indictment included eighty-six separate incidents of atrocity meant that the prosecution had to prove not only that a particular defendant was the leader of a unit and gave orders to subordinates to murder, but that he was also present at the particular place and time when the atrocities were to have taken place. To a certain extent, the way in which the indictment was laid out dictated the course the trial would take. On more than one occasion, the defense spent days attempting to prove that a particular defendant was "at home or in Berlin, or at his grandmother's funeral;" in short, anywhere but where the indictment indicated.[218] Had the prosecution kept the conspiracy charge, it would have been far easier to prove their implicit criminal behavior as individual members of a criminal organization dedicated to crime against a defined group, than as individuals responsible for a crime one group ultimately committed against another group.

[215] Roger S. Clark, "Crimes against Humanity," in George Ginsburgs and V.N. Kudriavtsev (eds.), *The Nuremberg Trial and International Law* (Dordrecht, Netherlands; 1990), 198–199.

[216] Taylor, *Final Report*, 73.

[217] Crimes against Humanity, amended Indictment, *TWC*, vol. 4, 15–21.

[218] Interview with Ferencz, April 24, 1997, 18.

3

Defendants

Since the twenty-[four] defendants were charged with one million murders, one would expect to see in the dock a band of coarse, untutored barbarians. Instead, one beheld a group of men with a formidable educational background.
Michael Musmanno[1]

Between 1933 and 1945, the Third Reich was responsible for the deaths of 20 million civilians, many of whom were killed during the war on the eastern front. To kill that many people took an enormous amount of manpower and, certainly, the four *Einsatzgruppen* units, along with reinforcements of German police and local auxiliary units, murdered their fair share of people – according to Nuremberg prosecution statistics, as many as 1 million between 1941 and 1943. Of the 3,000 *Einsatzgruppen* personnel, only two dozen were prosecuted by the Americans for their part in the murder of these civilians. Who were these twenty-four men indicted in July 1947 to stand trial in Case 9 of the Subsequent Nuremberg Trials? Were they ordinary men such as Christopher Browning's sample of members from Reserve Police Battalion 101, or do they fit into other perpetrator paradigms such as careerists, bureaucrats, or racists? The defendants were anything but ordinary in the sense that Browning meant: non-Nazified, older men from working-class backgrounds, who, in the field, succumbed to the pressures of the group, but who, under other circumstances, would not have become genocidal killers. Nor were they a random or representative sample of the general membership of the four units. Those selected for prosecution at Nuremberg were carefully chosen by the Americans precisely because they were *not* low-ranking members. They were elite leaders of the killing squads, who came from the offices of the SS and SD, and who were accessible to American authorities because they were already in custody or because they could be

[1] Musmanno, untitled, undated writings on the Einsatzgruppen trial, loose documents, MMP.

96

located and extradited from other occupation zones. Not representative of the rank-and-file then, they were representative of the larger leadership corps of the *Einsatzgruppen.*

In total, eighty-four men served as leaders of *Einsatzgruppen* units during their 2-year period of operation in the Soviet Union. Of these, fifteen were leaders of the four main groups; the remaining sixty-nine, were leaders of the sub-commando units or *Einsatz* and *Sonderkommandos.* Four of fifteen leaders from the main *Einsatzgruppen* and twenty of the sixty-nine leaders of the sub-commandos, or 28% of the entire leadership corps, were indicted in 1947. Admittedly, twenty-four is a small sample of perpetrators, especially when compared to the research of Michael Mann who examines data from 1,581 perpetrators from the entire spectrum of perpetrator groups. But this chapter is not intended as a quantitative study such as that offered by Mann.[2] Rather, this analysis is strictly focused on one subgroup of murderers, namely the leadership corps of the *Einsatzgruppen*, of which the twenty-four men examined here represent a statistically significant, albeit not random sample of that constituency.[3]

Aside from their leadership roles in the *Einsatzgruppen*, did the indictees have anything in common? For instance, were they long-standing party members, the so-called old fighters of National Socialism like Ohlendorf, or were they opportunists who joined the Party only after the Nazi seizure of power in 1933? Were they from lower strata of society, or were they the elite of Germany as were many members of the SS? Did they join the Party out of political conviction, for economic advancement, or to protest the failure of Weimar democracy?[4] Were they born after 1899 as were so many members and leaders of the Nazi's paramilitary organizations?[5] Some historians, such as Gerald Reitlinger, an authority on the SS, believe these men were misfits and losers, characterizing their lives as absolutely "bankrupt." Many had joined Heydrich's SD, Reitlinger asserts, because they had failed

[2] Michael Mann, "Were the Perpetrators of Genocide 'Ordinary Men' or 'Real Nazis'? Results from Fifteen Hundred Biographies," *Holocaust and Genocide Studies*, vol. 14, no. 3 (Winter, 2000), 331–366.

[3] *Ibid.*, 333–339.

[4] Many historians study the social composition of party membership. The earliest interpretations come from Hannah Arendt, *The Origins of Totalitarianism* (New York, 1951), George Mosse, *The Crisis of German Ideology: The Intellectual Origins of the Third Reich* (London, 1964) and Fritz Stern, *The Politics of Cultural Despair* (Berkeley, CA, 1961) and emphasize the irrational, anti-intellectual nature of Nazism, which appealed to marginalized groups during a time of national crisis. Others have identified class as the defining feature of National Socialism. Essentially, this group argues that lower middle-class Germans turned to National Socialism as a "third way" between capitalism and communism. This interpretation is best exemplified by Seymor Lipset, *Political Man: The Social Bases of Politics* (New York, 1960).

[5] Jens Banach, *Heydrichs Elite: Das Führerkorps der Sicherheitspolizei und des SD 1936–1945* (Munich, 1998), 325.

FIGURE 5. Defendants, USHMM Photo Archive Photo montage of 24 EGN leaders Paul Blobel (#s 09921), Erwin Schulz (09926), Gustav Nosske (09928), Walter Haensch (09931), Werner Braune (09932), Erich Naumann (09935), Heinz Jost (09936), Ernst Biberstein (09938), Walter Blume (09940), Adolf Ott (09941), Otto Rasch (09943), Eduard Strauch (09944),

FIGURE 5. (*cont.*) Eugen Steimle (09922), Franz Six (09923), Sandberger (09924), Felix Rühl (09925), Otto Ohlendorf (09929), Matthias Graf (09930), Heinz Schubert (09933), Willy Seibert (09934), Lothar Fendler (09937), Emil Hausmann (09942), Waldemar Klingelhöfer (09939), Waldemar von Radetzky (09945)

utterly in their chosen professions.[6] Highlighting the careers of a second-rate opera singer and an out-of-work dentist, Reitlinger insists the leaders of the *Einsatzgruppen* – including those indicted in 1947 – were the dregs of German society. Recent research would suggest that this depiction of the *Einsatz* and *Kommandoführer* is too simplistic. Certainly it is true that a good number of them had had difficulty finding jobs in the depression years (not so unusual during a period when one in three Germans was unemployed), it is also true that a disproportionate number of them were university trained – specifically in the profession of law – and a number of them even held doctoral degrees.[7] Of the fifteen *Einsatzgruppenführer* who worked in Russia between 1941 and 1943, six (40%) had earned doctoral degrees. And, of the sixty-nine *Einsatzkommandoführer*, sixteen (23%) held doctoral degrees; the rest had some university training.[8] These statistics strongly suggest that the leadership corps of the *Einsatzgruppen* comprised many men who were neither misfits nor failures; in fact, the opposite is true, as one historian has noted, they were more frequently "of above average intelligence, talent and ambition."[9] If not lay-abouts and rabble then, who were these men and why and how did they become involved in the activities of the *Einsatzgruppen*?[10]

---

[6] Gerald Reitlinger, *The SS: Alibi of a Nation, 1922–1945* (New York, 1957), 41. Reitlinger's characterization of the *Einsatzgruppen* leaders as failed members of society places him in the "Arendtian" school. Arendt, *Origins of Totalitarianism*, 311–312.

[7] Karl Dietrich Bracher, *The German Dictatorship: The Origins, Structure, and Effects of National Socialism*, trans. Jean Steinberg (New York, 1970), 274, notes that many of the Nazi leadership corps had led "unstable" lives before the Nazi seizure of power.

[8] Krausnick and Wilhelm, in *Die Truppe des Weltanschauungskrieges*, 360–364 and 639–644, state that Humbert Achamer-Pifrader (EG A), Heinz Jost (EG A), Walter Stahlecker (EG A), Erich Ehrlinger (EG B), Wilhelm Fuchs (EG A), Otto Rasch (EG C), and Max Thomas (EG C) held doctoral degrees. Benno Müller-Hill, "The Idea of the Final Solution and the Role of Experts," in David Cesarani (ed.), *The Final Solution: Origins and Implementation* (New York, 1994), 63 disagrees. Neither Jost nor Ehrlinger held doctoral degrees, but rather had studied law. Jost's SS Record and CV (NO 2896), in *Trial*, roll 9, frames 0626–0631, make no mention of a doctoral degree, but only parts of the document are legible. During testimony at trial and, in his sworn affidavits, Jost never said he had a doctoral degree although he did say he had passed both his junior and senior law examinations. See Eidesstattliche Erklärung, Jost, June 7, 1947, in *ibid.*, frame 0634.

[9] Wilhelm, "Die Einsatzgruppe A," 281–282. This agrees with Kater, *The Nazi Party: A Social Profile of Members and Leaders, 1919–1945* (Cambridge, 1983), 236, who concludes that "while the [German] elite was consistently over represented in the rank and file of the Party, this situation was more evident in the cadres: the higher the cadre, the greater the degree of elite overrepresentation." See also, Kater, "The New Nazi Rulers: Who Were They?," in Charles S. Maier, Stanley Hoffmann, and Andrew Gould (eds.), *The Rise of the Nazi Regime: Historical Reassessments* (Boulder, CO; 1986), 41–43.

[10] Some argue it would be more understandable if the murderers had been poorly educated. See, for example, Andy Logan, "Letter from Germany," *The New Yorker*, May 8, 1948 in the Papers of Andy Logan, NY Public Library Manuscript collection.

This analysis will show that many of their lives paralleled Ohlendorf's in that they joined the Nazi movement early and in a search of solutions to Germany's political, social, and economic problems. Others joined police organizations later, as a career move at a time when society offered them nothing else.[11] Some joined the Party out of conviction, many having cut their teeth on the activities of the *Freikorps* and other right-wing, nationalist organizations that proliferated after World War I and that offered violent solutions to Germany's social and political problems.[12] Frequently they joined the Party as young men – many while still university students – worked their way up through the ranks, eventually finding an occupation or niche where their particular skills were in demand.[13] Their trajectories show they were career-oriented go-getters, social climbers, and natural leaders like Ohlendorf. Many were born in the first decade of the twentieth century and as such were influenced significantly by shared experiences, most notably the privations brought on by World War I and the subsequent political upheaval generated by the loss of the war and the failed revolution of 1918–1920. This group unquestionably formed a generational cohort. Peter Loewenberg was the first scholar to draw our attention to the "generation of 1914" and make the psycho-social link between the success of the National Socialist movement and a generation of German youth. His argument is that the period between 1914 and 1920 had a permanent impact on the character of German youth; in short, it "turned" them into Nazis.[14] Since Loewenberg first published his research, a spate of work has been done on this particular cohort and a consensus seems to be emerging that the war created these young men. The distinction lies in how this transformation took place.[15]

---

[11] See Aronson, *Frühgeschichte von Gestapo und SD*, 199–217, who follows the careers of SD men such as Adolf Eichmann who rose from obscurity to prominence by chance. Eichmann began his career working in his father's mining company and later became a traveling salesman. He joined the SD at the beginning of 1934 and made a niche for himself as a so-called Jewish expert. Also revealing is Dieter Wisliceny's rise from theology student to Eichmann's deputy during World War II.

[12] On the *Freikorps* see Robert G.L. Waite, *Vanguard of Nazism: The Free Corps Movement in Postwar Germany, 1918–1923* (Cambridge, 1952). See also Peter Stachura, *Nazi Youth in the Weimar Republic* (Santa Barbara, CA; 1975) and Michael Stephen Steinberg, *Sabers and Brown Shirts. The German Students' Path to National Socialism, 1918–1935* (Chicago, 1973), who discuss the issue of pre-1933 youth involvement in nationalist organizations.

[13] For example see, Geoffrey Giles, "National Socialism and the Educated Elite in the Weimar Republic," in Peter D. Stachura (ed.), *The Nazi Machtergreifung* (London, 1983), 49–67 and *Students and National Socialism in Germany* (Princeton, 1985).

[14] Peter Loewenberg, "The Psychohistorical Origins of the Nazi Youth Cohort," *American Historical Review*, vol. 76, no.5 (December, 1971), 1481–1482.

[15] Andrew Donson, "Why did German Youth become fascists?" *Social History*, 31: 3 (August 2006), 337–358.

This chapter will offer a profile of the leadership corps of the *Einsatzgruppen* who were indicted for atrocities in 1947.[16] In doing so, I use Hilberg's paradigm of the perpetrators that situates the leaders of the *Einsatzgruppen* in the broader context of party members, particularly the leadership cadres of the SS. In an attempt to better understand the collective biography of this group of leaders, I will identify commonalities of the group. The analysis includes an examination of factors such as age, education, profession, religious affiliation, and party membership; attributes that historians of National Socialism have identified as significant markers of group identity. This chapter does not claim to offer a comprehensive empirical study of the entire membership of the *Einsatzgruppen*, although this is an area that clearly requires further attention; rather, the purpose of this analysis is to provide an accurate composite of the men in the dock at Nuremberg and in doing so, help us to better understand the collective "route to crime" of the leadership corps of the *Einsatzgruppen*.[17]

[16] For detailed, empirical studies of the social composition of members and leaders of the NSDAP see Kater's, *Nazi Party;* Stachura, "Who Were the Nazis? A Socio-Political Analysis of the National Socialist Machtübernahme," *European Studies Review* 11 (1981), 293–324; Thomas Childers (ed.), *The Formation of the Nazi Constituency* (London, 1986); Paul Madden, "Generational Aspects of German National Socialism, 1919–1933," *Social Science Quarterly* 63 (1982), 445–464 and Madden, "Some Social Characteristics of Early Nazi Party Members, 1919–1923," in *Central European History* 1:15 (1982), 34–56. For the most comprehensive empirical study of the composition of the SS leadership corps, see Herbert Ziegler, *Nazi Germany's New Aristocracy: The SS Leadership, 1925–1939* (Princeton, 1989). For analyses of the social composition of the SA, see Mathilde Jamin's, *Zwischen den Klassen: Zur Sozialstruktur der SA-Führerschaft* (Wuppertal, 1984) and Conan Fischer, "The Occupational Background of the SA's Rank and File Membership During the Depression Years, 1929 to mid-1934," in Peter Stachura (ed.), *The Shaping of the Nazi State* (New York, 1978), 131–159 and most recently, Bruce Campbell, *The SA Generals and the Rise of Nazism* (Lexington, 1998). Jens Banach, *Heydrichs Elite,* has analyzed and profiled the leadership corps of the Security Police and SD and George Browder, *Hitler's Enforcers* has examined the role of the SD in the Nazi system of terror. Peter Black, *Ernst Kaltenbrunner: Ideological Soldier of the Third Reich* (Princeton, 1984) is also an important contribution to the study of the men who led the paramilitary organizations of the Third Reich.

[17] No complete study has been done on the social composition or motivation of all *Einsatzgruppen* members or leaders. There are, however, several important studies of various aspects of their activities. For example, Angrick, *Einsatzgruppe D in der südlichen Sowjetunion,* (2003); Rossino, *Hitler Strikes Poland* (2003); Headland, *Messages of Murder* (1992); Ogorreck, *Die Einsatzgruppen und die "Genesis der Endlösung"* (1997); Krausnick and Wilhelm, *Die Truppe des Weltanschauungskrieges* (1981); Yaacov Lozowick, "Rollbahn Mord: The Early Activities of Einsatzgruppe C," in *Holocaust and Genocide Studies* 2:2 (1987), 221–241; Alfred Streim, "Zur Eröffnung des allgemeinen judenvernichtungsbefehls gegenüber den Einsatzgruppen," in Eberhard Jäckel and Jürgen Rohwer (eds.), *Der Mord an den Juden im Zweiten Weltkrieg* (Stuttgart, 1985), 107–119; Streim, "Zum Beispiel: Die Verbrechen der Einsatzgruppen in der Sowjetunion," in Adalbert Rückerl (ed.), *NS-Prozesse Nach 25 Jahren Strafverfolgung: Möglichkeiten-Grenzen-Ergebnisse* (Karlsruhe, 1971), 65–106; and Streim, "The Tasks of the Einsatzgruppen," *Simon Wiesenthal Center Annual* 4 (1987), 309–328.

Newcomers

Hilberg identifies three groups of perpetrators involved in genocide: the establishment, old functionaries, and newcomers. None of these various agencies on their own could have implemented and carried out the murder process, but taken together, Hilberg notes they "congealed into a massive machine" of destruction.[18] Indeed, genocide is a corporate act and as such the *Einsatzgruppen* formed but one part of the larger group of perpetrators. The leadership corps represent an even smaller subgroup of perpetrators, fitting primarily into Hilberg's newcomer classification, because they were neither the bureaucrats who came from established government agencies and ministries, nor were they the regime's old functionaries, the judges, doctors, lawyers, train operators, and members of the Order Police who participated in the destruction process in the field as well as from their desks.[19] Instead, the *Einsatzgruppen* leaders were what I would call a hybrid perpetrator; a mix of desk and first-hand murderers as their fieldwork never required them to the pull the trigger themselves, but they were physically present at the killing sites. Outside their fieldwork, they tended to be professional men. Unlike in the camp structures, no women participated in the activities of the *Einsatzgruppen* in the Soviet Union, although as the war progressed some wives of high-ranking SS officers did join their husbands on the eastern front. The *Einsatzgruppen* leadership corps consisted of German nationals, ethnic Germans, and even some foreigners who had come to Nazism because they had failed in their chosen professions, had been unable to secure employment, or had simply viewed Nazism as an attractive occupational choice. Many had adopted strong nationalist views in their youth and often-ethnic Germans were more nationalist than their national counterparts.[20] All felt an ideological affinity to Nazism.[21]

Newcomers, as the title suggests, were relatively young and impressionable; most were born in the first decade of the twentieth century.[22] Hilberg's newcomer classification corresponds with Wildt's generational cohort most of who were born in the first decade of the twentieth century as well, and who joined the ranks of the SD as a career choice. As Wildt has shown, the SD was the feeder organization for the *Einsatzgruppen*, and most of the Nuremberg defendants made their way into leadership roles in the *Einsatzgruppen* via their jobs in the offices of the SD. When the Nazis came to power in 1933, these men who were in their early to mid-twenties, were at loose ends, and had not yet made definite career choices. The oldest, Otto

[18] Raul Hilberg, *Perpetrators Victims Bystanders: The Jewish Catastrophe, 1933–1945* (New York, 1992), 20–26.
[19] *Ibid.*, 27–35.
[20] Mann, "'Ordinary Men,' or 'Real Nazis,'" 335.
[21] Hilberg, *Perpetrators Victims Bystanders*, 36–50.
[22] *Ibid.*, 39.

TABLE 2. *Age of Defendants**

Date of Birth		Name	Place of Birth
7 December	1891	Otto Rasch	Friedrichsruhe (Württemberg)
13 August	1894	Paul Blobel	Potsdam (Brandenburg)
15 February	1899	Ernst Biberstein	Hilchenbach (Westphalia)
4 April	1900	Waldemar Klingelhöfer	Moscow, Russia
27 November	1900	Erwin Schulz	Berlin (Brandenburg)
29 February	1902	Gustav Nosske	Halle (Saxony)
5 May	1903	Matthias Graf	Keltern (Württemberg)
9 July	1904	Heinz Jost	Holzhausen (Marburg – Westphalia)
3 March	1904	Walter Haensch	Hirschfelde (Saxony)
29 December	1904	Adolf Ott	Wardhaus or Waidhaus? (Bavaria)
29 April	1905	Erich Naumann	Meissen (Saxony)
23 July	1906	Walter Blume	Dortmund (Westphalia)
17 August	1906	Eduard Strauch	Essen (Westphalia)
4 February	1907	Otto Ohlendorf	Hoheneggelsen (Hanover)
17 June	1908	Willy Seibert	(Hanover)
12 August	1909	Franz Six	Mannheim (Württemberg)
11 April	1909	Werner Braune	Mehrstadt (Thuringia)
8 December	1909	Eugen Steimle	Neubulach (Württemberg)
11 October	1910	Emil Hausmann	(Württemberg)
8 May	1910	Waldemar von Radetzky	Moscow, Russia/Riga, Latvia
12 August	1910	Felix Rühl	Neheim (Westphalia)
17 August	1911	Martin Sandberger	Berlin (Brandenburg)
13 August	1913	Lothar Fendler	Breslau (Lower Silesia)
27 August	1914	Heinz Schubert	Berlin (Brandenburg)

* These data can be found in Prisoner Records, NARA RG 238, JAD, WCB, General Administration
Records 1942–1957, box 13, HICOG, Prisoner folders. See also, Krausnick and Wilhelm, "Kurzbi-
ographien," in *Die Truppe des Weltanschauungskrieges*, 639–643; and, SS Personnel Records of
all defendants, in *Trial*, rolls 8–11. Compare these dates with those of the SS officer corps especially
Table 3.3 and Figure 3.1, in Ziegler, *Nazi Germany's New Aristocracy*, 70–79.

Rasch (the leader of *Einsatzgruppe* C) was in his forties, whereas the
youngest, Heinz Schubert, an officer in Ohlendorf's *Einsatzgruppe* D, born
just as World War I began in August 1914, was still a teenager when the
Nazis seized power.[23]

Generational Aspects of the Defendants

One of the few social attributes historians of National Socialism agree upon
is that a disproportionate number of Nazi party members were young.[24]
As part of this larger cohort, the *Einsatzgruppenführer* indicted in 1947

[23] For information about birthdays, education, and party membership see Eidesstattliche
Erklärung of each defendant in M1019, rolls 1–3, 5, 8–10, 17, 22–23, 50–51, 55, 61,
67–69, and 71.
[24] See, for example, Paul Madden, "Generational Aspects of German National Socialism,
1919–1933," 452.

certainly were no exception. As Table 2 illustrates, youth was a salient feature of the leadership corps of the mobile security and killing units. That
so many of the *Einsatz* and *Kommandoführer* were born in the first decade
of the twentieth century is significant; similarity of age ensured common
experiences, which in turn influenced and helped shape their future political
ideas and activities.[25] Of the twenty-four defendants indicted, eighteen were
born between 1900 and 1910. An additional three were born between 1911
and 1914 and one was born in 1899. Only two, Otto Rasch (1891) and
Paul Blobel (1894) were adults when World War I began. In his study of
the SD and Security police, Jens Banach makes a clear distinction between
older and younger members. Those born after 1899 tended to be better
educated, having graduated from Gymnasia, followed by university training
where they were subjected to the radicalized teachings of their professors
making them more susceptible, he believes, to Nazism.[26] Excluding Rasch
and Blobel, 95% of the *Einsatzgruppen* defendants were of the same generation and as such were influenced significantly by shared experiences, most
notably World War I, and the subsequent upheaval generated by the failed
revolution of 1918–1920.[27] These hardships – hunger, disease, separation
anxiety from their parents, and political uncertainty – coupled with the perception that Germany had not lost the war and the harshness and perceived
humiliation of Versailles, as Lowenberg, Banach, Wildt, and Donson have
shown, helped shape the attitudes and future political affiliations of these
men.[28] It was probably inevitable that the young men who went to war
hoping to change what they considered a flawed society would be less idealistic when they returned. The brutal nature of trench warfare, the staggering
death toll, combined with the unexpected defeat and harsh peace settlement,
disillusioned many young Germans.[29] The vast majority of *Einsatzgruppen*
defendants do not fit into this category though, as they were too young to
experience the war first hand. Yet, without exception, all of them indicated
their lives had felt a significant impact from the war. If they were not direct
participants, how and why did the war have such a significant impact on
them?

[25] Madden, "Generational Aspects," 445–464, and Lowenberg, "Psychohistorical Origins,"
1457–1502, stress age and shared experiences as the most important factor for understanding
the attraction of German youth to National Socialism.
[26] Banach, *Heydrichs Elite*, 325–236.
[27] Lowenberg, "Psychohistorical Origins," 1465–1466, sees a direct relationship between date
of birth, shared experiences, and attraction to the NSDAP. This group constitutes what he
calls an "age cohort" defined as "the aggregate of individuals within a population who have
shared a significant common experience of a personal or historical event at the same time."
Whereas Madden refers to similar attributes as a "generation," Madden, "Generational
Aspects."
[28] Lowenberg, "Psychohistorical Origins"; Wildt, *Generation des Unbedingten*; and, Donson,
"Why did German Youth become fascists?" 337–358.
[29] For example, Robert Wohl, *The Generation of 1914* (Cambridge, 1979), 42–84, discusses
the effects of the First World War on German youth.

The impact of war on German society is well documented. What is less clear is the link between World War I and the subsequent genocidal violence that was perpetrated by members of the SS, SD, and Gestapo, in World War II. What we know with some certainty is that immediately following World War I, radical right-wing movements attracted young men, some of whom served in the war and some who had not, or who had only served a very brief time.[30] We also know that before 1933, approximately 50% of Nazi party joiners were too young to fight in World War I. It is probably not a coincidence that it was men born between 1900 and 1910 who comprised the preponderance of membership in the SS, SD, and Gestapo, and who ultimately "carried out [the] violence" of the regime.[31] A disproportionate percent of the leadership of the *Einsatzgruppen* fall into this age cohort; that is, young men born between 1900 and 1910. The question must then be asked: how did this group become so violent? If direct participation in the war did not barbarize these men, what did?[32]

One answer is unfulfilled and unrealistic national expectations which, nurtured by a regime that promoted aggressive nationalism and race hatred, created ideological soldiers of Nazism. It was this group who were then hand-selected to carryout the regime's genocidal policies. This is highlighted in defendant testimony. At their trial, the former leaders of the *Einsatzgruppen* all point to the war as a pivotal moment in their political development and this, they tell us, is what radicalized them. A war that most of them did not experience first hand essentially turned them into Nazis. As Michael Mann concludes, perpetrators "clustered toward the 'real Nazi' end of the spectrum"; the higher up the individual was in the Nazi hierarchy, the more likely he was to become involved in genocide.[33] The relationship between war and politics is clearly illustrated in the case of defendant Walter Haensch, leader of *Sonderkommando* 4b. Haensch was born into a middle-class family in Hirschfelde, Saxony.[34] His father, a physician, ensured the young man had a classical education at a Gymnasium. Because he was born in 1904, he was too young to fight in World War I. The war, nonetheless, had an immediate and lasting impact on his life. At trial, Haensch's attorney, Dr. Fritz Riediger, asked him how he became involved in politics. Haensch explained it was the direct result of the war. He told the court as a teenager he developed a political "psychosis" which he attributed to the war and resulting industrialization of the agricultural area where he lived. These changes,

---

[30] Donson, "Why did German youth become fascists," 337, finds that fascist movements were composed largely of young men who had not experienced World War I first hand.

[31] *Ibid.*

[32] *Ibid.*, 338. Donson argues that this generation had unreal expectations about Germany's military strength and that the shock of defeat in 1918 radicalized these young men.

[33] Mann, "'Ordinary Men' or 'Real Nazis,'" 358–59.

[34] Banach, *Heydrichs Elite*, 43 finds that the SD, Gestapo, and Security Police had a disproportionate number of personnel from the middle classes.

he noted, led to severe class divisions within his community.[35] When the war ended and the revolution broke out, he explained, the communists in his village held "meetings, propaganda speeches, [and] mass demonstrations." The chaos and terror perpetrated by the communists coupled with his belief that the left-wing was responsible for the defeat in the war led him to pathological hatred. He said that this political "psychosis" aroused in him such strong feelings of nationalism that he was impelled to action. This manifested in aggression directed thereafter against all leftist groups who he saw as betrayers of Germany. This is in keeping with Donson's findings, which note that fifty percent of members of the Party who joined before 1933 felt the same as Haensch.[36] Haensch's aggression turned to political action when he helped to found a nationalist youth organization whose goal it was to counter communism. The youth group merged with another national youth organization in 1919, and Haensch remained a member until 1922–1923, when he joined the *Jungdeutsche Orden* or German Youth Order, but he left this group after only two years because it did not provide the sense of community he desired.[37] This, too, is in keeping with Donson's conclusion that the success of German fascism was largely the result of the creation of a "militarist male youth culture" that developed before the war, but which in the face of defeat caused a complete psychic rupture among Germany's male youth.[38] In other words, the trauma of the lost war radicalized this group making fascism – a quasi-military movement – particularly appealing. As Haensch articulated it, World War I and the revolution that followed provided the impetus for his political activity as a youth, particularly his ardent anti-communist ideology and helped groom him as a young adult for a role in the radical ultra right-wing politics of the National Socialist movement.[39]

Unlike most of his co-defendants, Haensch openly admitted that joining the NSDAP was a well-considered move. He said he joined the Party in 1931, while he was still a student at university, because the NSDAP appealed to his brand of nationalism, promising to combat the communists who he believed were gaining control of politics in Germany and threatening to destroy the country.[40] Nazi ideology appealed to him. Years later, Haensch recanted this

---

[35] Although Haensch may have believed that the pronounced class divisions of his community were the result of the war, undoubtedly they already existed prior to this as they did all across Germany.

[36] Donson, "Why did German youth become fascists," 337.

[37] Abbreviated in SS Records as *Jungdo*, the *Jungdeutsche Orden*, originally a Freikorps organization, operated around Kassel and in Upper Silesia. See Waite, *Vanguard*, 203 n.73 and 210–211. Testimony, Haensch, December 2, 1947, in *Trial*, roll 4, 3227–3230; and, SS Record Haensch (NO 3261), in *ibid.*, roll 11, frame 0760.

[38] Donson, "Why did German youth become fascists?" 338–339.

[39] Waite, *Vanguard*, chapter 10, long ago identified the link between post World War I right-wing movements such as the *Freikorps* and, later, affiliation with the Nazis.

[40] *Ibid.*, 3232; and, SS Record Haensch (NO 3261), in *Trial*, roll 11, frame 0757. It should be noted that joining dates and party membership numbers do not necessarily correspond.

position, claiming he was duped by Hitler and "like many Germans . . . guilty of too quickly succumbing to the deceptions of the people in power."[41] The claim that he was deceived rings hollow, however, especially considering that his anti-communist political leanings were well developed before he joined the Party. His SS record also proves that his politics were already radicalized during the Weimar years. For example, he was known for publicly denouncing Marxism and the Versailles treaty as early as 1926. Far from being a puppet of National Socialism as he later claimed he was, Haensch was the perfect Nazi recruit; his SS record shows that, from an early age, he "frankly and actively stood up for the National Socialist 'Weltanschauung' and movement at any time and at any place."[42] Haensch found National Socialism; National Socialism did not find him. Like so many young German men of his generation, Haensch grew up with many negative attitudes toward the bourgeois state, parliamentary democracy, and the Jews. He would have been just as happy to see it destroyed. Haensch was representative of the defendants at large, whose goal it was to change (and later destroy) bourgeois German society. The war had politicized him.

Waldemar Klingelhöfer is another example. His upbringing demonstrates how important his formative years were in shaping his future political ideas. Klingelhöfer was slightly older than Haensch as he was born April 4, 1900, unlike Haensch, however, he was born in Moscow.[43] Between 1908 and 1915, he attended the (German-Protestant) Saint Peter and Paul church school in Russia. In 1915, his father was expelled from the country for being a German national; he moved the family back to Kassel, where his son continued his schooling until 1918.[44] In June of the final year of the war, at the age of 18 years, Klingelhöfer was drafted into the German army as an engineer with the 6th Replacement Company stationed in Silesia.[45] Donson notes that many supporters of fascism fit Klingelhöfer's profile; they spent the final months of the war in non-combat roles essentially staving off the inevitable, but not suffering the same privations (or trauma) as a soldier who served earlier and on the western front.[46] When the war ended, Klingelhöfer returned to Kassel to complete his education, which he did in 1919 receiving his *Abitur*

As Kater has noted, "Party membership numbers were not given out logically, that is sequentially," but we do know that low party numbers such as Ohlendorf's correspond to high party standing. Correspondence with Kater, October 18, 2000.
[41] Briefe, Wurm, May 12, 1948 in NARA RG 238, Advisory Board on Clemency, HICOG 1947–1950, Correspondence, box 10, Haensch folder.
[42] SS Record Haensch (NO 3261), in *Trial*, roll 11, frame 0760.
[43] Eidesstattliche Erklärung, Klingelhöfer, M1019, roll 35.
[44] Interrogation, Klingelhöfer, July 1, 1947, (NO 5846), in *Trial*, roll 12, frame 233; and, Testimony, Klingelhöfer, December 11, 1947, in *ibid.*, roll 5, 3800.
[45] Klingelhöfer, 20.6.1950, in B305/146 deutsche Kriegsverurteilte im Landsberg, Einzelfälle 1949–1950, BA; and, SS Record Klingelhöfer (NO 4809), in *Trial*, roll 11, frame 0671.
[46] Donson, "Why did German youth become fascists?" 337–340 and 356–358.

from the Wilhelm Classical Gymnasium. After graduation, Klingelhöfer devoted most of his time and energy to voice training; his passion was to become an opera singer. His schooling took him to Berlin, where he worked in a bank to finance his studies. Finally, in 1924 he embarked on a professional career as an opera singer, touring Germany giving concerts. With a view to supplementing his singing income, he studied to become a voice teacher and passed the state exam in 1928. Klingelhöfer pursued his singing career until 1934/1935 when an injury to his voice prompted him to take a job with the SD in Kassel.[47]

On the face of it, it may seem odd to find a refined and cultured individual such as Klingelhöfer embracing Nazism, but, in fact, he had been attracted to extreme right-wing ideology even when quite young. The expulsion of his family from Russia in 1915 and military service in the German army in 1918 made a vehement anti-communist and stalwart nationalist out of the young singer. When he returned from the front in December 1918, he promptly joined a veteran's organization, one used by the Kassel government to put down communist groups during the tumultuous years 1918–1920. Klingelhöfer's hatred of bolshevism and communism was serious and, like Haensch, he joined the *Jungdeutsche Orden* and, in the summer of 1920, he also joined the *Bewaffneter Bürgerschutz* or Armed Civil Guard of Upper Silesia.[48] Although Klingelhöfer had become thoroughly politicized in his youth, traveling and singing prevented him from taking an active part in the early Nazi movement, and it was not until June 1930, that he found enough time to join the Party.[49]

Many of Klingelhöfer's co-defendants had joined the Party for reasons identical to his, namely, as he stated on the witness stand, "to fight bolshevism." But Klingelhöfer was unusual in one way. While still singing professionally, he worked on translations. He put his knowledge of Russian to use translating into German a Russian, antisemitic treatise on the influence of Jews and Freemasons in the political development of Russia. The book was published in 1932 under the title, *Kampf der dunklen Macht* or *The Struggle of the Dark Power*. All in all, Klingelhöfer's singing career left him little time for party activity, but when his health put an abrupt end to his music career, on the advice of a friend he joined the SD fulltime in 1935, hoping he could use his language skills to his full advantage.[50] At first Klingelhöfer worked as an office clerk, but he was ambitious and, in 1937, he was promoted to *Referent* for Culture in *Amt* III-C. When war broke out in 1939, he was put in charge of a group assigned the task of analyzing the German population's attitude toward the war, the Reich, and its propaganda. He did this until

[47] Affidavit, Klingelhöfer, July 2, 1947, (NO 4235), in *ibid.*, roll 11, frame 0663.
[48] SS Record Klingelhöfer (NO 4809), in *ibid.*, frame 0671.
[49] *Ibid.*
[50] *Ibid.*

May 1941 when, because of his allegiance to the Party and his superior language skills, he was recruited for duty in the *Einsatzgruppen*.[51]

What about those who were younger, did their paths follow the same trajectory as Haensch and Klingelhöfer's? Certainly *Standartenführer* Walter Blume, born in 1906 in Dortmund, was influenced by the experiences of his youth.[52] At his trial, he claimed he had no particular political affiliation as a young man, but he later admitted to clemency officials that he had been introduced to right-wing extremist ideas at a fairly early age, while growing up in the Ruhr. The Ruhr is the industrial heartland of Germany, producing steel, iron, and coal; it was also the center of controversy after the war when the Weimar government was unable to make its reparation payments and the French and Belgians occupied the area in an attempt to take payment in kind. Blume witnessed the occupation first hand fueling his already pronounced nationalism. Like Klingelhöfer and so many others of his generation, to channel his anger he joined the *Bewaffneter Bürgerschutz*. During this period, he participated in armed struggles with local communist groups believing that the working classes had betrayed the nation. Young nationalists like Blume believed that the German defeat was the fault of the communists who had betrayed Germany by seeking a negotiated peace rather than doing their duty and fighting for their country. The myth of the war and occupation of the Ruhr turned Blume into an ideologue and vehement anti-communist at a very early age. Like so many of his peers, he turned to Nazism as a political party because it promised to solve all of Germany's problems that had resulted from the defeat in World War I. What comes through in Blume's testimony is that, like Ohlendorf, he harbored nationalist aims, yearning for German unity by destroying communism. He was convinced that Hitler in particular sincerely wanted to eradicate the class divisions in German society so that Germans could live in harmony. To this end he joined the Nazi Party May 1, 1933, and, thereafter, became a policeman-of-all-trades, someone who functioned equally well in the killing fields of the Soviet Union, as police chief in occupied Greece, or behind a desk in Berlin.[53] His youthful experiences had prepared him for leadership, action, and mobility.

Erwin Schulz is the final example offered to show how the myth of the war had an impact on the political choices of these young men. Schulz is on the margins of the 1914 generation in that he was born on its cusp in 1900. He attended Gymnasium like most of his cohort, but his studies were interrupted

---

[51] Interrogation, Klingelhöfer, July 1, 1947, (NO 5846), in *ibid.*, roll 12, frame 0234.

[52] Testimony, Blume, October 31, 1947, in *ibid.*, roll 3, 1754–1755. See also Eidesstattliche Erklärung, Blume in *ibid.*, (NO 4145), roll 8, frame 0059.

[53] Eidesstattliche Erklärung, Blume, June 29, 1947, (NO 4145), in *ibid.*, roll 8, frame 0060 and Wildt, "Spirit of the RSHA," 342–343.

for a brief time between April 1918 and February 1919, when he served as a volunteer infantryman in the German army during the final days of World War I.[54] Schulz's father was a soldier and when given the opportunity to serve his country he was enthusiastic. Schulz was a patriotic German whose wartime experiences transformed him into a German nationalist. As a result of the war he came to hate the working class, but especially their political representation, and when he returned home, like so many discharged and angry young veterans he took up fighting Socialists. He did this for a year, after which he was discharged from the army, finished his last term of school, and then went to university in Berlin. Originally, he wanted to study medicine, but was "frustrated by the economic consequences of the war" and, for reasons of "expediency," he studied political science and law for two semesters instead.[55] His university education did not quash his nationalism and, in the spring and summer of 1921, he helped to crush a Polish insurrection in Upper Silesia while serving in a *Freikorps* unit, an organization that undoubtedly helped to create a bond between many young nationalists of his generation.[56] In 1922, he was forced to withdraw from university because of financial difficulties. To support himself he took a job at a bank in Berlin. Like several of his colleagues during the great inflation, Schulz applied to the police for a job.[57] He was hired immediately and rose quickly through the ranks; by 1928, he had become such a good policeman that he was appointed instructor at the Bremen Police academy, where he worked until 1930.[58]

Schulz's SS record indicates he did not join the Party until May 1933. This date is consistent with many of his co-defendants, who also joined at the pinnacle of the Depression, but only after the Nazis were elected, suggesting some measure of opportunism.[59] At trial, he told the court he joined the Party because he was caught up in the frenzy of support for Hitler and he believed that the NSDAP and their values were perfectly in line with his own (here Schulz did not explain whether or not he was referring to specific policies

54 Eidesstattliche Erklärung, Schulz, May 26, 1947, (NO 3644), in *ibid.*, roll 8, frame 0294; and, SS Record Schulz (NO 4298), in *ibid.*, roll 11, frame 0771.

55 CV of Schulz, in SS Record Schulz (NO 4298) in *ibid.*, frame 0779 and Personal Statement for the Pardon Committee, Schulz, June 1950, in NARA RG 466, Prisons Division, Petitions, box 32, Schulz folder.

56 SS Record Schulz (NO 4298) in *Trial*, roll 9, frame 1187 and roll 11, frame 0770 and 0779.

57 Affidavit, Schulz, May 26, 1947 (NO 3644), in *ibid.*, roll 11, frame 0107; and, Testimony, Schulz, October 17, 1947, *ibid.*, roll 2, 905–907.

58 Trial Brief against Schulz, January 15, 1948, in John Mendelsohn (ed.), *The Holocaust. Punishing the Perpetrators of the Holocaust: The Ohlendorf and Von Weizsäcker Cases*, vol. 18 (New York, 1982), 92 and CV of Schulz, in SS Record Schulz (NO 4298), in *Trial*, roll 11, frame 0775.

59 Eidesstattliche Erklärung, Schulz, May 26, 1947, (NO 3644), in *ibid.*, roll 8, frame 0295; and, SS Record Schulz, in *ibid.*, roll 11, frame 0769.

or more general National Socialist traits, such as an emphasis on social order and control and nationalism).[60] Undoubtedly to mitigate his guilt, in court Schulz maintained that he had no political involvement with the Nazis prior to 1933, but his SS records indicate otherwise. Schulz was involved in intelligence gathering well before the Nazis came to power. In 1930, he worked for the Intelligence Division of the Bremen police, which dealt specifically with political counterintelligence. In June 1933, this division was transformed into the Secret State Police or Gestapo, and in November he was made Deputy Chief of the Bremen Gestapo. Schulz must have been a good intelligence officer because in May 1934 he was named Chief of the organization. It is highly unlikely that the NSDAP bosses would have hired Schulz for such an important position if he were, as he claimed, an unknown quantity. As it turns out, Schulz was no innocent bystander. Since 1931, he had been secretly working with local SS men to assist the Nazi takeover of the offices of the Bremen police.[61] His payoff came in 1935, on Hitler's birthday, when he became a member of the SS, undoubtedly hand-selected for his loyalty to the Party.[62]

Haensch, Klingelhöfer, Blume, and Schulz were by no means unique. Most of the leaders of the *Einsatzgruppen* tried at Nuremberg in 1947 were of the same generation and had similar experiences in the first two decades of the twentieth century, a time when the war and the failed revolution had a profound impact on their lives. Like an entire generation of German youth, these men were traumatized and shamed by the defeat of the war. Recent scholarship on this issue suggests that the war may have played a more important role in encouraging "militarist male youth culture" and ultimately "extreme violence" than once believed.[63] For instance, in her study of the concentration camp system, Karin Orth has shown that the "overwhelming majority" of SS camp guards also belonged to the "wartime generation," and like the *Einsatzgruppen* leaders, they were too young to experience the war first hand, but "gr[e]w up with its mythology." All of these men became important participants in the genocide perpetrated by the regime.[64] Members of the wartime generation had experience with right-wing violence well before they joined the Nazis as most had participated in radical youth groups immediately following the war, clear evidence that it was the loss of the war that trained these youth for political mobilization.[65] As a result, these young men were ready to be mobilized politically, and thus when the German economy crashed in 1929–1930 and the future looked

[60] Testimony, Schulz, October 17, 1947, in *ibid.*, roll 2, 915–916.

[61] Browder, *Hitler's Enforcers*, 45–46.

[62] CV of Schulz, in SS Record Schulz (NO 4298), in *Trial*, roll 11, frame 0775 and 0769; and, Eidesstattliche Erklärung, Schulz, May 26, 1947, (NO 3644), in *ibid.*, roll 8, frame 0295.

[63] Donson, "Why did German youth become fascists," 339.

[64] Orth, "The Concentration Camp SS," 307.

[65] *Ibid.*, 308.

particularly bleak – most had just reached the age when they would need to choose careers – they jumped at the chance to join a political party that promised them social mobility, economic improvements, and an ideology that reinforced their pre-existing right-wing nationalist political leanings.

Geographical Aspects of the Defendants

From where perpetrators came is a central question that has occupied historians of the Third Reich, but for which there is no consensus. Were the perpetrators drawn from the same geographic regions or did they come from all across Germany? Were they mostly German by birth or did they come from contested geographical locations, such as the border regions of the former German empire where ethnic Germans lived and extreme nationalism flourished? In his study, Michael Mann found that perpetrators were over-represented from certain geographical regions such as Alsace-Lorraine, the lost areas of Denmark and Belgium, and from Poland and other east European states where ethnic Germans lived in large numbers.[66] This does not seem to correspond with the distribution of the *Einsatzgruppen* leaders tried at Nuremberg, where only two of the twenty-four were born outside Germany.[67]

Waldemar Klingelhöfer and Waldemar von Radetzky were born in Moscow; however, Radetzky spent his formative years in Riga, Latvia, where he lived until World War II broke out. Both men had German parents and German was their mother tongue. That said, only Klingelhöfer was a refugee in the sense that his nationality forced him to leave Russia at the beginning of World War I (recall that his family moved back to Germany in 1915) and it was this status that turned him into a militant German nationalist. Radetzky, on the other hand, came to Germany in 1939, and then not as a refugee, RUSHA but voluntarily to continue work he had begun with the office in the east.[68] Klingelhöfer's experience conforms to Mann's findings that German "refugees" constituted the single most over-represented group of all perpetrators; whereas they made-up only 1% of the entire German population residing outside Germany as well as inside Germany proper, they constituted 6% of all perpetrators.[69]

Radetzky and Klingelhöfer told the tribunal at Nuremberg they had been drafted into the *Einsatzgruppen* because of their knowledge of Russian; they

---

[66] Mann, "'Ordinary Men' or 'Real Nazis,'" 343–344.
[67] For instance, Ernst Kaltenbrunner was Austrian. Hilberg, *Perpetrators Victims Bystanders*, 36–38.
[68] Erkundung, Klingelhöfer, 20.6.1950, in B305/146, Deutsche Kriegsverurteilte im Landsberg, Einzelfälle, 1949–1950, BA; Waldemar von Radetzky, 20.6.50, B305/147 in *ibid*.; and, affidavit, von Radetzky, (NO 4438), in *Trial*, roll 11, frame 0726.
[69] Mann, "'Ordinary Men' or 'Real Nazis,'" 345.

had been hired, they argued, merely as interpreters.[70] Even though both were fluent in Russian, this is almost certainly a half-truth. Radetzky had become affiliated with the NSDAP while still a youth when he joined the Latvian National Socialist movement, as did many ethnic German youth residing outside the Reich. On the other hand, Klingelhöfer was a committed anti-semite who had joined the Party three years before the Nazis took power.[71] These facts strongly suggest claims that they were not really perpetrators were, at best, a partial truth. It is more likely a combination of their language skills and devotion to the Party and its ideals that brought the two into the ranks of the *Einsatzgruppen*.

If ethnic German refugees were the most over-represented group, what about Reich Germans, what regions of Germany proper produced perpetrators? According to Mann's findings, the regions that bordered territories lost in 1918 produced the most perpetrators, with East Prussia and Upper Silesia being over-represented. Conversely, with the exception of Bremen and Osnabrück, the inner states of Germany proper produced the fewest numbers of perpetrators.[72] When compared with Mann's data, especially interesting is that among the leaders of the *Einsatzgruppen* tried at Nuremberg, with the exception of Adolf Ott who came from Bavaria, all the other defendants came from under-represented areas. Outside Mann, very few scholars have examined the role of geography in mass murder, suggesting a need for further investigation.

Confessional and Religious Aspects of the Defendants

In 1984, historian William Sheridan Allen observed that "religion [not class] proves to be the most decisive variable as to whether Germans voted Nazi or not."[73] Allen was commenting on sociologist Richard Hamilton's conclusion that generally the Nazis performed far better in Protestant areas than in Catholic, although in the elections of 1932 they did make some inroads into the Catholic community.[74] More recently, empirical studies

---

[70] Summary of Findings of the Advisory Board on Clemency to John McCloy, September 1, 1950, NARA RG 466, Prisons Division, box 6, Report of HICOG Advisory Board on Clemency, part II folder. See also affidavit, von Radetzky, (NO 4438), in *Trial*, roll 11, frame 0726; and, interrogation, Radetzky (1607-B), 25.7.46, in M1019, roll 55.

[71] CV of Klingelhöfer, in SS Record Klingelhöfer (NO 4809), in *Trial*, roll 11, frame 0671.

[72] Mann, "'Ordinary Men' or 'Real Nazis,'" 346.

[73] William Sheridan Allen, "Farewell to Class Analysis in the Rise of Nazism: Comment," in *Central European History* 17 (1984), 57.

[74] Much of the Nazi's electoral support came from the Protestant countryside, especially in areas where the population was 25,000 or less, whereas predominantly Catholic rural areas, and poorer districts of urban centres tended to vote against the NSDAP (in the countryside they voted for the *Zentrum* party and in cities they tended to vote for the left, either for the SPD (Social Democratic Party) or the communists). Hamilton, *Who Voted For Hitler?*, 38–41 and 420–423 and Childers, *The Nazi Voter*, 258–261.

have shown conclusively that confessional division was more pronounced among leaders of the SS than among German voters overall, where as many as 80% of the SS leadership were Protestant by birth.[75] Did the leaders of the *Einsatzgruppen*, who were similar in age and nationality and part of the SS and RSHA leadership corps, have similar religious backgrounds? Indeed, the preponderance were Protestant–Lutheran, not Calvinists.[76] So many in fact were Protestants that Catholics were actually under-represented in the leadership cadres of the *Einsatzgruppen*, particularly when compared to Nazi electoral support, party membership and, most importantly, to the SS leadership corps. In short, Protestants were over-represented among leaders of the *Einsatzgruppen* tried at Nuremberg.[77]

Of the twenty-four indicted *Einsatz* and *Kommandoführer* only one was Catholic, Heinz Jost. Except for his religious affiliation and the fact that he attained a higher position within the Party than many of his fellow defendants, he differed little from his co-defendants. Jost was born in 1904 in Holzhausen (near Marburg). His family was solidly middle-class and nationalistic, two other markers of young joiners of the Nazi movement. Jost's father Heinrich, a pharmacist by profession, was also a party member.[78] Like most of the other defendants, Jost joined the *Jungdeutsche Orden* while still in university and later became one of the leaders of the right-wing youth movement.[79] Not long after, he became involved in nationalist politics, he made the leap from student activist to a career in the National Socialist movement when he joined the NSDAP in 1928, at the age of 24 years. Jost's training as a lawyer helped his meteoric rise. He began his career as a legally trained civil servant in Hesse, where he worked with fellow lawyer Werner Best, who later drew him into work with the Gestapo. In 1933, he was made Police Director in Worms and a year later Best recruited him to the offices of the SD where the young lawyer was made responsible for the establishment of an office to monitor foreign intelligence. In May 1936, Jost became head of Department III 2 (Foreign Intelligence Services).[80] As was typical of most of the defendants, they recruited Jost in mid-1942 from the SD to command *Einsatzgruppe* A after the unit's original leader, Franz Walter Stahlecker, was killed.[81]

[75] Ziegler, *New Aristocracy*, 89 figure 3.5 and 83–92, notes that once these men joined the SS, most of them officially left their churches as prescribed by SS ideology. On the issue of the appeal of Protestants to the SA and SS, see Richard Steigmann-Gall, *The Holy Reich: Nazi Conceptions of Christianity, 1919–1945* (New York, 2003), 66.
[76] Steigmann-Gall, *Holy Reich*, xv.
[77] Childers, *Nazi Voter*, 113–115, 188–191, and 258–261; Hamilton, *Who Voted for Hitler*, 371–373, 382–385 and 485; & Steigmann-Gall, *Holy Reich*, 66.
[78] Testimony, Jost, October 21, 1947, in *Trial*, roll 2, 1129 and NO 2896, in *ibid.*, roll 11, frame 0525.
[79] Wilhelm, "Die Einsatzgruppe A," 282.
[80] CV of Jost," in SS Record Jost (NO 2896), in *Trial*, roll 11, frame 0525; and, Browder, *Hitler's Enforcers*, 201.
[81] Headland, *Messages of Murder*, 153–155.

The other twenty-three leaders came from denominational (mostly Evangelical-Lutheran) and nondenominational Protestant families, a far higher percentage of Protestants than in either the Party membership or the German population as a whole. Even though the overwhelming majority of the leadership corps of the *Einsatzgruppen* were Lutheran, confession does not seem to have been an important attribute, mainly because men who joined the SS were encouraged to leave the church of their birth, but remain non-denominational *gottgläubig* (believers in God); most of them recorded this fact in their SS-CVs.[82]

As a young man Himmler had been a devout Catholic; during the interwar period, however, his faith in Catholicism began to waver until he finally abandoned it altogether after the Nazis seized power.[83] It was not that the Reichsführer-SS wanted to eliminate all traditional religious institutions or force all SS men to abandon Christianity, but rather he hoped to create a new National Socialist pagan religion based on blood – a kind of "knight's order" that would supplant traditional religion for the elite members of the SS who were to become the leaders of the RSHA, Germany's new nobility.[84] Michael Wildt has asked to what extent Himmler's new utopian ideology was a form of political religion and whether or not the leadership of the RSHA was its missionaries. He has concluded that although they may not have embraced Himmler's new pagan faith, they were unquestionably missionaries of the political ideology of the regime as evidenced by their willingness to carry out racial policy with the zeal of true believers.[85] Wildt's conclusions seem to be borne out by the evidence. Even after the defeat of Germany in World War II, most of the *Einsatzgruppen* leaders tried at Nuremberg remained committed to SS-ideology, even though this meant it might cost them their lives, illustrating just how compelling SS ideology was for these men.

The real question though, and one that the literature does not deal with extensively, is whether or not SS and Nazi-ideology supplanted the more traditional religious views of these men. Presiding judge Musmanno, a Roman Catholic himself, was interested in the defendants' attitudes toward religion and repeatedly questioned them about their beliefs. Perhaps because of his own faith, he found it difficult to believe that genuine Christians (he never defines what he means by this) could also be mass murderers. Richard Steigmann-Gall has shown that Christianity does not provide "a barrier" to wrongdoing and in fact, the opposite may be true.[86] At trial, when asked about their religious convictions, most defendants responded that they had

[82] Ziegler, *New Aristocracy*, 86–87. Evidence of the strength of SS ideology can be found in the case of Adolf Eichmann. Hannah Arendt, *Eichmann in Jerusalem: A Report on the Banality of Evil* (New York, 1963), 252.

[83] Steigmann-Gall, *Holy Reich*, 106–107, 221, 129.

[84] *Ibid.*, 129 and Wildt, "Spirit of the RSHA," 333–335.

[85] Wildt, *ibid.*, 346–347.

[86] Steigmann-Gall, *Holy Reich*, 261.

no official church affiliation and subscribed to no particular theology, but they were still "believers in God."[87] The fact so many willingly gave up their formal ties to religious institutions – even Ernst Biberstein, a Protestant Pastor by training left the Church in 1938 – does not automatically support Ziegler's conclusion that the leaders of the SS were hardly "men of deep religious conviction"[88] Rather, what it shows is that humans have a unique capacity to compartmentalize their differing beliefs. However, without further directed research, we cannot know how these individual perpetrators felt about their faith and what impact, if any, it had on their behavior. That so many in the SS returned to their churches after the war suggests that perhaps they had never really abandoned their faith to begin with. In terms of understanding their collective paths to the murder, it seems that age, shared experiences, nationalism, and education are far more explanatory variables than religious conviction.

Education of the Defendants

Another commonality of the defendants is education. Not all were intellectuals of the same caliber and degree as Ohlendorf, but a good number had graduated from local Gymnasia and attended university for at least one semester.[89] Of the twenty-four men indicted, all but four or 83% had received their *Abitur* from a classical Gymnasium – the main path to university in Weimar Germany – a slightly higher percentage than the overall leadership of the RSHA.[90] Paul Blobel, head of *Sonderkommando* 4a and Waldemar von Radetzky, his Deputy Chief, had received diplomas from technical schools, whereas Heinz Schubert, an officer in Ohlendorf's *Einsatzgruppe* D and Adolf Ott, Commander of *Sonderkommando* 7b, received leaving certificates from *Realschule*. There is no equivalent in North America; the closest equivalent might be considered the completion of middle school.[91] After graduating from secondary school, seventeen of these men went on to some form of post secondary education. Twelve of the seventeen (50% of the total) completed a university education, a significantly higher percentage than for the total SS officer corps, where only 30% of SS officers were graduates of university, but somewhat lower than the overall leadership

---

[87] Testimony, Biberstein, November 20, 1947, in *Trial*, roll 4, 2741–2742 & 2700–2703; & testimony, Braune, December 1, 1947, in *ibid.*, 3206–3216.

[88] Ziegler, *New Aristocracy*, 86–87.

[89] Ziegler, *ibid.*, 114–115, notes that although education was not a prerequisite of membership in the SS, "there is no denying that a large share of the SS leadership was rooted in the educated bourgeoisie."

[90] Wildt, "Spirit of the RSHA," 339.

[91] For details of education see the SS Personnel Records of all twenty-four men, except Emil Hausmann, NO 4314, 3197, 3245, 3505, 3249, 4144, 4801, 3261, 2896, 4809, 2970, 3196, 4747, 3244, 3253, 4771, 3246, 2716, 4298, 2969, 4807, 4459, and 2966 in *Trial*, rolls 8–12.

of the RSHA, where about 66% had completed university.[92] Given the high level of educational attainment of the *Einsatz* and *Kommandoführer* tried at Nuremberg, it is clear they were the elite of an elite group; not only were they all better educated than the German population as a whole, but they were also significantly more educated than SS officers in general, who have been classified as the elite of the Nazi Party and where a good number of perpetrators came from.[93]

Empirical studies have shown that medicine and law had been the professions of choice for an overwhelming proportion of the leaders of the SS; for the leadership of the RSHA, career choices favored law and political science.[94] Whereas there were no medical doctors among the leaders of the *Einsatzgruppen* indicted in 1947 (medical doctors were tried separately), there were a number of lawyers and one political scientist. Law graduates constituted the single largest professional group. Of the twenty-four men indicted, eleven had studied law at university (46%) and nine (38%) had completed degrees, having passed at least the first law exam by 1933, which allowed them to practice their profession (Lothar Fendler did not complete his law examinations until 1942 and 1943).[95] Blume, Braune, Haensch, Jost, Nosske, Ohlendorf, Rasch, Sandberger, Strauch, and Fendler all had degrees in law, whereas Erwin Schulz had studied the subject, but did not complete the degree requirements.[96] Several members of this group had practiced law before the Nazi seizure of power in 1933. Most, because they were so young (five did not complete their law examinations until after the Nazi seizure of power by which time they had already taken jobs with the SA, SS, SD, or Gestapo) had never practiced their profession, because they had not had an opportunity to do so yet, or because they could not find jobs. There was probably a glut of lawyers in the SD because, during the Depression, the NSDAP offered them work.[97]

[92] Gunnar C. Boehnert, "The Jurists in the SS-Führerkorps, 1925–1939," in Gerhard Hirschfeld and Lothar Kettenacker (eds.), *Der "Führerstaat": Mythos und Realität. Studien zur Struktur und Politik des Dritten Reiches* (Stuttgart, 1981), 362 & Wildt, "Spirit of the RSHA," 339. Although a significant number of SS leaders had attended university, a much higher proportion than for the German population as a whole, many of them never completed their degrees. See Ziegler, *New Aristocracy*, 114–115. Compare Ziegler's statistics in Table 4.2, 115 to those of the defendants at Nuremberg.

[93] Ziegler, *New Aristocracy*, 113–115.

[94] *Ibid.*, 115–116 n69, finds that doctors constituted the single largest group of professionals within his SS officer sample, whereas Boehnert, *Jurists*, 262–263 puts law graduates in first place and Wildt, "Spirit of the RSHA," 339.

[95] These findings seem to contradict those of Gunnar Boehnert who states that only seven of the *Einsatzgruppen* leaders indicted in 1947 studied law. Boehnert, "Jurists," 165 n.25.

[96] Schulz studied law before he joined the NSDAP and Fendler did so afterwards. Bracher, *German Dictatorship*, 274, notes that large numbers of the Party elite studied at university, but many of them never completed their education. Schulz and Fendler are classic examples.

[97] Kater, *Nazi Party*, 67–68.

Not only were there a disproportionate number university graduates, but six of the defendants held doctoral degrees.[98] Walter Blume, described by Wildt as the typical RSHA leader, is a good example. He was the son of a schoolmaster, had studied law in Bonn, Jena, Münster, Berlin and Erlangen. By 1932, he had successfully completed his senior law examination, and in 1933, was awarded the Doctor of Law degree from the University of Erlangen.[99] His dissertation, submitted to the law school, dealt with property rights in divorce.[100] Werner Braune, arrested by British forces in Oslo, Norway in 1945 and an *Einsatzkommando* leader, also held a Doctor of Law degree.[101] Upon graduation from his local Gymnasium, he studied law first in Bonn, then Munich, and, finally, in Jena, where he passed his junior exam in 1930. Braune received his Doctor of Juridical Science from the law school at the University of Tübingen in October 1934 upon completion and submission of a dissertation on the legal problems of bankruptcy.[102] Walter Haensch held a doctoral degree in Law that he completed in 1936 at the University of Leipzig. His graduate work, a study of the organization of the police under the Nazis, was much more political than the research of Blume and Braune.[103]

Martin Sandberger, one of the youngest defendants in the dock at Nuremberg, was descended from a long line of Lutheran theologians, which helps explain why during clemency proceedings after the trial, Theophil Wurm, a prominent Evangelical Bishop from Württemberg, took up his cause.[104] Sandberger had also chosen law as his profession, studying at the Universities of Munich, Freiburg, Breisgau, Cologne, and Tübingen; he passed his junior exam in May 1933 and received his Doctor of Law from Tübingen in February 1934. His dissertation is, according to Benno

---

[98] There are no available statistics to compare this to the officer corps of the SS.

[99] Testimony, Blume, October 31, 1947, in *Trial*, roll 3, 1754–1755. See also Eidesstattliche Erklärung, Blume in *ibid.*, (NO 4145), roll 8, frame 0059.

[100] Blume's dissertation is titled, *Prozessuale Probleme bei der Beendigung des gesetzlichen Güterstandes während eines Prozesses des Ehemanns über eingebrachtes Gut der Frau*, Müller-Hill, "Role of Experts," 64.

[101] Case Record, Braune, April 27, 1948, in NARA RG 338, Landsberg, Records Relating to Executed Prisoners January 2, 1946–June 7, 1951, box 2, Braune folder.

[102] Testimony, Braune, November 25, 1947, in *Trial*, roll 4, 3006–3007 and 3010. Braune's dissertation was titled, *Gibt es ein Zwangsvollstreckung aus Verurteilungen zur Abgabe einer Willenserklärung*, Müller-Hill, "Role of Experts," 64.

[103] Testimony, Haensch, December 2, 1947, in *Trial*, roll 4, 3225–3226; Case Record of Haensch, in NARA RG 466, Prison's Division, Administrative and Medical Records, Landsberg, box 4, Haensch folder; SS Record Haensch (NO 3261), in *Trial*, roll 11, frame 0758; Haensch's dissertation is titled, *Weg zur einheitlichen Reichspolizei*, Müller-Hill, "Role of Experts," 65.

[104] Letter, Sandberger family to Clay, June 1948 in NARA RG 153 (AG), WCB, Nuremberg Administrative Records 1944–1949, box 11, 86-3-5 folder; and, testimony of Sandberger, November 7, 1947, in *Trial*, roll 3, 2141.

Müller-Hill, a "91-page apology for the social security system in Nazi Germany."[105]

The other two *Einsatzgruppen* leaders who held doctoral degrees, Franz Six and Otto Rasch, received their degrees from the faculty of arts and science rather than law. Six received his degree from the philosophy department at Karl-Ruprecht University in Heidelberg on May 6, 1934. His dissertation, *Die politische Propaganda der NSDAP im Kampf um die Macht* was an analysis of Goebbels's use of propaganda.[106] Finally, Rasch, who Chief Prosecutor Benjamin Ferencz thought suffered from a speech impediment because he was introduced to the former leader of *Einsatzgruppe* C as "Doctor Doctor," actually held two doctoral degrees.[107] He earned both from the University of Leipzig's Faculty of Arts and Science. His first dissertation, *Wohnungsmarkt und Wohnungspolitik in England in der Kriegs – und Nachkriegszeit* advanced an argument in favor of a free market economy, but little is known about, *Die verfassungsrechtliche Stellung des Preußischen Landtagspräsidenten*, his second doctoral study.[108]

Among the leadership corps of the *Einsatzgruppen* tried at Nuremberg, more than 80% had received their *Abitur* and 70% had some level of post-secondary educational attainment, not too different from that of some of the Party leadership in the RSHA, but certainly far above that for the Party membership as a whole or for the officer corps of the SS. The evidence presented strongly suggests that the leaders of the *Einsatzgruppen* constituted a highly-educated elite group within the cadres of the SS leadership and was in keeping with educational levels of the Security Police and SD who were highly educated elites themselves. Although clearly the elite, like the majority of the RSHA leadership, the *Einsatzgruppen* leaders were not traditional academic scholars removed from society and power, rather they were doers whose ideas were realized through their actions.[109]

The fact that so many of the leaders of the *Einsatzgruppen* were well-educated elites is significant to our understanding of how genocide was perpetrated, as Benno Müller-Hill has highlighted in his study of the link between educational attainment and perpetration of genocide.[110] Although there is no evidence that any of the *Einsatzgruppenführer* actually executed people personally, they gave the orders to do so and held power over life and death in Russia. They were not only high-ranking SS leaders, but more

---

[105] Sandberger's dissertation is titled, *Die Sozialversicherung im nationalsozialistischen Staat*, Müller-Hill, "Role of Experts," 65.
[106] Lutz Hachmeister, *Der Gegnerforscher: Die Karriere des SS Führers Franz Alfred Six* (Munich, 1998), 68–70 and on Six's early career at university see, 38–76; Müller-Hill, "The Role of the Experts," 65; and, Browder, *Hitler's Enforcers*, 179.
[107] Interview with Ferencz, April 24, 1997, 31.
[108] *Ibid.*
[109] Wildt, "Spirit of the RSHA," 340.
[110] Müller-Hill, "The Role of the Experts," 62–70.

TABLE 3. *Education of the Defendants**

Name	Secondary		Post Secondary	Completion Date
Biberstein, Ernst	Gymnasium	(1917)	Theological Seminary (College)	1921
Blobel, Paul	Technical School	(1912)	Architecture (Technical College)	1920
Blume, Walter	Gymnasium	(1919)	Law (University)	1929 & 1932
Braune, Werner	Gymnasium	(1929)	Law (University)	1932 & 1933
Fendler, Lothar	Gymnasium	(1932)	Dentistry (University)	Not completed
			Law (University)	1942 & 1943
Graf, Matthias	Gymnasium	(1920)	None/Merchant Apprentice	N/A
Haensch, Walter	Gymnasium	(1924)	Law (University)	1930 & 1934
Hausmann, Emil	Unknown	–	Unknown	Unknown
Jost, Heinz	Gymnasium	(1923)	Law (University)	1927 & 1930
Klingelhöfer, W.	Gymnasium	(1919)	Musical Academy (Professional Training)	1923
Naumann, Erich	Gymnasium	(1921)	None/Merchant Apprentice	N/A
Nosske, Gustav	Gymnasium	(1922)	Law (University)	1930 & 1934
Ott, Adolf	Realschule	(1920)	None/Merchant Apprentice	N/A
Ohlendorf, Otto	Gymnasium	(1928)	Law and Economics (University)	1931
Radetzky, W. von	Technical School	(1929)	None/Merchant Apprentice N/A	
Rasch, Otto	Gymnasium	(1919)	Law and Economics (University)	1933
Rühl, Felix	Gymnasium	(1926)	None/Merchant Apprentice N/A	
Sandberger, Martin	Gymnasium	(1929)	Law (University)	1933 & 1936
Schubert, Heinz	Technical School	(1931)	None/Clerk Apprentice	N/A
Schulz, Erwin	Gymnasium	(1919)	Law and Political Science (University)	Not completed
Seibert, Willy	Gymnasium	(1928)	Economics (University)	1932
Six, Franz	Gymnasium	(1930)	Political Science and History (University)	1934
Steimle, Eugen	Gymnasium	(1929)	Education and Languages (University)	1936
Strauch, Eduard	Gymnasium	–	Law (University)	1932 & 1935

* For general details of education see the SS Personnel Records of all twenty-four men, except Emil Hausmann, NO 4314, 3197, 3245, 3505, 3249, 4144, 4801, 3261, 2896, 4809, 2970, 3196, 4747, 3244, 3253, 4771, 3246, 2716, 4298, 2969, 4807, 4459, and 2966 in *Trial*, rolls 8–12. See also Eidesstattliche Erklärung of all defendants except Hausmann, NO 3824, 4145, 4234, 4144, 4844, 4151, 4235, 4150, 4146, 2857, 2993, 4749, 4149, 4438, 2891, 3055, 3841, 2859, 4546, and 4459 in *Trial*, rolls 8–12.

importantly in some ways, they were the leadership, the elite of the new German society. As Stanley Milgram discovered long ago, authority helps to ensure action. These men held more than one kind of authority in a society that used new party offices as well as traditional positions of authority to perpetrate genocide. When a university professor, an economist, a priest, a doctor, or a lawyer order executions, "they cannot be wrong," even more so in a society that was loathe to question authority, but instead, embrace it.[111] The collective biography of these men dispels the myth that educational attainment inoculates us against genocide. The opposite seems true.

Vocations of the Defendants

Certainly an impressive number of the leadership corps of the *Einsatzgruppen* was well educated; the majority were lawyers or legally trained, but what about those who were neither academics nor lawyers, were they also professionals or were they more in keeping with two-thirds of the officer corps of the SS who were not professionals?[112] Of the thirteen defendants who were not lawyers, three could be classified "professional" in that they had trained for specific vocations. The singing career of Klingelhöfer has already been discussed, the other two, Paul Blobel and Ernst Biberstein, have not.

The profile of Ernst Biberstein, who changed his family name from Szymanowsky in June 1941, because he feared he might be mistaken for a "Pole," is particularly interesting.[113] Biberstein was marginally older than his colleagues, born in 1899 in Hilchenbach, Westphalia, and was also one of the few so-called old National Socialists in the dock (he had joined the Party in 1926 and had membership number 40,718).[114] Like the majority of his co-defendants he graduated from a classical Gymnasium in the spring of 1917, but being slightly older also meant he was drafted into the German army immediately upon graduation, and spent a year and a half as an infantryman.[115] When Biberstein returned from the front in 1919, he began the study of Protestant theology in Kiel. He did so not because it was his calling, but rather, he told the court, because "it had been decided by my parents that I should become a clergyman," not a terribly cogent or

[111] *Ibid.*, 67–68.
[112] Ziegler, *New Aristocracy*, 116.
[113] Interrogation, Biberstein, June 29, 1947, (NO 4997), in *Trial*, roll 12, frames 0404-0405; and, SS Record Biberstein (NO 2901), in *ibid.*, roll 11, frame 0776.
[114] Testimony, Biberstein, November 20, 1947, in *ibid.*, roll 4, 2694; and, affidavit, Biberstein, July 2, 1947, in *ibid.*, roll 11, frame 0122.
[115] *Ibid.*, roll 4, 2690–2691; and, affidavit, Biberstein, July 2, 1947, (NO 4314), in *ibid.*, roll 11, frame 0122.

inspired reason for a career such as this.[116] In April 1921, he passed his first theological exam and, in November 1924, he was ordained a Protestant minister. His first posting was in Schleswig-Holstein, an area that produced scores of perpetrators.[117] Biberstein gave up his job as a clergyman as soon as the Nazis came to power. Because he had joined the NSDAP so early, he rose through the ranks quickly. In 1933, he was appointed Presiding Minister of the Provincial Protestant Church or *Kirchenprobst* in Bad Segeberg. In 1935, he left his congregation altogether to take a job as a "theological expert" in the Reich Ministry of Church Affairs, where he worked closely with the Gestapo as a liaison officer.[118] In 1936, he joined the SS and the SD because the prestige of this elite organization appealed to him and he relished the idea of becoming the only SS theologian among "all those lawyers" in the Gestapo.[119] The final move in his career came in December 1938, when he officially left the Church and, according to his testimony, never once regretted his decision.[120] Finally, in 1944, Biberstein joined the Gestapo and was appointed head of their Oppeln office.[121] He was transferred to Russia in the summer of 1942 to command *Einsatzkommando 6* of *Einsatzgruppe* C. He remained in that post for nearly one year and it was his activities during this time for which he was indicted. How did Biberstein go from theologian to leader of a mobile security and killing unit?

The presiding judge also wanted to know. In an unusually rhetorical style for a judge, Musmanno overstated the case against Biberstein and his transformation from theologian to murderer writing in his memoir that Biberstein "went the whole way and accepted office in the dreaded Gestapo which regarded the concentration camp as an ideal substitute for the church, and *Mein Kampf* as an improvement over the Ten Commandments."[122] Although Musmanno's characterization of National Socialism as a substitute religion is clearly an exaggeration, Biberstein's transformation from Protestant minister to Gestapo chief certainly raises serious and interesting questions about the nature of his beliefs and what motivated him to take such a radical step. This matter will be developed further in the next chapter, but what can be concluded now is that at the very least, Biberstein's career as a

[116] Testimony, Biberstein, November 20, 1947, in *ibid.*, roll 4, 2689–2690.

[117] *Ibid.*, 2693; affidavit, Biberstein, July 2, 1947 (NO 4314), in *ibid.*, roll 11, frame 0122; and, Mann, "'Ordinary Men' or 'Real Nazis,'" 344.

[118] *Ibid.*; and, Trial Brief against Biberstein, January 15, 1948, in Mendelsohn (ed.), *The Holocausts* vol. 17, document 8, 2–3.

[119] Testimony, Biberstein, November 20, 1947 in *Trial*, roll 4, 2740–2741. This supports Boehnert, "Jurists," 364–365, that "most legal[ly] trained [SS] officers served with the Gestapo/SD, that is in the security apparatus of the Third Reich."

[120] Testimony, Biberstein, November 20, 1947, in Trial, roll 4, 2741–2742.

[121] Trial Brief against Biberstein, January 15, 1948, in Mendelsohn (ed.), *The Holocaust*, vol. 17, document 8, 3.

[122] Michael Musmanno, *The Eichmann Kommandos* (London, 1961), 192–193.

Protestant pastor made him unique among his peers, and religious beliefs did not insulate him from becoming involved in the murderous activities of the Party.

The profile of the notorious Paul Blobel is no less intriguing than that of Biberstein. In the first place, Blobel was almost a generation older than most of the other defendants. His education and experience were also quite different. Unlike the majority of his co-defendants, he had neither completed his *Abitur* nor attended university prior to his work for *Sonderkommando* 4a. Rather, Blobel graduated from a vocational school or *Fortbildungsschule* and upon receiving his leaving certificate in 1912, spent the years leading up to the war as a carpenter's apprentice.[123] In 1914, he volunteered for the army as an engineer, and survived the four-year ordeal of trench warfare. He was discharged in 1918 with the rank of Staff Sergeant.[124] After the Great War, Blobel resumed training, first as a carpenter, then a building technician, and, finally, as an architect.[125] He found work as an architect a year after earning certification in 1924.[126] Blobel's dream of fashioning a career as a prominent architect crashed in 1929 however, when with the onset of the Depression he lost his job and had to rely on unemployment relief to survive.[127] He floundered for two years before joining the Party in July 1931. During testimony, Blobel told the tribunal that he was at the same time a member of the SPD (Social Democratic Party) and the SA, a claim that the prosecution found so outrageous they filed a brief to refute it. They argued that Blobel's statement, "irrelevant as it may be as to the questions in issue before the tribunal, deserves attention as it characterizes the defendant's boldness in perverting the truth."[128] But Blobel may well have been telling the truth; it was not so unusual for crossover memberships, at least early on in the history of fascism. He told American authorities after the war, that at the time he felt morally isolated and economically helpless; it appears that he may have decided to join the Party more to enhance his economic well-being than because he believed National Socialist ideology.[129] Once in the Party and after formally joining the elite SS organization in January 1932, Blobel quickly forgot his earlier dreams and instead worked his way

[123] Affidavit, Blobel, June 6, 1947 (NO 3824), in *Trial*, roll 11, 0139.

[124] SS Record Blobel (NO 3197), in *ibid.*, roll 11, frame 0718.

[125] Trial Brief against Blobel, January 15, 1948, in Mendelsohn (ed.), *The Holocaust*, vol. 17, 247.

[126] Testimony, Blobel, October 1947, in *Trial*, roll 3, 1493–1496; and, Eidesstattliche Erklärung, Blobel, June 6, 1947, (NO 3824) in *ibid.*, Prosecution Exhibits, roll 8, frames 0345–0349.

[127] Eidesstattliche Erklärung, Blobel, June 6, 1947, (NO 3824), in *ibid.*, frame 0345.

[128] Trial Brief against Blobel, January 15, 1948, in Mendelsohn (ed.), *The Holocaust*, vol. 17, 247–248.

[129] Petition for Clemency, Blobel," June 5, 1950, in NARA RG 466, Prisons Division, Petitions at Nuremberg, box 3, Blobel-Biberstein, Blobel folder. See also testimony of Blobel, October 28, 1947, in *Trial*, roll 3, 1493–1498.

up the SS ladder, joining the SD in 1935, and eventually becoming head of *Sonderkommando* 4a in May-June 1941.[130]

Not all defendants were academics, lawyers or professionals, the leadership corps of the *Einsatzgruppen* also included several non-professionals and nonintellectuals. Among those tried in 1947 – Matthias Graf, Erich Naumann, Adolf Ott, Waldemar von Radetzky, Felix Rühl and Heinz Schubert – had held nonprofessional, lower middle-class jobs in civilian life, such as refrigerator merchant and office clerk. With the exception of Naumann and Ott who had joined the Party before the Nazi breakthrough of 1929, typically these men were the lowest-ranking officers in the mobile security units who were tried at Nuremberg in 1947. It was in the offices of the RSHA that these defendants were offered a path to more prominent careers then they otherwise may have held in civilian life.[131]

Party Membership and Affiliations of the Defendants

Given the similarities in age, experience, religion, and education of so many of the leaders of the *Einsatzgruppen*, it is only natural that many joined the Party at approximately the same time (Table 4). Sixteen of the twenty-four defendants, two-thirds (66%) joined the NSDAP before the Nazis assumed power on January 30, 1933. The remaining eight, one third (33%), joined the Party later. Of those who joined before 1933, only four (17%) did so before the onset of the world economic depression in 1929: Biberstein, Jost, Ott, and Ohlendorf.[132] These men averaged just less than 26 years of age when they joined the Party, five years younger than the age of the average new member who was 31 years old.[133] The oldest, Otto Rasch, was 40 when he joined the Party, whereas Ohlendorf and Ott (both considered "Old Fighters") were still teenagers when they committed to National Socialism. Overall, statistically *Einsatzgruppen* leaders joined the Party much earlier in their lives than did the membership as a whole. This seems to reinforce Mann's findings, which suggest that the higher the rank, the more "real"

[130] Eidesstattliche Erklärung, Blobel June 15, 1946, in NARA RG 338, Landsberg, Records Relating to Executed Prisoners January 2, 1946–June 7, 1951, box 1 AB-BR, Paul Blobel folder; and testimony, Blobel, October 28, 1941, in *Trial*, roll 3, 1500.

[131] It is not surprising to find that under-qualified individuals, such as Naumann and Ott, held high-ranking positions, because they were long-standing party members. This conforms with Kater, *Nazi Party*, 230, and "The New Nazi Rulers: Who Were They?," 42–43, who concludes, "as a rule, the lower an individual's NSDAP membership number was, the greater was his peer-group standing in the Party and particularly in the leadership cadre. And since party rank correlated, positively with 'Old Fighter' status, the highest party cadres enjoyed not only the greatest authority but also the greatest measure of corporate stability and, in the last analysis, the most stable sense of collective identity."

[132] "Wanted Reports, OMGUS form 249," May 28, 1947, in NARA RG 238, OCCWC, Executive Counsel, Evidence Division, Office File 1945–1947, Entry 180 Nm70 box 1, Spare Copies of Wanted Reports folder.

[133] Ziegler, *New Aristocracy*, 60.

TABLE 4. *Joining Date of Defendants**

Joining Date		Name	Membership Number	Joining Age
October	1922	Ott, Adolf	2,433	18
28 May	1925	Ohlendorf, Otto	6,531	18
Unknown	1926	Biberstein, Ernst	40,718	27
1 February	1928	Jost, Heinz	75,946	24
1 November	1929	Naumann, Erich	170,257	24
1 March	1930	Six, Franz	245,670	21
1 June	1930	Klingelhöfer, Waldemar	258,951	30
9 November	1930	Rühl, Felix	408,468	20
7 June	1931	Haensch, Walter	537,265	27
1 July	1931	Braune, Werner	581,277	22
1 August	1931	Strauch, Eduard	623,392	25
1 October	1931	Rasch, Otto	620,976	40
1 December	1931	Sandberger, Martin	774,980	20
1 December	1931	Blobel, Paul	344,662	37
Unknown	1932	Hausmann, Emil	Unknown	22
1 May	1932	Steimle, Eugen	1,075,555	23
1 May	1933	Schulz, Erwin	2,902,239	33
1 May	1933	Seibert, Willy	1,886,112	25
1 May	1933	Blume, Walter	3,282,505	27
1 May	1933	Graf, Matthias	3,423,504	30
1 May	1933	Nosske, Gustav	2,784,256	31
1 May	1934	Schubert, Heinz	3,374,350	20
1 May	1937	Fendler, Lothar	5,216,392	24
1 December	1940	Radetzky, Waldemar von	8,047,747	30

* For these statistics see CV of Ott, (NO 4747); affidavits of Biberstein, July 2, 1947 (NO 4314); Klingelhöfer, July 2, 1947 (NO 4235); Nosske, July 29, 1947 (NO); Schubert, (NO 2716); Schulz, (NO 3841); Fendler, June 27, 1947 (NO 4144); and, Steimle, July 24, 1947, (NO 4459). See also SS Personnel Records of Blobel (NO 3197); Blume (NO 3245); Braune (NO 3249); Graf, (NO 4801); Haensch (NO 3261); Jost, (NO 2896); Naumann, (NO 2970); Ohlendorf, (NO 3196); Rasch, (NO 3253); von Radetzky, (NO 4771); Rühl, (NO 4808); Sandberger, (NO 3246); Seibert, (2969); Six, (NO 4807); Strauch, (NO 2966), in *Trial*, rolls 8–12. It is important to note that joining date and party membership numbers do not necessarily correspond. This would account for discrepancies between Rühl and Blobel's, whose number is lower even though he joined the Party later.

the Nazi, and the more "real" the Nazi, the greater participation rate in genocide.[134] Twenty of the twenty-four men indicted at Nuremberg, five-sixths (83%), were 30 years or younger when they joined the Party, whereas only 50% of those who joined between 1922 and 1932 were under 30 years.[135] What induced these young men to join at such a young age?

[134] Mann, "'Ordinary Men' or 'Real Nazis,'" 358–359.
[135] For detailed statistics of age and membership see Madden, "Generational Aspects," 453–454 Table 1 and Figure 1.

Any attempt to determine precisely why these young men joined the NSDAP is at best a difficult and hazardous task. Wildt, Lowenberg, Donson, and others who examine the social basis of various party organizations such as the SA, SS, and SD, have offered some insights, but what about the leadership corps of the *Einsatzgruppen*, can we draw any conclusions about what motivated this particular cohort to join the NSDAP? Defendant testimony, interrogation reports and affidavits, as well as SS records give us some insight into motivation. The two most important reasons cited by the defendants were opportunity and ideology. Opportunists such as Paul Blobel had already chosen a career (in Blobel's case architecture), but, because of the Depression, found themselves unemployed in the early 1930s. He joined the Party because it provided him an opportunity to work. He had had such difficulty finding a job in economically depressed Germany, he eventually gave up looking and joined the Party as an alternative career choice. Blobel was not alone, many of the future leaders of the *Einsatzgruppen*, most notably the youngest ones, had difficulty finding jobs in the years immediately before the Nazi seizure of power in 1933. As one scholar has aptly noted, "the young very often are the last hired and the first fired," making them particularly defenseless during times of economic hardship and high unemployment.[136] The NSDAP – in particular its paramilitary wings – offered these young men a chance to work when they otherwise would have been unemployed, and at a time when they were most vulnerable and most likely to be taken in by the entreaties and promises of the Nazis.

After 1933, opportunism played a more pronounced role in decisions to join the Party. Many highly trained professional men, especially newly accredited lawyers, found it difficult to practice their profession without becoming members of party associations. Gustav Nosske, born in 1902, was just such an opportunist.[137] His parents were civil servants, one a teacher the other a jurist, both self-declared nationalists.[138] After receiving his *Abitur*, Nosske went to university in 1925 to study political science and law.[139] He passed his junior law examination in 1933, just as the Nazis were taking power in Germany. During his university days he had attended several Party rallies, he told the court, but apparently at that time Nazism held no particular allure for him.[140] Nor did Nazi propaganda seem to influence his thinking as he found its contents to be far-fetched.[141] Rather, his main reason for joining the Party in May 1933 was to advance his professional

[136] Madden, "Generational Aspects of German National Socialism," 455.
[137] Eidesstattliche Erklärung, Nosske, June 29, 1947, in M1019, roll 50.
[138] Petition for Clemency, Nosske, June 26, 1950, in NARA RG 238, Advisory Board on Clemency, HICOG, Correspondence 1947–1950, box 10 (case 9 E212), Nosske folder.
[139] Nosske, B305/147, Deutsche Kriegsverurteilte im Landsberg, Einzelfälle 1949–1950, BA.
[140] Testimony, Nosske, December 4, 1947, in *Trial*, roll 4, 3428.
[141] Nosske, Statement to Advisory Board on Clemency, June 26, 1950, in NARA RG 238, HICOG, Correspondence 1947–1950, box 10 (case E212), Nosske folder.

standing. According to his testimony, he was in a financially precarious position in 1933 and wanted to practice law, but to do so he had to join the Party, which he did he confessed, "without any particular reluctance [or] enthusiasm."[142] Once in the Party, Nosske was offered a job with the Ministry of the Interior in Aachen. He worked there for a year at the end of which time he wrote his final law examination and then took a job with the Gestapo which, he told the court at Nuremberg, he had no "misgivings" about doing.[143] Blume had told a remarkably similar story: he joined the Party on the advice of a fellow lawyer who assured him that by doing so he would promote his career.[144]

The second most common reason cited by the defendants for joining the Party was ideological. Men such as Ott and Ohlendorf felt a strong affinity for the tenets of Nazism, Ott joining the Nazi movement virtually at its inception in 1922, and Ohlendorf three years later. At trial and under intense questioning, Ott confessed he had "always [been] a National Socialist at heart."[145] Not surprisingly, Ott came from Bavaria, the birthplace of National Socialism and an area of Germany over-represented by perpetrators.[146] When he joined the Party in 1922, he was working as a merchant apprentice, but he was so attracted to the nascent Nazi movement he volunteered for service in the SA immediately.[147] Ott was such a committed Nazi that at his trial he could not bring himself to lie about his adoration for Hitler and his loyalty to National Socialism, even though not doing so might cost him his life. When asked how he felt about the outcome of the war, he told the court he would have been happier had Germany won and Hitler survived.[148] Perhaps not all the defendants who joined the Party were as zealous and single-minded as Ott, yet they still supported the movement and its political objectives on ideological grounds.

Once in the Party, most defendants were quickly integrated into the Nazi system of power as many went to work in party organizations such as the SA, SS, SD, and Gestapo (Table 5). As Wildt has conclusively shown, *Einsatzgruppen* personnel came largely from the offices of the SD; this holds true for the *Einsatzgruppen* defendants, all of whom were members of the SD with the exception of von Radetzky who never officially joined.[149] Some worked very hard to advance their careers, others were less ambitious. There were those who gave up their civilian careers entirely to promote Nazi ideology,

---

[142] Testimony, Nosske, December 4, 1947, in *Trial*, roll 4, 3425–3429.
[143] *Ibid.*, 3429–3431; and, Eidesstattliche Erklärung, Nosske, June 29, 1947, in M1019, roll 50.
[144] Testimony, Blume, October 31, 1947, in *ibid.*, roll 3, 1757–1758.
[145] Testimony, Ott, December 11, 1947, in *ibid.*, roll 5, 3797.
[146] Mann, "'Ordinary Men' or 'Real Nazis,'" 344.
[147] CV of Ott, in SS Record Ott (NO 4747), in *ibid*, roll 11 frames 0677–0678.
[148] Testimony, Ott, December 11, 1947, in *ibid.*, roll 5, 3798.
[149] *Ibid.*

TABLE 5. *Joining Dates of the SA, SS, SD, and Gestapo**

Name	SA	SS	SS #	SD	Gestapo
Biberstein, Ernst	Not a Member	09.1936	272,962	1940	1935
Blobel, Paul	05.1931–01.1932	12.1931	29,100	1935	
Blume, Walter	06.1933–11.1936	04.1935	267,224	1935	1934
Braune, Werner	11.1931–11.1934	11.1934	107,364	1934	1936
Fendler, Lothar	Not a Member	04.1933	272,603	1939	
Graf, Matthias	Not a Member	03.1933	77,431	1940	
Haensch, Walter	11.1933–09.1935	08.1935	272,573	1935	
Hausmann, Emil	Unknown	Unknown	Unknown	Unknown	
Jost, Heinz	03.1929–07.1934	07.1934	36,243	1934	1933
Klingelhöfer, Waldemar	Not a Member	02.1933	52,744	1934	
Naumann, Erich	02.1930–06.1935	07.1935	107,496	1935	
Nosske, Gustav	06.1933–06.1936	07.1936	290,213	1936	1935
Ohlendorf, Otto	1925–1927	1926/27	880	1936	
Ott, Adolf	1922–1927	09.1931	13,294	1934	
Rasch, Otto	Not a Member	03.1933	107,100	1933	
Radetzky, Waldemar von	Not a Member	12.1939	351,254	Not a Member	1938
Rühl, Felix	11.1930–09.1932	10.1932	51,305	1935	1933
Sandberger, Martin	12.1931–04.1935	05.1935	272,495	1935–1936	
Schubert, Heinz	HJ1932–34	11.1934	107,326	1934	
Schulz, Erwin	Not a Member	04.1935	107,484	1935	
Seibert, Willy	Not a Member	11.1935	272,375	1936	
Six, Franz	11.1932–04.1935	04.1935	107,480	1935	1933
Steimle, Eugen	10.1932–04.1936	04.1936	272,575	1936	
Strauch, Eduard	08.1931–12.1931	12.1931	19,312	1934	

* These statistics come from SS personnel records, affidavits and interrogations of the defendants. See NO 4997; NO 4314; NO 3197; NO 3245; NO 4145; NO 3249; NO 4234; NO 4958; NO 4801; NO 4855; NO 3261; NO 2896; NO 4235; NO 4809; NO 5846; NO 2970; NO 4150; NO 3505; NO 2857; NO 4747; NO 4749; NO 4771; NO 4777; NO 4808; NO 2891; NO 3244; NO 3055; NO 4298; NO 2858; NO 4807; NO 3247; NO 2966 in *Trial*, rolls 8–12. And also Gesuch Felix Rühl, 12.06.1950 in NARA RG 238, Advisory Board on Clemency, (HICOG 1947–1950), box 11 case 9 E212, Rühl folder; Interrogation, Seibert, 11.03.1947, in M1019, roll 68; and Browder, *Hitler's Enforcers*, 46, 179, 201, and 222. Some of the SS membership numbers do not seem to make sense. For example, compare Naumann's statistics with those of Haensch. Both joined the SS at about the same time, yet, Naumann's SS membership number is significantly smaller than Haensch's.

whereas others seemed content to perform their part-time SS duties routinely as part of everyday life, displaying no particular zeal for the Party, its ideology or their own career advancement. Many historians have identified different behavioral patterns among the perpetrators, arranging them into sub-categories such as careerists, opportunists, and ideological soldiers. What type of perpetrators were the *Einsatzgruppen* defendants and how precisely should we classify them?

Classifying Defendant Political Careers

A few of the *Einsatzgruppen* leaders can be considered careerists, defined by Hilberg as individuals who had secure professions in pre-Nazi times, but who, because of all-consuming ambition and circumstances, chose Nazism as a way to advance their careers believing they could rise very quickly to positions of authority within the Party, men such as Adolf Eichmann proved to be.[150] Most defendants in the *Einsatzgruppen* trial were simply too young to be careerists in this sense – although Ernst Biberstein, the former Protestant pastor who left the Church to work for a government ministry, fits Hilberg's definition with ease. This is not to suggest that the leaders of the *Einsatzgruppen* were not career driven as the vast majority of them were highly ambitious young men like Ohlendorf, but rather simply that their motivation for joining the Party tended more toward ideology and opportunity, than for reasons of career alone. Like any system of classification though, individuals often fit into multiple categories.

Pure careerism may not have motivated many of the *Einsatzgruppen* leaders, but like other leaders from the RSHA, most of them certainly were ambitious young men, looking to make their mark on German society. Because they were so young when the Nazis came to power, often they had not yet decided on a career path. Some, like Ohlendorf and Six were political-academics, others such as Matthias Graf, were not. Different in their paths to National Socialism, most of these men still found a home in the SS and SD. Once firmly ensconced there, they rose quickly to positions of power, particularly if they had joined the Party early enough, as had Ohlendorf and Jost. Unemployed in 1933, with no alternative employment prospects, some joined the Party hoping to find a career. Lothar Fendler had good prospects in life, but chose the party because his circumstances encouraged him to do so.[151]

Fendler was one of the youngest defendants at Nuremberg, born the summer before World War I began. He had planned to become a dentist like his father and had even written his preliminary examination, but because of financial difficulties brought on by his father's illness was forced to withdraw from the program. Fendler wanted to help support his family, but at the time

---

[150] Hilberg, *Perpetrators Victims Bystanders*, 39.
[151] *Ibid.*, 30 & 40–45.

had no way to earn a living. When a friend offered him work in the SS in 1933, he accepted immediately and three years later when his father died, he joined the SD. Here, Fendler proved himself. He began his career as a switchboard operator, quickly moved up to become a clerk in the offices of Counter-Intelligence, and ended up in the SD main office.[152] Fendler's position in the SD afforded him the opportunity to complete his studies. In 1940 he began work on a law degree, which he hoped would land him a position in the Government bureaucracy. In 1943, he completed the final law examination and his future looked bright. It probably would have been had the Third Reich survived.[153]

Whereas all of the defendants demonstrate aspects of careerism and opportunism, many were also ideologically disposed and some became zealots, defined as professionals who had established careers prior to the Nazi seizure of power, but who gave up their careers to further the National Socialist cause. Eduard Strauch and Werner Braune fall into this category.[154] Braune was born in 1909 in Thuringia, an interior state of the Reich and one that produced few perpetrators.[155] Thoroughly middle-class, Braune had been apolitical during his school years, but became acutely aware of the weakness of Germany after the war. Nonetheless, he prepared for a career in law, receiving a doctorate in Juridical Science.[156] When he was introduced to National Socialism, his life was altered permanently.

Braune's introduction to National Socialism occurred in 1930, while he was studying at the University of Jena. He accompanied some of his fellow students to a party rally where he heard Hitler speak (his story is remarkably similar to Albert Speer's). So impressed was he by Hitler's passion, he forgot his middle-class sensibility and became politically active. He joined the NSDAP in 1931, and, in the opinion of one witness, did so because of his "idealism" and unwavering faith in the ideology of the Party, particularly its anticommunism.[157] Six months later he joined the SA setting himself on a political career path.[158]

[152] Letter, Fendler to the Clemency Board for the Nuremberg War Crimes Cases, June 26, 1950, in NARA RG 466, Prisons Division, Petitions for Clemency of War Criminals, box 7, Felmy-Flick, Fendler folder; testimony of Fendler, December 13, 1947, in *Trial*, roll 5, 3986–3988; SS Record Fendler (NO 4958), in *ibid.*, roll 11, frame 0763; and, affidavit, Fendler, June 27, 1947, in *ibid.*, 0761.
[153] Letter, Fendler to the Clemency Board for the Nuremberg War Crimes Cases, *ibid.*
[154] *Ibid.*, 39 & 45–47.
[155] Mann, "'Ordinary Men' or 'Real Nazis,'" 344.
[156] Testimony, Braune, November 25, 1947, in Trial, roll 4, 3006–3007 & 3010.
[157] Dr. V.A. Günther, Braune's spiritual advisor in Oslo and his advocate between 1948 and 1951, told Clay that Braune was a "man of sterling qualities, whose personality and character are high above the average." Letter, Günther to Clay, May 9, 1949, in NARA RG 238, Advisory Board on Clemency, HICOG 1947–1950, Correspondence, box 9 (Case 9 E212), Braune folder.
[158] Testimony, Braune, November 25, 1947, in *Trial*, roll 4, 3008–3009.

Braune decided to abandon his civilian career in law and in November 1934, joined both the SD and the SS, quite a bit earlier than many of his colleagues.[159] Like Ohlendorf, Braune worked under the direction of Dr. Reinhard Höhn in the office of domestic affairs, in the realm of law and administration.[160] Two years later, he joined the Gestapo where he worked until 1941. Braune received no fewer than five SS promotions – from Second Lieutenant to Lieutenant Colonel – because, as his SS file notes, he had a "strong character and a firmly established ideology," making him a perfect candidate for promotion.[161] Braune's extensive work with the SD prompted his transfer to Russia in 1941 to head *Einsatzkommando* 11b.[162] As part of group D, Braune's unit operated in the Crimea until the end of July 1942, when he returned to Germany and resumed his work in the Gestapo offices at Halle.[163] A year later, because of "his industry and comradely behavior," he was made head of the German Academic Exchange Service or *Deutscher Akademischer Austauschdienst* in Berlin. In December 1944, he was appointed Commander of the Security Police and SD in Oslo, Norway, where he stayed until the end of the war when he was arrested by allied forces.[164] Braune devoted his entire adult career to carrying out Nazi policy.

Einsatzkommando leader Eduard Strauch was one of the most brutal and sadistic of all the defendants. Not so unusual was that he was a lawyer who had studied theology at university.[165] He was well-educated and a lawyer by training, and he was also, without a doubt, a true party zealot who abandoned his career in law to work for the Party and advance its ideals, no matter the cost. Not once during the eight-month trial did Strauch express even an iota of remorse for his actions. Until the very end, he maintained that National Socialist racial policy must be carried out. Strauch was part of the generational cohort of *Einsatzgruppen* defendants born in the first decade of the twentieth century. After the war, his parents were hit particularly hard by the inflation that swept Germany, as his father was a factory foreman. For years, he and his brother worked to help supplement the family income

---

[159] SS Record Braune (NO 3249), in *Trial*, roll 111, frames 0860–0863.

[160] Testimony, Braune, November 25, 1947, in *Trial*, roll 4, 3011 & 3018. See also "Summary of Findings of Advisory Board on Clemency" to John McCloy, September 1, 1950, in NARA RG 466, Prisons Division, box 6, Report of the HICOG Advisory Board on Clemency, part II folder; and, "Information Sheets," Peck Panel, July 1950, in NARA RG 338, JAD, WCB, Records Relating to Positional Activities, box 1, Active Impact folder.

[161] SS Record Braune (NO 3249), in *Trial*, roll 11, frames 0862–0863.

[162] Testimony, Braune, November 25, 1947, in Trial, roll 4, 3031–3033.

[163] Closing Brief against Braune, January 1948, in Mendelsohn (ed.), *The Holocaust*, vol. 18, 4–5.

[164] Affidavit, Braune, July 8, 1947, in Trial, roll 11, frame 0850; SS Record Braune (NO 3249), in ibid., frame 0863; Testimony, Braune, December 1, 1947, in ibid., roll 4, 3125–3127; and Case Record of Braune, April 27, 1948, NARA RG 466, Prisons Division, Petitions for Clemency, box 3 Blobel-Buberman, Blume folder.

[165] Wilhelm, "Die Einsatzgruppe A," 282.

so they could attend school.[166] It was during this time that Strauch was politicized. He joined the *Jungdeutsche Orden* and remained a member until the end of 1927.[167] During this period, he also attended the University of Erlangen where he received his law degree from the faculty of Jurisprudence in 1930.[168] In 1931, Strauch joined the NSDAP and SA, and not long thereafter, the SS, because he felt it was a "better organization" than the SA.[169] During the Nazi struggle for power, Strauch was also in training for a career in law. In 1932, he passed his junior law examination and, in 1934, he was appointed Section Leader (*Abschnittsführer*) of the SD in Dortmund.[170] Strauch passed his senior law exam in 1935, which in the normal course of events would secure him a position in government, but by this time he had already fashioned a career within the SD and, in any event, he was so zealous in his new career that he gave up any idea of putting his legal training to use. When war came in 1939, Strauch performed front-line duty in an anti-aircraft unit in Poland for four months. When he returned to Germany in December 1939, he was appointed Government Councillor (*Regierungsrat*) and later was made High Government Councillor (*Oberregierungsrat*) for the Regional State Police in Königsberg.[171]

On November 4, 1941, Strauch received a teletype message from Heydrich reassigning him to Riga, Latvia where he was put in charge of *Einsatzkommando* 2 of *Einsatzgruppe* A under Stahlecker and, later, Jost.[172] In February 1942, he was made commander of the Security Police and the SD in Minsk, White Russia, or modern day Belorussia, and it was there he made a name for himself. Strauch's SS record notes that his work in Minsk was "outstanding," primarily because he was able to overcome "the most varied obstacles" and carry out the difficult task of "security."[173] This commendation came after 55,000 Jews were killed in ten weeks; all the murders were carried out under Strauch's command.[174] Strauch remained in Minsk until 1943, when he was made an intelligence officer of the Higher SS and Police and transferred to Belgium.[175]

What conclusions can be drawn about the social composition of the leadership corps of the *Einsatzgruppen* tried at Nuremberg in 1947 and did they

[166] Testimony, Strauch, January 13, 1948, in *Trial*, roll 6, 4908–4909.
[167] *Ibid.*, 4913–4914.
[168] Interrogation Nr. 1643-A, Vernehmung, Strauch, 4.8.1947, in M1019, roll 72.
[169] SS Record Strauch (NO 2966), in *Trial*, roll 11, frame 0538 and Testimony, Strauch, January 13, 1948, in *ibid.*, roll 6, 4914–4915.
[170] *Ibid.*, 4921.
[171] Strauch, (NO 2966), in *ibid.*, roll 11, frames 0538–0539.
[172] *Ibid.*, and, Testimony, Strauch, January 13, 1948, in *ibid.*, roll 6, 4930–4934.
[173] *Ibid.*
[174] Letter, Wilhelm Kube to the Generalkommissar Reichskommissar for the Ostland, August 10, 1942, (PS 3428), roll 11, frames 0550–0551.
[175] Interrogation, Strauch, (1643-A), 4.8.1947, in M1019, roll 72.

have a collective route to crime? What immediately strikes this reader is that the defendants were a remarkably homogeneous group, much more so than the officer corps of the SS, a considerably more heterogeneous group than once thought. The defining features of the *Einsatzgruppen* leaders were their youth, shared experiences in their formative years, high level of educational attainment, shared confession, and the remarkable similarity of their career paths. Because they were a generational cohort, most spent their formative years in Germany during a time of extreme uncertainty and social upheaval and, given the context of their youth, most were raised to adore the military and all it stood for, as well as embrace the chauvinist type of nationalism so popular during the day.[176] This had a significant impact on their lives and their worldviews. More than 90% of them grew up in the period after the First World War, too young to serve their country on the battlefield, but old enough to be impacted by its aftermath. The war, but especially the period immediately following it, with its accompanying economic chaos and national humiliation, helped politicize these youth. Given that the vast majority had a classical education in the Weimar education system seems to strongly suggest that their collective route-to-crime was through their educational experiences. Perhaps it is not a coincidence that such a large percentage of the leaders of the mobile killing units were exceptional; after all, they were charged with one of the most important tasks of National Socialism – the war against the Jews. In any society, Nazi or otherwise, people with proven track records are frequently selected to carry out important tasks. In the case of the *Einsatzgruppen* leaders, almost certainly they would have attained important jobs even if the Nazis had never seized power, because they were the elite of their generation.

[176] Wildt, *Generation des Unbedingten*, 23–28 & 41–142.

4

Defense

Despite all of the efforts of the prosecution, everybody could see that this man
was not a "monster."

Hannah Arendt[1]

Anyone who judges history solely by the standards of morality, even the history
of the Third Reich, who categorises the leaders of National Socialism . . . simply
as an "incarnation of evil" is putting barriers in the way of his/her access to
an understanding of their career and of historical events as a whole.

Ron Smelser and Rainer Zietelmann[2]

When I began researching this topic, I asked Benjamin Ferencz if he might
consent to an interview. I asked him specifically if we could talk about Otto
Ohlendorf. His immediate reaction was to ask if I thought Ohlendorf had
"horns and a tail." What does a man responsible for mass-murder look like,
a monster? Ferencz's question highlights a common tendency by scholars
and the public alike to characterize the perpetrators of genocide, particularly
Nazis, as "beasts," "devils," "monsters," or simply "madmen."[3] Certainly

---

[1] Arendt, *Eichmann in Jerusalem*, 54.

[2] Ronald Smelser and Rainer Zitelmann, "Introduction," in *idem* (eds.), *The Nazi Elite*, trans.
Mary Fischer (New York, 1993), 5.

[3] Early interpretations by psychiatrists and psychologists promoted the idea that perpetrator behavior was extraordinary. For instance, Gustav M. Gilbert, "The Mentality of SS
Murderous Robots," *Yad Vashem Studies on the European Jewish Catastrophe and Resistance* 5 (1963), 35–41, one of the prison psychologists at the IMT proceedings, examined
the defendants at length and concluded that the SS took normal individuals and turned
them into "murderous robots." He sees the SS men as machines, devoid of conscience, pro-
grammed to be obedient. Alongside the view of the SS perpetrators as automatons, is the
social-psychological view that SS perpetrators possessed "authoritarian personalities." The
nature of this personality type is bifurcated in that the individual has both the desire to hold
power over others as well as to submit to a higher authority. The classic statements on the
authoritarian personality are Erich Fromm's *Escape from Freedom* (New York, 1965) and
Theodor Adorno et al., *The Authoritarian Personality* (1969). On the issue of obedience to
authority, see Stanley Milgram, *Obedience to Authority* (New York, 1974).

it is tempting, even fitting to do so when describing their acts, but with the exception of Paul Blobel, they did not reflect the evil they had committed. Simplistic descriptions offer little in the way of explanation for the behavior of the perpetrators of genocide and we are left wondering what induced these men to participate willingly in one of the most brutal mass murders of the twentieth century.[4] Were they predators, racists, psychopaths, or otherwise morally and intellectually depraved? A completely satisfying answer to this question is almost certainly unattainable, human nature being so inscrutable.[5] Still, as the continuing debate on ordinary men versus ordinary Germans has shown, it is important for us to attempt to understand whether it was pure antisemitism or other factors that motivated these men to act as they did.

Unable actually to question the defendants renders the task of determining what motivated them difficult, doubly so because what evidence we do have comes from direct testimony in their own criminal trial, where few admitted outright that they had committed a crime.[6] When I asked Ferencz why the prosecution did not avail itself of the opportunity to discover what motivated these men, he pointed out that in 1947, "[he] didn't want to know these defendants as human beings. [He] didn't want to know their personal family history, their foibles, their ideology. [He] had evidence that

---

[4] Social scientists once believed that the Nazi perpetrators displayed abnormal personalities. Proponents of this view analyzed psychological data collected while the Nazi leaders were awaiting trial at Nuremberg and concluded they were pathological. See, especially, Florence R. Miale and Michael Selzer, *The Nuremberg Mind: The Psychology of the Nazi Leaders* (New York, 1975). Recently, certain social scientists have challenged this orthodoxy, arguing that there was no such thing as a homogenous Nazi personality type. For example, Eric Zillmer et al., *The Quest for the Nazi Personality: A Psychological Investigation of Nazi War Criminals* (Hillsdale, NJ; 1995), have re-examined the existing evidence on Nazi war criminals. Most notably is James Waller, "Perpetrators of the Holocaust: Divided and Unitary Self Conceptions of Evildoing," *Holocaust and Genocide Studies* 1:10 (Spring, 1996), 11–33, who argues that it is social and situational forces that fundamentally alter the personalities of ordinary men turning them into murderers.

[5] Henri Zukier, "The 'Mindless Years'?: A Reconsideration of the Psychological Dimensions of the Holocaust, 1938–1945," *Holocaust and Genocide Studies* 2:11 (Fall, 1997), 190–212, argues that sociological, psychological, and historical methodology must be combined if perpetrator mentality, and motivation are to be understood.

[6] Hilberg, "Sources and Their Usage," in Michael Berenbaum and Abraham J. Peck (eds.), *The Holocaust and History: The Known, the Unknown, the Disputed, and the Reexamined* (Bloomington, 1998), 6–7, stresses the importance of post-war testimony to our understanding of the Holocaust, but he issues a caveat, "the use of recalled events for the reconstruction of a history is important but limited. The accounts may be unreliable. Some of the witnesses, particularly if they were actual or potential defendants, withheld or plainly lied about the facts . . . we are all aware of these pitfalls. But what if we are interested in the witnesses themselves, their own experiences, what is it that they remember, and the structure or style of their testimony? If we are going to study the lives or personalities of all these contemporaries, our problems will be different, but not easier."

they were mass murderers, they were going to answer for that."[7] This highlights the fundamentally different aims of history and law. The existence or proof of a motive, whereas highly desirable for prosecutors, is not necessary for the conviction of a crime. In American criminal law, the existence of a motive is in fact "immaterial when guilt is clearly established."[8] Even though policy makers had promised that the Nuremberg trials were to serve the dual purpose of punishing the guilty *and* preserving the past, law prevailed. Short on time and manpower, and with political will waning, the Nuremberg prosecutors opted to move quickly with their case, prosecuting the *Einsatzgruppen* leaders in only two days, using an abundance of damning documentary evidence and eschewing live witnesses, they did not need to prove motive, it was built into their case.[9] In 1947, everyone believed that the Nazis murdered Jews because they hated them and everyone knew that antisemitism was a fundamental tenet of Nazi ideology. Where does this leave the historian who wants to understand motive then? How can trials help us to understand the world view of perpetrators and what motivated them?

In this instance, we have a surfeit of testimony because the presiding judge was deeply interested in the motivation of the defendants and fortunately the defense team put every defendant on the stand. During testimony, the tribunal asked probing questions about their legal defense, their motives, and their moral and religious views. The answers to these questions reveal much about the defendants and their personalities, and if we include interrogations and affidavits in the analysis, we can begin to understand what motivated these men to participate in the crimes of the Third Reich. Even though the most careful analysis of this information may not provide a definitive explanation of behavior, it does help in the construction of reasonably complete profiles of the men in the dock and opens promising avenues of investigation into why this group of men acted as they did. It also helps us to understand how the defendants were able to reconcile their roles as mass murderers and how they explained it in a public forum and to the court.[10] This is neither unimportant historically, nor in contemporary terms. Understanding how

---

[7] Interview with Ferencz, May 24, 1997, 2.

[8] http://legal-dictionary.thefreedictionary.com/criminal+law.

[9] Ferencz claims it was he who made the decision to call no witnesses, because it might be difficult to locate survivors and he felt witnesses were "unreliable . . . those who would testify against any Nazi defendant would be blinded by rage and pain. Besides," he emphasized to me, "I didn't need them. I was going to hang the murderous gang by their own documents." Letter, Ferencz to Hilary Earl, February 27, 1997. On the issue of the use of the *Einsatzgruppen* reports as legal evidence at the trial, see Headland, *Messages of Murder*, 159–176.

[10] For a guide to the literature on psycho-historical approaches to the study of personality see Waller, *Becoming Evil*, 3–134.

perpetrators of genocide account for their actions publicly may help us better understand their crimes at the time they were committed.

The uniform and stereotypical portrayal of SS personnel as monstrous ideological warriors was first challenged in the 1960s with the publication of Hannah Arendt's controversial, *Eichmann in Jerusalem.*[11] After observing Adolf Eichmann's trial in Israel, Arendt put forward the idea of the banal desk murderer. She depicted Eichmann as a relatively ambitious man who openly admitted he was neither a hater of Jews nor a first-hand killer, yet whose conscientious bureaucratic activities helped facilitate the murder of hundreds of thousands of innocent people. Because of these personality traits, Arendt concluded that Eichmann was neither mad nor a monster, but, rather, an ordinary albeit ambitious man, who committed extraordinary acts of evil.[12] Arendt's thesis is inapplicable in the context of shootings on the eastern front where the perpetrators killed their victims face-to-face. It was with the publication of Browning's *Ordinary Men*, that our understanding of the motivations and behavior of the men in the field was challenged. Now, based on the work of Klaus-Michael Mallmann, Ulrich Herbert, Andrej Angrick, Alexander Rossino, and others, we can see that a more complicated depiction of the SS men in the field is emerging.[13] Unfortunately, this picture does not allow for easy characterizations. Instead, it yields a myriad of personality types and variable factors that more accurately recreate the complex human reality of events on the eastern front.

It is in this spirit, and in an effort to answer the question of motivation and accountability that the following analysis of the comments and statements of the *Einsatzgruppen* leaders indicted at Nuremberg in 1947, is offered. This chapter does not purport to be a definitive answer to the question of motivation, more research in this area needs to be undertaken before such claims can be made, but rather its aim is to cast some light on the character traits, personalities, and motives of the men who directed the mass murder of Jews on the eastern front. This, coupled with an examination of defendant comportment at trial, particularly how they responded to the charge of

[11] Early challenges to the notion of a monolithic SS monster include Reitlinger, *The SS: Alibi of a Nation*, (1957) and Koehl, *The Black Corps* (1983).
[12] Arendt, *Eichmann in Jerusalem*, 247–248.
[13] See Gerhard Paul and Klaus-Michael Mallmann (eds.), *Die Gestapo im Zweiten Weltkrieg: 'Heimfront' und besetztes Europa* (Darmstadt, 2000); *idem* (eds.), *Die Gestapo: Mythos und Realität* (Darmstadt, 1995); Ulrich Herbert, *Best: biographische studien uber Radikalismus* (Bonn, 1996) and *idem* (ed.), *National Socialist Extermination Policies: Contemporary German Perspectives and Controversies* (New York, 2000); Widt, *Generation des Unbedingten*; Angrick, *Einsatzgruppe D in der südlichen Sowjetunion*; Rossino, *Hitler Strikes Poland*; Mann, "Were the Perpetrators of Genocide 'Ordinary Men' or 'Real Nazis'; and Isabel Heinemann, "'Another Type of Perpetrator': The SS Racial Experts and Forced Population Movements in the Occupied Regions," *Holocaust and Genocide Studies* 3:12 (Winter, 2001), 387–411.

mass murder, should begin to help us better understand what motivated this particular group of men to participate in the machinery of destruction when ordered to do so.[14]

As noted in Chapter 2, Otto Ohlendorf oversaw the murder of tens of thousands of people, and was at the same time a loving husband and father with a will of his own. Ohlendorf was not an automaton, but rather an active person with agency; in essence he was a very complex personality who was motivated to direct mass murders largely because of personal conviction. The truth is that Ohlendorf would not have carried out his orders so willingly unless he believed they were right. He was a man of conviction, motivated by belief in Nazi ideology, not in the Goldhagian-sense that he was brainwashed by the SS or unduly influenced by a society that promoted murderous antisemitic values, although undoubtedly societal norms as well as SS ideology influenced him on some level, rather he implicitly believed in the Nazi racial program and had for his entire adult life.[15] His ideas came out of a very specific German cultural, social, and political milieu, born of the postwar period and reinforced through the German educational experience. There were twenty-four defendants in the dock at Nuremberg. Were they all cut from the same cloth as Ohlendorf? If not, why and how did they act differently, what motivated them, and how did they respond to the charge of mass murder?

The names of the other defendants, save for a handful, are rarely heard today, even among students of modern German history. Few have likely heard of Matthias Graf, a former officer of *Einsatzkommando 6* or Lothar Fendler, the former Deputy Chief of *Sonderkommando* 4b. These functionaries do not rank very high on the scale of Nazi perpetrators, certainly not on the same plane as Hitler, Himmler, Göring, Heydrich or even Kaltenbrunner. Yet, they were responsible for implementing policies that resulted in the murder of nearly 1 million Jewish men, women, and children, approximately one-sixth of all the Jews who perished as a result of Nazi racial policy.[16] Were these men also fathers and husbands, young academics, and ideologues like Ohlendorf, or were they simply cold-hearted murderers, even sadists? Ordinary men, such as those described by Browning in his

[14] Long ago, Alfred Streim, the former director of the *Zentrale Stelle* in Ludwigsburg, called for a more complete history of the *Einsatzgruppen*, their role in the destruction of European Jewry, and their behavior during postwar trials. He noted that a study of this kind should "describe ... the pitiful way the perpetrators tried to justify and excuse their crimes," Streim, "Tasks," 320–321.

[15] For an interesting discussion of this issue, see de Mildt, *In the Name of the People*, 4–12.

[16] The exact number of Jews killed by units of the *Einsatzgruppen* has not been determined conclusively. Estimates range from as few as half a million to as many as 2 million. Hilberg estimates that 1.3 million Jews were shot by the *Kommandos* of the *Einsatzgruppen* and other police units, *Destruction*, 1215–1219.

landmark book on Reserve Police Battalion 101, the *Einsatzgruppen* leaders certainly were not. But neither were they all eager executioners as Daniel Goldhagen contends in his controversial analysis of perpetrator motives.[17] In some ways, they were social rebels who deliberately rejected the ostensibly bourgeois values of tolerance and heterogeneity in favor of racial cohesion and military might. They were the new breed of German nationalist and vehement anti-Marxists who subscribed to Nazi ideology or at least to its nationalist-racial elements as articulated (and practiced) during the war. They were also a new breed of killer, a cross between a desk and first-hand murderer, equally comfortable in their offices working on policy or in the field, applying it.

This chapter is organized into three sections. Each section represents one of three types of Nuremberg defendant: ideological soldiers, deniers, and conflicted murderers. This paradigm is the result of the perpetrators' characterizations of their own behavior in court. The first group, ideological soldiers, comprises a majority of the defendants, men who had no regrets about the role they played in implementing Nazi racial policy; morally, this group was able to reconcile their sense of right and wrong. None showed any outward sign of mental turmoil, either during the actual killing process, or later at trial. This group of defendants tended to publicly justify their actions during the war on ideological grounds, military necessity, or some other rationalization. During trial they demonstrated absolutely no remorse; instead they spent their time in court trying to prove that what they had done was justifiable, necessary, even right.

[17] Two broad classifications of killers are identified in the historiography on the motivation of the Nazi perpetrators: desk and first hand murderers. In his study of the Final Solution, Hilberg explains that the mass murder of Europe's Jews was made possible by fastidious administrators, desk murderers, who were removed from the killing process by bureaucracy. Although their behavior was unquestionably immoral, for a variety of reasons many did not comprehend the ramifications of their actions. First hand murderers, such as members of the *Wehrmacht* and the *Ordnungspolizei* knew their job was to kill enemies of the Reich. As such, their motives differed from desk murderers. Browning identifies situational factors such as coercion, obedience to orders, and group pressure as motives. Goldhagen argues that the perpetrators were ordinary Germans who were so indoctrinated with an eliminationist type of antisemitism that when the time came they were eager to murder. On the issue of motivation, see also Lozowick, "Rollbahn Mord," 221–241; Ruth Bettina Birn, "Guilty Conscience, Antisemitism and the Personal Development of some SS Leaders," *Remembering for the Future: Working Papers and Addenda Volume 2. The Impact of the Holocaust on the Contemporary World* (New York, 1989), 2083–2092; and Edward B. Westermann, "Ordinary Men or Ideological Soldiers? Police Battalion 310 in Russia, 1942," *German Studies Review* 1:21 (February, 1998), 41–68 and *Hitler's Police Battalions: Enforcing Racial War in the East* (Lawrence, 2005) who emphasize the role of ideology in motivating the perpetrators. For a first hand look at how the perpetrators viewed their crimes, see the chilling collection of documents compiled by Ernst Klee, Willi Dreßen and Volker Riess in *'Schöne Zeiten.' Judenmord aus der Sicht der Täter und Gaffer* (Frankfurt, 1988) trans. Deborah Burnstone, *'The Good Old Days.' The Holocaust as Seen by Its Perpetrators and Bystanders* (New York, 1991).

The second group, what I call "deniers," comprises individuals whose defense strategy was to admit to nothing at all.[18] Even under intense questioning by the prosecution and in the face of mountains of documentary evidence, they never once conceded that prosecution charges had merit. Because these individuals were unwilling to admit to any crimes whatsoever, it is difficult to determine motives for their behavior. They, nonetheless, merit some discussion, especially because their defense strategy was successful in the sense that none of the deniers were sentenced to death by the tribunal, who insisted on a public admission of guilt before rendering a death sentence.

The third and final group, "conflicted murderers," are the most complex and undoubtedly controversial of all the Nuremberg defendants. Conflicted murderers comprise two types of men: those who showed remorse for their actions after the fact (at trial), and those who exhibited signs of moral conflict during the murder process. First are those who, at trial, appeared to be somewhat contrite about the part they played in Soviet Russia during the war. The second type includes men who in outward appearance seemed to have had no qualms about carrying out their murderous orders, but who by all measures seemed to personally struggle to reconcile duty with morality.[19] In practice, these individuals carried out the racial policy of the Third Reich, but often turned to alcohol or some other form of escape to dull negative feelings. Even Hilberg notes that these conflicted types continuously struggled with "psychological difficulties," holding their emotions "in check but never" completely suppressing them.[20] Just because they were conflicted, however, does not mean they were remorseful and in no way do I mean to suggest their actions were less reprehensible than their colleagues. Rather, my aim is to illustrate the complexity of human behavior that until recently has been ignored in favor of simplistic characterizations of participants of genocide. I maintain it is vital that we attempt to understand individual behavior (as opposed to group behavior) because genocide continues today with no shortage of men willing to carry it out. If we can understand why this is the case, perhaps we can understand how to identify factors that lead to this outcome.[21] The men who showed remorse after the fact as well as those who demonstrated signs of mental instability or who succumbed to alcoholism thus comprise an important group of defendants.

---

[18] Adalbert Rückerl, *Die Strafverfolgung von NS-Verbrechen 1945–1978* (Heidelberg, 1979), 85–86, the former head of the *Zentrale Stelle* in Ludwigsburg, has noted that defendants were far more likely to confess to their crimes immediately following the war than they were years later when they were prosecuted by German authorities.

[19] Henry Lea, one of the interpreters for the *Einsatzgruppen* trial recalls that Blobel appeared quite collected at trial and not at all uncertain or conflicted about his actions.

[20] Hilberg, "The Nature of the Process," 16.

[21] James Waller reminds us that the one constant in all genocides is willingness for people to participate.

TABLE 6. Einsatzgruppen *Leaders**

Group	Commanders	Date of Command
EGN A	(Franz) Walter Stahlecker	June 22, 1941–March 23, 1942
	Heinz Jost	March 29, 1942–September 2, 1942
	Humbert Achamer-Pifrader	September 10, 1942–September 4, 1943
	Friedrich Panzinger	September 5, 1943–May 1944
	Wilhelm Fuchs	May 1944–October 1944
EGN B	Arthur Nebe	June 1941–November 1941
	Erich Naumann	November 1941–March 1943
	Horst Böhme	March 12, 1943–August 28, 1943
	Erich Ehrlinger	August 28, 1943–1944
	Heinz Seetzen	April 28, 1944–August 1944
EGN C	Emil Otto Rasch	June 1941–October 1941
	Max Thomas	October 1941–August 28, 1943
	Horst Böhme	September 6, 1943–March 1944
	Lothar Fendler (Deputy Chief)	May 1941–October 2, 1941
		March 1942–July 1942
	Matthias Graf (Deputy Chief)	June 1941–October 1942
EGN D	Otto Ohlendorf	June 1941–June 1942
	Walter Bierkamp	June 30, 1942–June 15, 1943
	Willy Seibert (Deputy Chief)	May 15, 1941–August 15, 1942

* These figures come from a variety of sources including, Krausnick and Wilhelm, *Die Truppe*, 644–646, 290–291; and, French L. MacLean, *The Field Men. The SS Officers Who Led the Einsatzkommandos – the Nazi Mobile Killing Units* (Atglen, PA; 1999), 36–130.

Ideological Soldiers

With few exceptions, the defendants at Nuremberg refused to acknowledge they had done anything wrong. To do so would have betrayed Hitler, the Party, the SS, and Germany. Instead, they introduced in court five basic arguments to explain their behavior.[22] First, there were those who maintained that they executed civilians because they were ordered to do so – the so-called superior orders defense.[23] This was one of the most common defense strategies. The argument of superior orders was closely linked and frequently

[22] Jürgen Matthäus, "What About the 'Ordinary Men'?: The German Order Police and the Holocaust in the Occupied Soviet Union," *Holocaust and Genocide Studies* 2:10 (Fall, 1996), 134–150, believes antisemitism is not enough to explain perpetrator behavior. He believes that both situational and long-term factors (ideology) played a role in transforming supposedly ordinary men into evildoers, and like the defendants at Nuremberg these men used rationalizations to justify their behavior after the fact.
[23] On the defense of superior orders, see Ferencz, "Brief for the Prosecution: Analysis of the Defenses Presented on Behalf of the Accused," February 1948, in *Trial*, roll 29, frames 0012–0018.

TABLE 7. Einsatzkommando *Leaders**

Group	Kommando	Commanders	Date of Command
EGN A	Sonderkommando 1a	Martin Sandberger	May/June 1941–Autumn 1943
		Bernhard Baatz	August 1, 1943–October 15, 1944
	Sonderkommando 1b	Eduard Strauch	December 3, 1941–June 1943
		Erich Ehrlinger	May 1941–December 1941
		Erich Isselhorst	June 30, 1943–October 1943
	Einsatzkommando 2	Eduard Strauch	November 4, 1941–December 2, 1941
		Rudolf Batz	June 1, 1941–November 4, 1941
		Rudolf Lange	December 3, 1941–1944
		Manfred Pechau	October 1942–unknown
		Reinhard Breder	March 26, 1941–July 1943
	Einsatzkommando 3	Hans Joachim Böhme	May 11, 1944–January 1, 1945
		Karl Jäger	June 1941–June 1943
		Wilhelm Fuchs	September 15, 1943–May 6, 1944
EGN B	Sonderkommando 7a	Erich Naumann	November 1941–Feb./March 1943
		Walter Blume	May/June 1941–September 1941
		Eugene Steimle	September 1941–January 15, 1941
	Sonderkommando 7b	Adolf Ott	February 15, 1942–January 1943
		Gunther Rausch	June 1941–January 1943
		Karl Rabe	January 1943–October 1944
	Einsatzkommando 8	Otto Bradfisch	June 1941–April 1942
		Heinz Richter	April 1, 1942–September 1942
	Einsatzkommando 9	Oswald Schäfer	October 1941–February 1942
	Vorkommando Moscow	Alfred Six	May/June 1941–August 20, 1941
		Waldemar Klingelhöfer	August 1941–December 1941
EGN C	Sonderkommando 4a	Paul Blobel	May/June 1941–January 1942
		Eugene Steimle	August 1942–January 1943
		Erwin Weinmann	January 1942–July 1942
		Theodor Christensen	January 1943–unknown
	Sonderkommando 4b	Walter Haensch	March 1942–July 1942
		Günther Hermann	Unknown–September 1941
		Fritz Braune	October 1, 1941–March 21, 1942
		August Meier	July 1942–November 1942
		Friedrich Suhr	November 1942–August 1943
		Waldemar Krause	August 1943–January 1944
	Einsatzkommando 5	Erwin Schulz	May/June 1941–end September 1941
		August Meier	September 1941–January 1942
	Einsatzkommando 6	Ernst Biberstein	September 1942–May 1943
		Erhard Kröger	June 1941–November 1941
		Robert Mohr	November 1941–September 1942
		Friedrich Suhr	August 1943–November 1943
EGN D	Sonderkommando 10a	Heinz Seetzen	Unknown–July 1942
		Kurt Christmann	August 1, 1942–July 1943
	Sonderkommando 10b	Felix Rühl (Officer)	May/June 1941–October 1, 1941
		Alois Persterer	May 1941–February 1943
	Einsatzkommando 11	Gerhard Best	Unknown
	Einsatzkommando 11a	Paul Zapp	June 1941–July 1942
	Einsatzkommando 11b	Werner Braune	October 1941–September 1942
		Bruno Müller	February 1942–October 1942
	Einsatzkommando 12	Gustav Nosske	May/June 1941–February 1942

* These figures come from a variety of sources including, Krausnick and Wilhelm, *Die Truppe*, 644–646, 290–291; and, French L. MacLean, *The Field Men. The SS Officers Who Led the Einsatzkommandos – the Nazi Mobile Killing Units* (Atglen, PA; 1999), 36–130.

cited in connection with the second argument: military necessity or, as it was also referred to, putative justification.[24] Those who claimed necessity or putative justification said they were legally justified because their actions were carried out in presumed self-defense on behalf of a third party, the German Reich, during a state of emergency (war). In other words, executing Jews and other civilians was presumed to be necessary under the circumstances. Some defendants maintained that if all Jews were not killed, they would likely retaliate. Even children had to be liquidated because one day they would grow up to be adults and seek revenge against those who had killed their parents.

The third argument put forward by the defendants was personal necessity. This meant that if they did not carry out their orders, they themselves would be punished, perhaps even executed.[25] The fourth defense was that their actions were legal. This defense was based on the idea that the victims were killed because they were guilty of crimes such as sabotage, partisanship, theft, or conspiracy. Many of the defendants who adopted this argument claimed that those who were killed had been found guilty of partisan warfare and robbery. Some defendants told the court they had held investigations into the criminality of their victims and not everyone was found guilty, those found to be innocent were allowed to live. The fifth and final argument put forward at trial was futility and powerlessness, by which the defendants meant that, although they did not want to kill civilians, they did so anyway. To say no to their orders was futile because they were otherwise powerless to stop it. Several defendants who used this defense told the court "if I did not do it, someone else would." They claimed they felt helpless to halt the process and therefore joined it instead.[26]

---

[24] On the issue of SS officers' defense strategies at Nuremberg, see former Nuremberg prosecutor Robert Kempner, *SS im Kreuzverhör* (Munich, 1964). Helge Grabitz, *NS-Prozesse. Psychogramme der Beteiligten* (Heidelberg, 1985) provides profiles of the Nuremberg defendants and their cases. An excellent and comprehensive analysis of Ohlendorf's defense strategy is Robert Wolfe, "Putative Threat to National Security as a Nuremberg Defense for Genocide," *Annals of the American Academy of Political and Social Science* 450 (1980), 257–285.

[25] Rückerl, *Die Strafverfolgung von NS-Verbrechen*, 81, notes that necessity was also a common defense in subsequent German trials. The *Zentrale Stelle*, which investigated the many claims of necessity found it could not substantiate even one case where refusing to carry out an order resulted in bodily harm to an individual. Grabitz, *NS-Prozesse. Psychogramme der Beteiligten*, 135–144 and Grabitz, "Problems of Nazi Trials in the Federal Republic of Germany," *Holocaust and Genocide Studies* 2:3 (Spring, 1988), 202–222, says that even with the assistance of pro-Nazi organizations such as *Stille Hilfe*, no defendant before a German court has succeeded in providing evidence that would support their claim of "imminent bodily harm." Also on this subject, see David H. Kitterman, "Those who Said 'No!': Germans who Refused to Execute Civilians During World War II," *German Studies Review* 2 (May 1988), 241–254.

[26] Prosecution Notes, undated, in RG 12.000, Drawer 24, WCT, box 2, Nuremberg Supplementary Material, BBF, USHMM; and, "Einsatzgruppen Case IX," in NARA RG 260,

That so many different explanations were put forward to explain defendant behavior is significant, and indicates that there was less coordination in defense strategies than some scholars have maintained. Legal strategies differed from defendant to defendant, but cross-examination proved that these defendants were motivated by a similar ideology, especially an extreme hatred of bolshevism and the desire and willingness to eradicate it by all means. So whereas they may have claimed obedience as their principal motive, the fact was that they were motivated to act because they believed what they were doing was right. This group can unquestionably be called "ideological."

Ohlendorf was the quintessential ideological soldier, yet, in many ways his case was also exceptional. He was the first of the *Einsatzgruppen* leaders to take the stand in 1947 and was the only defendant to disclose full details of his actions as well as those of his men. One scholar, noting Ohlendorf's honest accounting, has concluded that he displayed "a certain warped devotion to principle." He was an idealist – a character trait that did not escape the attention of both the presiding judge and the chief prosecutor.[27] Idealist or not, Ohlendorf was not the least bit reluctant to tell American officials about his role in the National Socialist machinery of destruction.[28] Two years before he was indicted, he had freely confessed that, under his command, *Einsatzgruppe* D had killed 90,000 people. He had also given prosecutors further details about the inner workings of the regime and the persons most deeply involved in its crimes. These early statements coupled with the discovery of the *Einsatzgruppen* reports, limited Ohlendorf's ability to put together a convincing defense when the time came, and it certainly precluded the use of denial as a defense strategy. Nonetheless he chose to plead not guilty to the charges levelled against him. On trial for his life, it is not surprising that he would defend himself any way he could and he opted to prove his innocence by convincing the court that his actions in Russia were governed entirely by superior orders and military necessity.[29] To this end, he sought to prove he had no personal animus toward his victims. Killing, he told the court, went against his inner convictions; he carried out his orders because it was his duty.[30]

OMGUS, Functional Offices and Divisions, OCCWC, publication of Proceedings of U.S. Military Tribunals at Nuremberg 1948–1949, box 104, Publication Information folder.

[27] Wolfe, "Putative Threat," 47 and Musmanno's comments to prosecuting attorney James Heath on October 14, 1947, in *Trial*, roll 2, 628–629. An idealist in the sense that Ohlendorf believed in his convictions. Interview with Ferencz, April 24, 1997, 10.

[28] Some historians have suggested that Ohlendorf's admission was prompted by his anger at German army officials who were trying to deflect responsibility for their murderous actions in the Russian campaign onto the SS, Wolfe, "Putative Threat," 47–48.

[29] Testimony, Ohlendorf, October 8–15, 1947, in *Trial*, roll 2, 477–770.

[30] *Ibid.*, 755. Ohlendorf told Musmanno on several occasions that he did not hate his victims, not even the Bolsheviks.

Ohlendorf's compromised situation put him in a precarious legal situation. It meant that he needed to illustrate to the court his lack of personal intent. In German criminal proceedings, the court distinguishes between perpetrators and accomplices by their level of intention. If the defendant harbored any ill-will toward their victim or if he intended to kill them, he was considered a perpetrator by the court and sentenced much more harshly than if he was merely an accomplice who was following orders. This also holds true in Anglo-American law where there are gradations of guilt, and those who have aforethought to murder are sentenced more harshly than those who kill unintentionally. That Ohlendorf seemed to be orienting himself toward the role of the accomplice suggests he believed he needed to make this distinction for the court.[31] To this end, he testified that he initially had been quite reluctant to accept a leadership position in the *Einsatzgruppen* when asked to do so in 1941.[32] In other words, he was neither a willing nor intentional participant in the early formation of the *Einsatzgruppen*. The problem with this line of argument was that it was not wholly convincing given his earlier admissions.[33] Ohlendorf was no fool though. He knew exactly the unsafe position in which he had placed himself. Because he had prematurely admitted to a leadership role in the killing operations, he now portrayed himself as a cog in the wheel. He told the court that Bruno Streckenbach (head of Office I Personnel in the RSHA) gave the order (frequently referred to by the defendants as the *Führerbefehl* or *Führer*-order) to carry out the liquidations. But, even Streckenbach, was not wholly responsible he testified, because authority to issue such an important order could only ever came directly from Hitler.[34] In other words, it was the chain of command that led to the murder of Soviet Jews. Neither Streckenbach nor Ohlendorf were responsible for the *Führerbefehl*. If anyone was guilty, surely it was Hitler himself.

The nature and the timing of the *Führerbefehl* are contentious matters among historians. Although many do not believe Ohlendorf's version of events, the fact remains that very little documentary evidence has emerged to decisively settle the issue of orders. Given the central importance of the *Führerbefehl* to the trial, and the complex issues surrounding its existence, the issue will be more fully addressed in the next chapter. For now, in terms of discussing defense arguments, it is important to note that the court

---

[31] On this issue, see Devin O. Pendas, *The Frankfurt Auschwitz Trial, 1963–1965: Genocide, History, and the Limits of the Law* (Cambridge and New York, 2006), 42–43 , 54–56, and 61–71 who discusses the prosecution of Nazi genocide in the context of the limitations of German law in the Frankfurt Auschwitz trial.

[32] Closing Brief for the USA against Otto Ohlendorf, January 1948, in *ibid.*, roll 29, 3; and, testimony, Ohlendorf, October 8, 1947, in *ibid.*, roll 2, 513.

[33] Affidavits, Ohlendorf, November 5, 1945 (PS 2620) and April 24, 1947 (NO 2890) in *ibid.*, roll 11, frames 0044–0045 and 0030–0033.

[34] Testimony, Ohlendorf, October 9, 1947, in *ibid.*, roll 2, 515 and 631–633.

accepted as fact Ohlendorf's version of the *Führerbefehl* and its timing. The court believed that there was an order issued by Hitler to liquidate civilians and that it was given to the leadership of the *Einsatzgruppen* before the invasion of the Soviet Union in the summer of 1941.[35] Importantly, the court also believed that this order explained the defendants' criminal actions; the *Führerbefehl* was the reason these men were on trial for crimes against humanity. No Hitler, no crime.

Ohlendorf was savvy. When asked how he felt about carrying out the *Führer*-order, he said that naturally he was opposed to it, he even protested to Streckenbach, but to no avail.[36] He was informed (by whom he did not say, presumably Streckenbach) that it was a direct order from Hitler and, as such, it had to be carried out. Furthermore, on the prosecution's charge of crimes against humanity, he did not believe the underlying purpose of Hitler's order was to murder Jews because they were racially or religiously inferior. Rather the purpose of killing the Jews was to destroy bolshevism in Russia where Jews "played a disproportionately important role."[37] In other words, killing Jews was an act of war. Killing children was militarily necessary too, he claimed, because they posed a possible security risk, especially when they reached adulthood and could avenge the death of their parents.[38] He had no choice but to obey the order because "no subordinate can take it upon himself to examine the authority of the supreme commander and chief of state," and in any event, anyone who dared refuse the order risked "immediate death."[39] Besides, he said, he always disagreed with the order to kill, but because it was his duty to do so, he carried it out "humanely" and without "excess," by which he meant humiliating the victims unnecessarily before death; his men shot the victims in military fashion, not for sport or pleasure.[40]

The first defendant to take the stand, Ohlendorf was also the only defendant the prosecution questioned at length about the morality of the Hitler order. On this issue Ohlendorf remained adamant. The order was wrong he explained, but it was nonetheless an order and as such he had to obey it. As to its morality, he never considered the matter one way or the other, he told the court, because it was not his place, as a soldier, to judge the *Führer* or his decisions, it was simply his duty.[41] Musmanno was totally unsatisfied with his answer. Wanting to learn more about Ohlendorf's views on the

---

[35] For example, Ferencz notes as late as 1950 that he had no doubt there was an order from Hitler. Letter, Ferencz to Nehemiah Robinson, July 31, 1950, RG 12.002.02.04 BBF, USHMM.

[36] Testimony, Ohlendorf, October 9, 1947, in *Trial*, roll 2, 631–633.

[37] *Ibid.*, 517–522.

[38] *Ibid.*, 528 and 662–665.

[39] *Ibid.*, 519 and 523.

[40] *Ibid.*, 523–524.

[41] *Ibid.*, 740–752.

FIGURE 6. Ohlendorf in court, USHMM photo archive (#43038)

morality of killing civilians he made the unusual move to pose a hypothetical scenario: if Ohlendorf had been given the order to kill his sister, would
he not have considered "whether it was right or wrong – morally – not
politically or militarily, but as a matter of humanity, conscience, and justice
between man and man?"[42] Ohlendorf refused the bait and did not answer
the question. He said it was like comparing apples and oranges, "it brings
a completely private matter into a military one; that is, it deals with two
events which have nothing to do with one another."[43] Clearly frustrated,
Musmanno insisted that Ohlendorf answer his question. Because Ohlendorf's defense rested on the idea of obedience to orders it is not surprising
that he eventually responded in the affirmative. As a soldier, he would have

[42] Cross-examination of Ohlendorf by Musmanno, October 15, 1947, in *ibid.*, roll 2, 750.
Aschenauer strenuously objected to the hypothetical question. Musmanno acknowledged
that under different circumstances such a question would not be allowed to be asked, but
given that this trial was "dealing with a charge of [genocide] . . . that has never been presented
in history of the human race," the question was allowed.
[43] Testimony, Ohlendorf, October 15, 1947, in *ibid.*, roll 2, 752.

executed his sister had he been ordered to do so he claimed – if not entirely convincingly.[44]

Ohlendorf was an intelligent and articulate man; he was also part maverick and a contrarian who rarely kept his opinions to himself. His need to express his views got him into trouble and at trial backed him into a corner. During his testimony he tried to portray himself as fundamentally opposed to Hitler's order to kill Soviet Jewry, whereas maintaining that he carried out the order because it was militarily necessary and his duty: a claim that is at best contradictory and at worst an outright lie. On the basis of what is known about his personality, it seems most unlikely that this independent-minded individual, who frequently voiced his opposition to National Socialist policies with which he disagreed (indeed, fashioned a career out of doing), would carry out an order he disagreed with so fundamentally. As noted earlier, Ohlendorf was willful and opinionated. He was not afraid to voice dissident opinions, even when they threatened to short circuit his career or land him in jail. On other matters he did not follow orders blindly. His often-stated views on those aspects of National Socialism with which he disagreed, in fact, earned him a reputation as an independent thinker rather than a passive follower. For instance, during trial he told the court that twice he had refused Heydrich's order to command an *Einsatzgruppe* and had suffered no adverse consequences. He also admitted that while he was leader of *Einsatzgruppe* D, he did not kill mentally ill persons, despite having been ordered to do so, because he did not agree with the order.[45] Even if this is untrue and his unit did kill the mentally ill, the fact remains that he painted a contradictory picture of himself to the court. He wanted the court to believe that he was, at once a man who made a career out of criticizing the weaknesses and foibles of the regime, hence an opponent of National Socialism, yet he was also an obedient soldier, who should not be held legally accountable for the crimes of the regime because he had no choice but to obey.

Ohlendorf's life is peppered with incidents in which he did not conform to established policy, all of which cast doubt on the validity of his defense. Early in his career, while working as Assistant Director at the Institute of World Economics in Kiel, he had landed in jail for teaching economic ideas contrary to National Socialist ideology and policy.[46] While working in the offices of the SD, he had several disagreements with Himmler, Ley, Goebbels, and Bormann, about the nature of Nazi policy, and as head of *Amt* III (Domestic Intelligence) he became a sort of devil's advocate, developing a reputation

[44] *Ibid.*
[45] *Ibid.*, 552.
[46] Lawrence D. Stokes, "Otto Ohlendorf, the Sicherheitsdienst and Public Opinion in Nazi Germany," in George Mosse (ed.), *Police Forces in History* (Beverly Hills, 1977), 234.

as the voice of opposition within high-ranking party circles.[47] Throughout his career as a National Socialist, Ohlendorf had been a maverick. To argue as he did in court that he could not disobey an order he disagreed with was entirely inconsistent with his previous record and totally out of character. Certainly, Ohlendorf was a committed National Socialist, but only when the commitment was to ideas that conformed to his personal beliefs. Ohlendorf did not blindly carry out orders; his actions, as always, were motivated by conviction. In the final analysis, any attempt to portray Ohlendorf as an "obedient soldier" fails. He was an independent player who carried out orders, in essence, for essentially ideological reasons.

Ohlendorf was not the only defendant to claim he acted because of superior orders but who, in reality, agreed fully with Nazi racial policy. Four others offered the same defense. Blume, Braune, Naumann, and Ott all conceded they supervised mass murder because they were ordered to. Space precludes a full discussion of all four men, but the case of Blume, is telling and is examined in some detail here.

Blume is a good example of the many *Einsatzgruppen* commanders who rose rapidly within the Party. He joined the SS in 1935 as an *Untersturmführer* and by 1941 had risen to the rank of *Standartenführer*.[48] Prior to joining the *Einsatzgruppen* in the spring of 1941, he held positions with the Dortmund police, the state police in Hannover, and the Prussian Secret State Police. In the late spring of 1941, while working in *Amt* I of the RSHA, Blume was notified he should proceed to Pretzsch, a town on the Elbe River, for police work. It was here that the *Einsatzgruppen* men assembled to prepare for Operation Barbarossa, and where Blume first learned of his assignment to head *Sonderkommando* 7a of *Einsatzgruppe* B under the authority of Arthur Nebe.[49]

When Blume found out the true nature of his assignment just days before the invasion of the Soviet Union on June 22, 1941, he claimed he recalled having mixed feelings. On the one hand, he agreed "in principle" with Nazi racial policy, that a solution to the Jewish problem was necessary, but on the other he did not "desire" a solution that included murder; rather, he hoped a program of forced emigration would suffice. Nonetheless, he conceded that despite his misgivings, he trusted Hitler fully and was certain he had considered all options carefully. Thus, his only "ethical" option, as a soldier who had pledged himself to the *Führer*, was to carry out the order. Besides, he reasoned, the true enemy was bolshevism and the "Jews of Soviet Russia were . . . the intellectual bearers of" that hated ideology.[50] Even

---

[47] *Ibid.*, 237 and 257; and, Testimony, Ohlendorf, October 15, 1947, in *Trial*, roll 2, 565.

[48] SS Record Blume (NO 3245), in *ibid.*, roll 11, frame 0629.

[49] Affidavit, Blume, June 29, 1947 (NO 4145), in *ibid.*, roll 11, frames 0046–0047; and, Testimony of Blume, October 31, 1947, in *ibid.*, roll 3, 1762–1763.

[50] Testimony, Blume, October 31, 1947, in *ibid.*, roll 3, 1768–1770 and 1761.

though he considered his task in Russia odious, apparently it never occurred to Blume that he might try to circumvent the order or to ask to be relieved of his commission; instead, he justified his actions to the court on military grounds.[51]

Blume, like Ohlendorf, argued that he was not criminally responsible for his acts or those of his *Kommando* because he was following orders. What seems to have motivated him was his genuine admiration of Hitler. He told the court that Hitler had a "courageous character" and "a great mission for the German people" and he would have done anything the *Führer* ordered.[52] While we know that many in the Third Reich "worked toward the *Führer*," Musmanno reminds us that charisma alone did not kill 1 million people. Human agency also played a role. The judgment states "that Hitler with all his cunning and unmitigated evil would have remained as innocuous as a rambling crank if he did not have the Blumes, the Blobels, the Braunes and Bibersteins to do his bidding, to mention only the B's."[53] In other words: no Walter Blume, no genocide.

During cross examination, Blume told the tribunal he found the work of the *Einsatzgruppen* distasteful, something Germans should not have to do. To this Musmanno quipped that if he found the job so repugnant, perhaps he should have falsified reports and lied to his superiors. Blume's consciousness had become so nazified that he believed it more nefarious to falsify records to his superiors than to shoot innocent people.[54] Blume may have been able to live with this task, but he worried the job might be too much psychologically for his men. To alleviate their anxieties and take their minds off their daily routine, he organized regular excursions for his men who were "particularly grateful," he noted, for the opportunity to play sports and sing songs after carrying out their murderous tasks.[55]

Blume's testimony rings hollow, however. It seems doubtful that he ever fully confronted the moral choices he had made by accepting a position of responsibility with the *Einsatzgruppen*. Rather, it appears that even with his life in the balance in a court of law, he was unable to mask his true beliefs. He supported Nazism and its ideology and he admired Hitler, for whom he would do anything. The only aspect of his job that he felt any reservations about was the brutalizing effect first-hand killing had on his men. In the

---

[51] *Ibid.*, 1772–1773.

[52] *Ibid.*, 1760 and Judgment, April 8, 1948, in *ibid.*, roll 29, 158.

[53] *Ibid.*, 159.

[54] Koonz, *Nazi Conscience* has shown that it took but a few years for the Third Reich to transform the morality of entire groups of people, including the SS.

[55] Musmanno, *Eichmann Kommandos*, 164. Christian Streit, "Wehrmacht, Einsatzgruppen, Soviet POWs and Anti-Bolshevism in the Emergence of the Final Solution," in David Cesarani (ed.), *The Final Solution: Origins and Implementation* (New York, 1994), n. 27, 116 notes that, on December 12, 1941, Himmler issued an order to the *Einsatzkommando* leaders to take care that their men did not become brutalized by their jobs.

end, it seems likely that Blume never confronted his own complicity; why else would he admit to his actions? Like many SS men at war's end, he fled to Austria to avoid arrest indicating some awareness that he might be held accountable for his wartime actions. He was captured in August 1945, but less than a year later was released from custody for unspecified reasons. He was re-arrested in June 1947 while working as a farmhand and charged with war crimes.[56]

Werner Braune was a youthful and well-educated ideological soldier who became involved in politics in 1930 while at university.[57] He tells the same story as so many of his generation: that he was utterly taken in by Hitler when he first heard him speak at a Party rally, so much so that he immediately became a committed National Socialist.[58] He worked for the SS and SD, and then in 1936, the Gestapo hired him. He worked for the Gestapo until 1941, when his extensive police work and his "strong character and firmly established ideology" prompted his transfer to Russia to head *Einsatzkommando* 11b of *Einsatzgruppe* D.[59] He soon discovered his job included the "difficult task" of murder.[60]

Braune followed Ohlendorf's lead admitting he was the leader of a *Kommando* that killed thousands of people. Speaking of the so-called Christmas massacre at Simferopol in December 1941, where thousands of innocent people were killed, Braune's counsel asked him if he supervised the executions. "Yes," he said unhesitatingly. The murders "took place under my responsibility."[61] Using a wall map Braune "obligingly and courteously" described the activities and areas of operation of the various *Kommando* units, "with the ease and detachment of a college professor lecturing to a class of students."[62] Like Ohlendorf, Braune justified his actions on the grounds of superior orders, stating that he considered himself a "small wheel in a large machinery," and had no choice but to obey.[63] Although Hilberg's metaphor may well be fitting, Braune accepted no personal responsibility nor expressed any remorse for his actions. Instead, he placed blame on his superiors, Hitler and Himmler, who had told him he would not be held

---

[56] Petition for Clemency, Blume, June 6, 1950, in NARA RG 466, Prisons Division, Petitions for Clemency, box 3, Blume folder.

[57] Case Record Braune, April 27, 1948 in NARA RG 338, Landsberg, Records Relating to Executed Prisoners January 2, 1946–June 7, 1951, box 2, Braune folder.

[58] Dr. Günther, Braune's spiritual advisor while imprisoned in Oslo and advocate between 1948 and 1951, told Clay that Braune was a "man of sterling qualities, whose personality and character are high above the average." Letter, V. A. Günther to Clay, May 9, 1949, in NARA RG 238, Advisory Board on Clemency, HICOG 1947–1950, Correspondence, box 9 (case 9 E212), Braune folder.

[59] SS Record Braune (NO 3249), in *Trial*, roll 11, frames 0860–0863.

[60] Testimony, Braune, November 25, 1947, in *ibid.*, roll 4, 3033–3034.

[61] *Ibid.*, 3094.

[62] Musmanno, *Eichmann Kommandos*, 135.

[63] Testimony, Braune, November 25, 1947, in *Trial*, roll 4, 3035 and 3047–3048.

personally responsible for his actions.[64] His direct superior, Ohlendorf was responsible for giving him the orders. Even his subordinate Erwin Schulz was partially responsible as head of a sub-Kommando.[65] For Braune, mass executions posed neither moral nor ethical questions, they were committed out of necessity; that is, because Hitler deemed it necessary to kill Russian Jewry, it was incumbent on him to carry out the order. Besides, Braune argued, the war in the east was against bolshevism and everyone knew that Jews and Bolsheviks were synonymous.[66] Braune had no qualms admitting he supervised executions because, like Ohlendorf, he agreed with National Socialist racial policy. That both Braune and Ohlendorf elected to explain their actions along military lines had tremendous repercussions; their courtroom strategy cost them their lives.

Erich Naumann, a deceitful individual whose defense strategy was blatantly evasive, was arrested in May 1945 by American forces while in hiding in Bavaria under the assumed name Rudolf Beegen. Not knowing who he was, the Americans released him. When his former secretary Marga Perl identified him in 1947, he was promptly re-arrested. As was common during this period to evade the allies, Naumann worked as a farm laboer.[67] Reports indicate he went farther than most to avoid detection, murdering his personal driver and assuming his identity.[68] Before his appointment to the *Einsatzgruppen*, Naumann had served the SS in a number of capacities. He had been head of Department III/2 of the SD Main Office and worked under the authority of Heinz Jost (leader of *Einsatzgruppe* A). In 1936, he had been made Section Chief (*Abschnittsführer*) in Nuremberg, and was promoted to *Oberabschnittsführer* in Stettin the following year. In 1938, he had held the same position in Austria until he was transferred back to Berlin and made an inspector of the Security Police and SD. Between September and November 1939 he served as head of *Einsatzgruppe* VI in Poland and was awarded the Iron Cross Second Class for his service.[69] Naumann received several other promotions finishing his career as a SS-*Brigadeführer*

[64] *Ibid.*, 3035.
[65] *Ibid.*, 3094.
[66] *Ibid.*, 3049.
[67] Identification of Prisoner, Dachau Detachment 7708 War Crimes Group, Case No: 12-3192-B, April 29, 1947 in NARA RG 238, OCCWC, Executive Office, Nuremberg Military Post, 201 Files 1945–1948, box 21, Naumann folder. An illustration of how common aliases were can be found in Rückerl, *Die Strafverfolgung von NS-Verbrechen 1945–1978*, 143–144 n.4.
[68] Investigation of Erich Naumann by Lt. Bohn of the CIC, Detachment 334, Unter-Traunstein, undated in NARA RG 238, OCCWC, Office File, Office File Materials, box 2, SS General folder.
[69] Krausnick, *Die Truppe des Weltanschauungskrieges*, 34; Testimony, Naumann, October 16, 1947, in *Trial*, roll 2, 806–808; Eidesstattliche Erklärung, Naumann, June 27, 1947 (NO 4150), in *ibid.*, roll 9, frame 0812; and, SS Record Naumann (NO 2970), in *ibid.*, frame 0817–1919.

and was awarded the Iron Cross First Class after returning from Russia.[70] On orders from Heydrich, he was made head of *Einsatzgruppe* B, replacing Arthur Nebe in November 1941. Given his service to the state, his contention at Nuremberg that he had to obey this order or be shot was less than convincing.[71]

Naumann served as head of *Einsatzgruppe* B (headquartered in Smolensk) until February–March 1943. The documentary evidence shows that Naumann's *Kommandos* killed tens of thousands of people. In the absence of any exculpatory evidence, his attorney, Dr. Hans Gawlik – an experienced Nuremberg attorney who had defended the SD at the IMT trial and who later was to become head of the *Zentrale Rechtsschutzstelle* (the Main Office for the Legal Protection of War Criminals) part of the Federal Republic's Justice Department,[72] mounted a defense designed to prove that the *Führerbefehl* to murder Soviet Jews, was issued before Naumann arrived in Russia.[73] According to this line of argument, Naumann was not responsible for the murders his *Kommando* carried out because he did not issue the order himself. Gawlik's defense of Naumann rested on a precedent set in a previous trial, the Milch case, where the judges ruled that knowledge alone was not sufficient to find one guilty of "crimes against humanity," rather one must have actually committed murder or at least have given the order to do so to be found guilty. By his own admission, Naumann had not personally killed anyone; therefore, Gawlik's goal was to demonstrate his client had never issued orders to kill.[74] Naumann did admit that those under his command killed people, but maintained this was done as a security measure in response to partisan activity resulting in the death of thirty-one of his men. He claimed the executions did not occur simply because the victims were Jews. Perhaps Naumann thought this line of defense valid because an important element of indoctrination of the *Kommandos* was to be told repeatedly that all Jews were partisans and all partisans were Jews.[75] One historian has contended that it would be a serious error to underestimate the significance of this type of indoctrination, for whether or not it was believed, it offered the perpetrators a legitimate military reason to commit murder, and thus

---

[70] *Ibid.*, 0817–0920.

[71] Testimony, Naumann, October 16, 1947, in *ibid.*, roll 2, 806.

[72] Gawlik took this position in 1949, when the German Basic Law made provisions for the establishment of a legal organization to help prisoners of foreign governments. Conot, *Justice at Nuremberg*, 464.

[73] This was a defense organization for German war criminals tried before foreign courts. The central office was located in Bonn. It was founded and funded by the German Government in 1949, as part of the Basic Law, but was administered by the Ministry of Justice and later the Foreign Ministry. See Ernst Klee, *Persilscheine und falsche Pässe* (Frankfurt, 1991), 131.

[74] Defense argument by Gawlik, for Naumann, October 16, 1947, in *Trial*, roll 2, 821.

[75] Testimony, Naumann, October 16, 1947, in *ibid.*, 828–830. According to Streit, *Keine Kameraden*, 121–122, participants of ideological training were taught that Jews, Bolsheviks, and partisans were indistinguishable.

helped them overcome any inhibitions they still might harbor about killing civilians.[76] It also offered them a legal defense after the war.

Even though Naumann and Gawlik tried their best to downplay his responsibility, the court already knew perfectly well he was concealing something. Naumann's duplicity is made clear in a letter he secretly gave to co-defendant Klingelhöfer the night Klingelhöfer had attempted suicide in July 1947. The letter was confiscated by American authorities and was entered into evidence against Naumann. It is worth quoting at length as it illustrates Naumann's knowledge of criminality:

Do not be bluffed during interrogations! Always be careful, even with the friendliest face! My statements until now:... The beginning of my tour of duty; end of November 1941. At that time there were no ghettos left in my area. The large scale executions of the first period fell into Nebe's time.... Troop Smolensk was led by some small Sturmscharführer or Unsturführer, whose name I do not know any more. Troop Smolensk belonged first to EK 9. The number of persons executed by Einsatzgruppe B was not registered in the Group Staff. I therefore cannot make any statements about this. I gave no more execution orders because these were already given by Heydrich and Nebe to the SK and EK B received 2 or 3 gas vans from Berlin which were not used by B and therefore, under directions of the RSHA, were given to C. Written reports went to Berlin about every three weeks. There was also no total of executions contained therein. They contained mainly a description of the situation from a Security Police point of view and a voluminous SD report. Beginning in spring 1942, the main activity of the Einsatzgruppe B changed to partisan reconnaissance and to the formation of police forces of indigenous persons (OD). This court has NO [his emphasis] original reports of Einsatzgruppe B and also no files; just information reports issued by the RSHA and these are incomplete. These reports were first issued in 1942. About your activity in Gahaisk and Smolensk this court has no records.[77]

This letter is an obvious attempt to influence Klingelhöfer's testimony. After reading the letter, the prosecution concluded that Naumann was attempting to conceal the truth and had not been, as he maintained, offering friendly advice to his colleague.[78] The court had ample reason to treat Naumann's testimony as suspect.

Naumann's testimony did not mask his guilt nor did it disguise the dark side of his character. During cross-examination Ferencz asked him whether or not he felt any "guilt or remorse." Initially, Naumann evaded the question, stating that everyone connected with the *Führer*-order experienced "considerable moral difficulties," but guilt or remorse, he thought for a moment and then stated, "no," he could only feel remorse for "crimes I personally commit. If I myself had carried out killings and cruelties then I would

[76] Streit, "Wehrmacht, Einsatzgruppen, Soviet POWs," 111.
[77] Letter, Naumann to Klingelhöfer, July 3, 1947 (NO 5450), in *Trial*, roll 12, frames 0380–0381.
[78] Testimony, Naumann, October 17, 1947, in *ibid.*, roll 2, 885 and Trial Brief for the USA against Naumann, January 1948, in Mendelsohn (ed.), *The Holocaust*, vol. 18, 70.

have to feel guilt and remorse. If I have carried out an order then I have no guilt at all, and therefore, no remorse."[79] He revealed a great deal more of himself when Musmanno asked if he agreed with the *Führer*-order or had any misgivings about it. He admitted that he did, in fact, agree with the order to kill Jews "because it was part of our aim of the war and therefore it was necessary." Musmanno recalled being stunned by Naumann's response as he had expected the defendant to respond as others had, to state that inwardly at least, they disagreed with it. With a judge who imagined that Naumann moved to Wagner's *Götterdämmerung*, it is not surprising that Naumann's fate was sealed.[80] His own testimony, coupled with the documentary evidence against him only added another nail in is coffin.

Heinz Jost did not rely exclusively on the defense of superior orders, instead he presented a baffling array of defenses, although for the most part he tried to avoid responsibility for his actions simply by denying that he did anything wrong. He told the court that while he disagreed with the Hitler order, he had to carry it out because his superior issued it, and he would be punished if he failed to do so. At the same time, he attempted to prove (unconvincingly) that he was emotionally conflicted by his actions in Russia. Because he relied on this strange amalgam of defenses, Jost's motivation is difficult to discern. It is clear that part of his defense was to prove he carried out his orders under duress. His defense strategy appears to have come out of desperation, saying whatever appeared strategic at the moment, hoping this would help him win an acquittal. Jost, like so many of his co-defendants was a lawyer; however, he had joined the NSDAP in 1928, much earlier than most of the others. By 1934, he was a chief in the Gestapo. Later Heydrich promoted him to *Amtschef*, first in the office of the *SD-Ausland*, and after the reorganization of the SD, to the top spot of *Amt* VI (Foreign Intelligence) of the RSHA.[81]

As head of *Amt* VI, an Old Fighter, and an SS-*Brigadeführer* Jost was a logical choice to command an *Einsatzgruppe*, but he somehow managed to avoid the assignment for nearly a year. It was not until the death of Walter Stahlecker, in the spring of 1942, that Heydrich appointed him *Gruppenchef* of *Einsatzgruppe* A, which was attached to Army Group North and whose area of operation was the Baltic region.[82] Jost testified that Heydrich catapulted him into the position as punishment for his "soft" disposition and persistent and extreme reluctance to supervise the gruesome tasks of the killing squads. Jost also claimed that Heydrich had promised

[79] Testimony, Naumann, October 17, 1947, in *Trial*, roll 2, 886.

[80] Musmanno, *Eichmann Kommandos*, 158–161.

[81] Testimony, Jost, October 21, 1947, in *Trial*, roll 2, 1133 and 1143; and, Information Sheet, Jost, 20.6.1950, B305/146, Deutsche Kriegsverurteilte im Landsberg, Einzelfälle, 1949–1950, BA. See also Höhne, *Death's Head*, 101 and 243–244.

[82] Testimony, Jost, October 21, 1947, in *Trial*, roll 2, 1155 and 1199; Wilhelm, *Die Truppe*, 285 and Interrogation Summary No. 2066, Jost, May 2, 1947, M1019, roll 32.

him his only tasks would be administrative and that he would not have to supervise executions personally.[83] Although this last claim is clearly untrue, it is possible that Jost was given the assignment as punishment, but it is more likely that Heydrich was attempting to help him rehabilitate his SS career. By taking on a leadership position in the *Einsatzgruppen* he could restore his prestige by doing "good work" for the regime, especially after being fired for incompetence as head of *Amt* VI in August 1941.

Jost suffered from both thyroid disease and rheumatism and at trial he appeared frail. He claimed both illnesses were a direct consequence of the stress of his job and the inner conflict he experienced while carrying out his orders in the east and that he believed murdering Jews was "unnecessary."[84] He claimed he had done everything in his power to have the order revoked even though he offered no evidence to support the claim. Further, he argued that he had no choice but to obey because Heydrich threatened him with death if he refused.[85] This argument completely contradicted his earlier claim that Heydrich had promised him he would not have to carry out any "executive actions."[86]

Desperate people do desperate things, and Jost, like the majority of the defendants, offered a bevy of arguments undoubtedly hoping beyond hope that the court would believe one of them. Jost was unconvincing in his claim of superior orders under duress, so he buffered it with the claim he suffered from a severe case of inner conflict. Nearly all his supporting evidence made the same case: he was a decent man devoted to National Socialist ideas, but he disagreed fundamentally with Nazi Jewish policy – in his "heart."[87] What evidence did Jost produce to prove his inner conflict? Werner Best, legal adviser to Reinhard Heydrich and, later, Reich Plenipotentiary in Denmark, testified that Jost was a weak person "burdened with inhibitions." According to Best, Heydrich found Jost's weakness distasteful and that is why he was dismissed as head of *Amt* VI.[88] Even though he was officially stationed

---

[83] Jost's assertion that he was being punished might very well be correct, because Heydrich had fired him from his position as Office Chief because of his incompetence. See Black, *Ernst Kaltenbrunner*, 177. Testimony, Jost, October 21, 1947, in *Trial*, roll 2, 1143–1144 and October 22, 1947, roll 2, 1149–1152; and, Trial Brief of the Prosecution against Jost, in *ibid.*, roll 29, 2.

[84] Musmanno, *Eichmann Kommandos*, 186–187 and Testimony, Jost, October 22, 1947, in *Trial*, roll 2, 1164.

[85] *Ibid.*, October 23, 1947, 1257 and 1262–1263.

[86] The defendants frequently distinguished between "executive" and other actions, the former meaning murder and the latter administrative duties.

[87] For example see affidavit, Arthur Deeken, September 29, 1947, in *Trial*, roll 26, frames 0713–0714; affidavit, Heinrich Eissfeller, October 4, 1947, in *ibid.*, frames 0715–0718; and, affidavit, Edgar Thomashausen, October 4, 1947, in *ibid.*, frames 0719–0728.

[88] Affidavit, Werner Best, October 16, 1947, in *ibid.*, frame 0751. Best's affidavit contradicts Walter Schellenberg's, who claimed Jost had been the subject of an internal investigation over illegal money-lending practices with a large banking house in Prague. When Heydrich found

in the east for nearly seven months, there is some evidence to suggest he did try to avoid his job as commander. Not only did he leave his group after only a few weeks at the front, but his personal physician, Dr. Wolfgang Wohlgemuth, testified that Jost suffered from a nervous disorder that resulted from the "discrepancy between [his] inner views and the demands of his office that resulted in mental tensions" and led to the "illness which [he] observed in Jost in 1941/42 and later."[89] Neither the tribunal nor the civilian psychiatrist who examined Jost accepted this diagnosis. Dr. Spradley, the American psychiatrist assigned to assess the mental health of the NMT defendants, went so far as to suggest that Jost was not conflicted at all, but rather he was a "cold, calculating type of individual" who displayed "sadistic" tendencies, and whose emotional world was bankrupt.[90] In the tribunal's view, Jost's credibility was compromised because of "irrefutable [evidence] that he was a principal in and an accessory to the extermination program in his territory."[91]

Martin Sandberger was another *Einsatzgruppe* leader with an education in law who became an ideological soldier of the Third Reich. Born in 1911 in Berlin, he grew-up in southwestern Germany, receiving a Doctor of Laws in 1935.[92] Sandberger worked for the Ministries of Justice and Interior before he joined the SD to serve as head of the Reich Student Leaders to promote the virtues of National Socialism.[93] In May 1941 he was transferred to the *Einsatzgruppen* after Heydrich ordered him to Pretzsch where he was made head of *Sonderkommando* 1a of *Einsatzgruppen* A.[94] On June 23, he and his *Sonderkommando* proceeded to Riga, Latvia, and in August to Reval, Estonia where he commanded his unit for two years.[95]

Although he did not deny knowledge of the order to murder the Jews, as did some of his co-defendants, Sandberger was extremely evasive and his responses were so convoluted that the tribunal often had difficulty making sense of them. He told the court he learned about the *Führerbefehl* while in Pretzsch, but he objected to it and asked his superior, SS *Brigadeführer* Bruno Streckenbach, if he could transfer to the *Wehrmacht* instead. Apparently,

---

out about this he was infuriated and the only thing that saved Jost from severe punishment, according to Schellenberg, was that he was an old Party member and Heydrich and Frau Jost were close friends. See Report on the case of Walter Friedrich Schellenberg, undated in NARA RG 238, OCCPAC, Schellenberg, box 50 E160, Schellenberg Report folder.

[89] Höhne, *Death's Head*, 404 and Affidavit, Wolfgang Wohlgemuth, January 15, 1948, in *Trial*, roll 26, fame 0854.

[90] Neuro-Psychiatric examination of Heinz Jost by Dr. Spradley, June 26, 1950, in NARA RG 466, Prisons Division, Petitions for Clemency, box 13, Jost folder.

[91] Judgment, April 8, 1948, in *Trial*, roll 29, 137.

[92] Eidesstattliche Erklärung, Sandberger, April 23, 1947, in M1019, roll 61; Testimony, Martin Sandberger, November 7, 1947, in *Trial*, roll 3, 2141; and affidavit, Sandberger (NO 2891), in *ibid.*, roll 11, frame 0591.

[93] Browder, *Hitler's Enforcers*, 222.

[94] Affidavit, Sandberger (NO 2891), in *Trial*, roll 11, frame 0591.

[95] Testimony, Sandberger, November 12, 1947, in *Trial*, roll 3, 2161–2166.

Streckenbach refused on the grounds of personnel shortages.[96] Throughout the trial, Sandberger, described as "round-faced and juvenile-looking," maintained his innocence claiming that on at least seven separate occasions he asked to be released from his duties in Russia.[97] This claim is suspect, however, because none of his co-defendants were forced to stay in the east for longer than a few months (Sandberger stayed for twenty-six months) and those who did stay for extended periods, such as Ohlendorf, did so by choice. Had Sandberger really desired to be relieved of his duties he could have asked for a release after a few months and very likely his request would have been granted.

Sandberger denied he was responsible for any illegal executions – his implication is that there is such a thing as a legal execution. He told the tribunal he never openly protested the *Führerbefehl*, even though he sincerely objected to it, because he feared disobedience or dissent would lead to his own "martyrdom." The truth is Sandberger never gave the order a second thought, believing it legal because it came directly from Hitler, who was in his opinion, the "supreme legislator."[98] Even in the face of numerous documents pointing to his culpability, he denied any wrongdoing whatsoever. He blamed the Estonian police and Home Guard for all "illegal executions," for they hated the Jews for the role they allegedly played in the communist takeover of their country.[99] The few executions his group carried out, he said, followed fair trials, the same procedure offered all suspected criminals, including Jews. They were executed, not because they were Jews, Sandberger insisted, but because after exhaustive investigations it was determined they were communist functionaries, and, therefore, a legitimate security risk.[100]

Sandberger's SS personnel record cites the "better than average intensity in his work" in the east and his "irreproachable politics" as reason for promotions he received when he returned from Estonia.[101] This strongly suggests that his account of the activities of his group was fictitious. Musmanno recalled that Sandberger "conveyed the impression of someone telling tall stories at a crowded bar," many of which were preposterous, especially Sandberger's claim that each individual slated for execution was entitled to, and indeed had his case reviewed. If those interned by his *Kommando* were found guilty, Sandberger maintained, they could appeal![102] That Sandberger thought the court would believe him seems outrageous, but to admit guilt

96 Testimony, Sandberger, November 7, 1947, in *ibid.*, 2152.
97 Musmanno, *Eichmann Kommandos*, 174.
98 Testimony, Sandberger, November 7, 1947, in *Trial*, roll 3, 2154 and 2157 and November 13, 1947, 2310.
99 *Ibid.*, 2184 and November 13, 1947, 2249–2253.
100 *Ibid.*; and, November 12–13, 1947, 2245–2265.
101 Memorandum, SS Standartenführer Ehrlinger, July 20, 1944 (NO 5045), in *ibid.*, roll 12, frames 0402–0403.
102 Musmanno, *Eichmann Kommandos*, 174.

would have been tantamount to questioning the convictions he had nurtured since his youth.

Quite telling of ideological soldiers was their demonstrable portrayal of the righteousness of their cause as well as their own infallibility. Ideology is a powerful motivator. It ensures a level of certainty that can only come when one relinquishes his own moral choice in favor of the prevailing one the ideology embraces. This group of defendants embodied a kind of cognitive dissonance that allowed them to convince themselves that killing Jews and other enemies of the state was the right thing to do. There can be no doubt that for these men, National Socialist ideology shaped their worldview and contributed significantly to their aberrant behavior. Even under intense cross-examination, these defendants remained certain about their ideological commitment to Nazism and its world view. Only this type of certainty can explain the conscience-clear willingness of a man like Ohlendorf, an academic by training and sensibility, who had neither police training nor a proclivity to militarism, to participate in the activities of the mobile killing units.

Also telling was that although ideology was an important motivator, none of these men took any responsibility for his actions. This seems out of character for ideologically motivated individuals, but can probably be explained by the fact that they were in a court, fighting for their lives. What is most surprising is that none was willing to tell the court, however mendaciously, that they were sorry for what they had done. Surely, they must have known that the prosecution was looking for an apology or if not that, any sign of remorse. Even decades after the fact, the chief prosecutor says "the one thing I missed most in Germany all the time I was there... was somebody to say, 'I made a mistake, I'm sorry... we shouldn't have done it.'"[103] Perhaps the tribunal would have been more lenient had these men offered some type of apology. These men knew they were fighting for their lives, yet they still refused to compromise their respect for and allegiance to the SS and Nazism.

Deniers

In the early part of the trial, the majority of defendants restricted their responses to standard defenses such as duty and superior orders, and were absolutely unwilling to offer alternative reasons for their actions. Only after the presentation of copious amounts of damning prosecution evidence and relentless questioning, did any of the defendants admit that they had participated in at least some executions. As we have seen, however, explanations for their behavior varied. Some said they were doing their duty and others claimed what they did was not illegal. Not all were opposed to their tasks;

[103] Interview with Ferencz, April 24, 1997, 11.

some argued that killing Soviet Jews was the solution to Germany's racial problems. But, there were also a number of defendants who, no matter how intense the questioning or how much evidence the prosecution marshalled, absolutely refused to admit they had done anything, let alone committed a crime. This group of defendants are referred to as deniers, and one such example was Gustav Nosske.

Nosske became head of an *Einsatzkommando* in May 1941.[104] According to the evidence presented in court, he remained in this position until late February or early March of the following year. His *Einsatzkommando* was attached to Ohlendorf's group D, but unlike his superior he consistently denied any involvement in murder. He told American authorities that "no executions of Jews, Gypsies or other members of 'racially inferior' minority groups were carried out" by his *Kommando* even though the court had already been told by Ohlendorf that they had.[105] While Nosske's *Kommando* may not have killed the large number of Jews that Paul Blobel's or Eduard Strauch's groups had, at least one *Einsatzgruppen* report (No. 178) stated otherwise, recording the murder of 1,500 civilians between February 16 and 28, 1942. Nosske's men had shot all the victims.[106] Despite this damning evidence, throughout the trial Nosske maintained his innocence until December 9, the last day of the cross-examination, when he begrudgingly succumbed to Musmanno's questioning and admitted that his unit "might be" responsible for the murder of as many as 244 people.[107] A tenuous acknowledgement at best, this is as far as he would go. Never did he admit to personally supervising any murders and he absolutely refused to be pinned down as to exactly how many persons were killed by his unit.

Clearly despised by his fellow inmates, Nosske was nicknamed the "SD swine." American interrogators felt he would do or say anything to shift the blame to others and seconded this characterization. He frequently cast aspersions on others while proclaiming his own behavior was beyond reproach. One interrogator said Nosske was

a thoroughly bad type, arrogant, unscrupulous, and hard; altogether he makes the impression of a man capable of anything and one who has thoroughly enjoyed his work in the Gestapo.... He is intelligent and shrewd and has done his best to withhold information which might in anyway show him or the Gestapo in a bad light.[108]

[104] Eidesstattliche Erklärung, Nosske, June 29, 1947 in M1019, roll 50.
[105] Interrogation Nr. 1500-B, Vernehmung, Nosske by Wartenberg am 29.6.47; and, Interrogation Summary No. 2608, Nosske, June 28, 1947 in *ibid.*, roll 50. See also, Testimony, Nosske, December 4–9, 1947, in *Trial*, roll 4, 3481–3685.
[106] Judgment, April 8, 1948, in *Trial*, roll 29, 189–190.
[107] Testimony, Nosske, December 9, 1947, in *ibid.*, roll 4, 3637–3667.
[108] Secret Final Report on SS Überstumbannführer Gustav Nosske, May 11, 1946 in NARA RG 238, OCCPAC, Reports and Interrogations 57–61, box 13 (NM 70), folder 57.

As might have been expected, Nosske refused to accept any personal responsibility for his *Kommando's* actions and blamed the victims for their own fate. He did acknowledge that executions were carried out by men under his command, but insisted they were entirely legal, because the individuals involved were saboteurs, who allegedly destroyed crops and farm equipment.[109] In his mind, he was innocent of all crimes, especially the crime of murder.

Another defendant who denied he had done anything illegal was the lawyer Walter Haensch, who had joined the Party in 1931 and worked in the RSHA until 1942 when he was sent to Russia by Heydrich to take command of *Sonderkommando* 4b of *Einsatzgruppe* C under the leadership of Max Thomas.[110] Haensch's stay in Russia was relatively short, lasting only six months, from mid-January to mid-June 1942 (during trial he claimed he did not arrive in Russia until mid-March, but the evidence indicates otherwise). During cross-examination Haensch was relatively open about his affiliation with National Socialism, admitting he was a member of the Party and in full agreement with its ideology. However, when questions arose about his activities with the *Einsatzgruppen*, his memory conveniently failed him. Haensch's defense was to be deliberately evasive and to "deny, deny, deny."[111] He claimed he knew nothing of the murder of Jews and denied any criminal wrongdoing by his *Kommando* while he was its leader. He told the tribunal that he "felt inwardly free and innocent" of all crimes, which allowed him to "mentally detach" himself "from the visual details of the war;" that is, to forget.[112] Haensch maintained his wall of silence throughout the trial and was one of the few defendants who did not succumb to Musmanno's relentless questioning, going so far as to claim that he knew nothing of the murder of Jews until July 1947, when he was brought to Nuremberg for interrogation, and even then it was his interrogator who told him of the Final Solution.[113] Haensch's silence could not prevent the evidence from speaking for itself. At least three Operational Situation reports (NO 3405, NO 3340, and NO 3240) referred to him by name as the *Führer* of *Sonderkommando* 4b and under his watch 3,401 persons were executed

[109] Testimony, Nosske, December 8, 1947, in *Trial*, roll 4, 3519.
[110] *Ibid.*, frames 0757–0760.
[111] Musmanno, *Eichmann Kommandos*, 182. See also Grabitz, *NS-Prozesse*, 109–119, who discusses the problem of denial among defendants in later German trials.
[112] Affidavit, Haensch (NO 4567), in *Trial*, roll 11, frame 0741. Waller, "Perpetrators of the Holocaust," 11–33, suggests that Haensch's reaction was not uncommon among perpetrators who had difficulty reconciling their moral perception of themselves with their immoral behavior. Forgetting was a defense mechanism employed to distance themselves from their actions. Some perpetrators even succeeded in permanently altering their inner selves, avoiding self-hatred and preserving their moral integrity.
[113] Testimony, Haensch, December 2, 1947, in *Trial*, roll 4, 3262.

between January 16 and February 14, 1942.[114] He said the reports were inaccurate. He could not be held responsible for executions in January and February as he was not in Russia at this time, he was in Berlin attending a birthday party, having his photograph taken, and visiting his dentist. He knew absolutely nothing about the murders, he maintained simply he was innocent.[115] Whether or not Haensch actually believed his denial would ensure a judgment of not guilty is a matter for debate. What seems more certain is that, like Ohlendorf, he believed in the rightness of Nazi ideology and when questioned about the morality of killing Jews, he said simply it was "necessary."[116]

After the trial, Haensch became obsessed with proving his innocence, so much so that he thought of little else. The prison warden at Landsberg recorded in 1954 that his health had "deteriorated somewhat mentally and physically because of his constant brooding over his innocence."[117] Even when given the opportunity to apply for parole he refused to do so, hoping that one day American officials would see their error and grant him the clemency he believed he deserved.[118]

Conflicted Murderers

The Nuremberg defendants were not all ideological soldiers, holding the same degree of conviction as Ohlendorf, who was unwavering in his certainty of the virtues of Nazi racial policy; some of the defendants did in fact suffer from psychological turmoil. Four of the defendants can be considered "conflicted murderers." Conflicted murders are those who exhibited signs of psychological imbalance during the perpetration of mass murder, which according to social psychologists *can* be the result of inner conflict experienced when individuals try to reconcile their moral beliefs with their immoral actions and those who showed remorse only after the fact. Paul Blobel is a classic example of the first type of conflicted murderer. As we saw in the previous chapter, he came to National Socialism during a time of economic stagnation in Germany, but did not make a name for himself until after being drafted into the *Einsatzgruppen* in 1941. In no time at all, he earned a reputation and notoriety as an efficient killer of Jews, even by

[114] *Ibid.*, 3255–3275.
[115] *Ibid.*, 3254–3255.
[116] *Ibid.*, December 4, 1947, 3406–3409.
[117] Institutional Record of Haensch, Landsberg, June 10, 1954, in NARA RG 466, Prisons Division, Petitions for Clemency for War Criminals at Nuremberg, box 9, Haensch folder.
[118] Attachment to institutional Report: Director's Personal Observations, June 10, 1954, in *ibid.* Haensch blamed everything, including the death of his father, the "broken heart" of his mother, and the poverty of his wife on the Russians. Letter, Haensch to the US High Commissioner, June 26, 1950, in *ibid.*

National Socialist standards. According to Musmanno's recollection, after Ohlendorf, Blobel was the most memorable personality in the dock. This was certainly not because of his charisma or good looks. Photographs of Blobel show an unkempt, unhealthy individual, who appears much older than his 53 years. In his usual flamboyant style, Musmanno recorded that Blobel "sat in the front row in the defendant's dock [with] his square red beard jutt[ing] out ahead like the prow of a piratical ship commanded by himself. His blood-shot eyes glared with the penetrating intensity of a wild animal at bay."[119] It was "hard to believe," Musmanno observed, "this ferocious-looking creature was once an architect handling weapons no more lethal than a slide-rule and colored pencils."[120]

As leader of *Sonderkommando* 4a, Blobel's unit was assigned to *Einsatzgruppe* C, which was commanded by Otto Rasch, and which operated in the southern Ukraine, the jurisdiction of the German Sixth Army under *Fieldmarshall* von Reichenau.[121] Blobel's *Kommando* killed tens of thousands of men, women, and children, and he was soon recognized for the efficiency of his operations. The most notorious massacre was at Babi Yar in 1941.[122] On the outskirts of Kiev, at the site of a large ravine, on September 29 and 30, Blobel's *Kommando*, together with the assistance of other police battalions and Ukrainian auxiliaries, massacred 33,771 Ukrainian Jews.[123] According to one witness, Blobel lost patience with the pace of the killing operation and frequently yelled at his men, from the top of the ravine, to speed up. To ensure the killings ran smoothly, Blobel worked his men in shifts, keeping them well supplied with liquor to dull their senses.[124] Years later, Kurt Werner, a member of *Sonderkommando* 4a reminiscing about Babi Yar said, "I still recall today the complete terror of the Jews when they first caught sight of the bodies as they reached the top edge of the ravine. Many Jews cried out in terror. It's almost impossible to imagine what nerves of steel it took to carry out that dirty work down there. It was horrible."[125] After the war, Albert Hartl, an employee of the RSHA, vividly recalled witnessing the Babi Yar massacre and recounted to American authorities how bizarre Blobel's behavior had been.[126] A year after the massacre while touring

---

[119] Musmanno, *Eichmann Kommandos*, 145.

[120] *Ibid.*

[121] Eidesstattliche Erklärung, Blobel, (NO 3824), in *Trial*, roll 8, frame 0346.

[122] On this subject see Ernst Klee and Willi Dreßen (eds.), *"Gott mit uns:" Der deutsche Vernichtungskrieg im Osten 1939–1945* (Frankfurt, 1989), 117–136; Lozowick, "Rollbahn Mord: the Early Activities of Einsatzgruppe C," 221–225; and Krausnick and Wilhelm, *Die Truppe*, 235, 237–238.

[123] Benjamin Ferencz, *Less Than Slaves: Jewish Forced Labor and the Quest for Compensation* (Cambridge, 1979), 14.

[124] Breitman, *Architect of Genocide*, 211–212.

[125] "Statement of Kurt Werner, member of Sonderkommando 4a," in Klee et al., *"The Good Old Days,"* 66–67.

[126] Hilberg, "The Nature of the Process," 30.

Russia with Blobel he remembered passing the ravine when he "noticed strange movements of the earth. Clumps of earth rose into the air as if by their own propulsion and there was smoke; it was like a low-tower volcano; as if there was burning lava just beneath the earth. Blobel laughed, made a gesture with his arm pointing back along the road and ahead, all along the ravine – the ravine of Babi Yar and said, 'Here live my thirty thousand Jews.'"[127]

Blobel's role in the Babi Yar massacre earned him a nomination by Heydrich for the War Service Cross Second Class.[128] It also enhanced his reputation as a most "efficient killer of Jews" as well as a "drunk and a monster" (apparently Blobel ended up in hospital as a result of excessive alcohol consumption following the killing spree at Babi Yar).[129] Two of his colleagues at Nuremberg, Eugen Steimle and Erwin Schulz, told American authorities that Blobel was a "bloodhound, brutal, without any inhibition, and not very well liked."[130] Rolf Wartenberg, the principal interrogator for the trial vividly recalled his first meeting with Blobel in 1947, and recalls feeling disgusted by him.[131] He seems to have been universally hated as a malicious and cowardly man. Blobel was so reviled that he was one of the few defendants who had difficulty securing affidavits from fellow SS and SD men attesting to his strength of character. The best defense he could mount at his trial was that the number of murders he was charged with was exaggerated; the actual number was in the range of ten to fifteen thousand, and not the sixty thousand the prosecution claimed. This was a defense, the tribunal noted, that "would anywhere be regarded as a massacre of some proportions, except in the annals of the *Einsatzgruppen*."[132] Fearing that the court might not accept his main argument, Blobel prepared a second line of defense: he claimed he spent much of the time he was in Russia in the hospital because of chronic illnesses, particularly dysentery, a condition exacerbated by heavy drinking.[133]

Even though Blobel probably suffered from a severe and prolonged case of dysentery in 1941, perhaps the true source of his health problems was the difficulty he had coping with his job. During cross-examination in October 1947, he admitted, after much prodding by Musmanno that his chronic

[127] Gitta Sereny, *Albert Speer: His Battle with Truth* (New York, 1995), 272 and affidavit, Albert Hartl (NO 5384), in *Trial*, Prosecution Document Book, roll 12, frame 0398.

[128] Christian Gerlach, "The Wannsee Conference, the Fate of German Jews, and Hitler's Decision in Principle to Exterminate All European Jews," in Omer Bartov (ed.), *The Holocaust: Origins, Implementation, Aftermath* (New York, 2000), 130.

[129] Sereny, *Albert Speer*, 270 and Lozowick, "Rollbahn Mord," 224–225.

[130] Affidavit, Steimle, October 29, 1947, in *Trial*, roll 3, 1617 and Interrogation Summary No. 2429, Schulz, June 12, 1947 in NARA RG 238, OCCWC, Executive Counsel, Evidence Division, Interrogation Branch, Interrogation Summaries, box 7, folder 2251–2325.

[131] Handwritten notes by Rolf Wartenberg, undated in RG 2005.347, Rolf and Hannah Wartenberg Collection, USHMM.

[132] Judgment, April 8, 1948, in *Trial*, roll 29, 152.

[133] Testimony, Blobel, October 30, 1947, in *ibid.*, roll 3, 1649–1650.

illnesses resulted from, the tasks he had to carry out; apparently it was not easy to murder for a living.[134] Blobel was not exaggerating. Murder was a gruesome business, particularly the use of the gas vans, which had been allocated to the *Einsatzgruppen* by Himmler to alleviate some of psychological stresses placed on the executioners when they had to shoot their victims. The use of the gas van proved just as psychologically taxing. Julius Bauer, Blobel's driver in *Sonderkommando* 4a, described their horrors and how Blobel used alcohol to cope with stressful and troubling situations.

The use of the gas vans was the most horrible thing I have ever seen. I saw people being led into the vans and the doors closed. Then the van drove off. I had to drive Blobel to the place where the gas van was unloaded. The back doors of the van were opened, and Jews who were still alive unloaded the bodies that had not fallen out when the doors were opened. The bodies were covered with vomit and excrement. It was a terrible sight. Blobel looked, then looked away, and we drove off. On such occasions Blobel always drank schnapps, sometimes even in the car.[135]

At trial Blobel's claims of psychological trauma were confirmed by his adjutant and frequent prosecution witness, *Obersturmführer* August Häfner. He stated that as early as July 1941, after the massacre of three thousand Jewish civilians (women and children included), Blobel displayed early signs of mental breakdown.[136] Häfner affirmed that:

Blobel had had a nervous breakdown and was in bed in his room.... He was talking confusedly. He was saying that it was not possible to shoot so many Jews and that what was needed was a plough to plough them into the ground. He had completely lost his mind. He was threatening to shoot Wehrmacht officers with his pistol. It was clear to me that he had cracked up.... [137]

Blobel's defense that he found his job mentally taxing enraged the presiding judge who told the defendant that it did not have to be that way, he could have done something, anything, to help those identified for murder. As Musmanno noted caustically, Blobel had chosen alcohol as a way to assuage his feelings of guilt. He could have avoided this altogether had he embraced a moral position and not carried out mass murder.[138] There can be no doubt that Blobel knew his actions in Russia were wrong. He was not

[134] *Ibid.*

[135] Julius Bauer quoted in Eugen Kogon, Hermann Langbein, and Adalbert Rückerl (eds.), *Nazi Mass Murder: A Documentary History of the Use of Poison Gas*, trans. by Mary Scott and Caroline Lloyd-Morris (New Haven, 1993), 61.

[136] Affidavit, August Häfner, November 10, 1947, and Document Book 2, Paul Blobel, Document No. 5, in *Trial*, roll 26, frames 0024–0032.

[137] SS-Obersturmführer August Häfner, Sonderkommando 4a, in Ernst Klee et al. (eds.), *"The Good Old Days,"* 111–112. During testimony Blobel admitted that, in July 1941, he was admitted to hospital in Lublin for a nervous breakdown. Testimony, Blobel, October 28, 1947, in *Trial*, roll 3, 1524. See also Affidavit, Häfner, November 10, 1947 in *ibid.*

[138] On the issue of disobedience to orders, see Kitterman, "Those who said 'No!'," 241–254.

able to rationalize his crimes on ideological or military grounds, nor could he bring himself to deny his horrible deeds at trial. The unavailability of coping mechanisms caused him such physical and mental torment that he had to find some way to cope. He did so by drinking heavily.[139] Today, we know that many people in violent situations suffer from what is called Post Traumatic Stress Disorder or PTSD, the symptoms of which mirror Blobel's. PTSD is not necessarily the result of inner or moral conflict; rather, it can be an extreme reaction to violence. Blobel's own response to the charges of crimes against humanity seem to hint that he knew what he had done was wrong, suggesting that although he may indeed have suffered from PTSD, he also showed genuine signs of inner turmoil. Blobel should have listened to his conscience and heeded his body's own warning. In 1950, he told a panel of American judges that "by taking a decision, a man makes of himself what he is: he creates or destroys his own moral personality."[140] Blobel was probably drawn into the killing process in spite of his inner convictions. Because of his weak nature and his need for acceptance he was unable to resist the pressures and do what was morally right. Rather, he ended-up overcompensating for his moral weakness by killing far more people, and with more vigor, than men who were more ideologically motivated. Only in April 1945, as the war was drawing to a close, did he realize that allied authorities were closing in and he might be punished for his crimes. To avoid capture, he obtained false papers under the name of Hermann Altenpohl (his wife's maiden name) and went to Salzburg to avoid capture.[141] Despite his efforts to conceal his identity, he was apprehended May 8 in Rastatt, Germany, and indicted for crimes against humanity.[142]

Few of the *Einsatzgruppen* leaders attained the same level of notoriety as Blobel, but there was one other who was equally as ruthless, but perhaps not as morally conflicted in his tasks, yet who nonetheless seemed to suffer from the effects of posttraumatic stress. Eduard Strauch, one of the most sadistic of the *Einsatzkommando* leaders had an alcohol abuse problem and early on in his career demonstrated clear signs of mental imbalance. His

---

[139] Blobel's reaction is in line with Birn, "Guilty Conscience," 2086 who writes, "It should be stressed here that SS leaders did not really feel they were innocent, while committing their crimes and that they had no reason to feel they acted under binding orders (*Befehlnotstand*). The German penal code was in force all the time during the Nazi era. On the contrary, they seem to have been well aware of the criminal nature of their deeds and to have hoped to get away with it."

[140] Petition for clemency, Blobel, September 12, 1950 in NARA RG 466, Prisons Division, Petitions for Clemency, box 3, Blobel folder.

[141] Case Record of Blobel, April 27, 1948 in NARA RG 338, Landsberg, Records Relating to Executed Prisoners January 2, 1946–June 7, 1951, box 1, Blobel folder. Rückerl notes that the SS furnished many such false papers to its members as the war neared its end. Rückerl, *Die Strafverfolgung von NS-Verbrechen 1945–1978*, 77–78.

[142] Eidesstattliche Erklärung, Blobel, June 15, 1947, in NARA RG 238, Landsberg, Records Relating to Executed Prisoners January 2, 1946–June 7, 1951, box 1 Ab-Br, Blobel folder.

ailments were the obvious result of his inability to overcome the mental strain of his work in Russia, whether this was the result of moral conflict seems doubtful. Unlike Blobel, who hinted at his negative feelings, Strauch never once expressed an iota of remorse for his actions. As a zealous National Socialist, he maintained throughout the trial and clemency period that Nazi racial policy was justified even though emotionally it took a heavy toll on him. George Browder notes that Strauch possessed the typical characteristics of an authoritarian personality, capable of overcoming the most difficult obstacles, yet unable to empathize with others. By all accounts, he was excessively judgmental, attaining a high level of formal education but possessing an underdeveloped level of "ethical maturity." His "cold bloodedness" did not protect him "from the resultant psychic strain [of killing]," and he even became one of the most merciless of all the *Kommando* leaders.[143] To admit his actions were wrong proved to be too heavy a burden for this committed National Socialist to bear.

Strauch was a stereotypical member of the *Einsatzgruppen* leadership corps, part of a generation of youth who grew up with the mythology of the war. He was a lawyer by training, and like Blobel had joined the Party at a time of great economic instability.[144] Also typical was that Strauch had been recruited to lead a *Kommando* while working in the RSHA. He was sent to Riga where he was put in charge of *Einsatzkommando* 2 of *Einsatzgruppe* A. In February 1942, he was made Commander of the Security Police and SD in Minsk.[145] While Strauch's leadership abilities earned him high praise with his superiors, he was ruthless. One incident in particular, involving the *Gauleiter* of White Ruthenia, Wilhelm Kube, stands out.[146]

In 1942, when the killing in Russia was at its peak, Kube accused Strauch and his men of especially barbaric behavior.[147] Apparently Kube himself had had no moral compunctions about murdering Russian Jews, but he was opposed fundamentally to the murder of German Jews.[148] Because of Strauch's attitude toward the murder of German Jews, Kube confronted

---

[143] Wilhelm, *Die Truppe*, 282 and for a more in-depth discussion of the authoritarian personality and social theory see Browder, *Hitler's Enforcers*, 158–170.

[144] On these subjects see *ibid.*; Testimony, Strauch, January 13, 1948, in *Trial*, roll 6, 4908–4909 and 4913–4914; Interrogation Nr. 1643-A, Vernehmung, Strauch, 4.8.47, M1019, roll 72; and, SS Record Strauch, (NO 2966), in *Trial*, roll 11, frame 0538.

[145] Testimony, Strauch, January 13, 1948, in *ibid.*, roll 6, ,4930–4934 and SS Record Strauch (NO 2966), in *ibid.*, roll 11, frame 0538.

[146] SS Record Strauch (NO 2966) in *ibid.*, roll 11, frame 0539.

[147] Wilhelm, *Die Truppe*, 554–557.

[148] Hilberg notes that Kube's moral barometer, unlike many of the perpetrators, was not flexible. He writes, "one reason why the person of *Generalkommissar* Kube is so important is that he had a firm line beyond which he could not pass. The line was arbitrary, and very advanced. He sacrificed Russian Jews and fought desperately only for the German Jews in his area. But the line was fixed. It was not moveable, it was not imaginary, it was not self-deceptive." Hilberg, "The Nature of the Process," 33.

him and accused his *Kommandos* of conducting a "fanatical campaign of liquidation," behavior that "was unworthy of a German."[149] Strauch was dumbfounded by Kube's attitude, declaring that, "it was incomprehensible [to him]...why Germans should fall out over a few Jews [even if they were German]." After all, he rationalized in a letter to his superiors, "all I was doing was my duty."[150] Strauch's relationship with Kube deteriorated further after Kube decided to launch an official complaint against Strauch and his men. Strauch was so outraged he wrote to the *Reichsführer-SS* outlining his dispute with Kube. In the letter, Strauch complained that Kube was an inept administrator and that he was hostile to the SS, SD, and police in the area. Strauch even questioned Kube's commitment to solving the Jewish problem, as he seemed to harbor sympathies for them. Apparently, Kube had once thanked a Jewish man for rescuing his car from a burning garage, and, on another occasion, had given candy to Jewish children. Worst of all, Strauch reported, Kube had used his knowledge as *Gauleiter* to help rescue some Jews! In Strauch's opinion, Kube's behavior was "traitorous." Because Strauch was at the front line of racial policy, criticism from behind the line was interpreted as a personal betrayal.[151] As one scholar has noted, "there was nothing so irksome [for a perpetrator] as the realization that someone was watching over one's shoulder, that someone would be free to talk and accuse because he was not himself involved [in the murder process]."[152]

Strauch's *Kommando* committed the kind of excesses that Ohlendorf had forbidden his men to engage in, although they killed fewer people than Ohlendorf's men had. To what extent his barbarous behavior was the result of a pre-existing psychological illness is difficult to say with certainty, although he was the only defendant at Nuremberg who exhibited genuine signs of mental collapse. Emil Hausmann had committed suicide in July 1947, before the trial began, and Waldemar Klingelhöfer had attempted suicide the same month, but survived. What we know with certainty is that even before his run-in with Kube, Strauch had had difficulties with his colleagues and, at trial, his mental capacities appeared diminished. He had great difficulty responding to the simplest questions from his defense attorney, and when he did respond his answers were frequently repetitive and confused; they made little sense.[153] The court knew he suffered from epilepsy, as the day of his arraignment he created drama by suffering a seizure in court.[154]

[149] Wilhelm, *Die Truppe*, 556.
[150] Strauch quoted in *ibid.*, 421.
[151] Letter, Strauch to the Reichsführer-SS and Chief of the German Police, July 25, 1943, in *Trial*, roll 12, frames 0053–0067.
[152] Hilberg, "The Nature of the Process," 19–24.
[153] For example, see Strauch's testimony on January 13, 1948, in which he had great difficulty responding to his attorney's questions concerning his education. In *Trial*, roll 6, 4907–4953. See also Wilhelm, *Die Truppe*, 282.
[154] Musmanno, *Eichmann Kommandos*, 141.

Strauch's seizures had been in abeyance during his youth, but returned with increasing frequency during stressful periods in his life, particularly during his incarceration after the war (interestingly, he did not suffer seizures while serving on the eastern front). Strauch's seizure prompted a physical and psychological evaluation to determine if he could survive a trial and whether he was capable of understanding the charges he faced. The medical board determined that "except for brief periods preceding, during and succeeding epileptic seizures" Strauch was perfectly capable of understanding the proceedings and was sufficiently lucid to participate in his own defense.[155] On the basis of this report the tribunal concluded that Strauch was "feigning" insanity to avoid responsibility for his crimes. In all likelihood Strauch's comportment was contrived to illicit sympathy with the court. That said, the evidence suggests he genuinely suffered from some form of mental imbalance but epilepsy was not the root cause. According to his SS Personnel record, he showed signs of diminished mental capacity, paranoia and aggression as early as March 1941. The report stated that his

emotional perception was not particularly developed. He finds it hard to imagine himself in other people's positions and, is rarely able to judge them conscientiously and correctly. This may well account for his mistrust towards his staff, an attitude which, in turn, renders him susceptible to tale-telling (sic.). His actions are predominantly instinctive and often scarcely influenced by reason. His reactions are impulsive and explosive. All that results in a decidedly unbalanced quality of his character, unfairness in managing men as well as discrepancy between his basic attitude and his actions. This also explains the fact that his decisions are often too hasty and ill-considered.[156]

Strauch's poor judgment, the evaluation continued, was exacerbated by the use of alcohol, particularly when he drank to excess which, by all accounts, was frequently.[157] It should be noted that the evaluators of Strauch's personality and mental state were not doctors, but they did have ample opportunity to witness his behavior and it was well known that he acted impulsively and had difficulty getting along with fellow SS men and other party officials. His relationship with Kube illustrates this quite effectively.

At trial, Strauch's testimony was garbled except when it came to his work, when his responses were remarkably coherent. He was a vehement antisemite and ultranationalist, and so imbued with National Socialist ideals that any display of humanity was to him a sign of weakness and betrayal of Nazism.

---

[155] "Physical and Mental Condition of Defendant, Eduard Strauch," in Judgment, April 8, 1948, in *Trial*, roll, 201–202 and Medical Report, Dr. Roy Martin to Evidence Division, September 4, 1947, RG 238, OCCWC, Executive Office, 201 files 1945–1948, box 32, Strauch folder. See also Musmanno, *Eichmann Kommandos*, 141 and ruling by tribunal, January 13, 1948, in *Trial,* roll 6, 4944–4945.

[156] SS Record Strauch (NO 2966), in *ibid.*, roll 11, frames 0539–0540.

[157] *Ibid.*

In a July 20, 1943 letter, he expressed resentment over criticism he had received concerning the behavior of his *Kommando* who had removed gold fillings from the teeth of captured Jews. This in itself was not such an unusual action. Rather, what was so odd was that the gold had been removed from people's teeth before they were killed, not afterward; barbaric behavior even by Nazi standards. Strauch saw this as neither sadistic nor wrong, because "expert physicians" had carried it out.[158] On another occasion, Strauch discovered that a group of Jews from Sluzk (near Minsk) were forewarned that resettlement was a hoax. To capture them, he created a ruse ensuring that executions would be carried out without incident. His Kommando murdered two thousand people in February 1943.[159] These incidents are emblematic of Strauch's worldview.[160] As he once said proudly, "sometimes we must fulfil hard and unpleasant tasks," but he always, "acted from conviction and loyalty [to his] leader."[161]

Whether or not Strauch's mental instability was feigned is questionable, but Waldemar Klingelhöfer's suicide attempt in 1947 was real. It will be recalled that Klingelhöfer spent his formative years in Germany and after the war had straddled two worlds: one in the realm of high culture, the other the politics of the far right.[162] Of course, this is not to suggest that these two worlds were incompatible, but the evidence seems to suggest that Klingelhöfer did not conflate them, preferring to be either a professional opera singer, or a politically active and professional Nazi. He joined the Party in 1930 and the SS two years later. Once his singing career came to an end, he joined the SD and it was while there that he was drafted to the mobile killing units.[163]

Like his co-defendants he was sent to Pretzsch at the end of May 1941, and was given the job of interpreter for *Sonderkommando* 7b of *Einsatzgruppe* B. In the field he participated in the advance on Minsk. Once the city was occupied, he was reassigned to the *Vorkommando* Moscow, at the time headed by co-defendant Franz Six. At some point after August 1941 when Six had left Russia (the exact particulars are unclear), Klingelhöfer was put in charge of *Vorkommando* Moscow. He headed the unit until December 1941 when he was reassigned. He stayed in the east an additional two years.[164] Between December 1941 and September 1943, he worked at *Kommando* headquarters in Smolensk, drawing up plans for the capture and control of Moscow. In addition to these duties, during his lengthy stay in Russia,

[158] Letter, Strauch to Commander of the Security Police and the SD–White Ruthenia, July 20, 1943, (NO 4317), in *ibid.*, roll 12, frames 0069–0071.
[159] Affidavit, Adolf Rübe, October 23, 1947, (NO 5498), in *Trial*, roll 12, frames 0072–0073.
[160] Testimony, Strauch, January 19, 1948, in *ibid.*, roll 6, 5244.
[161] Strauch quoted in Wilhelm, *Die Truppe*, 557.
[162] Eidesstattliche Erklärung, Klingelhöfer, M1019, roll 35.
[163] *Ibid.*, and testimony of Klingelhöfer, December 11, 1947, in *Trial*, roll 5, 3801.
[164] Vernehmung, Klingelhöfer, July 1, 1947, M1019, roll 35.

Klingelhöfer headed an "anti-partisan hunt" (May–June 1942), witnessed numerous executions and, in the autumn of 1941 was put in charge of requisitioning winter clothing for the men of *Einsatzgruppe* B.[165] In September 1943, he was transferred back to Minsk and then to Berlin in December.[166]

After Klingelhöfer was arrested (he turned himself in to British authorities on October 20, 1945) he was incarcerated in Bielefeld where he stayed until June 1947 when he was transferred to Landsberg for questioning by American authorities planning Ohlendorf's trial.[167] During his interrogation, but before he knew he was to be indicted, he confessed to many crimes.[168] He admitted that he was head of *Vorkommando* Moscow, whose crimes included the murder of Jews. With his confession and other evidence, the Americans indicted Klingelhöfer on July 1, 1947.[169] Five days later, in the early morning of July 6, his cellmate found him lying in a pool of blood. According to the on-duty physician, Klingelhöfer had spent several hours cutting a deep hole in the artery of his left wrist. Somehow he had obtained a rather large safety pin for this purpose (the National Archives in Washington, DC still has the pin attached to the physician's report). He was treated for heavy blood loss, but survived the ordeal.[170] The obvious question is why Klingelhöfer attempted suicide.

Ferencz believes that Klingelhöfer's suicide attempt was an expression of remorse for the role he had played in carrying out Nazi racial policy.[171] Although not an unequivocal expression of remorse or explanation for his behavior, Klingelhöfer's suicide note is somewhat contrite. He wrote,

Too late, unfortunately, after the collapse, I gained complete insight into the whole extent of the horrible blasphemy that was carried out here. Nevertheless, I ask that this [suicide attempt] of mine not be interpreted as an attempt to excuse myself in any way.... I am fully conscious of the fact that I must bear the consequences completely for my personal attitude and my acts. Still I will not burden my conscience with acts that are in complete opposition to the attitude I have again achieved.[172]

Corroboration that Klingelhöfer was repentant comes from prison officials who noted on his application for parole in 1955 and 1956 that, "the applicant has shown genuine remorse for many of his actions" and has "realized

[165] *Ibid.*
[166] Testimony, Klingelhöfer, December 11, 1947, in *Trial*, roll 5, 3819–3830 and interrogation, Klingelhöfer, July 1, 1947, in *ibid.*, roll 12, 0233–0236.
[167] Detention Report of Klingelhöfer, undated, in NARA RG 238, OCCWC, Executive Office, Nuremberg Military Post, 201 Files 1945–1948, box 16 Keip-Koenig, Klingelhöfer folder.
[168] As noted in Chapter 2, this was one of the main ways the prosecution collected evidence from the perpetrators.
[169] Testimony, Klingelhöfer, December 12, 1947, in *Trial*, roll 5, 3917–3918.
[170] Medical Report of Dr. Pflücker on Klingelhöfer, July 6, 1947, Nuernberg in *ibid.*
[171] Interview with Ferencz, April 24, 1997, 11–12.
[172] Suicide note of Klingelhöfer, July 4, 1947, (NO 5451), in *Trial*, roll 12, frame 0445.

that he was involved in a crime."[173] On the other hand, Klingelhöfer made only one public admission of guilt and that was the night in July 1947 that he tried to commit suicide.[174] His contrition was short lived. By the time his trial began (two months after his suicide attempt), he showed no sign of remorse. During direct testimony he denied everything he had said previously. He testified that he had known nothing about the murder of Jews, that he had never been head of *Vorkommando* Moscow, and that he did not supervise any executions – all facts he had confessed to in his pre-trial interrogation. When asked by Ferencz why he was recanting his earlier statements, Klingelhöfer stated that he had been "mixed up" when he had written it and did not have "all [his] logical thinking in order."[175]

Other evidence suggests that Ferencz may have misinterpreted Klingelhöfer's suicide attempt. His suicide note made reference to a letter that co-defendant Erich Naumann had given him secretly, two days after he was interrogated July 1, 1947. In the note, Naumann instructed Klingelhöfer what to say and not to say to his American interrogators. Rather than dispose of the note, Klingelhöfer decided to hand it over to American authorities, an unequivocal betrayal of a fellow SS officer.[176] Doing this caused Klingelhöfer great anxiety, and may have been the main reason for his attempted suicide. When asked how he felt about the incident involving his attempted suicide and the note from Naumann, he responded at trial,

Klingelhöfer: It was the general impression I had of the entire assignment that depressed me so much.

Ferencz: Were you depressed when you were here in Nuremberg in the jail and you had plenty of time to think about it?

Klingelhöfer: I was depressed, of course, but not only about my work in the East, and about the whole atmosphere there, but in general I was depressed about the collapse of the German Reich and about the things that I heard later on which I did not know anything about before. Those were the things that depressed me particularly.

Ferencz: Did you attempt to commit suicide while you were . . . in jail?

Klingelhöfer: Yes. That was as a result of sending [Naumann's] letter to Mr. Wartenberg [interrogator]. I had such an inner conflict

[173] Institutional Record of Klingelhöfer, January 27, 1955 and August 29, 1956, in NARA RG 238, OCCWC, Executive Office, Nuremberg Military Post, 201 Files 1945–1948, box 16 Keip-Koenig, Klingelhöfer folder.
[174] Letter, Naumann to Klingelhöfer, July 3, 1947, (NO 5450), in *Trial*, roll 12, frames 0380–0381. Naumann wrote that he told American authorities that he brought Klingelhöfer into his group B because of his language skills, but also because of "your inclination to drink deemed it necessary (I had to be frank here)."
[175] Testimony, Klingelhöfer, December 12, 1947, in *ibid.*, roll 5, 3917.
[176] Naumann's letter is part of the official record of the trial.

that I no longer realized whether I had acted in the right manner. On the one hand, I was trying to say the truth as far as possible, knowing the catastrophe which had happened and my responsibility for the development of things; on the other hand, I felt that I had to give away...a comrade, a former superior. In this state of excitement and in this conflict I found no way out, and my nerves were in such a bad state that I tried to commit suicide. I thought I could not live honestly this way...it upset me so much I did not know what [else] to do.[177]

The reason for Klingelhöfer's suicide attempt seems to be somewhere between remorse for his actions on the eastern front and regret for betraying a fellow SS officer.[178] If he had ever harbored any doubts about his job on the eastern front, his moral barometer was not sufficient to prevent him from carrying out his murderous tasks, nor did it allow him to admit to his crimes in court even after expressing some remorse in a suicide note he left for posterity. When his suicide attempt failed, he had to live with the repercussions of his actions on the eastern front as well as his betrayal of his own.[179] Klingelhöfer was truly a conflicted man.

The only other defendant at Nuremberg to appear at all troubled by his actions in Russia was Erwin Schulz, but the emotional turmoil he suffered had to do exclusively with the fact that women and children had been killed. Musmanno remembered him as "dignified" in appearance and "courteous in speech" and as such, he felt Schulz was somewhat out of place in the dock.[180] Intelligence reports set him apart him as a "man of complete integrity and possessing very high moral standards" who was "revolted by the 'barbaric and bestial behaviour'" of the *Einsatzgruppen*.[181] Schulz was the only defendant who had been a policeman by profession, and, by many accounts, he had been loathe to blindly implement Nazi racial policy, at least until he was sent to Russia in 1941.[182] Despite his apparent reluctance to act against his conscience, he received a total of six promotions between

[177] Testimony, Klingelhöfer, December 12, 1947, in *Trial*, roll 5, 3955–3956.
[178] Naumann's letter was a warning to Klingelhöfer not to tell American authorities too much. It is quoted on page 155. Letter, Naumann to Klingelhöfer, July 3, 1947 (NO 5450), in *ibid.*, roll 12, frames 0380–0381.
[179] *Ibid.*, 3957.
[180] Musmanno, *Eichmann Kommandos*, 176–177.
[181] Interrogation report of Schulz, FSX-004, May 25–31, 1945, in RG 319, G-2 Intelligence, IRR, box 202 & Confidential interrogation report of Schulz, May 25–31, 1945 in *ibid.*
[182] For example, see Schulz defense document numbers: 5, 7, 16, 21, 37, 49, 64, 65, 70, 88, 91, 92 and 93 in *ibid.*, roll 27. All these affidavits speak of Schulz as a fair and, in some cases, generous, police official who frequently challenged and even arrested individuals for excesses committed against Jews.

April 1935 and November 1942.[183] Before his work in the *Einsatzgruppen*, Schulz had performed various security tasks in Austria and Czechoslovakia and in 1940 he was transferred to Hamburg as an inspector of the Security Police and the SD.[184] Given his training in the police, Schulz was a logical choice for assignment to the east. While working in Berlin, Bruno Strecken-bach gave him the order to proceed to Pretzsch to train personnel. Schulz recalled that at the time, the role of the *Einsatzgruppen* had not been made known to him, and he speciously claimed he had assumed their task would be to attack England, not Russia.[185]

When he arrived in Pretzsch, Schulz was immediately put in charge of *Einsatzkommando* 5, remaining its head from May until early September 1941, a relatively short period compared to the time served by some of his co-defendants. During his testimony, he told the court that his *Kommando* had executed only eighteen people – as opposed to the 15,000 he was charged with murdering – all of whom were communists and partisans, and not specifically Jews. Schulz explained that for him the last straw came in August 1941, while he was stationed in Zhitomir. At that time his unit had received a particularly disturbing order from Himmler that directed that women and children were to be executed. Schulz recalled that he had been horrified by the suggestion that women and children were to be killed. He told the court that this was the first time he realized the true extent of the "dictatorial power" of Himmler and that he immediately wrote to Streckenbach, who was in charge of staffing and a person with whom he had a good relationship, asking to be transferred back to Germany as soon as possible.[186] Schulz's request for transfer was approved very quickly and without repercussions, but it did not sit well with Rasch, his superior, who viewed Schulz's request as a sign of weakness.[187] Schulz left the east on August 24 and was safely back in Berlin by the end of September 1941.[188] Although it is tempting to question Schulz's testimony, after all he was trying to prove his innocence and save his life, there is corroborating evidence to suggest that he was genuinely appalled by the order to murder women and children.

[183] Memorandum on Schulz, Himmler for SS Record, November 9, 1941 (NO 4957), in *ibid.*, roll 12, frame 0382.

[184] Affidavit, Schulz, December 20, 1945, (NO 3841), in *Trial*, roll 11, frames 0766–0767 and Trial Brief for the USA against Schulz, January 15, 1948, in Mendelsohn (ed.), *The Holocaust*, vol. 18, 94–95.

[185] Testimony, Schulz, October 17, 1947, in *Trial*, roll 2, 930.

[186] Testimony, Schulz, October 18, 1947, in *Trial*, roll 2, 954–955. George Browder discusses the concept of the transformation of values in individuals, or tansvaluation. In Schulz's case he sees this as having occurred during his stint in Russia. See Browder, *Hitler's Enforcers*, 42–43.

[187] Personal Statement of Schulz to the Pardon Committee, June 1950, in NARA RG 466, Prisons Division, Petitions for Clemency, box 32, Schulz folder.

[188] Testimony, Schulz, October 18, 1947, in *Trial*, roll 2, 958–964.

In 1945, after he surrendered voluntarily to American authorities, Schulz was interrogated.[189] At this point, he had no idea he might be indicted at some future date, giving this statement far more credibility than those he made later in 1947 when he knew he would have to defend himself and his actions in court. During the earliest interrogations, in 1945, he said he had asked to be released from his duties as commander of *Einsatzkommando* 5 in the fall of 1941 because he was distraught at the prospect of having to obey the "intensified orders for the ruthless extermination of the entire Jewish population." Furthermore, Schulz claimed he was bothered greatly by the prospect of having to shoot people himself. Apparently Rasch, his supervisor and a man with whom he did not get along, was particularly "ruthless" and thus demanded that *Kommando* leaders "participate personally in the shootings" in conformity with the policy of *Blutkitt* (essentially a murderous pact in which the blood of the victims unites the perpetrators).[190] Ten years later, he repeated this statement before a German court. He said that,

at the beginning of August 1941 the Einsatzkommandoführer of Einsatzgruppe C were ordered to report to Dr. Rasch...in Zhitomir. There Dr. Rasch revealed to us that Gruppenführer Jeckeln had delivered an order from Reichsführer-SS Himmler that from then on all Jews not engaged in work were to be shot along with their families. I was shattered when I heard this piece of news and I had absolutely no doubt that I could never carry out such an order. For this reason I wrote immediately to Gruppenführer Streckenbach, who was at that time head of personnel at RSHA, and asked him if I could come and see him in Berlin... Once in Berlin I described to Streckenbach what was going on in Russia... I also asked Streckenbach to have me released from my post.[191]

Schulz was released from his duties in the east and he suffered no adverse consequences.[192]

It is not possible to know definitively if Schulz really asked to be relieved from his post because he opposed the murder of women and children, although given the overwhelming number of affidavits testifying to his acts of kindness and his sense of generosity (unusual in the case of these defendants), it seems likely he did oppose such actions. The tribunal partially believed him, noting in the judgment that in Schulz's favor it can be said

[189] Personal Statement for the Clemency Committee of Schulz, Case Nr. 9, Ohlendorf u.a., Landsberg, June 1950 in NARA RG 238, Advisory Board on Clemency, HICOG 1947–1950, Correspondence, case 9, box 12 E212, Schulz folder.

[190] Affidavit, Schulz, December 20, 1945 (NO 3841), in *Trial*, roll 11, frame 0767. Schulz's contention concerning Rasch is corroborated by the affiant Karl Hennicke who also told American officials that Schulz had fallen out of favor with Rasch because he was viewed as "soft as an egg" on the Jewish question. See affidavit, Karl Hennicke, September 26, 1947 (Schulz Document No. 21), in *ibid.*, roll 27, frames 0807–0811.

[191] Erwin Schulz quoted in Klee et al. (eds.), *"The Good Old Days,"* 85–86. On the issue of disobedience to orders, see Kittermann, "Those Who Said 'No!'"

[192] Klee, *"The Good Old Days,"* 86.

that, "confronted with an intolerable situation he did attempt to do something about it."[193] In 1955, his parole supervisor "believed [in his sincerity
and admired] him for his honest and frank statements."[194] Schulz did confess that he was fully aware of the emotional impact murder had on his
men. He said he could see it in their faces, that they hated doing their job.
Perhaps many were conflicted about their inner feelings of disgust and their
strong sense of duty.[195] When asked, however, why his men continued to
murder innocent people when it troubled them so, he told the court that it
was, most likely, out of a sense of duty, something he himself knew well.

Schulz was never able to rid himself of the belief that obedience and duty
were cardinal virtues; even during his incarceration, he clung to these beliefs.
In 1953, in a report by prison officials to the Clemency Board for War
Criminals, the prison director noted that Schulz was "cooperative... and
extremely dependable." More telling was the last recorded comment, that
Schulz was "willing to do whatever we want," an attribute the prison official
seemed to regard as positive, but, one which, as we have seen, prompted him
to carry out orders, even orders that were personally repugnant to him.[196]
Even though Schulz refused to participate wholly in the war against the
Jews, irrefutable documentary evidence proves he was willing to supervise
at least some executions even if for only a relatively short period of time (two
months). Men like Erwin Schulz and Waldemar Klingelhöfer, although they
did acknowledge the monstrousness of the Final Solution they had participated in, they were still neither willing nor able to accept full responsibility
for their actions because in the end, duty was a stronger calling.

Like most of the defendants, even conflicted murderers attempted to justify, rationalize or otherwise explain their behavior when they appeared in
court and were forced to answer for their crimes.[197] This is not surprising
according to social psychologist James Waller. He contends that rationalization is by far the most common response of perpetrators to the charge that
they had committed heinous crimes. Social psychologists have shown that
human beings are incapable of living with severe internal moral conflicts
without suffering some type of psychic breakdown. Because of the need to
reconcile one's actions with one's moral compass, it is typically necessary
for wrong-doers to integrate or resolve their inner conflicts, most often by
changes in attitude that conform to behavior, or, in some cases, by blaming

[193] Judgment, April 8, 1948, in *Trial*, roll 29, 145.
[194] Memorandum, US Parole Officer, Control Visits of Schulz, July 1, 1955 in NARA RG
    338, JAD, WCB, Post-Trial Activities 1945–1957, box 6 US Parole Officer–Summarized
    Activity Reports, September 1954–June 1955 folder.
[195] Testimony, Schulz, October 18, 1947, in *Trial*, roll 2, 967.
[196] Institutional Record of Schulz, October 31, 1953, in NARA RG 466, Prisons Division,
    Petitions, box 32, Schulz folder.
[197] Ferencz, Brief for the Prosecution: Analysis of the Defenses Presented on Behalf of the
    Accused, February 1948, in *Trial*, roll 29, frames 0001–0017.

the victims themselves for their own demise.[198] This certainly describes the behavior of the majority of the defendants, especially the ideologically motivated men.[199] To be sure, men like Ohlendorf far outnumbered men like Schulz, Klingelhöfer, and Blobel in the leadership corps of the *Einsatzgruppen*. Even so, more research into this subject is needed and it should include a broader sample of men from all levels and ranks of the *Einsatzgruppen*, and not just the officer corps, to determine more fully the motivations of this group of perpetrators.

[198] Waller, "Perpetrators of the Holocaust," 16–18. Lozowick, "Rollbahn Mord," 232 agrees, writing, "reality was reinterpreted to fit preconceived rationalizations to justify a mass murder that had been decided upon independently of any 'reasons' or 'causes.'"

[199] This corresponds with Westermann, "'Ordinary Men' or 'Ideological Soldiers,'" 62–63, who found that unlike Browning's Battalion 101, the members of Police Battalion 310 were motivated largely by ideology because "the nature of warfare on the Eastern Front left little room for either ordinary men or ordinary life."

5

Trial

In my opinion, the records and judgments in these ... trials constitute a landmark in the development of international law, as well as a vital source of information upon the basis of which history can be written far more truthfully and fully than would otherwise have been possible. Their great importance will become more manifest as time goes on.

Telford Taylor[1]

A trial is, in part, a search for truth.

Monroe Freedman[2]

The *Einsatzgruppen* trial opened on September 29, 1947, at the Palace of Justice in Nuremberg, the same location that two years earlier had housed the landmark IMT. The trial began with the presentation of the prosecution's case led by the 27 year-old Chief Prosecutor, Benjamin Ferencz and it ended eight months later on April 10, 1948, when the tribunal rendered its judgment and passed sentences on the defendants. What distinguishes the *Einsatzgruppen* trial from the original Nuremberg trial – and all the other Subsequent trials for that matter – is that it was the only Nuremberg war crimes trial that dealt exclusively with the Final Solution to the Jewish Question. This makes it significant in the history of the Third Reich and the Holocaust. For such an important trial, one would expect a detailed presentation of the evidence of the crime by the prosecution. This did not happen. The presentation of the prosecution's evidence (mainly excerpts from the Operational Situational Reports of the *Einsatzgruppen* and sworn affidavits of the defendants – 253 exhibits in all) lasted less than two days, an unusually short time for such an important case, but also reflective of the strength of the evidence. The lion's share of the trial was taken up with the direct testimony of the defendants. The prosecution called virtually no witnesses;

[1] Taylor, Press Release, May 17, 1948, in *idem, Final Report,* 115.
[2] Monroe Freedman, *Lawyers' Ethics in an Adversary System* (New York, 1975).

other than Rolf Wartenberg, an interrogator for the OCCWC, and Francois Bayle, Commander of the Medical Corps of the French Navy, they relied exclusively on documentation to make their case.[3]

Admittedly, witnesses make for a more dramatic presentation of a case than documents, and there may have been plenty Ferencz could have called. Locating witnesses, however, involves time and money (war crimes investigators would have to be dispatched to the Soviet Union to track down witnesses), commodities the OCCWC was short on at the time. In any case, most of the defendants had admitted their crimes in pre-trial interrogations and, for those who had not, the *Einsatzgruppen* reports would prove their guilt. Thus, in the autumn of 1947, the Nuremberg prosecutors set out to prove – by documentation alone – that the men in the dock had participated in the worst crimes of the regime; they had committed crimes against humanity – what, today, we call genocide.

Who committed genocide, how it was carried out, when it was decided upon as a policy, and who made the decision are the issues that are at the heart of this trial. In spite of this focus, definitive answers to these questions are impossible to ascertain. More than half a century after the conclusion of this trial, historians still only agree on one issue: that the mass killing of Soviet Jews by units of the *Einsatzgruppen* beginning in the summer of 1941 marks a watershed in Nazi racial policy toward Europe's Jews. Beyond that, there is no consensus. Some view the *Einsatzgruppen*'s murderous activities in the summer of 1941 as the beginning of Hitler's plan for the Final Solution; others see it as a bridge between mass murder and total genocide, a kind of partial genocide that escalated thereafter. If the trial was about these important issues, why are we unable to say with some certainty when the order to kill all of Europe's Jews was made and by whom? The problem lies in a paucity of documentation about these questions. Although the prosecution had ample evidence to prove that the defendants had committed mass murder, they had no documentation to prove who ordered it, when, and under what circumstances. Was the order – referred to as the Hitler-order or *Führerbefehl* – given before the units were deployed in the Soviet Union on June 22, 1941, as Ohlendorf testified? Or, was it given later, in the late summer or early fall of 1941, some weeks or months after the SS-Security Police units departed from their assembly point in the town of Pretzsch as Erwin Schulz suggested it was?[4]

When exactly the order to murder all Soviet Jews – men, women, and children – was given is a matter of speculation and is part of the much broader intentionalist-functionalist debate that centers on the question of

---

[3] Rolf and Hannah Wartenberg Collection, RG 2005.347, USHMM.
[4] Browning, *Origins of the Final Solution* believes it was given sometime between August and December 1941.

whether Hitler had a blueprint to murder Europe's Jews.[5] The question arose largely because there is a lack of clear documentary evidence to prove when and by whom the decision for the Final Solution was made.[6] The absence of a clear record of the decision-making process has given rise to a surfeit of interpretations of the origins of the Final Solution.[7] Postwar

[5] At the trial the order to murder Soviet Jewry was at various times referred to as the "Hitler-order," the "Hitler-*befehl*," the *Führer*-order, and the "*Führerbefehl*." These forms are used interchangeably.

[6] Initially, there were two schools of thought concerning the origins of the Final Solution. Intentionalists such as Lucy Dawidowicz, *The War Against the Jews* (New York, 1975) and Gerald Fleming, *Hitler und die Endlösung: "Es ist des Führers Wunsch."* (Munich, 1982), strongly believe that there is a clear link between Hitler's early antisemitic ideology and his later antisemitic practice, they see a straight path from Hitler's hatred of the Jews to his policy of extermination. Proponents of this view refer to Hitler's writings and speeches that highlight his early commitment to annihilate the Jews. Hitler hated the Jews, millions were killed, and, therefore, Hitler's intentions had always been genocide. Intentionalists highlight the important role of Hitler in initiating murder. More moderate intentionalists such as Karl Dietrich Bracher, *The German Dictatorship* (New York, 1966) and Eberhard Jäckel, *Hitlers Weltanschauung: Entwurf einer Herrschaft* (Stuttgart, 1971) do not focus so much on the idea of a blueprint for murder as they do on the centrality of antisemitism in Hitler's worldview. They see the murder of the Jews as part of Hitler's long range goals; each policy he implemented, from the 1933 boycott to the invasion of the Soviet Union in 1941, was part of his overall goal to achieve a Europe free of Jews. Functionalists, on the other hand, de-emphasize the role of Hitler while emphasizing the function of other organizations. Adherents to this view argue the policy of extermination developed in stages. As the Nazis consolidated power, Jewish policy gradually radicalized, until 1941 and the invasion of the Soviet Union, when it was decided the best way to solve the "Jewish problem" was through mass murder. For classic statements on the functionalist position see Karl Schleunes, *The Twisted Road to Auschwitz. Nazi Policy toward German Jews 1933–1939* (Urbana; IL, 1990) and Uwe Dietrich Adam, *Judenpolitik im Dritten Reich* (Düsseldorf, 1972). In recent years, the debate has become less polarized, tempered by such nuanced interpretations as Browning, who classifies himself as a "moderate functionalist" and Philippe Burrin, *Hitler and the Jews: The Genesis of the Holocaust* (London, 1994) who calls his approach "conditional intentionalism." For elaboration of the terms initially coined by Tim Mason, see *idem*, "Intention and Explanation: A Current Controversy about the Interpretation of National Socialism," in Gerhard Hirschfeld and Lothar Kettenacker (eds.), *Der Führerstaat: Mythos und Realität. Studien zur Struktur und Politik des Dritten Reiches* (Stuttgart, 1981), 23–40. See also Ian Kershaw, *The Nazi Dictatorship: Problems and Perspectives of Interpretation* (New York, 1993), 80–107; Browning, "Beyond 'Intentionalism' and 'Functionalism': The Decision for the Final Solution Reconsidered," in *The Path to Genocide: Essays on Launching the Final Solution* (New York, 1992), 86–121 and "The Decision Concerning the Final Solution," in Browning, *Fateful Months*, 8–38.

[7] For overviews of interpretations concerning timing, see Browning, *Nazi Policy, Jewish Workers, German Killers* (Cambridge, 2000), 26–57. For specific positions on timing, see Christian Gerlach, *Krieg, Ernährung, Völkermord: Forschungen zur deutschen Vernichtungspolitik im Zweiten Weltkrieg* (Hamburg, 1998), 56–81; Ogorreck, *Die Einsatzgruppen und die Genesis der Endlösung* (1996); Peter Longerich, "Vom Massenmord zur 'Endlösung'. Die Erschießungen von jüdischen Zivilisten in den ersten Monaten des Ostfeldzuges im Kontext des nationalsozialistischen Judenmords," in Bernd Wegner (ed.), *Zwei Wege nach Moskau. Vom Hitler-Stalin-Pakt zum 'Unternehmen Barbarossa'* (Munich, 1991), 251–254; Burrin,

historians have had to rely on perpetrator testimony given during trial, especially that of Ohlendorf who claimed that Bruno Streckenbach, head of Office I (Personnel) of the RSHA, gave the brutal and murderous order, before the invasion of the Soviet Union in the summer of 1941.[8] Ohlendorf's testimony about the nature and timing of the *Führerbefehl* suggested to historians that the order was more than Hitler's "wish" or "desire," and was instead part of a well thought-out and concrete plan of genocide. Of course, testimony is not the only factor contributing to such a view. The minutes from the Wannsee Conference and other evidence have lent credence to the intentionalist argument as well, but certainly, Ohlendorf's statements on this issue had an impact on the subsequent development of this school of thought.[9]

The historical controversy about the timing and nature of the murderous order developed further when Alfred Streim, former chief prosecutor at the Central Office for the Investigation of National Socialist Crimes in Ludwigsburg, Germany, detected discrepancies in Ohlendorf's testimony. After reviewing a number of affidavits given by other members of the *Einsatzgruppen* during pre-trial interrogations, Streim concluded that the Hitler-order to murder all Jews had not been issued prior to the invasion of the Soviet Union in June 1941. Rather, it most probably had been given some weeks later, between early August and September 1941, the precise date of which cannot be determined without further evidence. Streim believes that *Einsatzgruppen* killings escalated from partial to total genocide sometime in the period between July and September 1941, but that the genocidal murder of Soviet Jews had not been planned at the outset of Operation Barbarossa as Ohlendorf had testified in 1947. From the evidence available, Streim concluded that Ohlendorf's testimony had been perjured; he had lied as part of a defense strategy to escape a death sentence by arguing the mitigating circumstance of superior orders. Since Streim highlighted the issue of timing in the 1980s, it has become a point of contention in the historiography on the origins of the Final Solution. And, although further research has helped clarify the issue, no definitive date for the order to murder all Soviet Jews has been established.[10] Nonetheless, research by leading scholars in the United States and Germany leans toward a functionalist interpretation.

Hitler and the Jews, 93–113; Ronald Headland, "The *Einsatzgruppen*: The Question of their Initial Operations," *Holocaust and Genocide Studies* 4:4 (1989), 401–412; and Lozowick, "Rollbahn Mord," 221–241.

[8] On the issue of documentation, see Peter Longerich, *The Unwritten Order: Hitler's Role in the Final Solution* (Port Stroud, 2001), 108–110.

[9] Mallmann, *Die Gestapo in Zweiten Weltkrieg*, 437–441, discusses this issue under the heading, the Ohlendorf-Legend.

[10] For a full account of the early debate about timing, see in particular Streim, "Tasks," 309–328 and Helmut Krausnick and Alfred Streim, "Correspondence," in *ibid.* 6 (1989), 311–346. See also, Krausnick et al., *Anatomy of the SS State* (Frogmore, England, 1973),

The timing and context of Ohlendorf's testimony is significant to our understanding of the evolution of the Final Solution.[11] British intelligence records and American interrogation reports that document Ohlendorf's earliest statements about his role in the genocide of Soviet Jewry call into question the prevailing functionalist interpretation. From the very beginning of his incarceration in May 1945, until his indictment in July 1947 and thereafter, Ohlendorf consistently said that he had received his orders prior to the deployment of the *Einsatzgruppen* in the Soviet Union in June 1941. If true, his claim of a pre-existing order means that the decision to murder all Soviet Jews was made before the invasion of the Soviet Union, not after it as functionalist historians have argued. Why should we take Ohlendorf's word about who gave the order and when? After all, he was a mass murderer and following his death many of his co-defendants from Nuremberg told German judicial authorities that Ohlendorf was lying.[12]

There is no question that Ohlendorf was not always honest. Upon his arrest, he constructed an image of himself that was not entirely accurate and thus the inclination is to distrust him and to assume he was perjuring himself to save his life. Historians and others who have questioned the veracity of his statements have argued that in the context of a trial that could result in his death, it is not surprising that he chose to argue superior orders. According to Article 8 of the *Nuremberg Charter*, if a defendant acted "pursuant to orders of his Government or of a superior," he is still legally accountable for his crime, but his actions "may be considered in mitigation of punishment if the Tribunal determines that justice so requires."[13] In other words, if the order to murder all Soviet Jews existed prior to the *Einsatzgruppen*'s deployment in June 1941, then the circumstances are mitigating, and whereas still legally responsible for the actions he carried out for the Reich, he might avoid a death sentence. Although legally plausible, the argument does not stand up for a number of reasons, not the least of which is that it ascribes a motive for lying that did not exist at the time Ohlendorf made his initial statement. Not only had the *Nuremberg Charter* not been signed when Ohlendorf made his first claims about his criminal activities, but the argument also

---

59–75; Streim, *Die Behandlung sowjetischer Kriegsgefangener im 'Fall Barbarossa': Eine Dokumentation* (Karlsruhe, 1981), 74–93 and "Zur Eröffnung des allgemeinen Judenvernichtungsbefehl gegenüber den Einsatzgruppen," in Eberhard Jäckel and Jürgen Rohwer (eds.), *Der Mord an den Juden im Zweiten Weltkrieg. Entschlußbildung und Verwirklichung* (Stuttgart, 1985), 107–119.

[11] For example see Bloxham, *Genocide on Trial*, 1–13 and Browning, "German Memory," 26.

[12] For example, Biberstein and his attorney Friedrich Bergold told German authorities that Ohlendorf lied about who gave the order to the leaders of the *Einsatzgruppen* as a defense strategy. See "Protokoll in der Gericht. Voruntersuchung gegen Bruno Streckenbach," by Bergold, 11.10.72 in ZSTL, 201 AR-Z 76–59, vol. 16, pp. 8387–8389 and "Protokoll in der gericht. Voruntersuchung gegen Bruno Streckenbach," by Ernst Emil Heinrich Biberstein, 4.05.72 in *ibid*, vol. 13, pp. 8058–8065.

[13] Article 8, *Charter of the IMT*, October 6, 1945, quoted in *TWC*, vol. 4, xiv.

184 The Nuremberg SS-Einsatzgruppen Trial, 1945–1958

presumes that Ohlendorf recognized that his actions were illegal and immoral, ignoring entirely his ideological and moral worldview and contradicting the nature of his personality. Additionally, when Ohlendorf made his initial statements in May 1945, he did not know he would be tried, nor did he know what documentation the Allies had to prove his guilt. We may never know with complete certainty whether he was telling the truth about the timing of the *Führerbefehl*, but this does not mean de facto that he was lying about it.

Some historians believe that accepting Ohlendorf's testimony as fact has resulted in the current historical debate – what Jürgen Matthäus has labeled the "myth" of the *Führer*-order.[14] Nuremberg testimony created and perpetuated the myth that the Final Solution began in earnest before the invasion of the Soviet Union on June 22, 1941, and far from elucidating the issue of timing, trial testimony has in fact "distorted the historical understanding of the Holocaust."[15] Did Ohlendorf lie? By thoroughly examining Ohlendorf's statements from first interrogation to his last, this chapter will explore the veracity of his statements about the timing and origins of the order. In terms of the historical record, it appears as if historians believed Ohlendorf's testimony because it came from a major, self-proclaimed participant in the Final Solution, who seemed to be more honest and straightforward than most of the accused. As Browning so aptly noted, assessing trial documents is always a judgment call.[16] Even though Ohlendorf was a self-confessed mass murderer, his personality was such that perjury appeared to be beneath him. As a witness, he seemed credible and a good source of historical evidence.[17] In the courtroom, facts of a case can be determined through direct testimony, but it is up to the tribunal to judge the reliability of the testimony.[18]

---

[14] Jürgen Matthäus, "A Case of Myth-Making: The 'Führer Order' During the *Einsatzgruppen* Trial, 1947–1948," unpublished article, USHMM, 1–20. I would like to thank Dr. Matthäus for kindly allowing me access to his findings on this subject. Two examples of what Matthäus is referring to can be found in Krausnick, who wrote in 1965 that "when the *Einsatzgruppen* were being formed in May 1941, their leaders ... were ... told about the *secret decree on shooting by word of mouth*," in idem, *Anatomy of the SS State*, 79; and, Robert Wolfe writing in 1980, "of all the Führer's orders, written and unwritten, signed and unsigned, this one ordering the "final solution of the Jewish question" is known as *the* Fuehrer Order," in "Putative Threat," n.52, 55. Klaus-Michael Mallmann, "Die Türöffner der 'Endlösung'," agrees with Matthäus, that Ohlendorf was the author of the myth of the Führerbefehl. In Paul and Mallmann (eds.), *Die Gestapo in Zweiten Weltkrieg*, 437–438.

[15] Matthäus, "A Case of Myth-Making," 3.

[16] Browning, "German Memory," 29–30.

[17] On the issue of the historian and use of trial documents to reconstruct historical narratives, see Browning, "German Memory, Judicial Interrogation, and Historical Reconstruction: Writing Perpetrator History from Postwar Testimony," in Saul Friedlander (ed.), *Probing the Limits of Representation: Nazism and the "Final Solution"* (Cambridge; MA, 1992), 22–36.

[18] On this issue, see Lawrence Douglas, "Wartime Lies. Securing the Holocaust in Law and Literature," in F. C. Decoste and Bernard Schwartz (eds.), *The Holocaust's Ghost. Writings on Art, Politics, Law and Education* (Edmonton, Alberta, 2000), 17–18.

Significantly for this story, Ohlendorf's comportment was such that the tribunal believed what he said because he was, they believed, the "very personification of . . . truth."[19] In any case, the timing of the order, whether promulgated in late June, July, or August 1941, was not germane to the prosecution's case.[20] Mass murders had been committed and the *Einsatzgruppen* leaders had been indicted. The task of the prosecution was to prove that the accused had committed these crimes, and the task of the court to determine if they had understood the illegal nature of the order. In other words, the timing of the order had little or no significant legal relevance for the prosecution's case.

Ohlendorf's testimony has directly contributed to the ambiguity of the historical record, especially to our current understanding of the events that led to the murder of Soviet Jewry in the summer of 1941. This should not be surprising given that one of the aims of the NMT was the exposure of Nazi criminality.[21] Establishing beyond a reasonable doubt what these men did, how they did it, and why, was not an unrealistic expectation given that in law, "the trial serves as the primary tool for securing a truthful picture of an historical event."[22] As Telford Taylor expressed it, "many of these [trial] documents now have a gloss on them in the form of supplementary testimony by the men who wrote them or who were mentioned in them, thus creating an immense overlay of additional information and comment that in many settings is of great historical importance."[23] Taylor and the other planners probably did not realize it at the time, but in the context of a legal proceeding, the dual goals of punishment and education are often incompatible.[24] After

---

[19] Musmanno, Review of Film, *Judgment at Nuremberg*, 1961, in Nuremberg Correspondence file 1445, in MMP. On the Hitler-order as fact see Eidesstattliche Versicherung des Rudolf Aschenauer, 11.11.1949, N642 (Aschenauer), box 62, Bundesarchiv-Militärarchiv, Freiburg (BA/MA from here forward). See also discussion between Musmanno and James Heath, October 14, 1947, in *Trial*, roll 2, 636–637.

[20] This short, six to eight week time frame is at the heart of the issue of timing.

[21] Taylor wrote that one of the purposes for publishing the records of the 12 Subsequent Nuremberg Trials was, "[t]o promote the interest of historical truth. . . . " See Taylor, *Final Report*, 101.

[22] Douglas, "Wartime Lies," 27–28.

[23] Taylor quoted in Headland, *Messages of Murder*, 177. Ferencz stated, "Most Germans are still unaware of the detailed events we shall account. They must realize that these things did occur in order to understand somewhat the causes of their present plight. . . . As we here record the massacre of thousands of helpless children, the German people may reflect on it to assess the merits of the system they so enthusiastically acclaimed." *Idem*, opening statement by the prosecution, September 29, 1947, *Trial*, roll, 1, 32–33.

[24] Michael R. Marrus, "History and the Holocaust in the Courtroom," in Gary Smith and Florent Brayard (eds.), *Vom Prozeß zur Geschichte: Die juristische und historische Aufarbeitung der Shoa in Frankreich und Deutschland* (Berlin, 2001), 1–35 argues that "trials cannot and should not be expected . . . to teach history." Compare with Douglas, *The Memory of Judgment. Making Law and History in the Trials of the Holocaust* (New Haven, 2001), 1–7, who thinks that war crimes trials can serve a didactic end and that they can inform historical narratives. The literature on war crimes trials and their didactic value is

all, criminal trials are adversarial, and testimony is most frequently given in an attempt to establish legal exculpation, not to document historical truth. By their very nature, criminal trials can act as strong impediments to the attainment of historical truth, when by excluding or altering historical facts a defendant can demonstrate innocence or a prosecutor, guilt.[25] Of course, the corrective to false or perjured testimony is a rigorous cross-examination, which is meant to detect discrepancies.[26] Facts introduced during testimony were often inaccurate and, not surprisingly, it is contested and distorted facts that are at the very heart of the current historical controversy over timing.[27] Thus, it is important to return to the context in which these issues were first spoken to determine if possible the nature of the distortions.[28]

No one disputes that the issue of the Hitler-order is of extreme importance historically. However, it is not the purpose of this chapter to investigate when, or even if, an actual order was given to the leaders of the *Einsatzgruppen*; this can be safely left to those who study and write about the origins of the Final Solution.[29] Yet, the issue is central to the trial, to ignore it would be remiss. The defense lawyers cite the order to justify and excuse the behavior of their clients in Russia; it was their defense. The judge and the prosecutor also saw it as integral to the trial because they believed it was *the directive*

---

a focus of scholarly attention. Examples include, Browning, "German Memory," 22–36; Leora Y. Bilsky, "When Actor and Spectator Meet in the Courtroom: Reflections on Hannah Arendt's Concept of Judgment," *History and Memory. Studies in Representation of the Past* 2:8 (Fall/Winter, 1996), 137–174; Jared Stark, "The Task of Testimony. On "No common Place: The Holocaust Testimony of Alina Bacall-Zwirn," *History and Memory. Studies in Representation of the Past* (1999), 37–61; Carlo Ginzburg, *The Judge and the Historian* (London, 1999); and, Bloxham, *Genocide on Trial* (2001).

[25] Not everyone agrees. Erich Haberer, "History and Justice: Paradigms of the Prosecution of Nazi Crimes," *Holocaust and Genocide Studies*, 19: 3 (Winter 2005), 487–519 argues that war crimes trials benefit historical inquiry.

[26] Douglas, "Wartime Lies," 27–28 writes that "Despite the elaborate evidentiary norms associated with this [legal] process, the trial in Anglo-American jurisprudence is governed by a relatively simple proposition: that facts be proved by firsthand testimony and that knowledge be produced by direct observation. This privileging of testimony, however, does not indicate a juridical faith in the veracity of the spoken word; quite to the contrary, Anglo-American jurisprudence attempts to control the spectre of mendacious or mistaken testimony through the rigors of adversarial confrontation."

[27] Whereas the existence and nature of the order were substantive issues at Nuremberg, today the controversy resides on the matter of *when* – before or after June 22, 1941 – and by *whom* – Heydrich, Himmler or Bruno Streckenbach – the order was given.

[28] Long ago Helge Grabitz, "Problems of Nazi Trials in the Federal Republic of Germany," *Holocaust and Genocide Studies* 2:3 (1988), 209, called for the continuation of trials against Nazi war criminals not only to punish those responsible, but also to better understand the historical facts brought out in them. More recently, Christian Gerlach, "The Eichmann Interrogations in Holocaust Historiography," *Holocaust and Genocide Studies* 15: 3 (Winter, 2001), 428–452 disagrees. He thinks war crimes trials obscure historical understanding.

[29] Gerlach, *ibid.*, 429, argues that war crimes trials "cannot serve as the exclusive, or even the main basis of an historiographical arguments."

that was at the heart of Hitler's racial war against the Jews. Depending on which side of the case you were on, the Hitler-order proved the defendants were innocent or it proved they were guilty. The issue is significant in still another sense. In this historically important trial the issues of history and testimony are of paramount importance. The marriage of these two mediums challenge the historian to examine the very nature of war crimes trial testimony and the standards by which today we assess testimony and use it for historical purposes.[30]

The issues here are complex; therefore, the chapter will be divided into three sections. The first section will trace the development of Ohlendorf's testimony on the issue of the *Führerbefehl* in the context of the trial, revisiting what he said and when he said it. The second section will place the *Führerbefehl* in the context of the *Einsatzgruppen* trial, to relate how the order was used as a defense strategy and how the strategy played out at trial. Finally, the chapter examines why and how the court came to view the order to murder Soviet Jews, the so-called *Führerbefehl*, as a singular policy, conceived of by the highest-ranking Nazi officials, directed against a distinctive racial group, but not part of the otherwise general destruction that resulted from the policies and actions of the Third Reich during the war. The material presented leads to the conclusion that the *Führerbefehl* was an important, even critical factor in determining the outcome of the trial; the defense used it to prove a lack of criminal intent, whereas the prosecution used it to prove that the defendants had perpetrated racial murder as specifically ordered by Hitler. In both instances, Ohlendorf played an important role.

Otto Ohlendorf, Early Interrogations, and the Question of Orders

Ohlendorf first articulated the matter of a *Führerbefehl* to murder Soviet Jewry in 1945, during early interrogations with the British who did not pursue the issue.[31] Instead, it was fleshed out during Ohlendorf's preparation for his testimony at the IMT. The discussion of the *Führerbefehl* began during his very first interrogation by the Americans on October 24, 1945, when he was asked outright whether or not he and the other leaders of the *Einsatzgruppen* had operated on their own initiative.[32] His answer was complicated. The leaders of the *Einsatzgruppen* had received their orders in

---

[30] Browning, "Daniel Goldhagen's Willing Executioners," in *History and Memory: Studies in Representation of the Past* 1: 8 (Spring/Summer, 1996), 88, warns that trial testimony is particularly problematic for the scholar who wants to reconstruct historical events. He believes that the use of trial testimony and interrogation records can produce, at best, a "minimum...narrative of events."

[31] Appendix 1, S.I.R. 1706, September 30, 1945 in RG 319, G-2 Security classified Intelligence and Interrogation Records, box 165A, Ohlendorf folder.

[32] Letter, Brookhart to Amen, October 24, 1945 in M1270, roll 13, 1–2.

Berlin prior to their deployment, he explained, but while in the field, aside from military issues, they did have some freedom and flexibility of action. By this he meant that different group leaders could employ different methods to carry out their assigned tasks but not, as some historians have suggested, that the *Einsatzgruppen* leaders decided on who and when to kill.[33] This behavior seems to conform to the earlier pattern followed by the *Einsatzgruppen* in Poland, who were given their orders prior to deployment, but who also had some flexibility of action during the course of the war.[34] Ohlendorf described in detail the organizational structure of the *Einsatzgruppen*, including the composition of the groups and their relationship to the army, and twice briefly he referred to orders. He said that the *Einsatzgruppen* received their orders to murder Soviet Jews on two separate occasions. The first time, he informed his interrogator, Lieutenant Colonel Smith Brookhart, the order was given verbally to the four leaders in early May 1941, just days before the mobile units crossed into Soviet territory.[35] At this time, Ohlendorf did not say who gave the order nor did Brookhart ask.[36] The second more familiar order was given directly by Himmler during the *Reichsführer's* visit to the eastern front in August 1941. Both orders unequivocally called for the murder of all Soviet Jews, and he stressed that although Himmler delivered the orders, both had originated with Hitler; hence, they were *Führer*-orders or *Führerbefehlen*.[37] It is important to bear in mind that during this early interrogation, Ohlendorf never explicitly revealed the contents of the first order, whereas he did tell Brookhart that the second order from Himmler called for the extermination of *all* Jews, without exception, in the Russian theater of war.[38]

Ohlendorf was interrogated October 25 for a second time. Before Brookhart could begin questioning him however, Ohlendorf spent some time correcting facts he had given the previous day. He had, he told Brookhart, mistakenly believed that Operation Barbarossa had begun in May, but after

---

[33] Interrogation, Ohlendorf, October 24, 1945, 1430–1700, NARA M1270, roll 13, 7–8 and 14.

[34] On *Einsatzgruppen* activities in Poland see Rossino, *Hitler Strikes Poland*, 234 who notes similarities between the campaign in Poland and the Soviet Union.

[35] Ohlendorf's recollection of the leaders of the four groups was incorrect. He initially identified Max Thomas as the leader of group C when the units were first formed in Pretzsch, but in fact Otto Rasch led *Einsatzgruppe* C in June 1941. Ohlendorf later corrected this error. See affidavit, Ohlendorf, November 5, 1945 (PS 2620), in *Trial*, Prosecution Documents, roll 11, frames 0044–0045. See also, Vernehmung, Ohlendorf by Brookhart and John Amen, November 26, 1945 in M1270, roll 13, 13.

[36] Interrogation, Ohlendorf, December 4, 1946, in TTP series 5; subseries 1; box no. 4; folder 51: NMT-OCCWC Evidence Division, Interrogation Branch – Interrogation Summaries N-Z.

[37] Vernehmung, Ohlendorf, October 24, 1945 in *ibid.*, 1–28. See also Interrogation Summary of Ohlendorf, October 24, 1945, in *ibid.*, roll 13, 3.

[38] Interrogation Summary, October 24, 1945, in *ibid.*, 3.

reconstructing the events he now realized he had been wrong.[39] He also implied that Hitler gave the directive to liquidate Soviet Jews long before Operation Barbarossa, but explained that Himmler waited to tell him about the *Führer's* decision (and his tasks) until approximately four weeks before the *Einsatzgruppen* were deployed.[40] Although it is unclear from the interrogation record, presumably here Ohlendorf was referring to the general assignment of the *Einsatzgruppen* in the east and not specifically to the *Führerbefehl* to murder all Jews.[41] Because Brookhart never asked for clarification, the record on this issue is unclear.

During these early interrogations Brookhart mainly sought to obtain specific details about the activities of the *Einsatzgruppen*, such as the precise manner in which the victims were killed and the bodies disposed of. Ohlendorf's claim that Hitler had given the order to murder did not seem out of the ordinary to Brookhart, which is hardly surprising considering allied presumptions about the hierarchy of the Reich and the power Hitler wielded in it. As one legal expert explains, an examiner, "whether he wishes it or not," always "base[s] his questions on his own assumptions regarding the events he has to clarify."[42] At this early date, trial officials had few details of what transpired on the eastern front, and the process of uncovering each new detail simply horrified British and American authorities.[43] Besides, before anyone could make a judgment about these events or assess their accuracy, the prosecuting authorities needed to gather basic information about what had happened. The case the Americans were preparing was based on the assumption that criminal decisions were conceived at the highest levels of the Party and thus Ohlendorf's claims merely confirmed their preconceived view that Hitler was at the center of the decision-making process with respect

[39] Vernehmung, Ohlendorf, October 25, 1945, in *ibid.*, roll 13, 1–2.
[40] *Ibid.*, 8 and affidavit, Ohlendorf (PS 2620), November 5, 1945 in *Trial*, roll 8, frame 0054 in which Ohlendorf stated: "Im Juni 1941 wurde ich von Himmler bestimmt, eine der *Einsatzgruppen* zu fuehren, die damals gebildet wurden, um den deutschen Armeen in russischen Feldzug zu folgen. Ich war der Chef der Einsatzgruppe D... Himmler erklaerte, dass ein wichtiger Teil (sic) unserer Aufgabe in der Beseitigung von Juden, Frauen, Maennern und Kindern, und kommunistischen Funktionaeren bestuende. Ich wurde etwa vier Wochen (sic) vorher ueber den Angriff auf Russland benachrichtigt."
[41] Richard Breitman, "Himmler and the 'Terrible Secret' among the Executioners," in Jehuda Reinharz and George L. Mosse (eds.), *The Impact of Western Nationalisms* (London, 1991), 77–97, argues that information concerning the murder of the Jews in the USSR was given on a "need to know basis" only, and then it was only given orally. Given Ohlendorf's high position, it is possible that he met with Himmler some weeks prior to the invasion.
[42] Arne Trankell, *Reliability of Evidence. Methods for Analyzing and Assessing Witness Statements* (Stockholm, 1972), 25–26.
[43] Whitney Harris, quoted in Hilary Gaskin (ed.), *Eyewitnesses at Nuremberg* (London, 1991), 177, recalled how horrified he was upon first hearing about the activities of the *Einsatzgruppen*.

to mass murder.[44] In this context, it makes sense that Brookhart would not have questioned Ohlendorf on the details of timing and intention. Instead, he listened intently while the former leader of *Einsatzgruppe* D willingly and dispassionately offered information about atrocities, always making certain that Brookhart was aware of how humane his method of execution had been compared to the practices of his colleagues who commanded the other three units.[45] Ohlendorf seemed "particularly anxious," Brookhart noted, to distinguish between those SS officers who acted under superior orders and those who did not, suggesting that killing under orders was somehow better than not. But again, Brookhart did not question how or even if it was possible for the SS units to take independent action, he merely accepted Ohlendorf's assertions at face value.[46]

What Streim may have identified as deliberate malfeasance by Ohlendorf, I see as an issue of memory. In these early interrogations at least, Ohlendorf's memory for detail was not always sharp. His mistake about the date of the beginning of Operation Barbarossa is but one example of his inability to recall specific dates, names, and locations.[47] His testimony is peppered with such qualifications as "if I remember rightly" or "contrary to my assumption of yesterday" or "I cannot remember" or "it must have been" or "I don't know anymore."[48] A careful reading of the interrogation record suggests that Ohlendorf's responses were not intended to be evasive or untruthful – at least not about the activities of the *Einsatzgruppen*. We know already that he had been unusually, perhaps even naively, cooperative with his captors, revealing much about the inner workings of the Nazi regime. As anyone's would, his recall suffered from the effects of time, remembering some details more clearly than others, and some not at all. To be sure, nearly six years had passed since the *Einsatzgruppen* had embarked on their fateful journey into Soviet Russia and Ohlendorf had not had the advantage of reviewing

[44] This idea is supported by Marrus, "The History of the Holocaust: A Survey of Recent Literature," *Journal of Modern History* 59 (1987), 120 who writes, "'Intentionalism,' it may be supposed, was born in Nuremberg in 1945, when American prosecutors first presented Nazi war crimes as a carefully orchestrated conspiracy, launched together with the war itself."

[45] Interrogation, Ohlendorf, October 24, 1945 in M1270, roll 13, 14–16; Interrogation Summary of Ohlendorf, October 24, 1945, in *ibid.*, roll 13, 3 in which Ohlendorf claims his job was to "prevent cruelties" one example of which was safeguarding the possessions of the victims until after they were executed or ensuring that the victims did not have to wait an excessive amount of time before they were shot.

[46] Vernehmung, Ohlendorf, October 27, 1945, and Brief of Ohlendorf Interrogation, Brookhart, October 29, 1945, in *ibid.*

[47] For a good discussion of human memory, reconstruction of events, and the law see Trankell, *Reliability of Evidence*, 20–23.

[48] Vernehmung, Ohlendorf, October 27, 1945; Brief of Interrogation, Ohlendorf by Brookhart, October 29, 1945 in M1270, roll 13; and, Interrogation, Ohlendorf by Colonel Tupikov (USSR), November 14, 1945, in *ibid.*, 1–7.

the vast array of documents the Allies possessed before he responded to questions during these interviews.[49] Psychological studies have also shown that time can seriously alter the memory of an event by allowing other events or influences to distort the perception of what transpired, even if the individual was an intimate participant. In some cases time has been shown to "create an entirely new memory" altogether.[50] But to suggest as some have, at this early date, that Ohlendorf was deliberately lying to his interrogators is a distortion of the evidence; it also ignores research that has shown the frail and subjective nature of human memory.[51] Most importantly, at this early date, there was no reason for Ohlendorf to be untruthful.[52] He was neither under indictment for war crimes himself nor was there any evidence of coercion (physical or otherwise) by American authorities. Because he had already confessed to supervising mass murder, there was little more he could disclose that would be more damaging should a legal procedure be mounted against him; when the order was given and by whom would not have been a factor one way or the other in his prosecution. Of course, all of this is not to suggest that Ohlendorf did not perjure himself in later testimony, but in October and November 1945, he had little reason to lie about the nature, timing, and delivery of the *Einsatzgruppen*'s orders. In any case, what was important for the legal process is that his captors believed him. I am in no way defending Ohlendorf here, but rather I am attempting to set the historical record straight and assess the likelihood that he was perjuring himself as Streim and others have argued. It is also important to highlight the fact that over the course of the next few months, Ohlendorf's description of the events surrounding the *Führerbefehl* did not change substantially. He remained rather vague about the details of the *Einsatzgruppen*'s initial orders at Pretzsch, but no one ever asked him to be more explicit, and as we shall see he was not one to evade a question. He plainly liked to talk, a lot. He spoke at length about the German army and its relationship to the

[49] In the summary of Ohlendorf's first interrogation, the author writes, "Ohlendorf says that his statements in the questionnaire he filled out (Exhibit A – Ohlendorf) are correct to the best of his knowledge, although he was given little time and no documents." See Interrogation Division Summary, October 24, 1945, in M1270, roll 13, 1. On the issue of the problem of memory, time lapse, and trial testimony, see for example, Brian A. Grosman, "Testing Witness Reliability," *The Criminal Law Quarterly* 5 (1962–1963), 318–327; Arne Trankell, *Reliability of Evidence*, and Sally M. A. Lloyd-Bostock and Brian R. Clifford (eds.), *Evaluating Witness Evidence. Recent Psychological Research and New Perspectives* (Toronto, 1983).

[50] Grosman, "Testing Witness Reliability," 322–323.

[51] For example, Alfred Streim believes that "Ohlendorf lied when deception was useful, and he spoke the truth when honesty was profitable," Streim, "Reply to Helmut Krausnick," *Simon Wiesenthal Center Annual* 6 (1989), 338–339.

[52] On this issue, see for example, Elizabeth F. Loftus and Katherine E. Ketcham, "The Malleability of Eyewitness Accounts," in Lloyd-Bostock and Clifford (eds.), *Evaluating Witness Evidence*, 159–171.

Einsatzgruppen, providing American prosecutors with damning and detailed information about the agreement between the German High Command and the RSHA concerning the formation of the *Einsatzgruppen* in the spring of 1941, evidence they later used against leading figures of the German military.[53]

In criminal proceedings, generally speaking, the more time that elapses between a criminal act and witness testimony about it, the less clear and reliable that testimony is judged to be by the court.[54] The opposite is true with Ohlendorf. The more he spoke about the *Führerbefehl* and its contents, and the more assertive and confident he became about it, the more willing the Americans appear to have been to accept his version of events as truthful.[55] After dozens of interrogations, Ohlendorf's recollection of events became more specific. Forgotten details were remembered, names recalled and new facts were added until his narrative became established legal facts. In spite of how forthcoming he had been, it was not until Ohlendorf was called as a prosecution witness in January 1946 at the IMT that he articulated the full contents of the groups' initial orders; even then, his statement, while legally compelling, was historically ambiguous.

Otto Ohlendorf, the *Führerbefehl*, and Testimony at the IMT

On January 3, 1946, Ohlendorf was brought to the Palace of Justice to serve as a witness for the prosecution in the trial of members of the German High Command, and the only representative of the SS on trial, Ernst Kaltenbrunner. The interrogations of the previous year formed the basis of his testimony. Colonel John Harlan Amen, the chief interrogator at the IMT who had personally conducted several of the earlier interviews with Ohlendorf, acted as examiner when Ohlendorf took the stand. He had Ohlendorf explain to the court how negotiations with the army and the RSHA resulted in the formation of the *Einsatzgruppen*, as well as outline the composition of the killing units and their relationship to the army. Ohlendorf told the court that the *Einsatzgruppen* were special military task forces (they were actually paramilitary forces) of the SS and police. At the beginning of Operation Barbarossa in June 1941, these motorized units were formed into four groups designated A, B, C, and D, and were officially assigned the task

---

[53] Testimony, Ohlendorf, January 3, 1946, in *Trial of Major War Criminals before the IMT*, vol. 4, 313.

[54] Grosman, "Testing Witness Reliability," 321.

[55] Grosman, ibid., 324–325, notes that "[j]uries may regard the assertiveness of the witness as a relevant test of his truthfulness," but that assertiveness is not always the best gauge of truth. On the issue of how to judge the accuracy of testimony see Gary L. Wells and R.C.L. Lindsay, "How do People Infer the Accuracy of Eyewitness Memory? Studies of Performance and a Metamemory Analysis," in Lloyd-Bostock and Clifford (eds.), *Evaluating Witness Evidence*, 41–55.

of providing security for German troops in areas behind the front line. In the context of war on the eastern front – where the enemies were ideological – security took on new meaning. On the stand, Ohlendorf explained how the *Einsatzgruppen* were expected to deal with Soviet Jews and communist functionaries, the main ideological enemies of Nazism. He told the court that "before their mission" RSHA Chief Bruno Streckenbach, had "orally instructed" the *Einsatz* and *Kommandoführer* to murder Jews and Soviet political functionaries.[56] It is important to note here that Ohlendorf did not state explicitly that the *Kommandos'* instructions were to kill *all* Jews, although this could certainly be inferred from his testimony; rather, he merely stated that Streckenbach told the leaders of the *Kommandos*, before their assignment, that Jews were to be liquidated.[57] It was during this testimony – and not during the *Einsatzgruppen* trial that took place two years later – that Ohlendorf first linked Streckenbach (who at the time was presumed to be dead) to the *Einsatzgruppen*'s initial orders.[58] Ohlendorf did so tangentially stating that it was Streckenbach who had orally "transmitted the [murderous] orders of Heydrich and Himmler" and Hitler to the leaders of the *Einsatzgruppen* three or four days before the invasion of the Soviet Union.[59] Herein lies evidence of the initial problem with Ohlendorf's testimony. For years, no one doubted its truth or content: Streckenbach had been the person who had delivered the fateful news to the leaders of the killing units and he had done it before the *Einsatzgruppen* were deployed. Only, as it turns out, Streckenbach was not dead. We know for a fact that Streckenbach had been present during the assembly and training of the *Einsatzgruppen* in Pretzsch in May and June 1941, but we cannot be so certain about what he said. When he returned from captivity in the Soviet Union, he denied he had transmitted the order to kill.[60] Although Ohlendorf did not expressly state that Streckenbach's instructions were *the* Hitler-order to murder *all* Soviet Jews, this is a reasonable inference to draw from his statement and it is certainly what historians have surmised.[61] Although Streckenbach's role in the transmission of orders has been the subject of

[56] *Ibid.*, 316–317.
[57] *Ibid.*, 316. Compare with Ogorreck's assessment, *Die Einsatzgruppen*, 48.
[58] Ogorreck, *Die Einsatzgruppen*, 51 and Streim, "Tasks," 313 notes that at the time of the IMT Streckenbach was secretly being held in captivity by the Soviets. Upon returning to Germany in 1955, he apparently denied to his friends and colleagues that he had delivered the Hitler-order. Allegedly he did not tell German prosecutors this, and, instead, remained silent because he did not want to betray colleagues who had recently secured clemency or parole. See also, Longerich, *Politik der Vernichtung*, 310–320 and Affidavits of Schulz, Blume, Rudolf Aschenauer, and Sandberger, 201 AR-\Z 76/59, vols. 6, 8, 16 and 18, *Zentrale Stelle*, Ludwigsburg.
[59] Testimony, Ohlendorf, January 3, 1946, in *Trial of Major War Criminals before the IMT*, vol. 4, 316, 340 and 353.
[60] Browning, *Origins of the Final Solution*, 226–227.
[61] Even though it was Ohlendorf who first linked Streckenbach to the *Einsatzgruppen*'s earliest orders in Pretzsch, it was Sandberger who told American authorities that he had heard a

intense scrutiny, the fact remains that the evidence is thin. Streckenbach denied any role in the transmission of the order, although Ohlendorf was not the only defendant at Nuremberg to state this. Martin Sandberger too told interrogators that Streckenbach gave the *Einsatzgruppen* leaders their orders in May 1941 in Berlin. Sandberger recalled that Streckenbach said: "it was the task of the Einsatzgruppen and Einsatzkommandos to safeguard the security of the country at all costs and by any means. Details were left to the leaders of the Einsatzgruppen, and owing to the complete uncertainty of future conditions, this unusual latitude as to their own judgment was given to the chiefs of the Einsatzgruppen."[62] Sandberger seems to be suggesting that it was up to the individual *Einsatzgruppen* leader to determine how best to deliver security.

As stated earlier, Streim was the first person to call into question the veracity of Ohlendorf's testimony. He assumed that Ohlendorf had "organized a conspiracy among the original defendants... to provide false testimony as part of a legal defense strategy."[63] The problem here is that Ohlendorf had no reason to lie in 1945–1946, or at least not about the timing and transmission of the *Führerbefehl*. He was not on trial himself and, therefore did not need to come up with a defense strategy – he was a witness for the prosecution, and besides he had said this from the beginning of his incarceration, before he ever suspected he would be on trial himself. Recent

speech by Streckenbach, in which the latter told of the impending invasion of the Soviet Union as well as the task assigned to the *Einsatzgruppen*. Interrogation Summary No. 2403, May 23, 1947 and No. 2519 in NARA RG 238, OCCWC, Executive Counsel, Evidence Division, Interrogation Branch, Interrogation Summaries, box 7 April 2, 1947–June 23, 1947, Summary 2401–2475 folder. Apparently this was a fabrication. Asked later why he made this false claim about Streckenbach, Sandberger did not offer a coherent or meaningful response. See Ogorreck, *Die Einsatzgruppen*, 52–53. Whether or not Sandberger's statement was influenced by Ohlendorf's testimony is difficult to determine. Streim suggests it was, noting that years later, Erwin Schulz leader of *Einsatzkommando* 5, related the following about Sandberger, the Hitler-order, and Streckenbach: "I met Dr. Sandberger frequently in the... [internment] camp. There we were able to listen to reports about the Nuremberg trials on the radio. One day Sandberger came to me and declared with great excitement that he had just heard on the radio that Ohlendorf testified at the Nuremberg trial of the major war criminals that Streckenbach had passed on the Führer order. But that cannot be true (Das stimme doch nicht)," Schulz claimed. "I also commented that I could not understand how Ohlendorf could make such a statement. I can no longer remember whether I also inquired at the time where and by whom he had been notified about the Führer order. Later, in Nuremberg, Sandberger asked to speak to me: he had meanwhile been enlightened (he did not say by whom) that Streckenbach had after all passed on the Führer order. Lapses of memory are certainly possible; perhaps even I could now remember that Streckenbach had passed on the Führer order. To assure that all members would march in step at Nuremberg, Sandberger obviously wanted to persuade me to give false evidence." Schulz quoted in Streim, "Tasks," n.31, 325–326.

[62] Interrogation, Sandberger, May 23, 1947, NARA RG 238, Evidence Division, Interrogation Summaries, box 7, summary 2401–2475 folder.

[63] Browning, *Origins of the Final Solution*, 227.

research supports Ohlendorf's version of events. For instance, we know that on June 12, 1941, during a visit to Munich, Hitler told the Romanian leader Ion Antonescu of German intentions to invade the Soviet Union and then kill all Jews in the newly conquered areas.[64] It is no coincidence that immediately following Antonescu and Hitler's meeting, the Romanians formed the equivalent of the *Einsatzgruppen* and in the opening months of Operation Barbarossa, murdered tens of thousands of Jews in Bukovina and Bessarabia, territories the Romanians wanted to reclaim for themselves.[65] If Ancel is right, Ohlendorf's original testimony – that the decision to murder all of Russia's Jews was planned before the invasion of the Soviet Union on June 22, 1941 – may also be true.[66]

We have another piece of evidence that may help clarify Ohlendorf's position at this time. It is an interrogation record of Werner Braune dated March 23, 1946, in Oslo, Norway, where he had been incarcerated since February 1945. Braune was the commander of *Einsatzkommando* 11b of *Einsatzgruppen* D and as such was directly answerable to Ohlendorf. When asked about the transmission of orders of kill Jews, Braune told his interrogators that there was no written order to do so, but that when he arrived in Russia in October 1941, Ohlendorf had informed him that "all Jews were to be executed." Ohlendorf was not the initiator of the order Braune insisted, but rather it was from Hitler directly or perhaps from the army. In any case, the idea was not Ohlendorf's. As commander of *Einsatzkommando* 11b, Braune took full responsibility for the atrocities committed by his unit.[67] This document is important to this story as Braune had no contact whatsoever with Ohlendorf at this time ensuring that his view was probably untainted. Moreover, it is doubtful that Braune knew what Ohlendorf had been telling the British and Americans, although he probably had heard of Ohlendorf's appearance at Nuremberg. That the men who were to lead these groups would be informed of their task before they were deployed is certainly not an unreasonable assumption to make, especially when a major (self-proclaimed) participant of the mass murder had offered this information as fact and helps explain why Amen did not pursue the issue further.[68]

[64] Jean Ancel, "The German-Romanian Relationship and the Final Solution," in *Holocaust and Genocide Studies*, 19: 2 (Fall 2005): 252–254.

[65] *Ibid.*, 257.

[66] *Ibid.*, 252–275.

[67] "Report on Interrogation of Ostubafü Dr. Braune, Werner, the KdS OSLO. Akershus Prison, Oslo – 23 MAR 46," Report No: PWIS (NORWAY)/93 in NARA RG 498, box 35. I want to thank Stephen Tyas for bringing this document to my attention.

[68] On this issue see Headland, "The *Einsatzgruppen*: The Question of their Initial Operations," 401–412, who argues that even if the so-called *Führerbefehl* was not given before Operation Barbarossa, at the very least the leaders of the *Einsatzgruppen* generally knew in June 1941 that their task in the Soviet Union was to murder Jews. Breitman, "Himmler and the 'Terrible Secret' among the Executioners," 80–81 agrees.

We cannot forget that Ohlendorf was a witness for the prosecution, not the defense. His testimony was meant to corroborate prosecution charges that the German Army had cooperated with the *Einsatzgruppen* in their brutal activities and that Kaltenbrunner–Heydrich's successor as head of the RSHA – personally had known of their criminal actions in Soviet Russia. Ohlendorf did not disappoint.

The prosecution could not have asked for a more credible witness than Ohlendorf, who was not only able and willing to divulge much information about the criminal workings of the regime, but did so convincingly.[69] His confidence during trial appeared to influence the court's perception of his testimony. As one judicial figure remarked, "whatever offenses Ohlendorf may have to answer for, he will never need to plead guilty to evasiveness on the witness stand [...] With a forth-rightness which one could well wish were in another field of activity, Otto Ohlendorf related how he received the Fuehrer-order (sic) and how he executed it."[70] From an "evidentiary standpoint," Taylor recalled in his memoir of the IMT proceedings, Ohlendorf's testimony was compelling; "a real blockbuster," he claimed.[71] Even the defendants against whom Ohlendorf was testifying believed he was stating the truth. Göring thought the former leader of *Einsatzgruppe* D had sold "his soul to the enemy," whereas Hans Frank and Walther Funk admired Ohlendorf for his honesty.[72] Whether or not Ohlendorf was seen as traitorous or a star-witness, there was no doubt in anyone's mind in 1946, this self-confessed murderer was speaking the truth.

Ohlendorf's testimony about the existence, timing, and delivery of the *Führerbefehl* at the IMT became his mantra. He would repeat this testimony in substance one year later in affidavits entered into evidence at his own trial and during direct testimony.[73] This evidence was so compelling and his testimony so assertive that those directly involved in his prosecution accepted his statements at face value. From that point onward, the existence of the *Führerbefehl* became a given and no further efforts were made to

---

[69] Taylor, *Final Report*, 60.

[70] Judgment, April 8, 1948, in *Trial*, roll 7, 132.

[71] Taylor, *Anatomy*, 246.

[72] Gilbert, *Nuremberg Diary*, 101 and Taylor, *Anatomy*, 248.

[73] For example, see his interrogation of November 15, 1946. Vernehmung, Ohlendorf by Wartenberg, November 15, 1946 in M1019, roll 50, 20–21; and, his affidavit of April 2, 1947 (NO 2856), in *Trial*, Prosecution Documents, roll 11, frames 0797–0798 of April 1947, in which he asserted, "On the basis of orders which were given by former Brigadeführer Streckenbach, Chief of Amt I of the RSHA, by order of the head of the RSHA, to the Chiefs of the Einsatzgruppen and the Kommandofuehrers at the time of the formation of the Einsatzgruppen in Pretzsch (sic) (in Saxony) and which were given by the Reichsführer SS to the leaders and men of the Einsatzgruppen and Einsatzkommandos who were assembled in Nikolajew in September 1941 a number of undesirable elements composed of Russians, Gypsies, and Jews and others, were executed in the area detailed to me." See also, Testimony of Ohlendorf, October 14, 1947, in *ibid.*, roll 2, 631–637.

FIGURE 7. Defendants in the dock, USHMM photo archive (#16813)

determine if events really transpired the way he stated. As historians we sometimes accept evidence uncritically, and if we want to understand our role in this controversy we need look no further than Ohlendorf's, which we accepted without corroboration.

Defense Arguments, the *Führerbefehl*, and Testimony at the *Einsatzgruppen* Trial

The trial of the *Einsatzgruppen* leaders began with their arraignment on September 15, 1947, at which time each defendant entered a formal plea of "not guilty, in the sense of the indictment."[74] What the accused meant by this became clear two weeks later when the trial began in earnest. The prosecution's case took only two days to present because the evidentiary basis of their case was entirely documentary, and, unlike in the IMT trial, each document did not need to be read into the record. The evidence against the defendants was overwhelming and, as far as the OCCWC was concerned, this was one of the easiest of the NMT cases to prepare. Incriminating evidence coupled with Ohlendorf's earlier confession to supervising mass murder

[74] See Arraignment, September 15 and 22, 1947, in *TWC*, vol. 4, 23–29. This became the standard response of war criminals to charges of mass murder. No one ever asked the defendants what they meant by this.

meant that the defense attorneys were forced to use imaginative arguments to prove their clients' innocence.[75] The large number of defendants who held different positions in the *Einsatzgruppen* compounded difficulties coming up with a common line of defense.[76] Whereas there is some evidence to suggest that Ohlendorf's attorney Rudolf Aschenauer attempted to coordinate defense strategy, the trial record indicates that all defendants and their counsel did not adhere to it.[77] Heinz Schubert recalled that Ohlendorf never told him how to behave during trial.[78] Certainly, many argued superior orders, but a variety of other strategies and creative applications of the law were employed in an attempt to prove their clients were not responsible for the crimes for which they were charged. Although this shotgun approach was probably necessary under the circumstances, rather than helping their clients, it created a sense of incredulity and desperation, ultimately weakening the presentation of their case.

Rudolf Aschenauer was a powerful force in the courtroom. As one of the youngest defense attorneys at Nuremberg, his behavior and dramatic appearance reminded Musmanno of a "Shakespearean actor."[79] Like so many of the German defense attorneys, Aschenauer fashioned his career at Nuremberg. After Ohlendorf, he represented hundreds of war criminals including Walther Funk, and, in 1963, he was one of the attorneys for Wilhelm Boger at the Frankfurt Auschwitz trial.[80] Even early in his career, he was dynamic. He made the opening statement for the defense at the *Einsatzgruppen* trial on October 6, when he laid out his client's case. He did not disappoint. To everyone's surprise, he did not deny his client's actions, but rather acknowledged that executions had occurred in the Soviet Union. They were defensive, however, carried out legally in *presumed* self-defense on behalf of a third party – the German Reich – during a *presumed* state of emergency; that

---

[75] *Ibid.*, 165.

[76] Prosecution Brief, February 1948, in *Trial*, roll 29, frame 0014. On the issue of a common defense, see Ogorreck, *Die Einsatzgruppen*, 53–55, who points to evidence that strongly suggests Ohlendorf did pressure the other defendants to plead a common defense of "superior orders" and "putative necessity."

[77] Among Musmanno's papers are a number of short essays he had written while in Nuremberg. One of these corroborates the charge that Ohlendorf attempted to direct the other defendants in the trial. Musmanno overstates the case when he writes, "By raising his right eyebrow he directs his co-defendants when they are on the stand. They follow his signals without exception, as though they were hypnotized. Without question he is their uncontested chief. – His name is Otto Ohlendorf." Excerpt from Musmanno, "Family Father and Mass Murderer," circa 1948, Capital Punishment file 1477, MMP.

[78] Statement, Heinz Schubert, November 20, 1972, ZSL. I want to thank Stephen Tyas for this document.

[79] Aschenauer was born in 1913, whereas the vast majority of the other defense attorneys were born between 1898 and 1910. Taylor, *Final Report*, 308 & Musmanno, *Eichmann Kommandos*, 119. For a summary of the legal issues involved in all of the Subsequent Nuremberg trials, see Lippman, "The Other Nuremberg," 1–100.

[80] Goda, *Tales from Spandau*, 64–65 and Wittmann, *Beyond Justice*, 284.

is, executions were necessary.[81] In American law this argument is referred to as putative justification or putative self-defense, which posits that an individual's criminal action is predicated on "the reasonable belief that a feared aggressor is about to attack."[82] The putative justification defense assumes that the crime committed "outweighs the harm of the offense – either because a greater harm is avoided or because a greater social interest is furthered."[83] Significantly for the defense, putative justification was an infrequently used legal argument in American law, but it was used in European legal proceedings.[84] Under normal circumstances, a lawyer would offer a defense arguing the accused did not commit the crime. However, because Ohlendorf had already said that he did, Aschenauer was forced to come up with a legal justification for the crime. With the putative self-defense argument Aschenauer aimed to show, in a complicated and, at times, confusing way, that otherwise criminal actions were legally justified because his client (mistakenly) believed he had acted in self-defense to protect Germany.[85] The accused had killed innocent civilians, Aschenauer told the court, but he did so believing his actions were for the greater good of the German Reich, not only to save Germany from bolshevism (the Jews), but also to ensure the continued existence of Germany which was mortally threatened by the war with the Soviet Union.[86]

As a second line of defense, Aschenauer (and the other defense attorneys) sought to prove that the leaders of the *Einsatzgruppen* took their

---

[81] It was impossible for Aschenauer to argue otherwise given the existence of the reports and the tribunal's ruling that they were authentic.

[82] George P. Fletcher, *Basic Concepts of Criminal Law* (New York, 1998), 88. Justification pertains to cases where an individual may legally use force to protect his person or property or the person or property of another. If the act is illegal, but was carried out for self-defense, it is justifiable and may prevail legally. On the other hand, the legal concept of "excuse" speaks to the culpability of the perpetrator of the criminal act. For example, if the perpetrator acted under duress in carrying out a criminal act, he cannot be considered personally responsible for his act. On the issue of justification versus excuse, see also George P. Fletcher, "The Right and the Reasonable," in Albin Eser, George P. Fletcher, et al. (eds.), *Justification and Excuse: Comparative Perspectives I* (Freiburg, 1987), 76–81, for German perspectives, see Winfried Hassemer, "Rechtfertigung und Entschuldigung im Strafrecht. Thesen und Kommentare," in *ibid.*, 175–227 and Claus Roxin, "Rechtfertigungs- und Entschuldigungs-gründe in Abgrenzung von sonstigen Strafausschließungsgründen," in *ibid.*, 230–262.

[83] Paul H. Robinson, "Causing the Conditions of One's Own Defense. Defense: A Study in the Limits of Theory in Criminal Law Doctrine," in *Justification and Excuse*, 660 n.3.

[84] On this defense see *Ibid.*, 103–109.

[85] Aschenauer, Opening Statement, October 6, 1947, in *TWC*, vol. 4, 60. German law has long recognized that a perpetrator may not be punished if his actions were committed because of "confusion, fear or fright." This does not alter the wrongfulness of the act, but legally it does mitigate personal blame. Albin Eser, "Justification and Excuse: A Key Issue in the Concept of Crime," in *Justification and Excuse*, 31 n.19 and 51–56.

[86] The legal basis for "necessity" comes from the notion that the action benefits society as a whole. For an explanation of the history of "legal necessity," see Fletcher, *Basic Concepts of Criminal Law*, 138–142.

orders from the military commanders of the German army to which their units were attached and that the so-called *Führerbefehl* compelled them to obey. This argument is exculpatory when it can be proved that an excusing condition existed in connection with the criminal act. In this case, it would have to be shown that either the accused did not know their conduct was wrong at the time of the crime or that their criminal actions were the result of coercion; that is, they did not have a choice or control over their own behavior.[87] Under CCL10, neither putative justification nor superior orders were admissible as defenses, yet, Aschenauer nonetheless hoped the tribunal would consider both, as they had long pedigrees in German law.[88] If the court did not find this defense compelling, he hoped they would legally excuse the defendants on the grounds that they were acting under duress on the orders of their superiors. Ostensibly, the defense attorneys hoped that the tribunal would consider obedience to orders proof of a lack of criminal intent and thus a mitigating factor and, not insignificantly, an important distinction in American criminal law. At best they hoped the defendants would be found legally not responsible for their criminal actions.[89] This was a dangerous strategy. By making these arguments Aschenauer implicitly acknowledged the criminal acts of the accused, placing the burden of proof on the shoulders of the defense whereas under normal circumstances all they would have to do is raise doubt.

To make their case the defense had to demonstrate that the defendants were soldiers, carrying out the most difficult of soldierly tasks – protecting their state – in a military fashion during the war.[90] Under any other circumstances, Aschenauer wanted the court to understand, the actions of the *Einsatzgruppen* would be considered criminal, but because of the state of emergency brought on by their presumption of a threat to Germany, their actions, while illegal, were both necessary and justified.[91] Aschenauer introduced expert testimony and entered into evidence the transcript of a radio broadcast by Stalin of July 3, 1941, in which the Soviet leader called for the most extreme measures against Germany, including partisan

[87] Robinson, "Causing the Conditions of One's Own Defense," 661 n.5.
[88] Aschenauer, Opening Statement, October 6, 1947, in *TWC*, vol. 4, 54–55. On the issue of putative self-defense in law see Fletcher, *Basic Concepts of Criminal Law*, 88–91.
[89] As attorney Willi Heim, Opening Statement, October 6, 1947, in *Trial*, 85 contended, had these men disobeyed their orders, they would have been subjected to military court martial and in all likelihood lost their own lives, and hence they had no choice but to follow orders.
[90] On the issue of the defense of superior orders, see, for example, Aubrey M. Daniel, "The Defense of Superior Orders," *University of Richmond Law Review* 3:7 (Spring 1973), 477–509 who writes about the case against Lieutenant William L. Calley, Jr., for his role in the My Lai Massacre in 1968. Daniel had been a prosecutor in the case and was very critical of President Richard Nixon for intervening.
[91] Aschenauer, Opening Statement, October 6, 1947, in *Trial*, 54–70. For an alternate analysis of the defense, see Wolfe, "Putative Threat," 46–67.

warfare and the total destruction of the German fascist state.[92] At the heart of Aschenauer's case was the argument that the defendants killed Jews because they believed it to be necessary. In his words, the "solution of the problem 'Bolshevism versus Europe' could only be brought about by a 'solution' of the Jewish problem and in . . . [the *Einsatzgruppen*'s] particular sphere, (sic) only by unreserved execution of the Führer-Order," that is, the mass murder of Soviet Jewry.[93] Aschenauer concluded that killing Soviet Jews could not be considered "part of a systematic program of genocide" as the prosecution contended, but rather it was the result of the defendant's belief that bolshevism as embodied in the Jews, posed a grave and immediate threat to the security and survival of Germany.[94] His argument was both misleading and inherently flawed. While these men undoubtedly took their orders from their superiors, they could hardly be considered soldiers, given their lack of military training and the political and ideological nature of their task. If the war on the eastern front really was military, the judgment asked, "why did the High Command not send military men to do it?"[95] The defense claim that the *Einsatzgruppen* murdered Jews to protect Germany from Soviet aggression (as articulated in Stalin's July 1941 radio speech) was implausible as well because Germany was the aggressor against the Soviets and not the other way around. If any nation could argue putative self-defense it was the Soviet Union. Given the lack of alternate strategies available to them, the defense opted for this line of argument despite its inherent flaws.

On the witness stand most of the men assisted in their own defense by claiming they believed that bolshevism and Jews were synonymous. For instance, Ohlendorf stated that he believed the Jews "played a disproportionately important role" in the Soviet state.[96] And, in what can only be seen as a pathetic and desperate attempt to prove the link between the two, he made the preposterous claim that "Jews who were executed went to their death singing *The Internationale* and hailing Stalin," as if singing confirmed that the Jews posed an imminent and grave threat to the Reich.[97] The putative self-defense argument proved unconvincing for the tribunal.[98] As they pointed out, Aschenauer should either defend Hitler's order as justifiable under the circumstance of total war or he should defend his client who testified that he carried out the order under duress because he objected to it on

---

[92] Ohlendorf Document 39, Transcription of Radio Broadcast of Joseph Stalin, July 3, 1941, in *Trial*, roll 26.

[93] Aschenauer quoted in Judgment, April 8, 1948, in *Trial*, roll 7, 69.

[94] Aschenauer, October 8, 1947, in *Trial*, roll 2, 521.

[95] Judgment, April 10, 1948, in *Trial*, roll 7, 102.

[96] Musmanno, *Eichmann Kommandos*, 111.

[97] Testimony, Ohlendorf, October 8, 1947, in *Trial*, roll 2, 522.

[98] Discussion between Musmanno and Aschenauer, October 15, 1947, in *ibid.*, roll 2, 759–765.

moral grounds.[99] But he should not argue both positions. Still, the tribunal did not set limits on the scope of the defense counsel's representation, in fact given the gravity of the charges, they acknowledged the defendant's right to put forth mutually exclusive defenses, yet they emphasized that in doing so both defenses were undermined.[100] As stated in the judgment, "one either justifies the Fuehrer-Order or one does not. One supports the killing of the Jews or denounces it," but by arguing them simultaneously both are "inevitably weaken[ed]."[101]

Werner Braune, head of *Einsatzkommando* 11b also opted to argue putative self-defense by making the link between bolshevism and the Jews, but his testimony was even less effective than Ohlendorf's. He told the tribunal that Hitler gave the order to murder the Jews in an attempt to save Germany, because "the Jews in the East were the decisive bearers of communism and its illegal manner of fighting."[102] As he understood it, "the vast majority of Jews supported Bolshevism." The tribunal was not convinced. Logically, the presiding judge stated if the majority of Jews supported bolshevism, of necessity a minority did not. Braune had to agree, but the number was small he said, perhaps as low as "ten, twenty, or thirty percent." Musmanno demanded to know why, if this were the case, all Jews were killed, including the minority who did not support bolshevism. Logic silenced Braune, whose only explanation was that "the possibility [to save them] did not exist."[103] For the tribunal this was demonstrable proof that the putative self-defense claim was fraudulent, Jews were not murdered to protect Germany from bolshevism, but rather to further Hitler's dream of creating a master race. The judgment stated that, "when it came to a Jew, it did not matter whether he was a member of the Communist Party or not," even if all the Jews in the Soviet Union had been shown to be Bolsheviks, killing them for holding divergent political opinions was still murder.[104]

The defense in any criminal trial has a duty to "zealously advocate" for their clients.[105] When the putative justification defense failed to persuade the court, defense counsel was compelled to argue their back-up case, superior orders. Technically, "superior orders" was not a permissible defense since CCL10 stipulated that it could only be considered in mitigation when sentencing. Perhaps because Musmanno was once a defense attorney himself and believed the defense should not be unfairly limited, in a highly unusual move, the tribunal interpreted the law liberally. They ruled that if a defendant carried out an order, even an illegal one, because not to do so brought

---

[99] *Ibid.*, 760.
[100] Judgment, April 10, 1948, in *ibid.*, roll 7, 60.
[101] *Ibid.*, 75.
[102] Testimony, Braune, November 25, 1947, in *ibid.*, roll 4, 3051.
[103] *Ibid.*, 3069–3072.
[104] Judgment, April 8, 1948, in *ibid.*, roll 7, 70 and 75.
[105] Freedman, *Lawyers' Ethics*, 9.

about physical repercussions, or if they had been physically coerced, or if they did not know carrying out their orders was illegal, then the defense of superior orders must be considered. Most of them raised the issue of their ignorance of law in direct testimony. Ohlendorf testified first. Under direct examination, he told the court of the involuntary nature of his assignment, emphatically stating that anyone who disobeyed the Führer "would have met immediate death."[106] Hitler's orders were so compelling he claimed without hesitation, that had he been ordered to do so, he would have murdered his sister.[107] At the same time Aschenauer tried to establish that the mission of the *Einsatzgruppen* was security, or as Ohlendorf put it, "to protect the rear of the troops by killing... all persons who would endanger... security," and as far as he knew, in doing so the goal was national survival not "racial extermination."[108] Some defendants supported the claim that refusal to obey Hitler's order would have resulted in very harsh punishment, even death in some cases. Because so many of the defendants had admitted to their crimes, the prosecution no longer had the burden of proof and thus they had no need to follow up on this issue.

Was Ohlendorf's testimony credible and was he really under threat to carryout illegal and immoral acts? To find out, American prosecutor James Heath, whom Chief Prosecutor Benjamin Ferencz characterized as "a fine southern gentleman," questioned Ohlendorf about the morality of the *Führer*-order.[109] Initially Ohlendorf was nonresponsive, but after some prodding, he admitted that he disagreed with the order, but as a soldier he followed orders and hence he had done nothing wrong.[110] Ohlendorf was tenacious, reinforcing the appearance of credibility, and even when his story began to show signs of inconsistency, Heath did not question him. For instance, after a rather heated exchange between the two, Ohlendorf changed his testimony, claiming the *Führerbefehl* was transmitted only once, before the mobile units had departed from Pretzsch and it remained in effect throughout the entire campaign against the Soviets, a departure from his earlier testimony when he told of a second instance in August 1941, when Himmler delivered the order in person.[111]

[106] Testimony, Ohlendorf, October 8, 1947, in *ibid.*, roll 2, 515, 521 and 526–527. He contradicted himself, ibid., 592 when he testified that he forbade executions by men who were emotionally unable to cope with the task of murder, sending them back to Berlin for reassignment.

[107] Testimony, Ohlendorf, October 15, 1947, in *ibid.*, roll 2, 740–752.

[108] Testimony, Ohlendorf, October 8, 1947, in *ibid.*, roll 2, 515–516 and 516–517.

[109] As Musmanno saw it, the true test of the credibility of the superior orders defense was not "the existence of the order, but whether moral choice was in fact possible." Musmanno, *Eichmann Kommandos*, 135. Ferencz, who is Jewish, believed it would be more effective if a Christian such as Heath cross-examined Ohlendorf. Interview with Ferencz, April 24, 1997, 3–4.

[110] Cross-examination of Ohlendorf, October 15, 1947, in *Trial*, roll 2, 740–752.

[111] Testimony, Ohlendorf, October 14 and 15, 1947, in *ibid.*, roll 2, 650 and 682–684.

The purpose of cross-examination is to illicit information or to test the credibility of witness testimony. In criminal trials, cross-examination is often a form of double-checking and is what the court uses to "separate truth from lies" and "memory from...invention."[112] Not only does a good cross-examiner detect inconsistencies, weaknesses, and exaggerations, but cross-examination is also one of the ways the court determines what is and is not a legal fact.[113] Why then, it must be asked, did no one on the prosecution team notice the inconsistencies in Ohlendorf's testimony? Part of the reason could have been the make-up of the prosecution team assigned to the *Einsatzgruppen* case. Chief of the prosecution team, Benjamin Ferencz was extremely bright. He had graduated from Harvard Law School and had studied under the renowned war crimes expert Sheldon Glueck. Immediately after graduation, he served in a combat unit and gained some practical experience when he was hired as a field investigator gathering evidence of war crimes for the army. Even though an excellent researcher, at the age of 27 years he had never had the opportunity to try a criminal case, let alone prosecute a case against major war criminals.[114] What Ferencz lacked in practical experience, however, he made up for with passion. Further, this was an open and shut case, the minor inconsistencies in Ohlendorf's testimony were irrelevant; Ohlendorf had already sealed his fate when he admitted to supervising mass murder. Heath, the member of the prosecution team assigned to cross examine Ohlendorf; was a seasoned attorney, but he was on the verge of being fired because of personal problems that Taylor believed compromised his ability to do his job effectively. Whether this had an impact on Heath's work in the *Einsatzgruppen* trial is impossible to tell. What is certain is that Ohlendorf did not buckle under Heath's questioning. Little is known about the two other attorneys, Peter Walton and John Glancy, except they were cast-offs, unwanted by the prosecution teams in other trials and were picked up by Ferencz, at the eleventh hour when Taylor gave his consent to indict the leaders of the mobile killing units.[115] Ferencz remembered that Arnost Horlik Hochwald, a Czech by birth, was the "only good" lawyer assigned to the case.[116] Hochwald had represented the Czech government at the IMT trial before being hired by Taylor's organization. By all accounts he was

---

[112] Douglas, "Wartime Lies," 29.

[113] *Ibid.*

[114] Despite the fact that the *Einsatzgruppen* trial was Ferencz' first case, he told me that he was confident of his abilities. Interview with Ferencz, April 24, 1997, 2–3.

[115] Ferencz, *Ibid.*, 3–5, states that Heath was a good lawyer, but was unable to "get down to the task" because of his problem and recalled that although Glancy and Walton were decent people they "were not competent lawyers." When the transcript of the trial was published in 1951, Heath was not listed as part of the prosecution team, but was instead referred to as "consultant," Prosecution Counsel in *TWC*, vol. 4, 11.

[116] Letter, Ferencz to Earl, February 27, 1997, 1 and interview with Ferencz, April 24, 1997, 4–5.

an excellent attorney, preparing "a highly effective euthanasia case," that linked "the killings of psychiatric patients with selections in the camps and X-ray sterilisation" for the prosecution at the Medical trial.[117]

In Ohlendorf the prosecutors faced a formidable opponent. He commanded attention and many people came to court just to catch a glimpse of a mass murderer whose story had been reported in newspapers. Musmanno recalled that like the allure of certain serial killers, some women even "sought to pass him notes offering encouragement and endearment."[118] Many believed his good looks and intellect made him a good man.[119] Certainly Ohlendorf is characterized as different (in a positive way) from his co-defendants and it is he who is cited most often in memoirs of the Nuremberg trials. He was confident and even audacious, presenting himself as assured and, above all, truthful; personality traits that when coupled with a weak cross-examination, did very little to discredit the defense of obedience to orders. Most notable though, was Ohlendorf's gift of speech, apparently possessing the narrative talents of a professional raconteur gave him a disarming presence. He was not an easy defendant to contend with, even for seasoned professionals. Whether others would have caught discrepancies in testimony is speculative, what is certain is that legally it did not hurt the prosecution because the tribunal had ruled that Ohlendorf's testimony at the original Nuremberg trial was admissible, and because he had already admitted to supervising mass murder, there was little else the court needed to convict him.

Not all defendants who took the stand came across as effectively as Ohlendorf and as far as the tribunal was concerned, only one needed to demonstrate the weakness of the superior orders defense for the entire argument to collapse. This occurred when Willy Seibert testified. Under direct examination by his attorney Hans Gawlik, Seibert explained that as a soldier his first duty was obedience. The presiding judge asked whether he understood that killing unarmed civilians without trial is murder under the recognized laws of war. Seibert responded that he "simply didn't know anymore" what was and was not murder during wartime.[120] After some thought he then concluded that killing because one was ordered to do so was not the same as murder.[121] Musmanno seemed stunned by Seibert's answer, and speculated to the court if perhaps Seibert had become so hardened and brutalized by his activities in the east that he could no longer distinguish between right and wrong: between killing during armed conflict and killing unarmed civilians

[117] Weindling, *Nazi Medicine and the Nuremberg Trials*, 136.
[118] Musmanno, *Eichmann Kommandos*, 106–107.
[119] Musmanno, "Family Father and Mass Murderer," undated, PPM.
[120] Testimony, Seibert, November 18, 1947, in *Trial*, roll 4, 2552.
[121] Musmanno, *Eichmann Kommandos*, 128.

without provocation during war.[122] Musmanno probed further, asking a hypothetical question, which in a criminal trial in the United States could have been grounds for an appeal but given the unusual latitude afforded the judges at Nuremberg, was well within his rights to do.[123] He wanted to know if Seibert were ordered, would he shoot his parents.[124] Seibert stumbled. He could not or would not respond to the question. As Musmanno recalled later, "the faces of the other defendants in the dock dropped. 'Why, you idiot,' they seemed to say, '*that* [superior orders] is our whole case.'"[125] Because Seibert refused to answer the question and Musmanno refused to allow the trial to resume until he did, the court was held in recess until the following day, at which time Seibert was instructed that he must answer the question.[126] The next day and looking exhausted from a night of no sleep, Seibert took the stand.[127] Musmanno repeated the question, "if . . . the military situation made it necessary for you, after receiving an order . . . from a superior officer, to shoot your own parents, would you do so?" In what can only be described as an agonizing moment, Seibert responded, "Mr. President, I would not do so . . . it is inhuman to ask a son to shoot his parents."[128] In one sentence Seibert, for whatever reason unwilling to lie, had destroyed the defense's case. Obedience to orders is not blind but has limits; a German soldier is not "a fettered slave," rather he is a "reasoning agent," and as such he does have some latitude for his actions. Some orders, particularly inhuman ones, the judgment importantly noted, may be disobeyed, and, because they could be disobeyed, the only reasonable conclusion the tribunal could draw was that the defendants had freely and with agency engaged in mass murder.[129]

Seibert's was not the only testimony to contradict Ohlendorf's on the issue of superior orders. Most historians of the Final Solution, when discussing the subject of timing, point to the testimony of Erwin Schulz as proof that Ohlendorf was lying about the nature and timing of the Hitler-order.[130]

---

[122] Testimony, Seibert, November 19, 1947, in *Trial*, roll 4, 2664–2665. See also, Musmanno, *Eichmann Kommandos*, 127–128.

[123] Musmanno took every available opportunity to directly question witnesses during the trial. In his memoirs, he smugly notes that he served as both judge and jury, *idem, Eichmann Kommandos*, 128.

[124] Cross-examination of Seibert by Musmanno, November 19, 1947, in *Trial*, roll 4, 2671–2673.

[125] Musmanno, *Eichmann* Kommandos, 129.

[126] Cross-examination of Seibert by Musmanno, November 19, 1947, in *Trial*, roll 4, 2674.

[127] Musmanno, *Eichmann Kommandos*, 132.

[128] Testimony, Seibert, November 20, 1947, in *Trial*, roll 4, 2676 and Judgment, April 8, 1948, in *ibid.*, roll 7, 79–81.

[129] Judgment, April 8, 1948, in *ibid.*, roll 7, 77 and Musmanno to defendant Seibert, November 20, 1947 in *ibid.*, roll 4, 2676.

[130] For example, see Ogorreck, *Die Einsatzgruppen*, 52; Streim, "Tasks," 214; Browning, *Fateful Months*, 17 & 19; and Burrin, *Hitler and the Jews*, 101–104. Interestingly, historians

Of all the defendants to take the stand and be questioned on the issue of superior orders, only Schulz did not confirm Ohlendorf's version of events. The prosecution did not probe into inconsistencies in his testimony because by the time Schulz took the stand they had already concluded that there was an order to murder all Jews and Hitler had issued it. Besides, Schulz was the only accused to challenge the orthodoxy and Ohlendorf's testimony appeared more credible than Schulz's to begin with.[131]

Schulz testified that everything he had done was legal, because all killings followed the international rules of war and were preceded by thorough investigations and trials. When asked by his attorney about the so-called Hitler-order, Schulz explained that the first time he had heard of it was during his interrogation on Good Friday in 1947, and it was Rolf Wartenberg, the prosecution's interrogator, who told him about it.[132] His assignment in the Soviet Union – which he seems to suggest had nothing to do with the Final Solution – was another issue. It was not until mid-August 1941, he stated, that he was given the order to murder *all* Soviet Jews including women and children, and then the order was given to him by Otto Rasch, the commander of *Einsatzgruppe* C, not head of Office I of the RSHA Bruno Streckenbach, as Ohlendorf had testified.[133] Moreover, he told the court, there was no mention of "extermination" or "final solution" when he was first assigned to lead a *Kommando*. Had he known beforehand that his job was to supervise killings, he insisted, he would not have taken the job in the first place.[134] Everything Schulz said on the issue of orders was at odds with Ohlendorf's testimony, which should have raised a red flag for the prosecutors. As Horlik-Hochwald's cross-examination demonstrates, the prosecution was reluctant to accept Schulz's version of events.

Horlik Hochwald: You made here a differentiation between the Hitler-order (sic) as testified to by the defendants Ohlendorf and Naumann and the order of Jeckeln which was handed down to you by Rasch?

Schulz: That is right.

Horlik Hochwald: ... will you tell the Tribunal where you see this *colossal difference* between these two orders?[135]

have overlooked the testimony of Adolf Ott, Testimony, December 10, 1947, in *Trial*, roll 5, 3716–3762, who tried to make the distinction between the Hitler-order to murder Soviet Jews and the Hitler-order to murder all European Jews. Even Taylor, *Final Report*, 69, did not distinguish between partial and total genocide, reporting that the objective of "the notorious 'final solution of the Jewish question' ... was nothing less than the extermination of European Jewry, was the basis of the 'Einsatz case'."

[131] Otto Rasch also disputed Ohlendorf's version but he did not testify.
[132] Testimony, Schulz, October 17, 1947, in *Trial*, roll 2, 933.
[133] *Ibid.*, October 21, 1947, 1073.
[134] *Ibid.*, October 17, 1947, 935.
[135] Emphasis supplied, *ibid.*, October 21, 1947, 1077.

Schulz did not take-up Horlik-Hochwald's challenge. His refusal or inability to respond with authority undoubtedly suggested to the prosecution that he was lying making Ohlendorf's version of events appear more credible. Ultimately Schulz's testimony helped reinforce the prosecution's belief that the defendants knew about their tasks before they were deployed in the summer of 1941. In any event, it made little difference when determining their guilt or innocence, as Hochwald pointed out, whether the order was given in Pretzsch by Streckenbach or a month later by Rasch in the Soviet Union, did not matter, it was still Hitler's order and innocent people still died.[136] Even had the prosecution been willing to entertain Schulz's assertions it is unlikely it would have had an impact on their case or the outcome of the trial, the point of which was to prove the defendants had committed mass murder, and not when they had been ordered to do so. While the court found Schulz's testimony unconvincing and self-serving, perhaps he and Ohlendorf were both telling the truth. Richard Breitman has argued that the decision to murder Soviet Jews was so sensitive and 'terrible' that it was given orally and then, only on a need to know basis. In practice this would have meant that the order was variable and that different *Einsatzgruppen* leaders received their orders at different times and from different people.

Schulz had testified that he received the order from Himmler via Rasch on August 10, 1941, and he believed the order was only for *Einsatzgruppe* C.[137] If we accept Breitman's argument, then it is conceivable that Ohlendorf, an Old Fighter with status, knew about the decision before many of his co-defendants, especially those who held positions of lesser importance and status in the Reich.[138] A variably timed order would also explain the contradictory and often confused testimony given on this issue during the trial. If correct, it may also mean that Ohlendorf probably did encourage those defendants who were not privy to this early information to adopt the same argument as he did. Had the defendants admitted that the order had been given at different times and by different people, it would also mean they would have had to admit that they were given some latitude regarding carrying out mass murder and this would have compromised their superior orders defense. To suggest however, as some have, that the men of the *Einsatzgruppen* did not know about the general nature of their assignment before they departed for the Soviet Union, is implausible and goes against all logical notions. After all, these were not soldiers by any classical definition of the term. None of them had had military training, or at least very little, as they themselves admitted. Professionally, they were lawyers, economists, and otherwise professionals, not military men. In practice they were political soldiers, called together to fulfil the most important ideological

---

[136] *Ibid.*, 1073.
[137] Testimony, Schulz, October 21, 1947, in *Trial*, roll 2, 1096–1098.
[138] See Breitman, "Himmler and the 'Terrible Secret' among the Executioners," 80–81.

task of the Third Reich. To suggest that they did not know they would be killing Jews, the avowed enemy of the Reich, requires almost a suspension of judgment.

Following Ohlendorf's lead, one by one, the defendants took the stand and testified that they were not legally responsible for the mass murder of Soviet Jewry, because they were soldiers, following orders they had to obey. Ohlendorf's detractors are correct in at least one sense after all.[139] Obedience to orders was a defense strategy, used in a desperate attempt to save the lives of mass murderers who otherwise had not a legal leg to stand on.

The defense attorneys faced an up-hill battle. Even experienced trial attorneys such as Freidrich Bergold who had acted as the principal attorney in the case against Erhard Milch and now represented Biberstein, had a difficult time finding credible explanations for his clients.[140] To be sure, putative self-defense and superior orders were not the only arguments put forward by the anxious defense team. Scores of different arguments were advanced during trial, many of which contradicted these two principal defenses. For instance, Franz Six posited a contradictory defense in which he maintained that while he was a professor and knew nothing of the murder of the Jews, he still tried his best to be released from duty as head of a *Kommando*.[141] When asked why he did not ask to be released from his duties, Klingelhöfer, Six's replacement, claimed it would have been futile and therefore he had not even tried.[142] Braune agreed with Klingelhöfer that it was pointless to evade one's duty, but also claimed that his actions were no worse than the Allies, who had indiscriminately killed thousands of German civilians during the war; he was only as guilty as the Americans.[143] Then, there were those defendants who claimed they had not killed innocent persons, only partisans, and then only after thorough investigations. Adolf Ott claimed that he had not killed any Jews because there were none left when he arrived in Russia in January 1942.[144] The most outrageous argument, however, came from those who claimed that had they not done the killing someone else surely would have.[145] Although unconvincing individually, combined,

[139] Streim, "Tasks," 313.

[140] *TWC*, vol. 2, 355–898.

[141] Testimony, Six, October 24, 1947, in *Trial*, roll 3, 1325–1335. Hermann Göring was the first of a long line of Nuremberg defendants to claim he knew nothing of the mass murder of the Jews. See testimony of Göring, in IMT, *Trial of the Major War Criminals before the International Military Tribunal, Nuremberg, November 14, 1945–October 1, 1946*, vol. 9 (Nuremberg, 1947), 628.

[142] Testimony, Klingelhöfer, December 11, 1947, in *ibid.*, roll 5, 3811–1812.

[143] Testimony, Braune, November 25, 1947, in *ibid.*, roll 4, 3042–44 and 3053.

[144] Testimony, Ott, December 11, 1947, in *ibid.*, roll 5, 3782.

[145] The tribunal found this argument particularly outrageous. Judgment, April 10, 1948, in *ibid.*, roll 7, 96.

FIGURE 8. Chief Prosecutor, Benjamin Ferencz in court, USHMM photo archive
(#09918)

all these varying arguments constituted what can only be considered a shotgun defense, adding to the appearance of desperation of the accused. As
a line of defense it was a complete failure. Efforts to coordinate strategy
not only failed to benefit their clients, it actually helped the prosecution.[146]
Testimony on the existence of the *Führerbefehl* confirmed what everyone
already knew, "there is no doubt [that] the order [to murder the Jews] was
issued by the Head of the State," proving that Jews were killed not because
they were communists or even because they were a threat to the Reich,
they "were killed simply because [they were] Jews."[147] As such, the tribunal
found the defendants guilty as charged, they had helped to carryout crimes
against humanity against particular ethnic groups, the Jews, the Gypsies,
and communist functionaries, and the *Führerbefehl* was their instruction to
do so.

---

[146] Ogorreck, *Die Einsatzgruppen*, 54–55 and Streim, "Tasks," 313 argue that Ohlendorf
tried to persuade his co-defendants to testify as he did. See also Longerich, *Politik der
Vernichtung*, 310–320.

[147] Discussion between Musmanno and Heath, October 14, 1947, in *Trial*, roll 2, 636–637
and Judgment, April 8, 1948, in *ibid.*, roll 7, 70.

FIGURE 9. Members of the prosecution team, USHMM photo archive (#16814)

The Prosecution, the *Führerbefehl*, and Genocide

If the defense believed that the existence of the *Führerbefehl* justified their clients' actions, how did the prosecution view its existence? Some indication is found in the indictment. It will be recalled that under count one, the defendants were charged with crimes against humanity, which were defined as "atrocities and offenses, including but not limited to, persecutions on political, racial, and religious grounds, murder, extermination, imprisonment, and other inhumane acts committed against civilian populations, including German nationals and nationals of other countries."[148] Unlike the indictment filed against the defendants at the IMT proceedings, crimes against humanity were not linked to crimes against peace or war crimes, but to the concept of genocide.[149] Under paragraph two, the prosecution had described the planned and systematic extermination of an identifiable ethnic or religious group including Jews, Gypsies, and Soviet officials, as crimes against humanity.[150] Interestingly, this is the opposite of how the international

---

[148] Amended Indictment, July 25, 1947, in *TWC*, vol. 4, 15.

[149] Indictment, IMT, *Trial of the Major War Criminals before the IMT*, vol. 1, 27–73.

[150] Amended Indictment, July 25, 1947, in *TWC*, vol. 4, 15–21. For an excellent discussion of the development of the crime of genocide in international law, see Schabas, *Genocide in International Law*, 1–101.

community would define it today, where genocide is seen as the larger, although less encompassing of the two crimes.

In 1945, genocide was a newly defined concept with arguably little precedent in international law, yet it was still briefly mentioned in article 6(c) of the IMT indictment in which the defendants were charged with "deliberate and systematic genocide, viz., the extermination of racial and national groups, against the civilian populations of certain occupied territories in order to destroy particular races and classes of people, and national, racial or religious groups, particularly Jews, Poles, and Gypsies."[151] Despite the inclusion of genocide in the indictment, the prosecution did not address the charge during the trial nor did the IMT mention it in its judgment, although it did invoke Ohlendorf and his testimony in its description of the persecution of the Jews.[152] The practice of genocide may well be "an old practice" as Lemkin had always maintained, but as a normative legal term it was not yet defined or widely used in 1945.[153] By the time of the *Einsatzgruppen* trial in 1947–1948 the term had gained wider currency (it was being discussed at length in the United Nations) and it formed an integral part of the indictment filed against the *Einsatzgruppen* leadership, to "characterize [their] activities . . . in Poland and the Soviet Union."[154] It was also simultaneously being heard in Case 8 of the NMT, the trial against Ulrich Griefelt and others in the Race and Resettlement Office who were eventually found guilty of genocide the first such case in history.[155] Certainly, the IMT indictment influenced the prosecutors of the Subsequent proceedings, but the inclusion of the charge also may have been the result of Lemkin himself who Ferencz recalls was present at Nuremberg in 1947 when the indictment against the *Einsatzgruppen* leadership was being written, but who is entirely absent from the documentary record otherwise.[156] Ohlendorf's pre-trial sworn statements about the *Führerbefehl* probably also provided impetus to include the descriptor in the indictment. The existence of the order to murder Soviet

---

[151] Quoted in Schabas, *Genocide in International Law*, 37–38. Crimes against humanity was count four of the IMT indictment, *Trial of the Major War Criminals before the IMT*, vol. 1, 65–67.

[152] Schabas, *Genocide in International Law*, 38.

[153] Lemkin quoted in *ibid.*, 27 & 24–25.

[154] *Ibid.*, 47–48.

[155] The defendants in Case 8 were indicted in July 1947 (as were those in Case 9), but Case 8 began in October, whereas the *Einsatzgruppen* trial began in September, but concluded in March, one month before the end of the *Einsatzgruppen* trial. See the "RuSHA Case," in *TWC*, vol. 4, 599–1173 and vol. 5, 1–177. See also Schabas, Genocide in International Law, 48–49.

[156] Interview with Ferencz, April 24, 1997, 9 and Lemkin, *Axis Rule in Occupied Europe*, 79. Schabas does not explain why or how the charge was included in the indictment against the *Einsatzgruppen* leadership, only that it was included.

Jewry, the prosecution believed, was proof that the murder of the Jews was not an accident, but rather premeditated and intended to eradicate the entire Jewish population of Soviet Russia, perhaps even Europe. The proof of the crime was contained within the so-called *Einsatzgruppen* reports, which the prosecution not only entered as evidence, but which also formed the basis of crimes against humanity, paragraphs six through nine of which detailed the exact number of murders, approximately 1 million, according to the prosecution's calculations of the *Einsatzgruppen* reports, clearly proving this was a crime of some magnitude.[157]

From Ohlendorf's earliest statements the prosecution concluded that the mass murders committed by the units of the *Einsatzgruppen* were part of a systematic plan to kill specific groups of the Soviet civilian population, and that the units had been formed for this purpose. As the prosecution made clear to the court, "[t]he actions of the *Einsatzgruppen* in the conquered territories will demonstrate the purpose for which they were organized," namely the genocidal mass murder of "undesirable" groups.[158] Even before the trial began, the prosecution had accepted as fact Ohlendorf's sworn testimony concerning the timing and nature of the *Einsatzgruppen*'s orders and had incorporated his testimony from the IMT trial into the indictment they filed against him. In the final reckoning, the prosecution turned his statements against him to prove that these murders were part of a master plan, hatched in the spring of 1941, to systematically destroy the Jews. The *Einsatzgruppen*'s actions, taken in conjunction with the Hitler-order, tended to confirm, rather than mitigate, the guilt of the accused in the minds of the prosecution team.

Before the trial had started, the prosecutors had already made up their minds about the *Einsatzgruppen* and the historic beginning of the Final Solution in the early summer of 1941. This notion was highlighted in the indictment, and it was frequently repeated throughout the trial. For instance, an affidavit of Walter Blume's admitted into evidence stated that "during the setting-up of the Einsatzgruppen and Einsatzkommandos during the months of May–June 1941 . . . we were already being instructed about the tasks of exterminating the Jews," implying that Nazi plans had always targeted Jews specifically.[159] Of course Ohlendorf tried to prove this was not the case. During his direct testimony, Musmanno asked him whether or not it was true that the task of the *Einsatzgruppen* was to execute groups of people because they were racially inferior. Ohlendorf appeared incredulous at the suggestion. Jews were killed, he conceded, not because they were Jews, but because they were enemies of the Reich. Their murder, in effect, was an act

---

[157] Amended Indictment, July 25, 1947, in *TWC*, vol. 4, 16–21.
[158] Opening Statement by the Prosecution, Ferencz, in *ibid.*, 37.
[159] Affidavit, Blume in *Trial of War Criminals*, vol. 4, 140.

of war. The task of the *Einsatzgruppen* was murder for security, not murder because of race.[160]

To this point Ohlendorf's defense had consisted of arguing that although he personally disagreed with the *Führer*-order, he carried out his murderous instructions, and this was legal because he had simply been following orders. Furthermore, the order, issued in response to an apparent emergency, was self-defense against an enemy who posed a grave security risk to the German Reich during the war.[161] In his cross-examination Heath discredited this line of defense by demonstrating that the murder of Soviet Jews and Gypsies was done for no other reason then, as he put it, "blood."[162] Ohlendorf insisted that the Jews were killed because they were Bolsheviks, and as Bolsheviks they posed a security risk to the Reich. Although more plausible for the Jews, his credibility was seriously challenged when it came to explaining the murder of Gypsies. Heath asked him directly on what basis Gypsies were killed. Ohlendorf had no answer. However, in an effort to sustain his basic defense he repeatedly returned to his argument about the Jews. Realizing the futility of the situation, he claimed that during wartime Gypsies were involved in espionage, partisan warfare, and sabotage and that is why they were killed.[163] Ohlendorf's vulnerability on this matter led Heath to conclude that, like the Jews, the "Gypsies" were murdered simply "because they were Gypsies."[164]

Although Ohlendorf desperately tried to maintain the fiction of murder out of necessity, some defendants were unable to sustain this argument under cross-examination. For example, Ott, claimed his *Kommando* only shot Jews who were found to be partisans and saboteurs. Yet, when asked whether some Jews were shot simply because they were Jews, he admitted that, "every Jew who was apprehended had to be shot. Never mind whether he was a perpetrator or not." This was the case, he told the court, because the *Führer*-order dictated it.[165] Even after confessing to the killing of Jews in Russia, he claimed that, "the *Fuehrer*-Order concerning the elimination of Jews was a complete surprise to me ... this *Fuehrer*-Order I first learned about here in Nuremberg."[166] Ott was the only defendant to attempt to distinguish between what we might call a partial and total genocide; that is, between a Hitler-order to murder Soviet Jews and *the* Hitler-order to murder *all* European Jews.

After nearly seven months of trial, the prosecution concluded that Jews, Gypsies, and communist functionaries were killed because their existence

---

[160] Testimony, Ohlendorf, October 8, 1947, in *Trial*, roll 2, 516–517, 528 and 559.
[161] *Ibid.*, October 8–16, 1947, roll 2, 487–752.
[162] Cross-examination of Ohlendorf by Heath, October 14, 1947, in *ibid.*, roll 2, 658–659.
[163] *Ibid.*, 658–660.
[164] *Ibid.*, 558–559.
[165] Ott quoted in Judgment, April 10, 1948, in *ibid.*, roll 7, 196.
[166] Testimony, Ott, December 10, 1947, in *ibid.*, roll 5, 3718 and 3762.

jeopardized the attainment of the Reich's ideological goals, linking the so-called Hitler-order to the *Einsatzgruppen*'s acts of mass murder in the Soviet Union. It was in their closing statement that they presented their case most succinctly, and it was surprisingly accurate. Antisemitism, they noted, was at the core of Nazi ideology. Although always persecuted, the outbreak of war in 1939 presented the Nazis with the perfect opportunity to bring their antisemitic doctrine to "its logical conclusion – the extermination of all Jews." Murdering an entire racial group was such a mammoth undertaking though that it required much planning and it was not until the summer of 1941, that the plan was "systematized" and operational. The plan included the formation of killing squads "at the outset of the Russian campaign," and the *Einsatzgruppen* reports chronicled the part the defendants played in it.[167] As the prosecution phrased it, "the documents make it clear beyond the slightest doubt where the truth lies – the order for the mass executions of Jews and political officials was given, and it was carried out."[168] The prosecution concluded that the evidence was compelling,

a German [military] victory would have enormously widened the scope of operations of the Einsatzgruppen and the holocaust would have been even more staggering...the crimes of the Einsatzgruppen were not, fundamentally, military crimes at all. They were not committed in order to make military victory possible. On the contrary, military victory was sought in order to put the victors in a position where these crimes could be committed. These crimes were a war objective, not a military means.[169]

The tribunal concurred. The murder of the Jews was unrelated to the security of Germany; rather, it was part of a planned "program of genocide."[170] Defense testimony regarding the *Führerbefehl* may or may not have been an attempt at self-exculpation. However, it is perfectly obvious that as a line of defense it was a total failure, and served mainly to demonstrate for the court that the mass murder of Soviet Jews was both planned and systematic.

From this example, it is plain to see that war crimes trials are complex forums. As such, they do not always provide complete accounts of the past and in this instance, trial testimony complicated our historical understanding of one of the most important elements of the Final Solution – its origins. This outcome highlights the divergent aims of law and history. By their very nature, criminal trials can be major barriers to the attainment of the historical record. Defendants who are guilty have a vested interest in excluding or distorting the truth and are likely to do so if they believe it could lead to an

[167] Closing Statement for the US, Case 9, The USA against Ohlendorf, et al., February 13, 1948, 1–2.
[168] *Ibid.*, 9.
[169] *Ibid.*, 16–17.
[170] Judgment, April 10, 1948, in *ibid.*, roll 7, 6 and 76.

acquittal. Clearly, this is what the defense attempted to do by arguing superior orders. Although due process and historical accuracy are not necessarily mutually exclusive, prosecutors and historians seldom ask the same questions, nor are they concerned with the same level of detail. As we have seen, it simply did not matter to the overall culpability of the accused whether or not they were given their orders in June, July, August, or September 1941. What resulted at the *Einsatzgruppen* trial was only an approximation of historical accuracy, with much left obfuscated or unexamined. If historians expect more from a legal proceeding, they will always be disappointed: law and history have different intentions and perhaps most critical of all, different contexts. The order to murder Soviet Jewry was legally important because the existence of such an order could be ruled exculpatory. But, as we saw in the last chapter, in 1947 the prosecution never seriously addressed the issue of motivation and, therefore, whether the defendants were following orders or acting on individual initiative was never considered, despite the availability of a legal framework for such a defense. In the end, the court never did take up this matter, disappointing the hopes of defense counsel. Of course, this is not to suggest that trial testimony is unworthy of historical consideration, but the experience of this and other trials of historic importance serve as a warning for historians. Testimony should be evaluated carefully, in the context of the trial it comes from. So, while it is often tempting to accept trial testimony as historically accurate, for the historian to do so is dangerous without considering the context in which that testimony was given.

6

Judge and Judgment

The perfect lawyer is the one who is at home in every trade, studied in every field of learning, visited every clime, lived with every people, fought in war, labored for peace, gathered flowers on the rugged mountain slope, penned poems to the sky, and loved in the light of the lambent moon. Universality is his name. He knows nature like a mother, science like a father – and the pages of the human heart turn under his sensitive fingers like the leaves of a treasured tome.

Michael Musmanno[1]

All the world's a court and its men and women merely judges and defendants.

Michael Musmanno[2]

In 1947, three prominent members of the American bar were appointed to Military Tribunal II-a to hear the evidence presented in the *Einsatzgruppen* trial: Richard Dillard Dixon, a judge of the Superior Court of North Carolina, recruited initially as Deputy Secretary General for all the Subsequent Nuremberg proceedings; John Joshua Speight a leading member of the Alabama bar; and Michael Angelo Musmanno, a Reserve Naval Captain and judge of the Court of Common Pleas, Allegheny County, Pennsylvania.[3]

---

[1] Musmanno, *Verdict!* (New York, 1958), 115.
[2] Musmanno, undated letter, Nuremberg Correspondence file 1445, MMP. Note: when I carried out research at the Gumberg library, Musmanno's papers were not indexed, cataloged, or organized. Some of the material was arranged by a file system he had devised before his death. In these instances, the name of the file and file number will be indicated, but where information was found outside of these files the reference will be cited as "loose documents."
[3] Military Tribunal II-a was later renamed Military Tribunal II. Memorandum, John Ray, Secretary General Military Tribunals, September 12, 1947 in NARA RG 153 (JAG), WCB, Nuremberg Administration Records 1944–1949, box 14, book 6 87-2 folder; Memorandum, to Lt. Col. Cross, WCB, USCC, Nuremberg, October 21, 1946, in *ibid*, box 3, book 4, 85-2 folder; and Letter, Patterson to Truman, December 23, 1946, in *ibid*, box 14, 87-2 folder.

Musmanno, the only member of the military appointed to the bench at Nuremberg, was also named presiding judge.[4]

Musmanno was at home in the courtroom.[5] He was a colorful and controversial figure, overly fond of the dramatic and a natural "showman."[6] If he were alive today you might expect to find him performing for the camera to satiate an overly large ego. Between 1946 and 1948, no such venue existed so he had to make-do with the courtroom at Nuremberg, which proved to be the ideal place for him to perform. Before serving as presiding judge in the *Einsatzgruppen* case though, he had served on the bench for two other important cases. The first was the trial of Erhard Milch (December 1946–April 1947) in which the tribunal sentenced the Field Marshal to life in prison for his part in the Nazi slave labor program. The second case he participated in was against Oswald Pohl and seventeen others from the SS Economic and Administrative Main Office (WVHA), who were charged with crimes committed in the concentration and slave labor camps run by the SS. Although happy to participate in both of these historic trials, Musmanno was never quite so satisfied as when he was center stage. The *Einsatzgruppen* trial proved the perfect setting for his personality, for it was as a presiding judge that he was able to silence Dixon and Speight and dominate the proceedings himself.[7]

Andy Logan, a columnist for *The New Yorker* magazine who was in Nuremberg after the war because her husband Charles Lyon was a prosecutor there, vividly recalled that even though the OCCWC for the Subsequent trials tried to recruit distinguished judges to serve on the bench, they were not always of the highest calibre.[8] Whereas there were some initial reservations about his appointment, Dixon was considered a capable jurist.[9] He had been a judge for the Superior Court of North Carolina and before serving on the bench at the *Einsatzgruppen* trial, had acted as an alternate judge for Tribunal IV, hearing the case against Frederick Flick. According to the American Secretary of War, Dixon was "highly regarded [for] his legal and judicial ability."[10] Speight, on the other hand, had no experience on the

[4] Memorandum, Louis Denfeld, Chief of Naval Personnel to Musmanno, October 10, 1946, Navy file 2340, MMP; Memorandum, Clay to Musmanno, September 10, 1947, in *ibid*; and, Letter, Musmanno to Joseph Sullivan, November 5, 1946, in Mark Clark file 1812, MMP.

[5] Despite Musmanno's long and colorful history as a jurist, and a full career as a writer, very little has been written about him.

[6] Interview with Ferencz, April 24, 1997, 29.

[7] Letter, Patterson to Truman, December 23, 1946 in WHOF, WCT at Nuremberg and Tokyo, HST.

[8] Andy Logan quoted in, *Witnesses to Nuremberg*, 201.

[9] Cable from OMGUS (Keating), undated, circa 1946, in NARA RG 466, Prisons Division, Security Segregated Records 1945–1947, box 10, WCT Correspondence 1946–1947 folder.

[10] Letter, Patterson to Truman, May 12, 1947, in WHOF, WCT at Nuremberg and Tokyo, HST.

bench before Nuremberg, but he was considered worthy of appointment because he had practiced law for more than thirty years and had also been Special Assistant to the Attorney General. He had been an alternate judge in both the Milch and Pohl cases before hearing the *Einsatzgruppen* case. In spite of his experience and credentials, Speight was seen as incompetent and at least two fellow judges at Nuremberg believed him to be "ineffective;" a mere "cipher," as one said.[11] It is difficult to determine the role that Dixon and Speight played at trial as they are almost entirely absent from the *Einsatzgruppen* trial transcript. Where they sat on the bench at other trials (for example, the Milch and Pohl trials) there is no evidence they directly participated in the proceedings. It is unfortunate that Dixon's papers contain no pertinent information about his Nuremberg days and Speight left nothing behind whatsoever. I asked Ferencz about the two men when I interviewed him and he claims they slept through the entire eight-month trial.[12] This may not be entirely accurate though. As Bradley Smith reminds us in his discussion of the IMT judgment, silence during trial does not necessarily translate to silence during deliberations. At Nuremberg, each judge had an equal vote in determining the guilt or innocence of defendants, and as we know from the U.S. Supreme Court, some judges talk, whereas others write. Even though the documentary record is sparse, Dixon and Speight cannot unequivocally be said to be unimportant to these proceedings, yet it is difficult to write them into the historical record when it is Musmanno's public performance that stands out in both the official record and in his personal papers. He left behind a voluminous archive of his life, including every letter he wrote, the drafts of all of his books, and all of his Nuremberg material. And, although his record may not be a complete reflection of Tribunal II's deliberations, it is the only record we have. What it tells us is that publicly Dixon and Speight are far less participatory in the trial than Musmanno. The presiding judge was so riveted by the proceedings he wrote an unsolicited letter to Rebecca West expressing his amazement at her boredom with the IMT. For him, no matter how long a case, the courtroom was a place of drama, not monotony.[13] After Ohlendorf who was extremely charismatic and voluble, Musmanno's was unquestionably the loudest and most frequently heard voice in court. He participated in every phase of the proceedings, sometimes as judge, sometimes as prosecutor, and sometimes as mentor to the defense attorneys. Not surprisingly then, from the very beginning he dominated in most aspects of the trial. The judicial license Musmanno exercised may not

[11] Memorandum, W. H. Schroder to Col. Robinson and Alvin Rockwell, November 22, 1946, in *ibid.*; and, Memorandum, Charles Sands, Acting Secretary General, to OMGUS Chief of Staff, December 15, 1946, in *ibid.*
[12] When I asked Ferencz what kind of men Speight and Dixon were, he replied, "quiet!"
[13] Musmanno, undated note to himself regarding Rebecca West's, *Train of Powder* (New York, 1955), 546–547, Memoranda and Notes Nuremberg file 1247, MMP.

have been tolerated in an American criminal proceeding; however, given the unprecedented nature of the Nuremberg proceedings and the extraordinary circumstances under which the trials were held, it is hardly astonishing that liberties could be, and were taken by the judges, especially by a judge such as Musmanno.

The part the judge plays in any criminal trial is vital. In the case of the Subsequent proceedings, the function of the judge was of even greater importance because there were no jurors and because the laws under which the defendants were indicted and tried were quite flexible, providing the judges a great deal of latitude with respect to evidence, procedure, and process.[14] Under Article 17 of the *Charter*, for instance, tribunals were given the power to interrogate and question defendants.[15] They also had sole discretion concerning evidence, as they were "not bound by technical rules."[16] Rather, tribunals were mandated to "adopt and apply ... expeditious and non-technical procedure, and [to] admit any evidence which it deems to have probative value."[17] The nature, scope, and flexibility of the rules opened the way for a dominant personality to control the proceedings. Not one to shy away from the spotlight, Musmanno did precisely this.

To draw attention to himself, Musmanno sometimes turned the courtroom into his own personal stage, using outbursts of humor and sarcasm – often lost on the defendants. This behavior infuriated the prosecution who, given the grave nature of the charges, were "trying to convey a sombre atmosphere" in the courtroom.[18] Musmanno understood the historic nature of Nuremberg, and this, coupled with his exceptionally large ego, may account for his determination to leave his mark.[19] Once described as "his own best press agent," he took advantage of every opportunity to make his voice heard, whether in the courtroom, in the written judgment, to the press, or in his personal correspondence.[20] Musmanno even wrote a book about his experiences at Nuremberg.[21] Important to our understanding of the *Einsatzgruppen* trial is that Musmanno used his position as presiding judge to stage manage the trial, to determine what was admitted as evidence, and

---

[14] See especially U.S. Military Ordinance No. 7, Articles 2–10 in *TWC*, vol. 15, xxiii–xxvi.

[15] Articles 17 and 18, *Charter of the IMT*, October 6, 1945 in *ibid*., xiv.

[16] Article 19, *Charter*, in *ibid*., xvi.

[17] *Ibid*.

[18] Interview with Ferencz, April 24, 1997, 6.

[19] Letter, Musmanno to Lt. Commander Ann Brennen, December 11, 1946 in Navy file 2340, MMP. Musmanno referred to Nuremberg as "the Bar of History itself." *Idem, Eichmann Kommandos*, 90.

[20] Alfred Santangelo, New York House of Representatives, "Justice Michael Musmanno, Nemesis of Nazis, and a Man of the People," *Congressional Record – Appendix*, May 18, 1961, A3554, Loose Documents, MMP.

[21] Musmanno erroneously believed that the *Einsatzgruppen* were under the authority of Adolf Eichmann, even testifying such at Eichmann's trial. He was also a publicity opportunist, using the Eichmann trial to sell his story to publishers.

ultimately to help determine its outcome. Much to the surprise of the defense, he came to the bench prepared to listen to the evidence. His experiences as a defense attorney had shaped his judicial worldview and profoundly influenced his subsequent behavior on the bench.

Before coming to Nuremberg in 1946, Musmanno had had an extremely successful career. Eleanor Roosevelt remembered him as "a man passionately dedicated to the welfare of the underprivileged,"[22] and some of his political and judicial colleagues agreed that he was a "champion of true justice," who could not rest "until all wrongs had been righted."[23] To right a wrong is what Musmanno had attempted to do in 1927, when he represented convicted murderers Nicola Sacco and Bartolomeo Vanzetti. His experience defending these men was a watershed in his career. But Musmanno's motives were not always so highly regarded. His incessant red baiting in the 1950s, coupled with questionable behavior at Adolf Eichmann's trial in 1961 has tarnished his reputation as a jurist; one scholar has even suggested he became a fascist later in life.[24] The record is clear; Musmanno was at the forefront of the anti-communist witch-hunt in Pittsburgh during the 1950s, using his courtroom as a way to expose communists and their sympathizers.[25] So bad was his behavior that, on several occasions, Musmanno was reprimanded by the Pennsylvania Supreme Court.[26] His behavior seems to have gotten worse over time and was not limited to his own courtroom. As Stephan Landsman has noted, at Eichmann's trial in Jerusalem in 1961, Musmanno was so badly behaved that the court ruled he was a hostile witness. Here he eschewed all "rules of evidence," giving "dubious" testimony about Eichmann's role in the Final Solution.[27] It seems that Musmanno had agreed to testify at Eichmann's trial not because he had anything valuable to offer the court as a witness, but rather because he wanted to promote himself and the Nuremberg memoir he was trying to get published. He went to Jerusalem in 1961 armed with hearsay evidence, maybe even lies, designed to implicate Eichmann in the activities of the *Einsatzgruppen* hoping that the press from the trial would secure him a publication deal. This incident highlights an important negative quality in Musmanno that cannot be ignored at the outset. Throughout his career, but especially after Nuremberg, he often sacrificed truth for self-promotion, a troubling character trait for a judge.

[22] Eleanor Roosevelt, undated, quoted in "Biographical Outline Pennsylvania Supreme Court, Justice Michael A. Musmanno," Biographical Jan–June 1969 file 940, MMP.
[23] Jacob K. Javits, U.S. Senator, undated, quoted in *ibid* and David L. Lawrence, Governor of Pennsylvania, undated, quoted in *ibid*.
[24] David Caute, *The Great Terror. The Anti-Communist Purge under Truman and Eisenhower* (New York, 1978), 218.
[25] *Ibid.*, 216–223.
[26] *Ibid.*, 218.
[27] Landsman, *Crimes of the Holocaust*, 80–81.

Although Musmanno's unorthodox style and disregard for the truth has garnered criticism, contemporaries praised his work at Nuremberg. In February 1948, *Die Zeit* called him the most "momentous" presiding judge since Justice Lawrence chaired the IMT and, in April, the same paper reported that he was the only judge at Nuremberg to whom the defendants expressed their thanks for the fair manner in which he conducted the trial.[28] *Der Spiegel* had reported that even against defendants such as Ohlendorf and other SS leaders, Musmanno's judicial conduct at trial was flawless.[29] Expressions of appreciation and praise were rare at Nuremberg, especially by the Germans whose press coverage of the Subsequent Proceedings was extremely critical.[30] Yet, Musmanno's behavior caught the attention of the German press, perhaps because the defense team gave him an eighteen-inch bronze statue of a penguin as a token of their respect for his conduct of the trial.[31] An odd gift to say the least, but one that symbolized their appreciation of his now famous *Penguin Rule,* which dictated that the defense would be permitted to enter into evidence any and all material that might prove the innocence of their clients, including the social life of the Antarctic penguin, if it would help.[32] The *Penguin Ruling,* as it came to be called, was intended to offer the defense every possibility to refute the serious charges against their clients.

---

[28] Untitled article, *Die Zeit*, February 26, 1948, Loose Documents (Scrapbook), MMP and untitled article, *Die Zeit*, April 1, 1948, in *ibid.*

[29] Untitled article, *Der Spiegel*, March 9, 1948, in *ibid.*

[30] Examples of German newspaper articles critical of the trials include, "Urteil oder Racheakt? Landesbischof Wurm gegen Nürnberger Gerichtsmethoden," *Allgemeine Zeitung*, May 15, 1948; "Bischof Wurm gegen Nürnberg," *Rhein-Echo*, June 10, 1948; "Kritik an Nürnberg," *Nordwest-Zeitung*, May 15, 1948; "Anklagen ohne Beweise," *Telegraf*, May 21, 1948; "Die Grundlagen der Nürnberger Prozess: Dr. Alfred Seidl über die Einwände der deutschen Verteidiger," *Die Neue Zeitung*, May 23, 1948; "Die Männer in roten Jacken: Ein Beltrag zum Rechtsbewußtsein unserer Zeit," *Hamburger Abendblatt*, November 18, 1948; and, "Verbrecher oder Märtyrer?" *Stuttgarter Nachrichten*, June 12, 1948. These articles and many more can be found in Nachlass Landesbischof D. Theophil Wurm, Bestand D1/IV (Nachkriegszeit), Kriegsverbrechen Bd. 289–336, NL Wurm, LKA. German criticism of the Nuremberg trials was not limited to the press, it also includes the collection of legal essays edited by Benton and Grimm, *German Views of the War Trials* and two widely distributed pamphlets by Rudolf Aschenauer, "Zur Frage einer Revision der Kriegsverbrecherprozess," (Nuremberg, 1949) and *idem*, "Landsberg," (Munich, 1951). Finally, see an in-depth criticism of the U.S. war crimes trials written by high-ranking German church officials and some of the Nuremberg trial attorneys, "Memorandum by The Evangelical Church in Germany on the Question of War Crimes Trials before American Military Court," (Stuttgart, 1949), in NARA RG 238, Advisory Board on Clemency, HICOG 1947–1950, Correspondence and other Records 1950, box 4, General folder.

[31] The inscription on the statue reads "Presented to Navy Captain Michael A. Musmanno by German Defense Lawyers in appreciation of the Penguin Rule, Nuremberg 1946–1948." The statue is part of Musmanno's official collection located at Duquesne University, Pittsburgh, Pennsylvania.

[32] Musmanno, *Eichmann Kommandos*, 246–247.

Musmanno largely contained his ego during the *Einsatzgruppen* trial, adjudicating the overwhelming documentary evidence against the defendants as objectively as he was able. At Nuremberg, at least, he seemed committed to ensuring that the trials he participated in were not foregone conclusions or *fait accomplis*, publicly stating that even mass murderers were entitled to fair treatment under the law. He adhered to the American legal precepts that "every man is presumed innocent until proved guilty. . . . [and] that the prosecution has the burden of proof and must prove the guilt of the accused beyond a reasonable doubt," although as we saw in chapter 4, the defense relinquished these rights when they argued putative justification.[33] In 1947, he was certain that the gravity of the charges demanded that the tribunal weigh all the evidence carefully and that reason should prevail. Although the defendants and their crimes were the centerpiece of the trial, it was the presiding judge who directed and shaped the proceedings. Because Musmanno took such an active and leading role in the proceedings, it is necessary to examine his background, legal career, and personality in order to fully understand the course of the trial and especially its outcome.

Musmanno before Nuremberg

Michael Angelo Musmanno was the seventh of eight children born to a devoutly Catholic Italian immigrant couple, on April 7, 1897, in Stowe Township, Pennsylvania, a mill and manufacturing community six miles outside of Pittsburgh on the Ohio river.[34] His father, Antonio, had immigrated to the United States to provide for his large family, working first as a coal miner, then a railway-worker, and finally as a policeman. A drunk driver killed his mother Maddelena while he was still a boy, which undoubtedly explains why he was the first judge in the United States to sentence drunk drivers to prison terms.[35] To help support his family, Musmanno began working in the coalmines at 14 years of age, but his father strongly encouraged him to acquire an education and thus he attended school at the same time.[36]

---

[33] "Summary Statements from the Judgments of the Tribunals, or from Concurring or Dissenting Opinions on Procedure, Practice, and Evidence," in *TWC*, vol. 15, 98.

[34] Musmanno refused to divulge the true date of his birth. Some documents identify it as 1900, but the date given on his military service records is 1897. He died in 1968. Letter, Patterson to Truman, December 23, 1946, in WHOF, WCT at Nuremberg and Tokyo 1945–1948, HST.

[35] Conversation with A. E. Lawson, a Pennsylvania attorney who grew-up in Stowe Township, November, 2001; and, Biographical Information Musmanno, in "Michael A. Musmanno and the Modification of the 1794 Sunday Laws of Pennsylvania," loose documents, MMP. Musmanno's book, *Listen to the River* apparently details the life of his mother and father, but I could not locate it anywhere, all traces of it seem to have vanished.

[36] Biographical Information Musmanno January–June 1968, Biography file 940, MMP.

Working excessively hard as he did growing up in Pennsylvania was one of the defining features of Musmanno's adult life.

Musmanno also demonstrated a lifelong passion for learning, earning an astonishing seven degrees from five different universities, and all before the age of thirty years. Most of his degrees were earned in universities in the Washington, D.C. area, where he could work during the day and attend night classes, only interrupting his studies briefly to serve as an infantryman in 1917 when the United States entered the war.[37] He earned a B.A. and M.A. from George Washington University, followed by a Bachelor of Laws from Georgetown, Master of Laws and Master of Patent Laws both from National University, and then a Doctor of Juristic Science from American University. His final degree was earned outside the United States, a Doctor of Jurisprudence from the University of Rome in 1925.[38] Later in his career, he also studied criminology at Harvard and Notre Dame although he did not receive degrees from either university.[39]

While in Washington, Musmanno honed his oratorical skills, joining the Delta Sigma Rho fraternity – renowned for producing excellent debaters. In 1932, he put his debating expertise to use when he publicly debated the question, "Does Man Live Again?" with the celebrated jurist Clarence Darrow at Carnegie Hall in Pittsburgh.[40] Musmanno worked on his elocution throughout his career, priding himself on how effectively he could capture audiences with his speech. This strikes me as surprising after hearing his voice on tape, but perhaps in person he sounded better. From an early age "worry and hard work" were Musmanno's motivators; attributes he believed to be key ingredients "to success."[41] If hard-work was his trademark, it was his obsessive desire for victory, his hunger for notoriety, and a naive idealism that were to shape the early part of his career as a lawyer.

After completing some of his university education, he returned to his home in Pennsylvania in 1923 to take the state bar exam. Typical of Musmanno's life-long work habits, he spent nineteen hours a day for nearly two months preparing for the exam, constantly fretting that he might fail. He was so concerned about his performance that when he found himself slipping into exhaustion he would go to the nearby train station, a noisy and bustling spot, where he could stay awake to study.[42] In May 1923, Musmanno wrote his exam and in July he was officially admitted to the Pennsylvania bar. Despite his success, he had difficulty finding a job. He was so desperate

---

[37] Musmanno, *Verdict!*, 27 and "Biographical Outline of Musmanno," Biography file 940, MMP. Neither of these sources explain where Musmanno served during the war. Lawson recalls that Musmanno was in Europe. Conversation with A. E. Lawson, November 2001.

[38] "Biographical Outline of Musmanno," in *ibid.*

[39] *Ibid.*

[40] Musmanno, *Verdict!*, 14 and 177.

[41] *Ibid.*, 177.

[42] *Ibid.*, 28–29.

for employment that he considered options other than the law and applied to teach at no fewer than sixty-two different educational institutions. All turned him down. While looking for work as a lawyer, he was also churning out fictional short stories and legal articles by the dozen, hoping to be published. During this period he published an article on amendments to the American Constitution in the *New York Times*, earning him his first remuneration – thirty-five dollars – and proffering a great amount of pride.[43] Like a gambling addict, this small success encouraged him to continue his writing career, a vocation he courted until the end of his life.

At times Musmanno's preoccupation with writing upstaged his career as a jurist. In total, he published fifteen books (not including volumes of his legal opinions which number in the dozens) on topics as diverse as his legal career, his battle against communists in America, and his experiences at Nuremberg.[44] Two of his books, *Black Fury*, a fictionalized account of his struggle for justice against the corrupt coal and iron police in the Pennsylvania coalfields, and *Ten Days to Die*, the story of Hitler's last days in the Reich Chancellery bunker, were made into feature films.[45] Musmanno's writing was very important to him, nurturing his ever-present desire for fame. There is no question he fancied himself a good writer, though the reality was he was not. The plots of his books are overly dramatic and immature, the result of a trite and self-absorbed writing style. That said, his novels allowed him to feed his appetite for the dramatic, a quality that came to define his style as a judge as well.

A perusal of Musmanno's written work reflects his passion for drama. All of his publications, including his legal opinions, are replete with references to Shakespeare, his knowledge of which was acquired while a student in Washington where he worked as a supernumerary with several different

---

[43] This article was later expanded and turned into a book, *Proposed Amendments to the Constitution*, and published by the US House of Representatives. Musmanno, *Verdict!*, 30–31.

[44] Musmanno's publications include: *After Twelve Years*, which chronicles his experiences as a defense attorney in the Sacco-Vanzetti trial; *Listen to the River*, about his Italian parents; *Ten Days to Die*, based on interviews he conducted at Nuremberg concerning the last ten days of Hitler's life; *The Soldier and the Man*, a biography of General Mark Clark who Musmanno worked for during World War II; *Across the Street from the Courthouse*, a recounting of Musmanno's red-baiting after the war; *The Eichmann Kommandos*, a memoir of his experiences as presiding judge at Nuremberg; *Justice Musmanno Dissents*, Musmanno's dissenting opinions while on the bench of the Pennsylvania Supreme court; *Verdict!*, Musmanno's autobiography as a lawyer; *The Story of the Italians in America*; *World War II in Italy*; *An American Replies*, a response to the perceived defamation of the Italian people; *Columbus was First*, an argument refuting the authenticity of the "Vinland Map"; *That's my Opinion*, excerpts from Musmanno's dissenting and majority opinions; and, *The Glory and the Dream*, the story of Abraham Lincoln.

[45] *Black Fury* was written in 1935 and republished in 1966. *Ten Days to Die* was published in 1951 and made into the film *Der Letzte Akt* in 1955.

Shakespearean theatre companies.[46] His novels are also rife with references to the sea, another of his great loves. His books tend to convey a sense of adventure, some are about overcoming adversity and all seem to end in victory for the heroic protagonist, usually himself or a client who had been unjustly accused. Sometimes his writing is genuinely quite humorous, using puns as a narrative tool, at other times it is unintentionally comical, the result of an exaggerated and verbose writing style. But, the defining feature of almost all of his writing, particularly his autobiographical works, is heroic melodrama. To achieve this, he relies heavily on hackneyed metaphors, dramatic language, and exaggerated scenarios that inevitably create a sensationalized rendition of the facts. His writing is reminiscent of modern day pulp fiction – "over the top" – and tellingly, a style for which he was quite proud.

Although Musmanno believed he had an obligation to write for his colleagues in the legal profession, his real audience was the man on the street.[47] To appeal to both constituencies, he took dramatic license and allowed accuracy to go by the wayside because, in his view, it "distracted" from the "excitement of the narrative."[48] Musmanno's attitude toward facts has thus always been somewhat distorted. For instance, his book *Ten Days to Die* was expressly written "to fill an historical void" by clarifying the details of Hitler's death in the Reich Chancellery bunker. To elucidate this historical event, he claims to have interviewed more than 200 witnesses who had direct knowledge of Hitler's death. Yet, the end product, although an interesting and compelling story, cannot be verified as accurate as he provides no notes, no bibliography, and no reference to the personal interviews he conducted. His memoir of the *Einsatzgruppen* trial, inappropriately titled, *The Eichmann Kommandos*, is another example. The original version of the book, written while in Nuremberg, was first titled: *The Biggest Murder Trial in History*, and makes no reference whatsoever to Adolf Eichmann. Musmanno could not find a publisher for the book in 1948 and the manuscript ended-up on his shelf. Twelve years later, when Eichmann was kidnapped in Argentina by Israeli agents and brought to Israel to stand trial, Musmanno seized the moment to publish the memoir. He had been asked to testify as a witness for the prosecution at Eichmann's trial. Never one to miss an opportunity to advance his interests, he linked the *Einsatzgruppen* and their murderous activities directly to Eichmann. In the revised version, Musmanno claims that Eichmann was both the brain behind the creation of the *Einsatzgruppen* as

---

[46] *Ibid.*, 206–207. Musmanno believed that Shakespeare was "the most powerful writer that ever traced poetic drama across paper." See Musmanno, *An American Replies to a Defamation of the Italians* (Florence, 1965), 20.

[47] Julia Edwards, "Sailor on the Bench," *Weekend*, April 24, 1948, in *Einsatzgruppen* Trial 1947–1948 Clippings, Photos, Record of Defendants and Listing of Sentences, Nuremberg Clippings file 2150, MMP.

[48] Musmanno, "Preface," *Ten Days to Die* (London, 1951), unpaginated.

well as the planner of their murderous activities. Of course, this is not true, but he nonetheless states it as fact.[49] Musmanno could have gotten away with these changes had he called the book historical fiction, that he pretended it was true, is extremely troubling but clear evidence that the truth was not as important to him as drama.[50] Writing "impressionistically rather than as a scholar," *The Eichmann Kommandos* makes for theatrical reading: by altering the original memoir and placing himself at the center of the narrative, he gives the impression that he single-handedly prosecuted, tried, and convicted the defendants.[51]

Even with the added drama, Musmanno's writing is not very good, his autobiographical books standing out as particularly awful. One reader complained that the biography of his mother and father was "unquestionably the worst book I have ever attempted to read."[52] Whereas his prose style prevents any of his novels or autobiographical works from being classified as good literature, these same practices had the opposite effect on his written legal opinions. His humor, metaphors, drama, and imagination do add significant color, making for engaging reading, rather than the dry legalistic style of most judicial opinions. As one jurist familiar with Musmanno's legal career has said, his "style is so fascinating that one easily finds himself reading for enjoyment."[53] Imaginative legal writing was one reason the written judgment of the *Einsatzgruppen* trial was so well received; it also helped him land his first job as a lawyer.

---

[49] Musmanno, *Eichmann Kommandos*, 53–60, see especially pages 56–57 where Musmanno writes, "Eichmann conferred with Himmler and Himmler conferred with Hitler. Eichmann's recommendations were accepted and the Einsatzgruppen organization was born. Thus, in the early part of 1941, Hitler directed Himmler, Heydrich and Eichmann to recruit mobile bands of executioners which were to accompany and follow the German armies.... [f]or men to lead the Einsatzgruppen Heydrich asked Eichmann for recommendations. Eichmann looked for men with exceptional ability and with a capacity for Semitic destruction as intense as his own. He found the ideal men for top leadership in Walter Stahlecker, Arthur Nebe, Otto Rasch and Otto Ohlendorf."

[50] "US Judge Stirs Eichmann Trial," *The New York Times*, May 16, 1961, Loose Documents, MMP and Landsman, *Crimes of the Holocaust*, 81.

[51] Musmanno's love of drama explains the appeal of the 1961 film, *Judgment at Nuremberg*, a fictionalized account of the NMT starring Spencer Tracy and Marlena Dietrich. Other Nuremberg participants were critical of the film's lack of historical accuracy. For example, Letter, Ferencz to Horlik-Hochwald, January 10, 1961, in RG 12.000, Drawer 11, Biographical Material, box 2, Correspondence re: Film *Judgment at Nuremberg* (sic) 1960–1961 folder and Letter, Henry Lea to Ferencz, December 10, 1989, BBF, USHMM.

[52] Letter, Robert (last name illegible) to Alvin Rockwell, OMGUS, July 21, 1948, in Alvin Rockwell Papers, HST.

[53] Abraham Freedman, "The Dissenting Opinions of Justice Musmanno," *Temple Law Quarterly* 30 (1957), 253. Steven Spector, "Judicial Activism in Prose: A Librarian's Guide to the Opinions of Justice Michael A. Musmanno," *Law Library Journal* (Spring, 1994), 311–321 has written about Musmanno's legal prose, particularly his dissenting opinions as a member of the Pennsylvania Supreme Court from 1952 to 1968, calling his writing "enjoyable."

Musmanno began his career in law in 1923, when he was 26 years old. John R. K. Scott, a Philadelphia litigator of local fame, had noticed Musmanno's article on the constitution in the *New York Times*, and hired him as a defense attorney for his firm.[54] He quickly made a name for himself. Musmanno's courtroom theatrics, earned him a reputation as a showman reaffirming his belief that, "to be a lawyer without knowing Shakespeare (sic) would be like being a musician without burning a candle to Beethoven."[55] His frequent melodramatic and sappy performances to juries, which he referred to as "the dramatic third act," coupled with his oratorical skills almost always proved successful in the courtroom.[56] He was so good at captivating juries and gaining their sympathy that he won the first forty-two cases he tried.[57]

As do many young lawyers, Musmanno threw himself into his career, working extremely long hours. He was no ordinary apprentice though. He took everything to the extreme, even forgoing a social life in order to read legal judgments and prepare cases for his firm.[58] This was a practice Musmanno had begun in youth and continued throughout his career. Of this practice, one of his colleagues at Nuremberg claimed he had,

never s[een] anyone work with the ardor, the continuity and thoroughness which Captain Musmanno brought to his judicial tasks... for the last five months I know that [he] has been depriving himself of rest and sleep... so that the work could be done and the job completed.[59]

When his winning streak came to an end he was devastated. So over-whelmed by his failure he impetuously tendered his resignation, dramatically

---

[54] Musmanno, *Verdict!*, 12–13 and 31–32.

[55] *Ibid.*, 209.

[56] *Ibid.*, 218. As Musmanno grew older he increasingly came under attack for his arrogant and verbose style of public speaking, a method of oratory that one of his public relations managers warned him was out of date and "old school technique." See Letter, Terry Parker, Public Relations to Musmanno, August 31, 1961, Buick Bats file 1811, MMP.

[57] Musmanno, *Verdict*, 9–23, 33–45 and 67–68.

[58] One newspaper reported that Musmanno never found time to marry because the women who were interested in him took one look at his attitude toward work and "kept on running." Edwards, "Sailor on the Bench," *Weekend*, April 12, 1948, in Einsatzgruppen Trial 1947–1948, Clippings, Photos, Record of Defendants and Listing of Sentences, Nuremberg Clippings file 2150, MMP.

[59] Letter, Speight to John Sullivan, Secretary of the Navy, April 13, 1948, in Lucius Clay file 1138, MMP. One newspaper reported that Musmanno worked at the Palace of Justice in Nuremberg from eight-thirty a.m. to eleven p.m. daily, only to return to his room at the Grand Hotel where he continued working until 2 a.m. See Edwards, "Sailor on the Bench," in Einsatzgruppen Trial 1947–48, Clippings, Photos, Record of Defendants and Listing of Sentences, Nuremberg Clippings file 2150, MMP. Not only did Musmanno work on the *Einsatzgruppen* case, he also claims to have interviewed hundreds of witnesses to write *Ten Days to Die*. While at Nuremberg he wrote *Listen to the River* and was a judge at two other trials as well.

proclaiming that as the person "responsible for the defeat, I personally experience the most intense personal chagrin and mortification . . . I suffer in the realization that I have lost for you, you who have placed so much confidence in me."[60] Musmanno's inability to cope with failure, and his incessant need to please those in authority, highlights an important contradiction in his personality: he was a man who possessed both a fragile ego and an exaggerated sense of self. Both of these personality traits defined Musmanno, who not only strove for success and recognition out of fear of failure, but who also expected it. It was his inability to cope with failure that prompted his temporary abandonment of the law in 1924. At this juncture in his life, no amount of pleading by his colleagues or employer – who thought him an excellent junior lawyer – could console him. A week after his resignation in 1924 he boarded a ship and sailed to Italy.[61]

While abroad Musmanno was a frequent visitor to the Italian courts, which brought him into contact with several prominent Italian jurists, who encouraged him to continue his study of the law in Rome.[62] To do this, Musmanno needed money. As he had done in Washington earlier, he took on several different jobs at once. He worked as an extra in the film *Ben Hur*, then being shot in Italy, he had a small role in an opera, he taught English to Italians, and he wrote for Rome's English daily where he got to meet Mussolini and ride the Duce's horse. A picture of this encounter is in his collection, although given his later political inclinations and his role as a Naval Captain in World War II, no mention of meeting Mussolini is made in any of his written work.[63] While at the University of Rome, he studied under the criminologist Enrico Ferri, but he also took courses from former Italian prime ministers, Vittorio Emmanuel Orlando and Francesco Nitti.[64] In June 1925, Musmanno received a doctorate in Jurisprudence from the University of Rome. His thesis, for which he supposedly earned 110 percent, was a comparison between the American and Italian jury systems.[65] His adventure complete, Musmanno visited Paris and London before setting sail for home.

Reinvigorated, and back in Pennsylvania, Musmanno decided to resume his career. While pounding the pavement in search of employment, he was asked to represent a coal miner who had been unjustly arrested and beaten by

---

[60] Musmanno, *Verdict*, 70–71. Musmanno had drafted a letter of resignation upon losing his first case, but a colleague in his firm encouraged him not to submit it.

[61] Musmanno, *An American Replies*, 9, was written and published while in Italy. The book is a response to Italian parliamentarian, Luigi Barzini's, *The Italians*, in which the author derides Italian Americans as scoundrels, who lack honor. Outraged that anyone would defame Italian-Americans, Musmanno wrote the book, because of his "love of the truth."

[62] Musmanno, *Verdict!*, 81.

[63] One reference to this encounter can be found in "Interview with Michael A. Musmanno," undated, Nuremberg Correspondence file 1445, MMP.

[64] Musmanno, *An American Replies*, 9–10.

[65] Musmanno, *Verdict*, 82–86.

the corrupt and brutish police organization of the coal and iron magnates. This proved to be the beginning of a long battle against the tyranny and injustice of the coal and iron industry in Pennsylvania and eventually led to the film *Black Fury* produced by Warner Brothers, staring Paul Muni and later the book by the same name.[66] The case earned Musmanno a reputation as a fighter for the "little man," and he was subsequently offered (by an individual sympathetic to his cause) free office space in Pittsburgh to open his own law practice.[67] His defense of the coal miners marked the beginning of his career as a defense attorney who fought against systemic injustice, frequently in personal injury cases, but also against corrupt institutions in civil society. His new career appealed to his ego.[68]

Early on in his career, we can see the beginnings of what might today be called a narcissistic personality. While still a youthful idealist, Musmanno also fundamentally believed he had the power to save people from injustice and he actively sought out those who he believed were wrongly accused. Even at this early date Musmanno exhibits troubling signs of a skewed legal ethic, openly admitting – even boasting – he was not interested in representing individuals whose guilt was ambiguous.[69] As he put it, the "true lawyer is not the one who pleads any case regardless of the right or wrong of it. Such indiscriminate championing can only blunt one's appreciation of the important distinction between justice and injustice, and eventually it may deaden the moral sensibility of the heart."[70] How Musmanno determined a client's innocence or guilt he never explains, but he seems to have genuinely believed that good lawyers have a greater social purpose than merely defending their clients to the best of their ability. Clearly driven by an insatiable ego, Musmanno sought to fight perceived injustice, a trait he held onto throughout his life and one he later brought to his work on the bench in the United States.

The defining moment of Musmanno's early career came in 1927, when the famous case against Nicola Sacco and Bartolomeo Vanzetti (more commonly known as the Sacco-Vanzetti case) came to a head seven years after they originally had been sentenced. Sacco and Vanzetti, Italian immigrants and labor activists (at the time they were viewed as a threat to established political and economic norms because both had links to the anarchist movement), were sentenced to death by electric chair by Judge Webster Thayer, in

---

[66] The film preceded the book, which was not written until much later. Typical of Musmanno's penchant for the dramatic, he fictionalized the Pennsylvania coalminers' strike of 1925–1928.

[67] Musmanno, *Verdict!*, 105–115.

[68] *Ibid.*, 218–219. Musmanno received the Legion of Merit medal awarded to individuals for meritorious conduct in the performance of outstanding service to the U.S.

[69] On the issue of professional ethics see Freedman, "Code of Professional Responsibility," in *Lawyers' Ethics*, 132–238.

[70] Musmanno, *Verdict!*, 237.

Dedham, Massachusetts's county court. According to Musmanno and others, the two men were treated unjustly by a system that favored the upper classes and political tradition over the working classes and labor activism. They were tried, convicted, and executed not because they were guilty of the crime, but rather because they were immigrants and anarchist troublemakers and those in positions of power wanted to make an example of them.[71] The peculiar irony here is that the man who set out to defend them was later to become an overzealous cold warrior himself. Musmanno became such a passionate anticommunist that during the early cold war he denounced many people to federal authorities for their alleged ties to the communist movement in the United States eventually testifying against them in court. He also corresponded with J. Edgar Hoover who Musmanno repeatedly praised for his work ferreting out communists from American society. His main contribution to the anticommunist movement however, was authoring the "Musmanno Act" which outlawed the Communist Party in Pennsylvania. Sacco and Vanzetti's links to the anarchist movement seemed unimportant to Musmanno at this early date, but had their case come to his attention in the 1950s, it is doubtful that he would have been as sympathetic.[72]

As Musmanno recounts the story, the two men, Sacco a shoemaker, and Vanzetti a fishmonger, had been mistakenly indicted, tried, and convicted for first-degree murder in Braintree, Massachusetts. The state prosecutor had argued that they were responsible for planning and executing the theft of $15,000 from a local shoe factory on April 15, 1920, and, in the course of the crime, had murdered the factory paymaster and security guard. For this, they would have to pay with their lives. For Musmanno, all of the evidence in the case pointed to their innocence, but the Massachusetts authorities were determined to uphold the conviction and carry out the death sentences. As the years passed, and the injustice of their conviction became increasingly apparent, they became the *cause célébre* for many working-class and fair-minded people across the United States. This included Musmanno.[73] For Musmanno, the maltreatment of Sacco and Vanzetti was a grave inequity. The case against these two working-class Italian immigrants offended his

[71] The Sacco-Vanzetti case has generated a great deal of interest over the years. The literature on the subject is too vast to list here, but some examples are Roberta Strauss Feuerlicht, *Justice Crucified. The Story of Sacco and Vanzetti* (New York, 1977); Francis Russell, one of the first to call into question the innocence of Nicola Sacco wrote *Tragedy in Dedham: The Story of the Sacco-Vanzetti Case* (New York, 1971) and *Sacco and Vanzetti: The Case Resolved* (New York, 1986); and Joseph B. Kadane and David A. Schum, *A Probabilistic Analysis of the Sacco and Vanzetti Evidence* (New York, 1996).

[72] "Biographical Sketch of Pennsylvania Supreme Court Justice Michael A. Musmanno on the subject of Americanism," Biography file 940, MMP and Letters, Musmanno to Hoover, October 26, 1959, January 21, 1960 and Hoover to Musmanno, July 25, 1957, October 19, 1959, and February 1, 1960 in Anti-Communist file 1288, MMP.

[73] Musmanno, *Verdict!*, 239–258.

sense of American justice, which he had naively assumed to be incorruptible. As the son of Italian immigrants made good, he believed in the American dream. His earlier experiences with the coal and iron police taught him that if one worked hard enough, justice would eventually prevail. Thus, when he learned of the circumstantial nature of the evidence against Sacco and Vanzetti and the selective way in which it was used, he was outraged by a judicial system that was being misused to keep the poor men down.[74]

Musmanno followed the case for years, since his days as a student in Washington. In 1927, when he learned the two men would be executed imminently, he closed the doors to his private practice in Pittsburgh, boarded a train to Massachusetts, and became involved in the case even though the two men had not retained him. Musmanno claims he took the case for reasons of "universal justice," to right this legal wrong.[75] A more cynical person might say he took the case at the eleventh hour because he wanted publicity. Both are probably true. Musmanno had never shied away from hard work, but this case was definitely an uphill battle. Along with a team of lawyers, he threw himself into his work to secure pardons, stays of execution, and retrials. This was the first time his hard work did not pay off and, on August 10, 1927, Sacco and Vanzetti were electrocuted in a small Massachusetts prison.[76] Musmanno witnessed their deaths.

The execution of Sacco and Vanzetti in 1927 altered Musmanno's perspective of the judicial system forever. He had discovered that it was fallible; that good people do not always win. He wrote despairingly of his experience,

I learned that right does not always triumph though the heavens fall; I ascertained that in the law there could be a wrong without a remedy. Nor did it appear that all those entrusted with administering American freedoms were worthy of that trust. In the very cradle of America I had seen individual human liberty and life itself suffocated under the blankets of personal greed, political ambition, and unqualifiable (sic) infamy.[77]

Musmanno vowed to change the system. To do this, he ran for a seat in the Pennsylvania State Legislature winning the 1928 election by a narrow margin. He ran again in 1930 and won with a landslide victory.[78] While in the legislature, Musmanno tried to change the dated laws that governed the coal and iron police. Although he was not immediately successful, his dreams were realized in 1935, when the Governor of Pennsylvania repealed the legislation after the film *Black Fury* caused such a public outcry over the

---

Ibid., 240.
Ibid.
Ibid., 239–293. Musmanno, *After Twelve Years*, is about the case. Louis Joughin and Edmund M. Morgan, *The Legacy of Sacco and Vanzetti* (New York, 1948), 352–353, highlight Musmanno's sloppy scholarship.
Musmanno, *Verdict!*, 293–294.
Ibid., 293–323.

injustices perpetrated by the coal industry, that had he not acted he would have lost his seat.[79] He also became a vocal advocate for the abolition of the death penalty.[80]

Musmanno had opposed the death penalty since 1925, when he joined the American League to Abolish Capital Punishment after deciding that the state used capital punishment as a form of social control for the less privileged who did not have the means to protect themselves.[81] He came to this realization first hand, when he defended a seventeen-year-old boy, Albert Carelli, the son of a friend of his father's who was wrongly accused of a saloon hold-up and the murder of its bartender.[82] Musmanno was successful in appealing the conviction and death sentence, saving the boy from the electric chair. In another case three years later, he wrote the Governor of New York, Alfred E. Smith, asking for a commutation of the death sentence for his client Ruth Snyder who was found guilty of killing her husband. This case was more ambiguous than the Carelli case, but Musmanno felt strongly that the defendant's guilt was irrelevant. Capital punishment, he argued, should be abolished because two wrongs do not make a right.[83] Musmanno succeeded in winning a reprieve for Snyder too.

Musmanno remained a strong and vocal opponent of the death penalty throughout his life, which on the surface seems to contradict his later behavior at Nuremberg, where he sentenced defendants to death. Yet, his actions at Nuremberg were no disavowal of his conviction, despite the seeming divergence from his previous position. Musmanno's opposition to the death penalty rested neither on principle nor on morality. What bothered him so much was the possibility of the miscarriage of justice. He found it intolerable that innocent people were executed because of a fallible legal system that did not always acquit the innocent.[84] As the Sacco and Vanzetti case so clearly demonstrated to him, "nothing, absolutely nothing, can ever be done to right the wrong done these innocent men . . . they are dead: irretrievably, incurably and uncompromisingly dead . . . yet they were innocent."[85] Two innocent people lost their lives and he could not tolerate the possibility it

---

79 Musmanno recounts the details in *Black Fury*, 371–374. See also *Verdict!*, 323. Lawson argues that Musmanno deserves a lot of credit for the changes imposed to the coal and iron police system, and this should be considered one of his legacies. Conversation with A. E. Lawson, November 2001.

80 Musmanno had been a member of the American League to Abolish Capital Punishment since 1925, but became more active after the execution of Sacco and Vanzetti in 1927.

81 Musmanno, "Death Penalty does not Prevent Crime," Letter to the Editor, *New York Herald Tribune*, May 1963 in Capital Punishment file 1477, MMP.

82 Musmanno, *Verdict!*, 115–124 and Letter to Musmanno, undated and unsigned, Capital Punishment file 1477, MMP.

83 Letter, Musmanno to Governor Alfred Smith, New York, 1928, *ibid.*

84 Musmanno, "Death Penalty does not Prevent Crime," in *ibid.*

85 Musmanno, "Is it Possible to Execute Innocent Men?" Address to Annual Conference of the American League to Abolish Capital Punishment, New York, April 26, 1940 in *ibid.*

might happen again.[86] Such an individual serving as presiding judge in the "biggest murder trial in history," ensured that death sentences would not be considered lightly.

The Road to Nuremberg

In 1934, Musmanno was elected judge of the Allegheny County Court of Common Pleas, Pennsylvania where he served on the bench until December 1941, when the United States officially entered World War II. Musmanno's career as a judge at the county and state level was as eventful, colorful, and controversial as had been his career as a defense attorney. His personality was so expansive and his showmanship frequently so outrageous, that had he been born to this generation he might well have had his own court television show. On one occasion he sentenced himself to three days in jail because, as he later explained, he "wanted to see what [prison was] like."[87] He also became somewhat famous for his "campaign against drunk drivers" when he actively and harshly punished hundreds of individuals to six months in jail, a level of punishment for drinking and driving unheard of at the time, but undoubtedly prompted by his mother's premature death at the hands of a drunk driver.[88] In one twelve month period he doled out more than 481 sentences, enough to have him temporarily suspended from the bench.[89] Musmanno spent nearly eight years as a judge in the Court of Common Pleas, until he was called up for duty.[90] As a forty-three year old extreme patriot he had enlisted in early 1940 in the U.S. Naval reserves.[91] He was called to active duty on January 2, 1942, less than one month after the bombing of Pearl Harbor and was given the rank of Lieutenant Commander. Not many details are known about his Navy career, what is known is that he did not see action until sometime in 1943, during the allied campaign in Italy.[92] During this period, Musmanno was wounded twice, once in February 1944, during the Battle of Minturno for which he received

---

[86] Musmanno, "Death Penalty does not Prevent Crime," in *ibid.*

[87] Alfred Santangelo, New York House of Representatives, "Justice Michael Musmanno: Nemesis of Nazis, and a Man of the People," *Congressional Record – Appendix*, May 18, 1961, A3554, Loose Documents, MMP. See also, Musmanno, "I went to Prison," *Shadows* 1:11 (Salem, Oregon, July 1946), 7.

[88] Conversation with A. E. Lawson, November, 2001.

[89] Santangelo, "Justice Michael Musmanno," *Congressional Record*, 1961, A3554, Loose Documents, MMP and, Musmanno, "I went to Prison," 7.

[90] Letter, C. W. Nimitz, Navy Department Bureau of Navigation, to Musmanno, July 29, 1941, Navy file 2340, MMP.

[91] Memorandum, Chief of Naval Personnel to Musmanno, August 16, 1940, Navy file 2340, MMP; and, Letter, Patterson to Truman, December 23, 1946 in NARA RG 153 (JAG), WCB, Nuremberg Administration Records 1944–1949, box 14, 87-Z folder.

[92] Memorandum, Musmanno to Naval Staff Personnel Officer, December 12, 1946, Navy file 2340, MMP.

the Bronze Star for Valor, and again later in 1944, when he was wounded by shrapnel at Mount Formichi.[93]

During the Italian campaign, Musmanno was Naval Aide to General Mark Clark, who commanded the American Fifth Army and later the allied Fifteenth Army Group. When the Allies liberated the southern Italian city of Sorrento, Musmanno was made Military Governor of the Sorrentine Peninsula. How he obtained this position is unclear. While Military Governor, he developed an intense fondness for the Italians of the region, viewing them paternally and in need of his help. Unlike the accolades he received during his days fighting for the underdog as a defense attorney, as a military commander in charge of an occupation government, his actions were frequently questioned and heavily scrutinized. On one occasion, Musmanno commandeered a ship in Bari to obtain olive oil for the population of Sorrento who were out of this staple. While leaving the harbor, the ship was bombed and sunk, but he managed to save several crew members and was subsequently decorated for bravery by the King of Italy.[94] After the olive oil debacle, more serious incidents of insubordination followed. He became the subject of investigation when he challenged a British general over the requisitioning of Benedetto Croce's house in Sorrento. When the British general attempted to take Croce's house by force, Musmanno fiercely and boldly protected the aging Italian liberal and his home. The confrontation led American investigators to question Musmanno's allegiance to the United States, and accused him of harboring an "Italian complex." After a year-long investigation, Musmanno was found guilty of "flouting orders which do not agree with his interpretation of conditions and . . . constant[ly] befriending and championing . . . Italians."[95] Not wanting any negative publicity, the Navy transferred him out of Italy altogether. He accompanied Clark to Austria where the General was named American High Commissioner.[96]

In Vienna, Clark assigned Musmanno to the presidency of review courts known as the United States Board of Forcible Repatriation. The Americans established these courts as a way to avoid an agreement they had signed with the Soviets and British at Yalta in February 1945, in which it was decided that at war's end the British and Americans would assist

93 "Biographical Sketch of Musmanno on the subject of Americanism," Biography file 940, in MMP.
94 *Ibid* and Musmanno, "The Monitor and Merring," July 1941, Navy file 2340, MMP.
95 Naval Report, March 1944, Navy file 2340, MMP. The Navy investigated Musmanno and it was decided not to pursue charges against him, because it would have brought unwanted negative publicity to the British. See memorandum, R. D. La Marr (Captain) to Musmanno, December 17, 1943; Letter, SFT to RC and MG Section, Headquarters ACC, April 30, 1944; Letter, Edgar Hume, Allied Military Headquarters to Allied Control Commission, May 23, 1944 all letters in Navy file 2340, MMP.
96 Musmanno, notes to himself, undated, Soviet Board file 1101, MMP.

the Soviets in forcibly repatriating Soviet citizens who refused to return to their homeland voluntarily.[97] Following the mass-suicide of sixty Russian ex-patriots who American and British soldiers had forced to board a train bound for Moscow, the American authorities concluded that urgent action was necessary.[98] Clark agreed to establish a review board whose job it would be to hear arguments from individuals who did not want to be repatriated to the Soviet Union. Musmanno and three other judges served on these boards.[99] For nearly a year, Musmanno traveled the Austrian countryside, going from DP camp to DP camp, hearing stories of Russians who had no desire to return to the Soviet Union. Perhaps foreshadowing his later aggressive campaign against communists in America, Musmanno did his utmost to protect those refugees who came before him, but inevitably he had to send some people back to the Soviet Union even though he understood that in all likelihood they would be exiled to Siberia.[100] Musmanno's work in Austria came to an end in September 1946, when he was sent home a fully decorated Naval Commander. His sojourn was short-lived, however.[101] Even before he was discharged from the Navy, he received word that he had been reassigned to work under Admiral William Glassford to review the cases against the German naval commanders Karl Dönitz and Erich Raeder currently being tried at Nuremberg.[102] Acutely aware of Nuremberg's historic importance, Musmanno happily returned to Germany.

Since its inception in the autumn of 1945, Musmanno had been following the IMT closely, he had even written a series of articles on the trial for a Pittsburgh newspaper. Never one to miss an opportunity for notoriety, he asked the Military Government for permission to interview imprisoned former Nazis to determine the circumstances surrounding the death of Hitler. His superiors in the Military Government granted him free access to imprisoned war criminals as long as the interviews did not interfere with his Navy duties. In his spare time, between 1946 and 1948, Musmanno interviewed more than 200 witnesses to Hitler's last days

[97] "Musmanno Transferred from Italy to Austria," *Pittsburgh Gazette*, July 28, 1945, Scrapbook 1946–1949, Loose Documents, MMP.
[98] Memorandum, General McNarney to Commanding General, Seventh US Army, January 31, 1946, Soviet Board file 1101, MMP.
[99] Musmanno, notes to himself, undated, in *ibid.*
[100] *Ibid.* See especially Musmanno, *Across the Street form the Courthouse* (1954), recounts his experiences as a judge on the Board as well as his personal battle against communism in America.
[101] Letter, James G. Fulton to Clay, September 13, 1948, General Clay file 1138, MMP.
[102] Musmanno, *Eichmann Kommandos*, 48; Letter, Musmanno to Henrietta Sherwood, October 16, 1946, Admiral Glassford file 1186, MMP; "Judge Musmanno to Return in Fall. Services Requested at Nuremberg Trial," *Pittsburgh Press*, June 25, 1946; and, "Musmanno Recalled by Navy to Nazi Trial, *Pittsburgh Press*, 2 October 1946 in *ibid.*

that culminated in the publication of *Ten Days to Die* in 1951.[103] It was while working for the Navy in Nuremberg that Musmanno was asked and appointed to the bench of the NMT. His appointment was as much a case of being in-the-right-place-at-the-right-time, as it was from his professional qualifications.

As mentioned earlier, one of the major obstacles American authorities encountered in planning the Subsequent Proceedings was recruiting staff. Very early on in the planning phase, the Americans discovered that many of the high-profile candidates they selected for work at Nuremberg simply did not want to go to Europe for extended periods of time. The problem was compounded when the pool of potential candidates was restricted by the newly appointed Supreme Court Chief Justice Fred Vinson who denied federal court judges leave to serve at Nuremberg. Even had many of these jurists been able to go to Nuremberg, the attitude of the American judiciary had shifted and no longer did all view Nuremberg as a positive advancement of international law.[104] Vinson's decision meant that judges would need to be sought from state courts, even then the OCCWC had difficulty manning all the tribunals with experienced justices.[105]

Judges were recruited in the United States by the Department of the Army who submitted names of candidates to OMGUS for approval.[106] To ensure integrity and fairness, OMGUS officials wanted judges "of [the] highest calibre,"[107] who were capable of presiding over the "novel and complicated" Subsequent Proceedings.[108] Although the OCCWC was not assigned a role in recruiting judges, Taylor did make his voice heard regarding the types of judges to be recruited. He was adamant that civilian rather than military justices be recruited. Even though the tribunals were technically labeled military, one of the major tasks of those appointed would be to write opinions of their judgments. Given this was not standard practice in military hearings, Taylor preferred the use of civilian judges whose jobs regularly required them to do so.[109] Taylor was not alone in his concerns;

[103] Copies of these interviews are in Musmanno's personal papers.
[104] Peter Maguire, *Law and War: An American Story* (New York, 2000), 149–150.
[105] Letter, Patterson to Truman, November 7, 1946, Subject File: Foreign Affairs File (Germany–Nuremberg War Crimes), PSF, HST.
[106] Taylor, "Nuernberg Trials: War Crimes and International Law," in *idem, Final Report*, 156–157.
[107] Cable from OMGUS to AGWAR, November 20, 1946, in NARA RG 466, Prisons Division, Security Segregated Records 1945–1947, box 10, WCT, Correspondence 1946–1947 folder.
[108] Memorandum, Taylor to the War Department, September 2, 1946, RHJ Papers, box 10 NG WCT, OF, US Chief of Counsel, Subsequent Nuremberg Trials, folder 2.
[109] The rules that governed the NMT dictated that opinions accompany judgments. Article 26 of the *London Agreement* in Taylor, *Final Report*, 29 and 35 stated that tribunals must "give the reasons on which [the judgment] is based."

others in the Military Government also seemed to have doubts about the ability of military men to carry out such historically important tasks. As Clay awkwardly expressed on one occasion,

because of the very difficult legal problems and complicated subject matter which will necessarily be involved, we . . . doubt if retired Army officers would have the requisite legal experience and background to establish historically the record of utmost legal consideration in these cases.[110]

When Musmanno's name was put forward as a candidate for judge, there were some concerns about his military standing. Taylor worried about the "appropriateness of [a] naval officer with [the] rank of commander sitting on [a] tribunal which may be called upon to try field marshals and high ranking generals."[111] Despite these apprehensions, Musmanno received high recommendations for the job. General Clark, the Mayor of Pittsburgh, and the Dean of the Georgetown Law School where the Department of the Army had been looking for judges, endorsed his appointment.[112] It was Colonel David Marcus, the individual in Washington in charge of recruiting personnel for Nuremberg, who personally told Taylor that Musmanno would be an excellent candidate for the job.[113] Such high recommendations coupled with Musmanno's civilian legal experience and recent position on the review board of the Navy, was enough for the Military Governor and Taylor to agree to Musmanno's appointment.[114] Initially Taylor wanted Musmanno as an alternate judge, but Musmanno's position was elevated when Geoffrey Keyes, Lieutenant General of the US Army, wrote to Alvin Rockwell, Associate Director of the Legal Division of OMGUS, suggesting that Musmanno's "experience and background," made him eminently qualified for a post of presiding judge.[115] While Musmanno was not immediately named presiding judge, he was appointed on January 10, 1947, by Executive Order 9819,

[110] Memorandum, Clay to War Department, September 4, 1946 in NARA RG 153 (JAG), WCB, NA Files 1944–1949, box 1, 85-1-76 folder.

[111] Memorandum, Taylor to War Department, November 21, 1946, in NARA RG 466, Prisons Division, Security Segregated Records 1945–1947, box 10 WCT, Correspondence 1946–1947 folder.

[112] Memorandum, War Department, No. 86237, November 23, 1946, in *ibid.*

[113] Letter, Marcus to Taylor, undated, Navy file 2340, MMP.

[114] Memorandum, Commander Talbot, May 12, 1946 and Memorandum, Louis Denfeld to Musmanno, October 1, 1946, in *ibid.* See also Letter, Clay to James Fulton, October 5, 1948, Lucius Clay file 1138, MMP, in which Clay writes, "It is because we determined as a matter of policy that these tribunals would not be composed of military personnel but would be composed of experienced civilian jurists so that the record would be crystal clear as to the nature and justice of the trials. Captain Musmanno was the only one of the judges who was in military service. For this reason, I accepted him in uniform only because of his long experience as a civilian jurist."

[115] Letter, Geoffrey Keyes, U.S. Army Commanding, to Alvin Rockwell, OMGUS, December 8, 1946, Navy file 2340, MMP.

to sit as one of three judges hearing the case against German Field Marshal Erhard Milch.[116] In accordance with the prestigious position at Nuremberg, the Navy promoted Musmanno to Captain.[117] A year later, after having sat in judgment on two tribunals and in the process of presiding on a third, Musmanno requested that the Navy raise his rank "one more notch" to Commodore to eliminate the "incongruity" between his rank of Captain and that of four of the defendants in the *Einsatzgruppen* trial who outranked him as Generals. The Navy declined his request.[118]

While Musmanno was hearing the Milch case, the Office of Chief of Counsel found itself in particular need of judges. Given these shortages and the reputation that Musmanno had already earned as a workhorse, it is not be surprising that he was asked to sit as a judge in the case against Oswald Pohl. Without reservation, he accepted the position. While Pohl's trial got under way, the indictment against the *Einsatzgruppen* leaders was filed and the trial was scheduled to begin in September 1947. The perennial problem of staffing again confounded the OCCWC. Never one to pass up a chance for fame, and without any family or children in the U.S. to demand his return, Musmanno accepted the position as presiding judge in the trial against Otto Ohlendorf and the leaders of the mobile killing units. On September 10, 1947, Lucius Clay, officially appointed Musmanno presiding judge for Military Tribunal II-a to hear the evidence in the *Einsatzgruppen* trial.[119]

Musmanno at Nuremberg

Musmanno's comportment at Nuremberg was remarkably consistent. Evidence for this can be found in the transcripts of both the Milch and Pohl cases, where he was a member of the tribunals, but not their presiding judge. The record shows from the beginning he had been an exceptionally active participant in all proceedings, questioning witnesses regularly and during the Milch trial he took exceptional delight when he had the opportunity to question the former Armaments Minister, Albert Speer, at length about the slave-labor program and his understanding of international law.[120] Musmanno's behavior made quite a strong impression on some in the Nuremberg community. One youthful participant recalled that

[116] Truman, Executive Order 9819, January 10, 1947, in NARA RG 260, OMGUS, Functional Offices and Divisions, OCCWC, box 99, SPD Memos folder. See also *ibid* in Navy file 2340, MMP.
[117] Letter, Patterson to James Webb, Director Bureau of the Budget, December 21, 1946, WHOF, 325-B, IMT, HST and "Musmanno Heads Nuernberg Court: Navy Vet Jurist to Try High Nazis," *The Pittsburgh Press*, November 17, 1946, Nuremberg Correspondence file 1445, MMP.
[118] Letter, Musmanno to James Fulton, September 30, 1947, Lucius Clay file 1138, MMP.
[119] Memorandum, Clay to Musmanno, September 10, 1947, Navy file 2340, MMP.
[120] *TWC*, vol. 2, 502–509.

he considered Musmanno a "hero," because of his unwillingness to take "nonsense" from the defendants.[121] A more mature observer thought his behavior was simply "comical."[122] However one remembered Musmanno, what is certain is that he flourished at the *Einsatzgruppen* trial. From the first day of proceedings, he established his total authority in the courtroom, a sign that he was both comfortable in his role as presiding judge as well as intensely interested in the course of the proceedings. On the first day of arraignment, Otto Rasch, who suffered from Parkinson's disease collapsed in a "paralytic attack." Soon thereafter, Eduard Strauch stood up to answer to his name and suffered an epileptic seizure, dropping "to the floor as if hit with a pistol shot."[123] Refusing to be distracted or allow any delays in the trial, the presiding judge simply ordered Strauch and Rasch removed from the courtroom and continued arraigning the defendants as if nothing had happened. Later that day, Musmanno reversed established procedure for the tribunals when he refused to grant defense counsel a two-to-three week recess after the completion of the prosecution's case. Musmanno viewed the request as frivolous, and an unnecessary waste of time, a likely "delaying tactic" he stated.[124] That first day he established his authority vis-à-vis the defense and the prosecution, making certain that both groups knew he was in charge.

His first ruling was to deny the prosecution's motion to screen a film blatantly prejudicial to the defense. The film in question was a short documentary that graphically depicted mounds of corpses being placed in mass graves for burial. The bodies were those of Soviet Jews presumably, killed by the units of the *Einsatzgruppen*. The film was grisly and controversial and had already been shown during the IMT trial, causing great emotional outbursts by the defendants there.[125] The prosecution wanted to use the film as proof of the murderous activities of the defendants. Some judges might have allowed the film into evidence as was the case with the IMT, but Musmanno ruled against the prosecution, noting that the tribunal believed the film did not implicate any of the defendants individually or directly and therefore it had no evidentiary basis and could not be screened in court. Besides, Musmanno added, "personally . . . I could not in any way use that

[121] George Krevit, quoted in *Witnesses to Nuremberg*, 75.
[122] Andy Logan quoted in *ibid.*, 201.
[123] Noah J. Jacobs, "The Biggest Murder Trial in History," undated, 16, in Material to Review while Reading of Biggest Murder Trial in History file 249, MMP; and "Arraignment," *TWC*, vol. 4, 26.
[124] "Arraignment," *ibid.*, 27–28.
[125] Letter, Ferencz to Defense Information Center, RE: Documentary Motion Picture USSR 81, September 22, 1947, in NARA RG 260, OMGUS, OCCWC, Secretary of Nuremberg Military Tribunals 1946–1949, box 139 607.3–609.3 folder. On defendant's reactions to the film at the IMT trial, see Gilbert, *Nuremberg Diary*, 45–49. Lawrence Douglas, The *Memory of Judgment*, 11–37, covers the history of the film in detail.

exhibit in the disposition of this case, because I closed my eyes [in horror] after the first five minutes."[126]

Musmanno's ruling on the film set the tone for the trial. Most frequently, he sided with the defense. Along with the now famous *Penguin ruling* he was willing to overlook prosecution counsel's many legitimate objections to the scope of defense evidence. One such instance occurred during the case of Walter Blume, whose principal defense was that he was following orders not simply for military reasons, but also because he adored Hitler and believed his *Führer* could do no wrong. Günther Lummert, Blume's attorney, asked the court to accept an affidavit by an Austrian Catholic Bishop which would provide a "window through which" the court could "get a view of the psychological conditions of Germany under Hitler" and thereby try to understand Blume's unnatural devotion to the *Führer* and his subsequent behavior in Russia. When the issue of Blume's attitude to Hitler was raised, the prosecution vehemently objected to the submission of the affidavit as irrelevant to the charge of murder. Musmanno disagreed and ruled that the affidavit was admissible. Although this infuriated the prosecution, it helped to create an atmosphere of fairness in court.[127]

Another example in which Musmanno ruled for the defense was during the cross – examination of Lothar Fendler, Deputy Chief of *Sonderkommando* 4b. In this case, Dr. Süss, one of the assistant attorneys working for Erwin Schulz, wanted to ask Fendler a question about an issue that had been raised during direct examination but which had not been brought-up during his cross-examination. Under American criminal procedure, this practice would have been impermissible and Horlik-Hochwald, one of the more seasoned prosecution lawyers at Nuremberg, rightly objected. Even though Musmanno took judicial notice that Horlik-Hochwald was "absolutely right," as supreme authority in the courtroom, he decided he would "pay no attention" to the objection and allow the question anyway. Exercising his discretion and bending the rules of procedure was typical behavior of Musmanno at trial.[128]

Musmanno's role in the courtroom was not limited to ruling on motions. He frequently voiced his own opinion when a defendant made, what seemed to him, an outrageous statement. One such instance, was during the cross-examination of Paul Blobel, a defendant with whom Musmanno had difficulty hiding his irritation. In an attempt to justify his role in reprisal murders in the Soviet Union, and to illustrate they were a natural part of war, Blobel defiantly pointed out that it was a "well known fact" that General Dwight Eisenhower had ordered that for each American killed, 200 Germans would

[126] Ruling by Musmanno, October 3, 1947, in *Trial*, roll 2, 257.
[127] Exchange between Lummert and Musmanno, November 4, 1947, in *Trial*, roll 3, 1844–1845.
[128] Musmanno ruling on prosecution motion, December 15, 1947, in *Trial*, roll 5, 4116–4117.

be executed in retaliation. Musmanno seemed to take the accusation personally and expressed his outrage by embarrassing Blobel in front of the court.

Musmanno: You say there is a well known order of General Eisenhower that two hundred were to be executed to one?

Blobel: All the German people know, your Honor, that an order was given by General Eisenhower that for every one American killed, two hundred Germans are to be shot.

Musmanno: ...do you say that every German and every defense counsel here knew of such an order?

Blobel: ...I am convinced that many of the defense counsel knew of this order.[129]

Musmanno demanded that Blobel, "point out one [person in the courtroom] who will make the statement."[130] Musmanno waited a moment, looked around the courtroom, but not one person raised their hand or acknowledged Blobel's claim. He again demanded to know if the defendant still believed that all Germans knew of such an order. Blobel meekly whispered, "no."[131] Dissatisfied with the defendant's retraction, Musmanno insisted Blobel "make an apology for having cast this aspersion upon the [good] name of General Eisenhower, who up until this very time has earned the respect of not only those in his services on the Allied side, but even the respect of the foe."[132] According to Musmanno's recollection of the exchange, Blobel "wilted" under his relentless pressure, stating for the record that, "under the circumstances, I have to beg your pardon."[133] Blobel's pathetic contrition seemed to satisfy the presiding judge.

Musmanno's natural inclination toward showmanship, his ease when speaking publicly, as well as his desire for justice, prompted him to become involved in the trial on a regular and daily basis.[134] He not only presided as judge, he frequently took on the role of prosecutor as well, especially when he felt that a defendant was being less than frank. In these instances, he would relentlessly question a defendant until he either recanted his testimony or admitted to his actions. As one observer keenly noted of Musmanno's cross-examination skills, he had the ability to get at the heart of an issue by asking "penetrating questions...[which] always hit the mark."[135] Musmanno's questions were often asked when the prosecution counsel was unable to elicit a desired response from a defendant. However controversial this behavior

[129] Exchange between Musmanno and Blobel, October 30, 1947, in *Trial*, roll 3, 1728–1729.
[130] Musmanno, *Eichmann Kommandos*, 154.
[131] *Ibid.*, 154–155.
[132] Exchange between Musmanno and Blobel, October 30, 1947, in *Trial*, roll 3, 1732.
[133] *Ibid.*; and, Musmanno, *Eichmann Kommandos*, 156.
[134] *Ibid.*, 82–83.
[135] Letter, James Fulton to Clay, September 13, 1948, Lucius Clay file 1138, MMP.

was for a judge, he never regretted or apologized for his actions, always maintaining his right to question witnesses. As he repeatedly noted, "no witness is compelled to take the stand if he does not wish to, but once he takes the stand, he is subject to cross examination and then, if he volunteers statements, certainly those statements are open to inquiry," even by the presiding judge.[136] He also made a practice of questioning witnesses because their "believability has to be tested" and if the prosecution was unable to perform this function, it was his duty to probe deeper in order to ascertain the facts of the case and the motivations of a defendant and thereby determine their innocence or guilt.[137] Not surprisingly under the circumstances, in almost every instance where Musmanno did this; it was in an attempt to unearth how the defendant ethically, morally, and personally viewed the order to kill. Musmanno did so, he told the defendants one day in court, because this was "the only way the issue [of conscience] can be decided by the tribunal" and thus it formed an important part of the tribunal's judgment and as shall be shown, the sentences as well.[138]

Musmanno's exchange with Werner Braune was typical of his courtroom behavior and is worth examining to illustrate the point.

Musmanno: What was your inner reaction to this Fuehrer-Order to kill defenseless people, women and children?

Braune: I rejected this order innerly.... What I am trying to express is that I innerly objected to having defenseless people killed and shot, and I cannot imagine that there is any human being who does not feel in this inner struggle.

Musmanno: Was it the feeling that this order was unethical?

Braune: This question has been asked here repeatedly and it is difficult for me to answer.[139]

Not satisfied with Braune's sidestepping of the issue, Musmanno demanded that the defendant explain what kind of inner objection he had to the *Führerbefehl*. As was typical of most of the defendants under cross examination, Braune avoided the question and instead stated quite generally that "there are human beings who could kill defenseless people and go about their affairs and sleep at night...who could kill defenseless people and not [have] any...regret."[140] Musmanno would not let the matter pass and insisted that Braune explain his own personal feelings and not those of some other, anonymous commander. Giving in somewhat to the pressure, Braune admitted that during "normal times" he believed that killing defenseless

[136] Musmanno, *Eichmann Kommandos*, 178.
[137] Ibid., 200.
[138] Cross examination of Braune by Musmanno, November 25, 1947, in *Trial*, roll 4, 3052.
[139] Ibid., 3040.
[140] Ibid., 3042.

people was indeed unethical, but that the war on the eastern front was "different," it was a war until the death. Besides, he continued, the order to kill the Jews came from Hitler who he believed was not only above international law, but who also had the right "by the [German] constitution to decide about war or peace and therefore... to decide about the lives of millions of people."[141] In other words, Braune believed that the order to murder Soviet Jews was not only legal but also justified under the circumstance of total war.

Neither satisfied nor convinced by Braune's explanation about his inner feelings Musmanno tested the defendant's contention that he inwardly objected to the order. He wanted to know why, if Braune objected to the order so much, he did not attempt to evade it. Braune told the court that he did not arrive in Russia until 1942, a full year after the killing spree had begun, and, therefore, there was no point in evading the order because the *Kommando* he supervised was already conditioned to carry it out. Besides, he said, his superior, a commander who outranked himself, had tried to have the order rescinded, but even he could do nothing to stop the carnage. Musmanno pushed further, wanting to know why, if he and Ohlendorf were so close, he did not confide in him and ask for his help. To which Braune replied,

Braune: Herr Ohlendorf would not have understood me at all if I had come to him and said, 'please send me home, and let somebody else do this very difficult task instead of me.' I believe Herr Ohlendorf would have considered me a shirker if I had done this and he would not have had the slightest understanding in spite of our good relation.

Musmanno: Well then, you were more afraid of being considered a coward than to take the chance in asking him to relieve you from this task which you found so onerous and distasteful?

Braune: No, your Honor. I was convinced that there would be no point in it, and that Herr Ohlendorf would not have been able to do anything.

Musmanno: Well, then you decided what his answer would be without even putting the question to him?[142]

Obviously Braune had forgotten that Ohlendorf had earlier testified that he personally sent men who expressed or displayed their inability to deal with their tasks, back to Germany. The presiding judge had not forgotten. Besides, the prosecution had entered evidence that showed that while Braune was working in Norway, he had repeatedly gone against Reich orders without suffering any consequences. Musmanno wondered whether Braune was "more humanitarian in Norway than in Russia." No, he concluded, the

---

[141] *Ibid.*, 3046.
[142] *Ibid.*, 3062.

difference was that with the Jews, "there was no one to take up their cause and, therefore, there was nothing [for Braune] to fear in killing them."[143] Musmanno concluded that Braune was lying and, in an attempt to irrefutably demonstrate this, he pursued another avenue of questioning.

He asked whether or not Braune believed Hitler's propaganda, that the Jews were the bearers of bolshevism. "Yes," Braune said that to the best of his knowledge the leadership and administration of the Soviet state was largely, almost 90 percent he thought, Jewish in composition. "Well," Musmanno reasoned, "if the Jews carried the flag of Bolshevism and played the active part which you have indicated, then they were definitely enemies and dangerous enemies . . . weren't they?"[144] He was trapped by the judge's logic. Either Braune had to argue that killing Jews was militarily justifiable in the course of total war or that he knew the order was morally wrong and that is why he objected to it. Arguing both positions weakened his case. Realizing the direction of Musmanno's questions, Braune attempted to avoid the trap.[145] Musmanno found his response untenable. If Braune really had inner misgivings about the order to murder the Jews as he claimed, surely he would have made some attempt to ease his guilty conscience. To find out, Musmanno asked,

Musmanno: Did you ever excuse one Jew just because there may have been some doubt as to whether he was a participant in communism or not?

Braune: No, your Honor.[146]

Braune had failed the test and Musmanno had his answer. Like so many others, this defendant carried out his orders without remorse. He killed people he knew to be innocent because Hitler ordered him to do so and because they were Jews, the defendant had lied to the tribunal, never feeling any inner misgivings.

Musmanno also used tenacity and aggression to test the credibility of defense arguments. In the case of Walter Blume, he did so during the defendant's direct testimony. Dr. Günther Lummert, one of the less experienced attorneys at trial, was attempting to show that a suicide attempt by the defendant in early 1947 was the result of American ill treatment during internment, prior to trial. Blume had tried to kill himself while in prison, Lummert argued, because he was afraid of being physically harmed by his captors. Clearly annoyed by the suggestion that Americans used torture, Musmanno tested the assertion.

---

[143] Musmanno, *Eichmann Kommandos*, 138–139.
[144] Cross-examination of Braune by Musmanno, November 25, 1947, in *Trial*, roll 4, 3064–3065.
[145] *Ibid.*, 3066.
[146] *Ibid.*, 3074.

Musmanno: Well, it was just a blow or two given in anger. Isn't that about what it was? ... I am not trying to justify it, witness ... I am only trying to get at the facts ... it was just a blow struck in hatred?

Blume: Yes.

Musmanno: You really didn't feel any ill effects of it after the actual striking?

Blume: Not of a special kind. [Just] the general pain.

Musmanno: There was no attempt on the part of this interrogator ... to permanently disable you?

Blume: No.

Musmanno: You didn't have to have any medical treatment, did you?

Blume: No.

Musmanno: So you exaggerated in your own mind what had happened to you, and made that the basis for a suicide attempt, didn't you?

Blume: I only wanted to express, ... that the psychological pain of the situation moved me very much.

Musmanno: Well, were you so touched by a slap or two – that you having been a soldier all these years–that because of this temporary humiliation ... you wanted to commit suicide?

Blume: Your honor, it was not only one or two blows; it took quite some time.

Musmanno: Well, whatever they were, they weren't bad enough to cause you to be hospitalized ... Now, do you want to tell us that you, a big, strapping fellow who had been through a war ... would want to commit suicide just because someone struck you with his fists?

Blume: Your Honor, I had assumed that this would continue, this ill-treatment, after the interrogation, I was, of course, over-whelmed by the fact that when questions were asked as to names of comrades, and I thought that I would be thus put into a forced situation, and I was afraid of all this.

Musmanno: You were afraid that you would have to divulge some information which might implicate your comrades. Is that what I understand?

Blume: Yes. I thought I would not be hard enough, perhaps, to bear it in the long run.[147]

Musmanno forced Blume to admit that his suicide attempt was not the result of fear of intimidation and brutality by his captors, but rather fear of retribution from his colleagues in the event that he betrayed them during the beating!

[147] Exchange between Musmanno and Blume, November 4, 1947, in *Trial*, roll 3, 1827–1830.

Along with cross examination, one of Musmanno's favorite techniques to force an answer to a question (often a very incriminating one) was to put the defendant in a provocative hypothetical situation, an unusual practice in an American criminal proceeding that could be cited as grounds for an appeal, but a technique which Musmanno nonetheless employed regularly at Nuremberg.[148] Only one defense attorney, Dr. Hans Gawlik an experienced lawyer who had represented Waldemar Hoven in the Medical trial, ever challenged this practice and it ended with Musmanno dressing him down in court. It is interesting to note, that although the defendants frequently ignored or sidestepped sensitive questions posed by the prosecution, when Musmanno exerted his authority, they almost always answered his questions, even damaging hypothetical ones suggesting that even in a courtroom authority impels obedience. This was no less true for Ohlendorf who for three days had been avoiding Heath's questions about his job. Each time Heath asked Ohlendorf about his personal feelings, he obfuscated. Musmanno, who thought it imperative to know how the leaders of the mobile killing units viewed their work, stepped in. To test Ohlendorf's principal defense that he legally had no choice but to carry out the order, Musmanno insisted Ohlendorf answer a hypothetical question: under the circumstance of total war, if he were ordered to murder his sister, would he do so? Ohlendorf wasted no time with his response. Able to think on his feet quickly and probably fearful of jeopardizing his defense of compulsion to superior orders, he told the court that if he were ordered to, he would indeed murder his own sister.[149] Most defendants were not as adept as Ohlendorf at dealing with Musmanno's questions highlighting Ohlendorf's unique ability to use legal arguments to mask his moral responsibility. Willy Seibert found himself in a similar situation as Ohlendorf, but he was unable to lie as easily.

Testifying on his own behalf, Seibert made the same claim as many defendants, that Hitler's order to murder could not be considered illegal because all orders from the head of state were legal. Viewing himself as both "judge and jury," Musmanno set out to determine Seibert's worldview and thus he posed an impossible hypothetical situation.[150]

Musmanno: Let us suppose you received an order directly from Hitler... that you were to execute the chief of the *Einsatzgruppen*. Would you execute that order?

Seibert: No, I would not have carried it out.

Musmanno: Well, then, suppose you received an order to shoot a 12-year-old Jew. Would you shoot him?

Seibert: I cannot say.

[148] Musmanno, *Eichmann Kommandos*, 202.
[149] Testimony and cross-examination of Ohlendorf, in *Trial*, roll 2, 740–752.
[150] Musmanno, *Eichmann Kommandos*, 128.

Musmanno: You had no trouble in answering that you would have refused
to shoot Ohlendorf, but you have some hesitation in saying
whether you would have refused to shoot a Jewish boy of
twelve. And the answer, would you say, is that Ohlendorf
means something to you, but a 12 year old Jewish lad means
nothing – except the abstract inhumanity of wiping out an
innocent child?

Seibert: No, this is not what I want to say.

Musmanno: Well, let us suppose a situation where your superior officer
tells you that the situation is such that the only way we can
get out of it is for you to shoot your parents. Now, that's an
order.... are you going to live up to [it] or not?[151]

Not reflected in the official trial transcript, but according to Musmanno's
recollection of events, Seibert was agitated by this question. His dilemma
was that he would either have to admit he was inhuman enough to kill his
parents or he would have to abandon the defense that he had no choice but to
follow orders. Seibert apparently looked to Gawlik for direction. Seeing the
damage such a question could do to the defense, the attorney for Naumann
stood-up and objected that under German and American criminal procedure,
such hypothetical questions are inadmissible.[152] Eschewing conventional
process, Musmanno demanded that the defense attorney prove his objection.
Gawlik said he would get back to him when he located the evidence and
he quickly left the courtroom returning a few minutes later with a copy
of *Wharton's Law* – an American legal text that states that hypothetical
and speculative questions can be asked, but only if they are based on the
facts of the case. Clearly exercising his courtroom authority, Musmanno
disagreed with Gawlik's interpretation of facts; in his view, knowing the
extent to which a defendant would go to follow an order went to the heart
of the case. If the prosecution could not do their job, he would because lives
were at stake and he needed to make certain that he had all of the facts
in the case before he rendered judgment. Musmanno overruled Gawlik,
although he gave the defense attorney the right to object, small comfort for
a defense whose entire case rested on the issue of compulsion to superior
orders.[153] Seibert's reprieve was thus short-lived, and he was instructed to
answer the question, "would he kill his parents if ordered to do so?" For
whatever reason Seibert refused to answer. Musmanno decided to give him
until morning to think about it. Musmanno recalled that the courtroom was
"abuzz" with speculation: "would [Seibert] be better off by hypothetically
slaying his mother and father or by outrightly disgracing his lawyer," who

---

[151] Exchange between Musmanno and Seibert, November 19, 1947, in *Trial*, roll 4, 2670–
2671.
[152] Musmanno, *Eichmann Kommandos*, 129.
[153] Exchange between Musmanno and Gawlik, November 18, 1947, in *Trial*, roll 4, 2611.

had introduced the subject of superior orders in the first place.[154] Had this been television, it would have made for a dramatic pause.

The next morning the courtroom was full to overflowing with spectators interested in Seibert's moral dilemma.[155] Musmanno gave the defendant a moment to compose himself and repeated the question. Would he kill his parents if ordered to do so? The courtroom was silent. Seibert, looking worn-out, simply responded, "no, Mr. President, I would not do so."[156]

Musmanno: Then there are some orders which are issued by the chief (sic) of state which may be disobeyed?

Seibert: It is inhuman – to ask a son to shoot his parents... I would not have obeyed such an order.

Musmanno: Now, suppose the order came down for you to shoot the parents of someone else, let us say, a Jew and his wife... it is established beyond any doubt that [they] have not committed any crime... the only thing that is established is that they are Jews and you have this order... would you shoot the parents?

Seibert: Your honor, I would not shoot these parents.

Musmanno: Yes, so therefore, this order issued by the Fuehrer to kill all Jews indiscriminately did not have to be obeyed by the German soldiers in your estimation.[157]

In this way, Musmanno tested each and every defendant. Some, like Seibert buckled under pressure, others refused to submit to his authority. Years later Musmanno explained the absurdity of arguing superior orders, noting that, "if a soldier is required... to put into effect the most patently unjust order, his superior officer could order him to shoot himself and the soldier would have to turn his gun on himself, or otherwise be shot for disobeying orders!"[158] In Seibert, Musmanno had demonstrated the weakness of the superior orders defense: if agency existed as Seibert testified it did, an individual could not hide behind the legality of superior orders as had Ohlendorf, but rather he had to take legal responsibility for the moral choices he made.

Even those who said they did not follow orders such as Walter Blume maintained, damaged the defense of compulsion because in doing so they reinforced the fact that they could make moral choices without fear of reprisal.

Musmanno: ... according to your statement, you did not execute all Jews?

Blume: No.

Musmanno: So therefore, you did not follow the Fuehrer-Decree?

Blume: No, not to that extent.

---

[154] Musmanno, *Eichmann Kommandos*, 132.
[155] *Ibid.*, 132–133.
[156] Testimony, Seibert, November 19, 1947, in *Trial*, roll 4, 2676.
[157] Exchange between Musmanno and Seibert, November 20, 1947, in *ibid.*, roll 4, 2676.
[158] Musmanno, *Eichmann Kommandos*, 134.

Musmanno: You were very fond of Hitler at the time weren't you?

Blume: Yes, your Honor.

Musmanno: You adored Hitler?

Blume: Yes, your Honor.

Musmanno: Then, why did you not follow his order which was very expressly given to you?

...

Blume: ... in this particular moment I deviated from the path of my duty.

Musmanno: You lied to your adored leader?.... By your actions, not by words... but by your actions you told a lie, an untruth, to your adored leader, Adolf Hitler... answer that!

Blume: One can formulate it so, your Honor.

...

Musmanno: How do you feel about Adolf Hitler today? Do you still think he was the perfect man you believed him to be?

Blume: The results speak against it, your Honor.[159]

One by one, Musmanno challenged defense arguments and in the process helped to discredit the defense of compulsion to superior orders.[160]

Even though Musmanno frequently and enthusiastically questioned defendants for more information, he also offered unsolicited advice to the more inexperienced defense attorneys, who were at a serious disadvantage.[161] From the first day of trial, he made suggestions about how to defend their clients, even recommending who and when they should call witnesses.[162] He stepped in when he believed that the defense should have objected to the way their defendants were being cross-examined and in several instances he used humor to train the defense in the art of procedure. In one instance Seibert was being cross-examined by Peter Walton who asked the defendant to look at a document. Just as Seibert located the document, Gawlik jumped from his seat objecting. Musmanno thought this odd timing, noting that Walton "hasn't put a question yet. What are you objecting to?" To which Gawlik responded, "I object to any question that might refer to this document." In his usual humorous way, Musmanno retorted, "you say you object to any question he might put regarding this document. Suppose the question shows that your client is innocent? Would you object to that?" Gawlik acknowledged that perhaps he should "wait" before he objects.[163]

---

[159] Exchange between Musmanno and Blume, November 4, 1947, in *Trial*, roll 3, 1860–1863.

[160] Musmanno, *Eichmann Kommandos*, 166–167.

[161] Landsman, *Crimes of the Holocaust*, 52–53.

[162] Musmanno to defense attorneys, October 6, 1947, in *Trial*, roll 2, 290–291.

[163] Exchange between Gawlik and Musmanno, November 20, 1947, in *Trial*, roll 4, 2684–2685.

During the direct testimony of Erwin Schulz, Musmanno had to prevent one assistant defense attorney, Dr. Oskar Ficht who was an assistant defense attorney and had also assisted in the Pohl trial, from making the case even worse for Walter Haensch. Ficht had asked Schulz whether or not Haensch was an exemplary employee and carried out his job well. Musmanno felt compelled to point out to Ficht that when he asked Schulz how well Haensch performed in his work he was "not talking about a street car conductor (sic)," but rather a person "who is charged with the execution of an order which involved the killing of human beings. Now, if you ask '[if [Haensch] was conscientious in the discharge of his duty, if he did it well,' and [Schulz] replies, 'yes, he did it well, and sometimes even did better than was expected for him,' and if we are thinking of that order we must assume that he killed more people than the order required of him to kill, so I merely want to call to your attention that when you use generic language of that kind that is capable of an interpretation not so favourable to your client."[164] Ficht seemed appreciative of Musmanno's comments.

Musmanno's behavior in the courtroom did not always reflect the grave nature of the trial and the seriousness of the charges. As we saw with his writing earlier in this chapter, he frequently used sarcasm and made jokes to lighten the moment in the courtroom. This was the case when Heinz Jost, one of the most reviled of all the *Einsatzgruppen* leaders, took the stand. When Jost spoke Musmanno observed that,

since we have been sitting here, our greatest difficulty with witnesses has been that they speak too rapidly. Now this present defendant is a refreshing contradiction to that, in that he speaks slowly, and I am just hoping that we don't all go to sleep, because of the very leisurely manner he is testifying.[165]

He found room for humor during the testimony of Franz Six too, but it appeared to be lost on the German-speaking defendant. The former SS-Brigadier General had testified that he had committed no crimes in the Soviet Union; rather, he stated he was a university professor, sent to Russia to collect archives, protect churches and to instill culture in the local population. Never, he claimed, had he received or carried out the *Führerbefehl* to murder. To test Six's credibility, Musmanno asked him what he would have done had he received the order to murder Jews. Like Seibert before him, he initially refused to answer the question, and then thought better of it and told the court he would need additional time to consider his answer. He was given three days to think it over. When Six took the stand again, he said he could only answer a hypothetical question with a hypothetical answer. He could answer the question as a professor, a philosopher, and as a soldier, but he could not answer as a defendant. To which Musmanno dryly

[164] Musmanno to Ficht, October 20, 1947, in *ibid.*, roll 2, 1043.
[165] Musmanno to the Court, *ibid.*, 1140.

commented, "your name may be Six, but you are here only as one man. You will reply directly." Six, oblivious of the play on his name in English, stated that hypothetically, if given the order he would refuse to obey it, an answer that immediately threw the other defendants and their counsel into an uproar.[166]

Despite these humorous punctuations, Musmanno was acutely aware of the seriousness of the crimes. He felt a tremendous burden in his job as presiding judge and wanted to be absolutely certain that he had all the facts of the case. This was the main reason he spent so much time questioning each defendant. Had he not done so, he may not have been able to formulate a judgment he could live with. As each defendant took the stand, he thus made a point of questioning his testimony and drawing his own conclusions. After nearly six months of trial testimony, he felt satisfied with the facts established. The trial was coming to an end. On February 13, 1948, the prosecution presented its closing arguments and the defendants made their final pleas to the court. This practice was not part of Anglo-American law, yet defendants were granted this right because it conformed to continental and German trial procedure and had been incorporated into CCL10. All of the defendants except Biberstein, Braune, Sandberger, and Strauch availed themselves of the opportunity to address the court, which, on the whole, was notable only for its banality. The most eloquent closing statement was Ohlendorf's. Musmanno was so arrogant though, that he recorded for posterity how appreciative he was of Ohlendorf's public recognition that his trial had been fair and he remembered thinking, he hoped that the "erudite and profound" lead defendant would speak longer, so captivating was his speech.[167] Once all of the defendants had made their final pleas, the advocacy portion of the trial was over and the court adjourned so that the judges could confer.

The Judgment

On May 8, 1948, *New Yorker* columnist Andy Logan wrote, "there have been times lately when it seemed as if the 'So What?' sign were hanging in the Nuremberg courtroom."[168] Logan was referring to the discouraging fact that the tribunals in the Krupp and RuSHA cases had just acquitted a number of clearly guilty individuals. This did not escape the attention of the Chief Prosecutor Telford Taylor who, in his *Final Report to the Secretary of the Army*, noted that with the conclusion of each NMT, "sentences

---

[166] Excerpt from trial, undated, Nuremberg Correspondence file 1445, MMP and exchange between Musmanno and Six, October 24 and 27, 1947, in *Trial*, roll 3, 1369–1415.

[167] Musmanno, *Eichmann Kommandos*, 252–253. Henry Lea, an interpreter at the trial remembered Ohlendorf's closing statement differently: he described it as "absolutely hair-raising." See Letter, Henry Lea to Ferencz, November 24, 1989, RG 12.000, Drawer 24 WCT, box 2, folder Nuremberg Supplementary Materials, BBF, USHMM.

[168] Andy Logan, Letter from Germany, *New Yorker*, May 8, 1948, 65-4-5, Andy Logan Papers.

FIGURE 10. The Judges (Speight, Musmanno, and Dixon) of Military Tribunal II-A, USHMM photo archive (#16815)

became progressively lighter."[169] This was not the case with the *Einsatzgruppen* trial, where two-thirds of the defendants received death sentences and this even though the presiding judge strongly and actively opposed the death penalty. In the same report, Taylor noted that "the conclusions and reasoning of the judgments [in the Subsequent trials] are...far more important than the sentences" because the written judgments were meant to contribute to the future development of international law.[170] Nuremberg, Taylor clearly hoped, would set a legal precedent. As Stephan Landsman has noted, however, this was probably an unrealistic aim under the unique circumstances of Nuremberg, where the "conditions were so idiosyncratic" that "to replicate them" would be virtually impossible.[171] Yet, Nuremberg has stood the test of time. It is a significant departure from past practice and is held up as the new standard bearer of justice in the face of continuing atrocity.[172] As the only trial to deal exclusively with the crimes associated with the genocidal murder of the Jews, what is the legacy of the *Einsatzgruppen* trial judgment and how and what does it contribute to international law?

[169] Taylor, *Final Report*, 92.
[170] *Ibid.*, 90–91 and 93.
[171] Landsman, *Crimes of the Holocaust*, 49.
[172] *Ibid.*, 49–50.

Although it is a lengthy legal document containing the most pertinent legal arguments relating to the trial, unfortunately, the judgment was not the "brilliant contribution to international law" one observer claimed it was or Taylor hoped it would be.[173] Written exclusively by Musmanno, the judgment attempts to make sense of the criminal history of the *Einsatzgruppen* and the significance of their acts, no small feat in 1948 when very few people really understood the mammoth SS organization let alone the specialized role of the *Einsatzgruppen* in the evolution and execution of the Final Solution.[174] Although the judgment falls short of such grandiose aims, it does offer a contribution to our historical understanding of what transpired on the eastern front between 1941 and 1943, providing numerous examples of *Einsatzgruppen* activities and thus leaving an important record of their crimes. The judgment also offers some insight into the character, personality, and motives of the defendants, by outlining their responses to the origins, tasks, goals and methods of the *Einsatzgruppen*. Finally, it examines the defense of "superior orders," and attempts to clarify the nature of the charge of "crimes against humanity," although in neither case does it do a very satisfactory job. The judgment may be more memorable for what it does not do, than for what it does. What the 228-page judgment does not attempt is to situate the organization of the *Einsatzgruppen* as part of a larger police and paramilitary structure, nor does it contextualize their relationship to the more pervasive Nazi project of European-wide murder. Even though the tribunal recognized that this case was unprecedented and historically important, they failed to articulate the novel crimes of the defendants and move beyond examples of individual murder to examine the collective nature of the crime and the individual's relationship to the state in carrying out the crime of genocide.[175] The focus on individual acts may be the result of the larger Nuremberg aim of holding individuals responsible for the crimes of the regime, and not the entire nation.[176] In any case, judges, like all Nuremberg employees, were under tremendous pressures to expedite the process in 1948.[177] In the end, as the final statement on the genocidal crimes of the *Einsatzgruppen*, the judgment is simply disappointing.

Unlike the IMT, we have no record of the judges' deliberations for the *Einsatzgruppen* trial. However, we do know that Dixon, Speight, and

---

[173] Letter, James Fulton to Clay, September 13, 1948, in Lucius Clay file 1138, MMP, and Letter, Clay to Musmanno, October 9, 1948, Lucius Clay file 1138 in which Clay writes, "I am grateful to you for your contribution which has lived up in every way to the American tradition of justice."

[174] I could find few references to Speight or Dixon's contribution to the Judgment even though they were mandated to participate in it. Military Ordinance No. 7, Article 2(h) in *Trials of War Criminals under Law No. 10*, vol. 15, xxiii–xxiv.

[175] Judgment, April 8, 1948, in *Trial*, 38 rolls, roll 7, 139.

[176] *Ibid.*, 60 and 61.

[177] *Ibid.*, 4.

Musmanno worked together to review the 6,895 pages of trial transcript and the 984 documents to reach consensus on the guilt or innocence of each defendant and that it took them the better part of a month to do so suggesting it was not as open and shut a case as the prosecution thought.[178] In the two other cases that Musmanno had served as judge, he wrote "Concurring Opinions."[179] Both were substantial pieces of legal writing, the opinion in the Pohl case could even be considered insightful. There was no parallel in the *Einsatzgruppen* case where outside the tribunal's main judgment, there are no additional opinions filed by either Dixon or Speight.[180] As presiding judge, and probably the best versed in the facts and evidence of the case, Musmanno undertook the task of writing the opinion and judgment. While the document was not solely his, it has his stamp all over it.[181] Acutely aware of the potential of the judgment as precedent for international law, Musmanno took the job seriously. He also believed it could serve didactic ends as a way of illustrating for the German people the true "character of those who were their leaders."[182] To this end, the judgment offers a character study of the defendants who, it is noted in the beginning of the document, were neither duped nor brainwashed into their murderous actions, but rather were free agents who acted out of their love for Germany and their commitment to Hitler and National Socialism, at best a kind of Goldhagian analysis of German cultural values and behavior.[183]

The tribunal felt that Germans needed to know how educated men, who were otherwise described as honest, friendly, and good-natured, could "willingly" and "enthusiastically" commit such heinous crimes against defenseless civilians.[184] Relying on the contents of the *Einsatzgruppen* reports as well as the testimony of the defendants, the judgment notes that the defendants acted for a variety of reasons.[185] One was the irresistible nature of Hitler, who was so charismatic that some defendants enthusiastically carried-out his wishes. It will be recalled that many defendants expressed their reverence and adoration for Hitler at trial. Sensing that something more was at work in the minds of the defendants, the judgment concluded that extreme nationalism and the spectre of the "unbridled domination" of

[178] Musmanno, *Eichmann Kommandos*, 254.
[179] "Concurring Opinion by Judge Michael A. Musmanno in Milch Case," *TWC*, vol. 2, 797–859 and "Concurring Opinion by Judge Michael A. Musmanno in Pohl case," *TWC*, vol. 5, 1064–1163.
[180] In the Milch case Fitzroy Phillips also filed a "Concurring Opinion," albeit much shorter than Musmanno's. *TWC*, vol. 2, 860–878.
[181] Letter, Musmanno to Ferencz, April 13, 1948, in RG 12.000, Drawer 11 Biographical Material, box 1, folder C Biographical Material Job Related Personnel File 1946–1955, BBF, USHMM.
[182] Musmanno, *Eichmann Kommandos*, 254–255.
[183] Judgment, 5.
[184] *Ibid.*, 125.
[185] *Ibid.*, 47.

Germany also seduced these men to commit extraordinary acts of evil.[186] Part of that nationalist ideology was the unique and specific hatred of Jews based on their race. One of the major defenses put forward was that of putative self-defense under the condition of presumed necessity: killing Jews was a pre-emptive strike to protect Germany from bolshevization.[187] But the defense never proved how Jews "were bearers of Bolshevism," nor how "this translated into an attack on Germany."[188] And, given that no Jewish lives were spared, even if the victim did not embrace bolshevism, the court could only reasonably conclude that Jews were murdered not to protect Germany from the threat of bolshevism, but "simply because" they were Jews.[189] Nazi ideology had made murder "a matter of blood and nothing could save the person with Hebrew arteries," Musmanno dramatically wrote.[190] When it came right down to it, although some defendants may have complained about their gruesome tasks, all agreed with their orders and carried them out in what may only be described as a shockingly routine manner.[191] In its explanation of defendant motivation, the judgment makes three important empirical observations: first, human beings can become inured to any job, even mass-murder. Second, nationalism is a powerful force that encouraged the most well educated elites of German society, such as were the leaders of the *Einsatzgruppen*, to participate in mass murder. Finally, it observed that the Jews were the special targets of murder.

Even though the judgment takes notice of all the victims of the *Einsatzgruppen*, particularly striking is its emphasis on the special nature of the crimes against the Jews. The indictment had charged the defendants with crimes against humanity for their murder, yet during opening statements, the prosecution emphasized that the crimes committed by the *Einsatzgruppen* were "more than murder," it was genocide by which they meant the denial of "whole peoples" the right to exist.[192] To be sure, it appears that the tribunal understood that the crimes of the *Einsatzgruppen* leadership on the eastern front were aimed at the Jewish population specifically, as on so many occasions they noted this. They also seemed to have grasped the grand scale of the atrocity, yet, they never formulated a clear definition of the crime in the judgment, all the more surprising given that all three judges had heard evidence in SS trials that dealt with other elements of the crime against the Jews. Even without an exact explanation, the judgment captures, in a fragmented way, the essence of Nazi criminality against the Jews in the Soviet Union. In page after page of the judgment, the tribunal emphasized

---

[186] *Ibid.*
[187] *Ibid.*, 67–68.
[188] *Ibid.*
[189] *Ibid.*, 70.
[190] *Ibid.*, 87.
[191] *Ibid.*, 20, 21, 26, and 47.
[192] Ferencz, opening statement to the court, September 29, 1947, 33.

to the reader that the task of the *Einsatzgruppen* was the complete destruction of Soviet Jewry and no matter how much the perpetrators attempted to mask their crimes through the use of deceitful language, it was clear that this was "only macabre window dressing" used to disguise the murder of "all Jews."[193] That Jews were the special targets of Nazi policy was a basic observation that framed the judgment. In spite of this though, the tribunal found the defendants guilty of the more traditional crime of murder; never did the judgment mention the crime as the murder of one group by another group. Thus, the tribunal missed an opportunity to significantly contribute to innovations in international law. The crime of genocide would remain for future tribunals to grapple with.

Along with its explanation of perpetrator motivation, the judgment also provided a narrative of the genesis and functioning of the *Einsatzgruppen*. Ohlendorf had clearly made an impression here, as it was his version of events that made their way into the official record. The *Einsatzgruppen* leaders had been given their orders in Pretzsch by Bruno Streckenbach and Heydrich later in Berlin" had reiterated them.[194] Most importantly, the crimes for which these men were charged were the direct result of the "notorious Fuehrer-Order" which in May 1941 directed the defendants to murder all Jews, Gypsies, the insane, Asiatic inferiors, communist functionaries and asocials, including women and children.[195] The defendants were not furnished with a "precise definition" of any of these groups and because of this "were authorized to take executive measures on their own responsibility" to determine who was and was not a member of one of these target groups.[196] In the course of explaining how the defendants came to their tasks, the judgment unwittingly identified two important elements of genocide: the intention to kill specific groups (the so-called *Führerbefehl*) and the identification of those victim groups by the perpetrators.

The judgment did not offer anything new in terms of its interpretation of "war crimes" or "membership in organizations declared criminal by the IMT," although it was assumed if it could be shown that a defendant had attempted to leave a criminal organization before September 1, 1939, he could not be found guilty.[197] Where the tribunal made a contribution to law was in its clarification of what constituted crimes against humanity.[198] The *London Charter* had severely limited crimes against humanity to acts "committed in the execution of or in connection with crimes against peace

---

[193] Judgment, 13 and 51.

[194] *Ibid.*, 6.

[195] *Ibid.*, 6–8. Musmanno reiterates this as fact throughout the judgment. For example, see *ibid.*, 27–28.

[196] *Ibid.*, 6–7 and 8.

[197] *Ibid.*, 109–111.

[198] On the issue of Nuremberg's contribution to developing law for *crimes against humanity*, see Lippman, "The Other Nuremberg," 90–99.

and war crimes."[199] But under CCL10, this limitation was removed, allowing the tribunal jurisdiction to try all crimes, whether they were committed during the war or independently thereof.[200] The tribunal defined humanity universally, as all peoples, of all countries, regardless of nationality or geographic boundaries. As the judgment phrased it, "humanity is man itself."[201] Furthermore, the tribunal ruled that crimes against humanity were "acts committed in the course of wholesale and systematic violation of life and liberty," and as such came under international jurisdiction, especially when the state involved in these crimes was "unable or ha[d] refused to halt the crimes and punish the criminals," as was the case in the Soviet Union during the war.[202] Foreshadowing future international legal efforts, the tribunal finally ruled that "crimes against humanity" have no national jurisdiction and as such everyone must work together to build "a tower of justice, a tower to which the persecuted and the downtrodden of all lands, all races and all creeds may repair." Nuremberg was the foundation of that "tower" in the "Law of Humanity."[203] The judgment concluded that while Nuremberg represented the first time "international tribunals have adjudicated crimes against humanity as an international offense," this was by no means to suggest that the crime was new. Man had the right, indeed, the obligation to "maintain a tribunal [which] holds inviolable the Law of Humanity, and, by doing so, preserve the human race itself."[204]

Individual Judgments

The individual judgments were, on the whole, straightforward. No attempt was made to elucidate individual crimes; there were far too many to record, nor was all of the evidence against the defendants presented. Rather, the judgments addressed the specific charges of criminality presented in the indictment and, in most cases, offered the reader a short summary of the defendant's crimes, his defense of the charges, followed by an explanation of the court's findings on guilt.[205] As can be seen in Table 8, all of the defendants with the exception of two were found guilty on all counts suggesting the evidence was more than convincing. It is no coincidence that the two who were found not guilty, Felix Rühl and Matthias Graf were the lowest-ranking members of the *Einsatzgruppen* indicted. Despite their noticeably lower rank, the charges against Rühl and Graf were the same as those against the other defendants, yet the evidence against them was not nearly as direct or convincing, in fact it was mostly circumstantial. To

[199] Judgment, 114–115.
[200] *Ibid.*
[201] *Ibid.*, 113–114.
[202] *Ibid.*, 114.
[203] *Ibid.*, 116.
[204] *Ibid.*, 115–116.
[205] *Ibid.*, 133.

TABLE 8. *Judgment and Sentences**

Defendants	Crimes/Humanity	War Crimes	Membership	Sentence
Biberstein, Ernst	X	X	X	Death by Hanging
Blobel, Paul	X	X	X	Death by Hanging
Blume, Walter	X	X	X	Death by Hanging
Braune, Werner	X	X	X	Death by Hanging
Fendler, Lothar	X	X	X	10 Years
Graf, Matthias	Not Guilty	Not Guilty	X	Time Served
Haensch, Walter	X	X	X	Death by Hanging
Jost, Heinz	X	X	X	Life Imprisonment
Klingelhöfer, Waldemar	X	X	X	Death by Hanging
Naumann, Erich	X	X	X	Death by Hanging
Nosske, Gustav	X	X	X	Life Imprisonment
Ohlendorf, Otto	X	X	X	Death by Hanging
Ott, Adolf	X	X	X	Death by Hanging
Radetzky, Waldemar von	X	X	X	20 Years
Rühl, Felix	Not Guilty	Not Guilty	X	10 Years
Sandberger, Martin	X	X	X	Death by hanging
Schubert, Heinz	X	X	X	Death by hanging
Schulz, Erwin	X	X	X	20 Years
Seibert, Willy	X	X	X	Death by Hanging
Six, Franz	X	X	X	20 Years
Steimle, Eugen	X	X	X	Death by Hanging
Strauch, Eduard	X	X	X	Death by Hanging

* *Ibid.*, 130–228.
NB: X = Guilty

be found guilty of the graver charges the tribunal wanted evidence that both men had acted as commanders of their units in the absence of their leaders.[206] The prosecution's case here was flimsy. Field reports that neither identified them specifically as holding leadership roles, nor identified them as being present at the crimes coupled with questionable affidavits simply was inadequate to prove guilt beyond a reasonable doubt.[207]

In Rühl and Graf's favor was also their rank. As Musmanno awkwardly phrased it in the judgment, their low rank did not "automatically" place them in positions "where ... lack of objection" to the executions "in any way contributed to the success of any executive operation."[208] Graf's situation was even more favorable than Rühl's as he never commanded a unit nor was he a commissioned officer, whereas Rühl was an officer and may have commanded a unit, although the evidence simply was not there to prove it.[209] While the judgment never disputed the fact that Graf and Rühl's units killed civilians, in a case dealing with the upper echelons of the SS, the

[206] *Ibid.*, 217–218.
[207] *Ibid.*, 219.
[208] *Ibid.*, 220.
[209] *Ibid.*, 225.

tribunal found it unlikely that they would have been present at officers' meetings, or privy to information regarding the planning and preparation of the mass murders, elements of the crime that they insisted on for the other defendants.[210]

If the tribunal had difficulty with the Graf and Rühl cases, it had no trouble whatsoever determining the guilt of defendants such as Ohlendorf, the evidence against these individuals was straightforward and they had admitted to supervising the killing of thousands of civilians. Whereas adjudicating the cases of those less voluble and forthcoming or those who simply denied they had done anything, was, of necessity, more involved and lengthy. This was the case with the leader of *Einsatzgruppe* A. The evidence against Jost came almost exclusively from the *Einsatzgruppen* reports. Although it did not name him directly, one of the Operational Situation Reports stated that up-to-and-including March 29, 1942, *Einsatzgruppe* A had killed in excess of 100,000 people. The prosecution contended that because Jost was leader of that group, he was responsible for its victims. The most damning evidence against him was a report dated April 24, 1942, which recorded the murder of 1,272 persons by *Einsatzgruppe* A as well as naming Jost directly in the participation of the slave labor program in White Ruthenia.[211] Jost had offered a variety of defenses; foremost was his outright denial of participating in "the execution of the Führer-Order." He also claimed that he was never present during any killings, and he was not aware of the criminal purpose of the *Einsatzgruppen*.[212] The tribunal did not believe him, noting that it found it "extraordinary" that given the *Einsatzgruppen's* long-standing orders to murder, that his unit would suddenly cease doing so just as Jost arrived to command the unit.[213] On the issue of the *Führerbefehl* it "was in effect prior to Jost's arrival at Riga" in March 1942, and since Jost had never revoked it, he was still responsible for the acts committed by the group that he commanded. In the end, the only evidence Jost had was his testimony; he could provide no documentary proof to counter the prosecution's evidence and therefore, he too was found guilty of all three counts in the indictment.[214]

Of the leaders of the sub-*Kommando* units of the *Einsatzgruppen*, the tribunal's findings against Franz Six are fairly typical. Because Six never admitted to any crime whatsoever – it will be recalled that his defense strategy was to deny everything – it made the tribunal's job more difficult. At trial Six portrayed himself as a man of moral honesty dedicated to teaching and research, and nothing more. The tribunal did not believe Six, finding much lacking

[210] *Ibid.*, 226.
[211] *Ibid.*, 134, 135, 136.
[212] *Ibid.*, 133–134.
[213] *Ibid.*, 135.
[214] *Ibid.*, 137.

in both the professor's defense as well as in his character.[215] Evidence indicated that Six was more committed to carrying out Nazi racial policy than he was willing to acknowledge at trial. He had voluntarily joined the Party in 1930 while still a graduate student, had joined the SA in 1932, and the SS and SD in 1935, eventually achieving the high rank of *Brigadeführer*.[216] While this in itself was not enough to convict Six, the prosecution did have evidence to suggest that he was more than a mere "collector of archives" as he maintained. Operational Situation Report No. 73, of September 4, 1941, in particular detailed some of the activities of *Vorkommando* Moscow. The report noted that Six's *Kommando* was responsible for the murder of 144 persons and an additional 46 persons, of whom, 38 were Jewish intellectuals residing in the Smolensk Ghetto.[217] Like other defendants, Six's attorney attempted to show that while *Vorkommando* Moscow may very well have committed these acts, Six was not with the unit then, rather he had already returned to Germany.[218] More damning were the activities that Six participated in, namely his "scientific" work. In one speech from April 1944, Six spoke on the Jewish question in which he stated that his "solution" would be their "physical elimination... which would deprive Jewry of its biological reserves." At trial Six denied that he was the author of the remarks, but he did admit to being present at the meeting.[219] Other circumstantial evidence included Six's promotion to *Oberführer* that his SS-Personnel Record stated was for "outstanding service in the east."[220] Despite the large amount of circumstantial evidence, his refusal to admit to anything forced the tribunal to conclude that it was impossible to determine with "certitude," that Six "took an active part in the murder program" in the Soviet Union. They did however agree that he had engaged in "atrocities, offenses and inhumane acts against civilian populations," and therefore, like the vast majority of his colleagues, was found guilty of "crimes against humanity" and "war crimes."[221]

Sentences

As Musmanno, Speight, and Dixon deliberated, it became clear that they would be required to impose death sentences on some of the defendants.[222] Although Musmanno had already made morally vexing decisions when he had helped pass judgment in the trials against Oswald Pohl and Erhard

[215] *Ibid.*, 147–148.
[216] Six was actually appointed leader of *Vorkommando* Moscow in late May 1941.
[217] Judgment, 148–149 and Arad et al. (eds.), *The Einsatzgruppen Reports*, 120–125.
[218] Judgment, 149.
[219] *Ibid.*, 150.
[220] *Ibid.*, 150–151.
[221] *Ibid.*, 151.
[222] Musmanno, *Eichmann Kommandos*, 257.

Milch, both of whom received death sentences, he was not presiding in either of these trials. As presiding judge in the *Einsatzgruppen* trial he felt more morally and spiritually taxed than he had previously and wanted to be certain that he had done a decent job supervising a fair and impartial trial. But the issue of the death penalty, something he had inveighed against throughout his career as a defense attorney in the United States weighed particularly heavily on his conscience; he apparently found it an "intolerable burden."[223] Despite all he had heard and seen in court, he still held to the view that the defendants were human beings and the thought of ending their lives filled him with dread. In an early draft of his memoir of the trial (which was subsequently eliminated in the published version), he admitted that he had gotten to know the defendants so well during the trial that he could not view them as "beasts," rather he found many of them "personable individuals" and this made the task of sentencing "particularly painful."[224] He spoke especially fondly of Ohlendorf, who he regarded as possessing "courage and character [as well as] some strand of moral fortitude," and he worried about the time when he would have "to look this man in the eye and tell him he was going to die."[225] Musmanno spent many sleepless nights thinking over his dilemma, ultimately turning to an old friend, U.S. army chaplain Francis Konieczny for guidance.[226]

Toward the end of March 1948, once the committee work was completed and the judgment written, Musmanno asked Konieczny to assist him in finding a "retreat" where he could "dwell in meditation and prayer."[227] The chaplain recommended a monastery about thirty miles outside Nuremberg. Musmanno spent some weeks at the retreat under the spiritual guidance of Father Stephan Geyer and Father Carol Mesch. The latter spoke both Italian and German and thus acted as Musmanno's interpreter in his discussions with Father Geyer. Musmanno also invited a close friend from his days in Sorrento, Lieutenant Guiseppe Ercolano who served to keep him isolated from all "secular" affairs so that he could do some "soul-searching" before he was required to hand down sentences.[228] It was while at the monastery that Musmanno found the necessary peace of mind to accept death sentences.

Musmanno had talked at great length to Geyer and Mesch, and was forever grateful for their help during these "very trying days," yet, he never

---

[223] Letter, Musmanno to Ferencz, April 13, 1948, in RG 12.000, Drawer 11 Biographical Material, box 1, Folder C Biographical Material Job Related Personnel File 1946–1955, BBF, USHMM.

[224] Musmanno, draft of *Eichmann Kommandos*, March 14, 1959, 81, in Memoranda and Notes file 247, MMP.

[225] *Ibid.*, 82.

[226] Noah J. Jacobs, "Justice Musmanno and the Death Sentence: An Article on the Sentencing in the Einsatzgruppen Case," *Venerdi*, September 1, 1961, Einsatzgruppen file 1691, MMP.

[227] Musmanno, *Eichmann Kommandos*, 257–258.

[228] *Ibid.*, 258–259.

revealed the content of the discussions with these men.[229] One can surmise that their discussions concerned his feelings about the death penalty and the dilemma imposing it caused him. To be certain Musmanno never had any difficulty reaching a decision on the guilt of the defendants as he found the trial evidence quite sufficient.[230] Determining sentences was another matter. Although we may never know exactly how the tribunal reached its decisions on the death penalty, there is one clue that cannot be overlooked. For each death sentence passed, the defendant in question had admitted to the crime of murder.[231] In no instance was a defendant who had refused to admit to his crimes in front of the tribunal sentenced to death. For example, Ohlendorf admitted to killing 90,000 people in his testimony before the IMT, and at his own trial while he claimed the number was inflated, he never recanted entirely. Blobel said the estimated 33,000 killed at Babi Yar was and exaggeration, but admitted to killing somewhere between 10,000–15,000 people. Blume and Sandberger admitted to killing people, but they said they had no choice. Braune admitted to the Simferopol massacre. Haensch admitted that he supervised executions, but he could not remember how many exactly. Ott told the court he carried out between eighty and one hundred executions. Naumann told the court the *Führerbefehl* was correct and carried out his orders accordingly although he thought the figure of 135,000 victims was probably too high. Biberstein said that he went to executions to experience the sensation. Schubert admitted to supervising the execution of 800 people. Willy Seibert admitted to being Ohlendorf's deputy. Although his testimony was jumbled, Strauch admitted to carrying out his orders. Klingelhöfer admitted he hoped that Hitler had won the war and that he carried out his duties. Each one of these men was sentenced to death. Those who did not admit to killing anyone (Fendler, Nosske, Radetzky, Rühl, Schulz, and Six) were spared the hangman. Never admitting to the court to killing a single person, Jost was the only leader of the parent organization of the *Einsatzgruppen* not to be sentenced to death. In this sense, Musmanno was true to himself and his earlier position on the death penalty as he had articulated it during the execution of Sacco and Vanzetti twenty years earlier: he abhorred the punishment because it was irrevocable and the system was imperfect. In choosing this path, Musmanno may well have reached a compromise with himself. He could pass the harshest of sentences on those who had confessed their crimes, and, at the same time, sentence those who did not confess to prison terms and still live with himself knowing that at the very worst, someone who may have been innocent had not lost his life.

[229] *Ibid.*
[230] *Ibid.*, 146.
[231] Notes to himself, 1948, Material to be read while Reading Manuscript of Biggest Murder Trial in History file 249, MMP.

Musmanno returned to Nuremberg to pass sentences on the defendants. He prepared himself for the day, since he knew that his "sensitive spirit would suffer a horrible wrench when the moment would arrive."[232] To make his task as easy as possible, when each defendant arrived via an elevator from the basement, he planned to read from a prepared text, and keep his reading glasses on which blurred his distance vision and made objects appear "vague and undistinguishable."[233] In this way, he hoped to distance himself from each individual defendant. Ohlendorf was fittingly the first to appear before the reconvened tribunal on April 10. Flanked by Staff Sergeant J. L. Henderson of Houston, Texas, and Private Joe Dodds, of Baton Rouge, Louisiana, Ohlendorf appeared small and powerless, certainly not what one would expect of a man who had perpetrated such tremendous wrongdoing. When he was told that that he had been found guilty of all three charges and the tribunal was sentencing him to death by hanging, Ohlendorf accepted his fate stoically.[234] Before he turned to leave, however, he briefly bowed to the tribunal in a gesture of respect. Following Ohlendorf, one by one each defendant emerged from the basement of the courthouse to face the tribunal and hear his punishment. In all, the tribunal sentenced fourteen defendants to death, two more than had been sentenced to death at the IMT trial and more than any other tribunal convened at Nuremberg. Two defendants were sentenced to life terms and five to prison terms of ten to twenty years. One defendant, Matthias Graf, who the court found had not participated in any executions and whose role in the murderous operation was a minor one, was released with time served.[235] With the twenty-two sentences read in open court, the *Einsatzgruppen* trial was officially over.

[232] Musmanno, draft of *Eichmann Kommandos*, p. 83, March 14, 1959, Memoranda and Notes file 247, MMP.
[233] *Ibid.*, 86.
[234] Logan, Letter from Germany, *New Yorker*, May 8, 1948, 65-4-5, Andy Logan Papers.
[235] Judgment, 225–228.

7

Aftermath: From Perpetrators of Genocide to Ordinary Germans

This inmate is somewhat reserved. He is at no time a trouble maker and endeavours to make the best of things. He seems devoted to his faith and his family; he is anxious to get released, reestablish his home, and pursue his profession. He is a model inmate and possesses the qualifications to make a good adjustment in a free society.

Robert Karicher, Prison Director[1]

If I had all the facts I now have, I might have reached a more just result.

John McCloy[2]

The work of Tribunal II at the *Einsatzgruppen* trial officially ended with the pronouncement of sentences on April 10, 1948. For the defendants of course, the story did not end there. Rather, a new, lengthier, and far more favorable ordeal – for all but four of the convicted – was just beginning. Their legal story would not be complete until 1958 when, only ten years after they originally had been sentenced, the last of the *Einsatzgruppen* leaders tried at Nuremberg was released from prison.

What went so horribly wrong to allow some of the most active and notorious perpetrators of the Third Reich to be released back into German society so soon after they were punished? This is a difficult question to answer because the *Einsatzgruppen* trial was part of a larger process that became enmeshed in the politics of the post-war period and, therefore, is difficult to isolate. What we can say with certainty is that between 1948 and 1958 the context changed. The most drastic and important transformation was that of the political landscape. Former allies were now enemies and icy

---

[1] Robert Karicher, Prison Director, Landsberg, commenting on the prisoner Ernst Biberstein WCP # 1420, August 23, 1957 in NARA RG 466, Prisons Division, Administration and Medical Landsberg, box 1, Biberstein.
[2] McCloy quoted in a letter, Ferencz to Martin Gilbert, November 10, 1989, RG 12.000, Drawer 24 WCT, box 2, Folder A John J. McCloy file, BBF, USHMM.

relations with the Soviet Union defined and conditioned the foreign policy of the United States. The cold war seriously affected American policy toward Germany and, by extension, its war crimes policy there. The war criminals issue became politicized and the fallout from the cold war meant that little-by-little American leadership lost its political will to carry through with the punishment of the former enemy, opting instead for a *quid pro quo* that guaranteed German political support against the Soviets. It was during this crucial period that Germans regained their political confidence, especially after they won their sovereignty in 1949, and, as a result, some nationalist-minded groups began massive and organized campaigns to free convicted war criminals. These groups, among them Nuremberg defense attorneys, the Catholic and Protestant clergy, and other "pro-German" lobbyists, argued that the men who were convicted in foreign courts were not war criminals at all, but rather good German soldiers who had merely followed orders.[3] These groups believed that the Nuremberg trials, as well as the American army's military trials were acts of political vengeance and therefore not legit-imate; those sentenced by American tribunals should be granted pardons and released from prison. These two factors – a changing political climate and a resurgent German nationalism – coalesced and resulted in the gradual erosion of punishment, first through the establishment of a commission to review the army's military war crimes trials, followed closely by an Ameri-can Senate review of war crimes trial procedure, then an executive review of all sentences, and finally two clemency panels that were established in 1950 to review sentences in both the Dachau military trials as well as the twelve Subsequent Nuremberg Proceedings. The cumulative effect of these reviews was a massive reduction of sentences and the release of a good number of those tried at Nuremberg. All but four of the *Einsatzgruppen* defendants were released from prison; the other four were eventually hanged at Lands-berg war crimes prison, along with Oswald Pohl, on June 7, 1951.[4] How this gradual but radical shift in policy came about, and how the life sentences of the *Einsatzgruppen* leadership turned into freedom is examined below.

Appeals for Clemency

As with the original IMT trial, the Americans did not make any provisions for the establishment of an appellate court in which those convicted in the

---

[3] Other groups included the National Council for the Prevention of War, Stille Hilfe, and prominent individuals, mainly attorneys.

[4] Landsberg prison was designated war criminals prison no. 1 by the Americans. Hitler was incarcerated there after his failed putsch attempt and it is where he wrote *Mein Kampf*. It was also the prison where nearly 1,000 convicted war criminals were housed following their trials by the U.S. army and the Nuremberg tribunals. Klee, *Persilscheine und falsche Pässe*, 72–73 and 75.

NMT could launch appeals of their convictions and sentences.[5] Article 26 of the Nuremberg Charter and Article 15 of American *Military Ordinance No. 7* stated that the judgments of the tribunals "shall be final and not subject to review," yet both documents also made room for the possibility of sentence reductions at the executive level.[6] Whereas the *Nuremberg Charter* provided for the possibility of sentence reduction by the unanimous consent of the quadripartite Control Council for those tried by the IMT, under *Ordinance No. 7* – the law under which the Subsequent Trials were conducted – sentence reductions were the sole prerogative of the American Military Governor, who was given "the power to mitigate, reduce or otherwise alter the sentence[s] imposed by the tribunal[s]."[7] There was an important codicil to all of this, however. Article 18 of *Ordinance No. 7*, also stated that death sentences could not be carried out "unless and until confirmed in writing by the Military Governor," and that the Military Governor was empowered to defer the death sentence of anyone he believed could be of value in future prosecutions of war criminals.[8] In other words, the Military Governor had to review the sentences before they were executed. Under the circumstances of the post-war period, especially with American and British emphasis on reviving the German economy, sentence review was not a top priority and thus it took time. Yet, the intention of these provisions was never, as Robert Jackson noted, "to authorize anything in the nature of an appeal from the tribunal's sentences or a re-examination of the law or the decision on the facts," as the tribunal's judgment was final.[9] But a court of last resort is exactly how the defense attorneys at Nuremberg came to interpret Article 17 and Lucius Clay's office of Military Governor.[10] Almost as soon as each trial ended, the convicted men deluged Clay with appeals for sentence reviews. In the case of the defendants in the *Einsatzgruppen* trial, twenty of the twenty-one convicted men filed appeals almost immediately, little more than two weeks after they had been sentenced on April 10, 1948. Only

---

[5] Letter, Jackson to Howard Petersen, September 12, 1946, Office Files, Allied Control Council Directives, box 98 US CCWC, RHJ Papers. See also Smith, *Judgment at Nuremberg*, 299–300; Tusa and Tusa, *The Nuremberg Trial*, 479–480; and Conot, *Justice at Nuremberg*, 498–507.

[6] Article 26 and 29, Charter of the IMT, October 6, 1945, and Article 15 and 17, Military Ordinance No. 7, October 18, 1946, in *TWC*, vol. 4, xvi and xxvii.

[7] Article 17, "Military Ordinance No. 7," October 18, 1946, in *ibid.*, xxvii.

[8] *Ibid.*, xxvii–xxviii. Ohlendorf attempted to evade the death penalty by testifying for the prosecution at the trial of the OKW. Untitled article, *Christ und Welt*, August 20, 1948, D1/332, NL Wurm, LKA.

[9] Letter, Jackson to Petersen, September 12, 1946, RHJ Papers.

[10] On the issue of sentence reviews see Brief, re: Regulation No. 1 under Military Government Ordinance No. 7 as Amended by Military Government Ordinance No. 11, April 8, 1947, in NARA RG 260, OMGUS, Executive Office, The Office of the Adjutant General, Military Government Ordinances 1945–1949, box 640, ord No. 1–18, Ordinance No. 7 folder.

Gustav Nosske did not appeal his sentence at this time, but did so soon thereafter.[11]

The petitions filed on behalf of the convicted *Einsatzgruppen* leaders were, in the main, a reiteration of issues of fact and law already established at the trial, and therefore the content of the petitions were not grounds for review. But these men were desperate, fighting for their lives, and they filed petitions regardless of the conditions laid out for doing so. For example, Werner Braune's appeal was partially based on the argument that although he carried out the *Führerbefehl* to murder Soviet Jewry, he morally objected to it. The petition stated that Tribunal II did not take this "fact" into consideration. Of course the tribunal had dealt with this issue in the judgment, but found it to be moot when a defendant made no effort to evade the order. At trial, Braune had admitted he had made no attempt to evade or avoid the order.[12] Braune's petition also claimed that the evidence presented at the trial "clearly established that refusal to obey a Hitler order would have meant certain death," for him.[13] Again, this issue had been dealt with extensively at trial where absolutely no concrete evidence was presented by the defense to prove this claim. Several of the defendants had admitted that refusal to carry-out an order, even a Hitler order, most frequently resulted in transfer, and not death as Braune's petition held.

Ohlendorf's appeal for clemency, filed by Dr. Rudolf Aschenauer (later an active and vocal lobbyist to free war criminals who made a career out of defending imprisoned war criminals), differed somewhat from the others, making a number of specious arguments that hardly warranted review let alone pardon.[14] For instance, Ohlendorf's petition included the argument that the prosecution had overestimated the number of murders the defendants had committed: the *Einsatzgruppen* had not killed 1 million people as the indictment charged, but only 450,000. This, in Aschenauer's legal opinion, was a distortion of history and given one of the stated purposes of the trial was to create an historical record, should command a pardon for his client.[15] Aschenauer also argued that the tribunal's judgment was faulty because it did not take into consideration that the *Einsatzgruppen* had other tasks besides that of killing, such as record collection, security and intelligence work. Again, this represented a distortion of the truth and

[11] *Nuernberg: United States of America v. Otto Ohlendorf et al. War Crimes Trials Records of Case 9* (Special List 42), compiled by John Mendelsohn (Washington, 1978), 176–178.

[12] Petition for Clemency, Braune, April 26, 1948, 2–3, in NARA RG 466, Petitions for Clemency or Parole at Nuremberg, box 4 Bobermin-Creutz, Braune folder.

[13] *Ibid.*

[14] [14]Klee, *Persilscheine und falsche Pässe*, 78–80 intimates that Aschenauer not only defended war criminals, but that he also helped filter money into the hands of former Nazis.

[15] Petition for Clemency, Ohlendorf, April 26, 1948, 7–8, in NARA RG 466, Petitions for Clemency or Parole at Nuremberg, box 8, Ohlendorf folder.

warranted pardon in his view.[16] Inundated with petitions for sentence reviews, clemency and pardons such as these, Clay, who had always supported the war crimes trials, set out to review the convicted's requests.[17] He did not announce the results of his reviews until a year later in March 1949, by which time German opposition groups to the war crimes trials had organized themselves and were at the height of their campaign of pressure to discredit the American war crimes trial program and force Clay to pardon all war criminals regardless of their crimes, even the leaders of the *Einsatzgruppen*.

Just as the *Einsatzgruppen* trial was wrapping-up in the spring of 1948, substantial German opposition to the American war crimes trials was developing. Serious opposition began when irregularities in the U.S. army's "Dachau trials" were detected. The most problematic was the Malmédy trial. In May 1946, seventy-four former SS men were brought to the American prison at Dachau and were tried by the U.S. army for the murder of eighty-four American prisoners of war in Malmédy, Belgium, during the Battle of the Bulge in 1944.[18] Almost immediately following the conclusion of the Malmédy trial, German attorneys for the convicted men filed complaints that were sent to Clay, and to several Republican senators in the U.S. The complainants argued that the convictions in the Malmédy trial were gained unlawfully, through "trickery, threats of violence and other methods of coercion and duress."[19] As this was potentially embarrassing, the Americans could hardly ignore such serious accusations, thus both the Military Governor and the U.S. Senate held separate investigations into the conduct of the army's trials. Whereas these events might seem unrelated to the *Einsatzgruppen* trial – a judicial procedure carried out by a different American organization and under different laws – the army's Malmédy trial is important because its effects were wide-ranging, having an impact not only on the army's trials and sentences, but ultimately all of the Nuremberg trials as well. Ironically, it was the Malmédy massacre that initially inspired Americans to conduct war crimes trials in post-war Germany to begin with, and now it was the trial of those involved in the massacre that would lead

---

[16] *Ibid.*

[17] Memorandum Clay to Oliver Echols, War Department, June 28, 1946, RG 338, JAD, WCB, General Administration Records 1942–1957, box 1, 1946 folder; Bloxham, *Genocide on Trial*, 27 & Tom Bower, *Blind Eye to Murder. Britain, America and the Purging of Nazi Germany – a Pledge Betrayed* (London, 1995), 313.

[18] Justus Doenecke, "Protest over Malmédy: A Case of Clemency," *Peace and Change* 2:4 (1977), 28. See also, John Mendelsohn, "War Crimes Trials and Clemency in Germany and Japan," in Robert Wolfe (ed.) *Americans as Proconsuls. United States Military Government in Germany and Japan, 1944–1952* (Carbondale, IL; 1984), especially 248–250.

[19] Memorandum, James Costello to Theater JA EUCOM, May 1948, in NARA RG 338, JAG, WCB, Post-Trial Activities 1945–1957, box 9, Bishop Wurm folder. For a discussion of the problems of the army's Malmédy trial, see especially, Bower, *Blind Eye*, 300–326.

to the disrepute of the American war crimes trial program and ultimately
bring the entire judicial process down. The investigations into the conduct
of the Malmédy trial mark the beginning of the end of the punishment of
Nazi war criminals by the United States. With the cold war setting in, and
American political resolve waning, certain groups of German nationalists,
led most vociferously by some high-ranking Catholic and Protestant bishops
and German defense attorneys, recognized that the opportunity to strike was
at hand.[20] This is precisely what they did, and with great tenacity.[21]

Opposition to the Nuremberg Judgments

The earliest and most vocal opponents of the American army's trials, as
well as the Nuremberg trials, were some of the nationally-minded German clergy, a group one scholar considers to have been the "most effective
helpers of National Socialist [war] criminals."[22] Indeed, without the active
and "pesky" lobbying of the German clergy, it is doubtful if any revision of
sentences would have occurred.[23] Four of the most outspoken critics were
the Catholic auxiliary bishop of Munich, Johannes Neuhäusler, who had
been incarcerated in a concentration camp by the Nazis in 1941, a fact
that he always made mention of when lobbying on behalf of convicted war
criminals and a position that offered him a "moral advantage."[24] Theophil
Wurm, bishop of the Evangelical Church of Württemberg, whose anti-Nazi
pedigree was not as pure as Neuhäusler's and whose son was an early
joiner of the Nazi party, was the most vocal opponent from the Evangelical
Church.[25] Wurm also was instrumental in helping several of the convicted

[20] On the issue of the German clergy's role in helping convicted war criminals, compare Klee, *Persilscheine und falsche Pässe* and Michael Phayer, *The Catholic Church and the Holocaust, 1930–1965* (Bloomington, 2000) and "The German Catholic Church after the Holocaust," *Holocaust and Genocide Studies* 2:10 (Fall 1996), 151–167. Klee is far more critical of the bishops' behavior regarding war criminals than Phayer.
[21] Klee, *Persilscheine und falsche Pässe*, 77–78, points out that the German clergy became involved in the war criminals issue as a result of several factors, including a perceived attack on Christian rituals in Landsberg prison as well as the alleged transgressions in the Malmédy trial. See also Letter, August Eckardt to Wurm, February 20, 1949, D1/293, NL Wurm, LKA.
[22] Klee, *Persilscheine und falsche Pässe*, 7. See also, Daily Intelligence Digest # 133, "Clergy Continues to Favor Cause of Interned Nazis," March 15, 1946, in NARA RG 260, OMGUS, Information Control Division, Opinion Survey Branch, box 145, Daily Intelligence Digest folder and Letter, Wurm to Justice Lawrence, September 19, 1946, D1/272, NL Wurm, LKA.
[23] Phayer, *Catholic Church*, 143.
[24] Bower, *Blind Eye*, 319.
[25] Klee, *Persilscheine und falsche Pässe*, 14–15 & 61–71 and Phayer, *Catholic Church*, 138–144. Wurm's son was found to be a follower by the denazification court in Wiesbaden and was sentenced to one year in prison. Letter, Wurm to Ambassador Murphy, January 19, 1949, D1/272, NL Wurm, LKA.

Einsatzgruppen leaders. The Catholic Cardinal of Cologne, Josef Frings, who had initially supported the punishment of war criminals, but changed his mind when he discovered the Vatican opposed punishment, was also an active lobbyist.[26] And finally, Hans Meiser, the Evangelical *Landesbishof* of Bavaria, whose links to Nazism were most pronounced of all the bishops. He worked closely with Wurm who inspired his own lobbying.[27] Meiser worked to free convicted war criminals, by publicizing all rumors of maltreatment of prisoners at Landsberg, even if they were unfounded.[28] All four clergymen became involved in the debate over war criminals during the period of controversy surrounding the army's Malmédy trial. In turn, they solicited the support of other influential Catholic priests and Protestant pastors, German defense attorneys, and some pro-German, American organizations to help in their battle against what they viewed as blind American vengeance.[29] To coordinate their lobbying efforts, in the spring of 1949, they established the Committee for Church Aid for Prisoners or *Komitee für kirchliche Gefangenenhilfe.*

On the legal front, the German bishops employed the assistance of former Nuremberg attorneys to help in the campaign to discredit the war crimes trials. Rudolf Aschenauer was foremost among those active in the opposition movement. Aschenauer, a young and ambitious lawyer from Munich and former Nazi party member, was a devout Catholic and had a close relationship with Bishop Neuhäusler as his legal advisor.[30] In March 1949, the German bishops worked with Aschenauer to establish the *kirchliche Gefangenenhilfe,* an organization whose main aim was to legally assist so-called destitute war criminals housed in Landsberg prison.[31] The Protestant and Catholic churches financed the welfare organization and they retained Aschenauer and fellow attorney Georg Fröschmann (a personal friend of *Landesbishof* Meiser, Nazi party member, and member of the SA) as their principal attorneys whose job it was to offer legal advice to the Landsberg prisoners.[32] The two lawyers officially began their work in May 1949. It was

---

[26] Phayer, *Catholic Church,* 143.

[27] Klee, *Persilscheine und falsche Pässe,* 13.

[28] Frederic Spotts, *The Churches and Politics in Germany* (Middleton, 1973), 8–11.

[29] Report on Bishop Wurm (sic) to the Secretary of the Army, May and September 1948, in NARA RG 338, JAD, WCB, Post-Trial Activities 1945–1957, box 9, Bishop Wurm folder.

[30] Klee, *Persilscheine und falsche Pässe,* 78–79.

[31] "Komitee für kirchliche Gefangenenhilfe," *Süddeutsche Zeitung,* March 27, 1950, 305/94 Kriegsgefangenen Allgemeines 1950, BA; and, Klee, *Persilscheine und falsche Pässe,* 79.

[32] Memorandum, Special Agent Joe R. Cox to the JAG, re: Rudolf Aschenauer and the Church Aid Society, September 5, 1950, 1–5, in NARA RG 338, JAD, WCB, General Administrative Records 1942–1957, box 5, Aschenauer folder; and, Letter, Evangelical Landeskirchenrat to Rudolf Weeber, May 24, 1949, D1/293, NL Wurm, LKA. For synopses of Aschenauer and Fröschmann's postwar activities, see the reports by the CIC, Internal Route Slip, October 10, 1950, in NARA RG 338, JAD, WCB, General Administration Records 1942–1957, box 5, Aschenauer folder.

not long before Aschenauer's client list reached a ridiculous 683 worthy, but apparently very poor, convicted war criminals. By comparison, Fröschmann had only 150 clients.[33] Aschenauer persuaded many of the convicted men to become his clients when he told them his services were free of charge as the *kirchliche Gefangenenhilfe* would cover all their legal expenses. He gained clients precisely because of his backing by the churches as well as having some connections with sympathetic and influential U.S. Senators and Congressmen. The work of the *kirchliche Gefangenenhilfe* helps explain why so many ex-Christian Nazis returned to the church during this period.[34] In addition to his legal work, Aschenauer produced several propaganda pamphlets one of which was titled, "The Question of a Revision of the War Crimes Trials" (*Zur Frage einer Revision der Kriegsverbrecher Prozesse*), which was surprisingly similar in content and tone to the hundreds of letters written by German bishops to American authorities.[35]

Between 1948 and 1951, Neuhäusler, Wurm, Meiser, Frings, and many others, actively lobbied the U.S. army, the Military Governor, and, later, the High Commissioner, calling first for the establishment of an appellate court to review the army's Dachau trials, and soon after the same for the Nuremberg trials.[36] Most importantly for the fate of the convicted *Einsatzgruppen* leaders, they demanded sentence reviews for all the convicted men in Landsberg, the Bavarian prison, which the Americans used to house and execute the convicted and condemned Nuremberg war criminals and where Neuhäusler was spiritual advisor.[37] Wurm, in particular, personally lobbied on behalf of several of the condemned *Einsatzgruppen* leaders, those such as Eugen Steimle and Martin Sandberger, who had been prominent and active members of the Evangelical church before the Nazi "seizure of power," when they renounced their faith in order to participate actively in the Nazi regime and its police organizations.[38] These clergymen took up the work of freeing

[33] Klee, *Persilscheine und falsche Pässe*, 80 and Letter, Weeber to Frederick Libby, February 11, 1949, D1/293, NL Wurm, LKA. Bower states that Fröschmann had over three thousand Landsberg inmates on retainer at one point, *Blind Eye*, 320.

[34] *Ibid.*, 6–7.

[35] Aschenauer, *Zur Frage einer Revision der Kriegsverbrecher Prozesse* (September 1949) can be found in NARA RG 338, JAD, WCB, General Administration Records 1947–1957, box 5, Aschenauer folder.

[36] For example see the statement by Wurm and Neuhäusler, May 1948, untitled, D1/293, NL Wurm, LKA, in which they outline their grievances concerning the trials. See also, Letter, Wurm, Meiser, Bender, Wüsemann, and Niemöller to Clay, May 20, 1948, D1/289, *ibid*; and, Letter, Wurm to Charles Lafollette, May 21, 1948, D1/289, *ibid*.

[37] On the issue of German opposition and Catholic bishops see Buscher, *US War Crimes Trial Program in Germany*, 91–94.

[38] Walter Haensch wrote to Wurm directly begging for his assistance. He swore "before God" that he was unfairly sentenced to death, because he had not killed anybody nor had he ordered any of his men to do so. Letter, Haensch to Wurm, May 13, 1948, in NARA RG 238, Advisory Board on Clemency, Correspondence, box 10, Haensch folder. Wurm also

some of the most notorious mass-murderers of the Third Reich because, as they convinced themselves, these men were not war criminals, but "decent human [beings]," and the trials were simply not fair.[39] Not only were they vengeful and an expression of victor's justice, but the laws under which the defendants were tried were *ex post facto* and, worst of all they argued, the Americans lacked the "moral authority" to try these men.[40] Nearly every complaint the bishops filed with American authorities was based on the word of the defendants themselves, and in not one instance did they produce any concrete evidence of maltreatment of the convicted war criminals.[41] To free the war criminals, they initiated letter-writing campaigns, lobbied American officials, and used the press to call into question the jurisdiction and integrity of American war crimes policy, especially convictions, all during a period when the American political leadership was seriously concerned about reintegrating Germany back into the community of nations as a bulwark against communism.[42]

took up the case of Eugen Steimle. Letter, Erich Meyer to Frau Steimle, April 12, 1948, D1/311.6, NL Wurm, LKA, and Letter, Dekan (signature illegible) to Weeber, June 7 1949, in *ibid*. The wife of Eduard Strauch had her minister, pastor Meiswinkel write to Wurm to ask for assistance, Letter, Meiswinkel to Wurm, June 10, 1948, D1/311.7, NL Wurm, LKA.

39 Vermerk, Wurm, September 1, 1950, "Mein Besuch in Landsberg zum 9. August 1950," B305/148 Deutsche Kriegsverurteilte in Landsberg Einzelfälle, BA; and Letter, Wurm to Robert Kempner, March 30, 1948, D1/289, NL Wurm, LKA.

40 By "moral authority," Wurm meant that the Americans had secured convictions through "criminal methods," such as torture and extortion. See Letters, Wurm to Kempner, January 28, and May 5, 1948, D1/289, NL Wurm, LKA.

41 For instance, see "Complaint against the American War Crimes Trials," by Meiser, January 5, 1949, in NARA RG 338, JAD, WCB, Post Trial Activities 1945–1947, box 11, Bishop Meiser folder in which Meiser accused Ferencz of threatening potential defense witnesses with the promise of extradition to the Soviet zone if they testified on behalf of a defendant. He was also accused of having defense witnesses dismissed from their jobs and of illegally searching witness's apartments. Meiser charged Rolf Wartenberg, the chief interrogator for the NMT, with depriving defendants of sleep before they were interrogated, of altering affidavits, and threatening defendants so as to extract confessions from the accused. Meiser did not produce any evidence to substantiate his complaints. The judge advocate's office investigated all of Meiser's accusations and found them to be "grossly exaggerated and unfounded." Letter, J.L. Harbaugh, Jr., Judge Advocate, to John Raymond, January 18, 1949, and Memorandum, to the associate Director Legal Division OMGUS, undated, in NARA RG 466, Prisons Division, Security Segregated Records, box 10, War Crimes Trial 1949 folder.

42 For example, on December 6, 1948, Neuhäusler initiated a letter-writing campaign to Clay concerning prison conditions and accusations of abuses of prisoners at Landsberg. Clay immediately ordered Taylor to investigate. He concluded that although "prisons are not health resorts," conditions at Landsberg were "generally satisfactory." Taylor's findings did not mollify the Catholic bishop who continued to complain of the unfair treatment of convicted war criminals. See Memorandum, Taylor to Clay, re: Inspection of War Criminal Prison No. 1 (Landsberg), June 3, 1949, in NARA RG 466, Prisons Division, Administrative and Medical Records Landsberg, box 1, Nuremberg Subsequent Proceedings Medical Reports folder. Wurm lobbied Clay for the creation of appellate court. Because Clay refused

Although the Americans had absolutely no intention of creating an appellate court as the German clergy hoped, they were initially somewhat sympathetic and understanding of the bishops' attempts to assist their fellow countrymen, no matter how misplaced they believed their support was for the convicted war criminals.[43] The intense lobbying by the bishops reaped partial rewards almost immediately.[44] On July 30, 1948, the American Secretary of the Army (formerly the Secretary of War) Kenneth C. Royall, a known opponent of the American war crimes trial program in Germany, announced he was ordering a stay of execution of all death sentences handed down in the army's Dachau trials, at least until further review of the proceedings were carried out.[45] In the meantime, Royall appointed a commission that was to be headed by Justice Gordon Simpson, a judge of the Supreme Court of Texas, to investigate the German accusations.[46] After investigating 139 death sentences, the Simpson Commission, as the investigative body was referred to, recommended that twenty-nine of those sentenced to death by the army's Dachau tribunals have their sentences commuted to prison terms.[47] The Commission did not find that the Dachau trials were unfair; they did however conclude that in some instances justice would be better served if some of the death sentences were commuted to life terms.[48] More importantly, the Commission recommended the establishment of a clemency and parole board to deal with all of the army's trials and those convicted in them.[49] Immediately following the Simpson Commission's decision, on October 15,

to establish one, Wurm and the Nuremberg defense attorneys embarked on a media campaign to gain public support. Various newspaper articles, D1/332, NL Wurm, LKA, and memorandum, Major Joseph L. Haefele to Theater JA, September 16, 1948, in NARA, RG 338, JAD, WCB, Post-Trial Activities 1945–1957, box 9, Bishop Wurm folder.

[43] "Complaint against the American War Crimes Trials," by Hans Meiser, January 5, 1949, in NARA, RG 338, JAD, WCB, Post Trial Activities 1945–1947, box 11, Bishop Meiser folder.

[44] Letter, John Raymond to Wurm, June 7, 1948, D1/290, NL Wurm, LKA.

[45] Letter, Wurm and Meiser, Wüstemann and Bender, and Letter, Niemöller to Royall, August 1948, D1/291 and file 272, NL Wurm, LKA; "US Will Probe Dachau Trials," *Stars and Stripes*, July 30, 1948, D1/333, in *Ibid*; and, Memorandum, Royall to Forestall, November 23, 1948, Foreign Affairs File, HST. Royall had served as defense counsel in the now infamous Nazi Saboteurs Case in which eight Nazis had gone to the United States to commit acts of sabotage during the war.

[46] *Ibid.*

[47] Letter, Wurm to John Foster Dulles, October 16, 1948, D1/292, NL Wurm, LKA; and Wurm, "Memorandum by the Evangelical Church in Germany on the Question of War Crimes Trials before American Military Courts" (copy No. 2, 1949), 18–19, in NARA RG 238, Advisory Board on Clemency, HICOG 1947–1950, Correspondence and other Records, box 4, General folder (from here forward simply Memorandum by the Evangelical Church).

[48] Letter, Gordon Simpson to Weeber, Oberkirchenrat, November 10, 1948, D1/292, NL Wurm, LKA.

[49] Mendelsohn, "War Crimes and Clemency," 249–250.

1948, executions resumed at Landsberg prison at the rate of ten men every Friday.[50] Between October 1948 and February 1949, 104 men were executed at Landsberg.[51] Simpson's recommendations for the establishment of a clemency and parole committee, and the commutation of death sentences was not enough to placate the German bishops who wanted nothing short of a complete reversal of the program.[52]

To add fodder to their case, not long after the Simpson Commission rendered its decision, the verdict in Case 11 of the NMT (America v. Ernst von Weizsäcker et al.) was handed down and it was not unanimous. Excluding the IMT, after the completion of eleven trials, a dissenting opinion was finally registered. In von Weizsäcker's case, the presiding judge called into question his colleague's judgment and ultimately the sentence of the former State Secretary of the Foreign Office.[53] This judgment was more than enough evidence to convince the German clergy that along with the army's proceedings, all war crimes trials carried out by the United States, including the Nuremberg trials, were tainted.[54] They would not be satisfied until every single war criminal from both the army's trials as well as the Nuremberg proceedings, was released from prison. As one official in the Judge Advocate's office summed up the problem,

apparently it is the feeling... of these higher church officials that if one error is discovered to have been committed in one case, or if it is disclosed that one accused may have been sentenced upon insufficient evidence or to have received too severe a sentence, or if it is shown that one accused may have suffered some mistreatment while held in custody before trial, then all the trials are bad and must be held for naught. It is not enough that the one error has been corrected, that the accused unfairly convicted has been released, that the too severe sentence has been appropriately reduced, but because of such mistakes all of the convicted war criminals should be released.[55]

In the logic of the clergy, if one judge in one trial found fault with the proceedings, surely the other trials must also be flawed.

---

[50] Letter, Wurm to Dulles, October 16, 1948, D1/292, NL Wurm, LKA; and Letter, Weeber to Simpson, October 28, 1948, D1/293, in *ibid.* When the executions resumed many of the Landsberg prisoners began a four-day hunger strike. Memorandum, Wade Fleischer to Colonel Harbaugh, October 25, 1948, in NARA RG 338, JAD, WCB, Landsberg, box 5, Landsberg 201 1948 folder.

[51] Bower, *Blind Eye*, 315.

[52] Dissenting Opinion in Case XI, USA v. Ernst von Weizsäcker et al., in *Memorandum by the Evangelical Church*, 41–49.

[53] *Ibid.*

[54] Letter, Wurm to L.W. Goebel, President of the Evangelical and Reform Church, February 23, 1949, D1/293, NL Wurm, LKA.

[55] Internal Route Slip, JA, re: Complaint against the American War crimes Trials by Meiser, January 5, 1949, in NARA RG 338, JAD, WCB, Post Trial Activities 1945–1957, box 11, Bishop Meiser folder.

The dissenting opinion in von Weiszäcker's trial inspired a new round of lobbying. The repeated petitions coupled with Clay's desire to "free [his] successor from this thankless task," (he would be stepping down as Military Governor in July) the American Military Government's Legal Division recommended to Clay that he review the Nuremberg sentences immediately. Like Musmanno earlier, Clay was loathe to confirm any death sentence if there was any doubt whatsoever as to a defendant's guilt.[56] Thus, he had always insisted on personally reviewing the cases of each condemned man. Review cases is exactly what he did with the help of a team of attorneys. On March 4, 1949, he found no basis whatsoever to grant clemency or mitigate the sentences of any of the *Einsatzgruppen* leaders, but rather reaffirmed thirteen of the fourteen death sentences.[57] Only Heinz Schubert's sentence was not confirmed as Clay was still considering commuting it to life imprisonment because of his "low rank, his subordinate position and his youth."[58] After some reflection, however, he rethought his position and soon thereafter affirmed Schubert's sentence. Despite Clay's affirmations, all sentences were stayed pending the results of petitions to the United States Supreme Court for writs of habeas corpus filed by Aschenauer and paid for by the *kirchliche Gefangenenhilfe.*[59] In June 1949, in a four to four decision, the Supreme Court denied jurisdiction of the petitions. By this time, the political climate in Germany and Europe had changed and the political will to carry through with the program was waning. The Department of the Army, under Royall, stayed all pending executions in the army's military trials as well as Nuremberg. Royall's decision to do this, as one scholar has noted, was the death knell for punishment of Nazi war criminals as it "consciously handed the pro-German lobby in America and the Nazis in Germany an official licence to attack the whole war crimes trial program."[60] To make

[56] Bower, *Blind Eye*, 309–310.
[57] Memorandum, OMGUS to Taylor, March 5, 1949, in NARA RG 338, JAD, WCB, General Administration Records 1942–1957, box 4, War Crimes 201 File vol. 4 folder; and, Press Release, Office of Military Government for Germany, March 7, 1949, in *ibid* RG 238, Advisory Board on Clemency, HICOG Correspondence, box 3, General File Case No. 9 folder.
[58] Memorandum, Raymond to Clay, February 26, March 4, March 11, 1949, in NARA RG 466, GR 1949–1952, box 15, 321.6 War Criminals 1949–1952 folder and memorandum to Clay, re: Review of the Sentences Imposed by United States Military Tribunal II, Sitting in Nuremberg, Germany, in Case No. 9, circa February–March 29, 1949, in NARA RG 466, Prisons Division, War Criminal Case Files, box 4, Case 9 folder and Press Release from OMGUS, March 7, 1949, in NARA RG 238, Advisory Board on Clemency, HICOG Correspondence, box 3, General File Case No.9 folder.
[59] When a petition is filed with the U.S. Supreme Court in a death sentence case, a stay is almost always granted while the court is considering the petition. Memorandum, OMGUS to the Chief of Staff, U.S. Army, February 6, 1949, in NARA RG 338, JAD, WCB, General Administration Records 1942–1957, box 4, War Crimes 201 Files vol. 4 folder.
[60] Bower, *Blind Eye*, 311.

matters worse, the Americans were in the process of replacing Clay with a new High Commissioner, John McCloy, whose outlook toward the war criminals question had changed significantly since his initial involvement in the formation of the IMT in 1945.[61] McCloy would play a decisive role in reversing sentences in the twelve NMT and especially in the *Einsatzgruppen* case.

Not long after Clay affirmed all of the death sentences in the *Einsatzgruppen* case, the U.S. Senate formed its own committee to investigate the army's Malmédy trial. Senator Raymond Baldwin of Connecticut was the committee's chairman.[62] Their aim was to examine the methods by which confessions were obtained, to investigate allegations of irregularities in the conduct of the trial, and finally to consider whether or not any of the cases were improperly handled by the courts.[63] The committee did not complete its work until September, by which time the German Basic Law or *Grundgesetz* which outlawed the use of capital punishment, had been implemented and Konrad Adenauer had been elected the first chancellor of the new German Federal Republic. These political changes also brought about a change in American personnel and their attitudes toward the war criminals issue. The Military Government was replaced with the Office of the High Commission for Germany, which was created in June 1949, three months before the Federal Republic came into being. The new head of the HICOG, as the High Commission was referred to, was John McCloy. The Baldwin Commission's work coupled with the changing political environment gave renewed hope to those campaigning to save the convicted war criminals from the hangman. Beginning in March and gaining full momentum in June 1949, Aschenauer and Fröschmann as well as many others flooded the Military Governor and then the High Commissioner with requests for clemency for the convicted men of Landsberg.

John J. McCloy and the War Criminals Problem

When McCloy replaced Clay in 1949 as the American representative in Germany, sixteen Nuremberg prisoners remained on death row at Landsberg prison. Included among these were all fourteen of those sentenced to death in the *Einsatzgruppen* case as well as Oswald Pohl, former head of the WVHA, the main economic office of the SS in charge of the administration of the concentration camps, and Franz Eirenschmalz a colleague

---

[61] Internal Route Slip, Headquarters, European Command, June 3, 1949, in NARA RG 338, JAD, WCB, General Administration Records 1942–1957, box 4, War Crimes 201 File vol. 4 folder, and memorandum, OMGUS to JA, June 10, 1949, in *ibid*, Landsberg, box 6, 201–1949 folder. See also, Schwartz, "McCloy and the Landsberg Cases," 434–436.

[62] Letter, George Dix to Weeber, March 31, 1949, D1/293, NL Wurm, LKA.

[63] Letter, Raymond Baldwin to Frederick Libby, April 14, 1949, D1/293, NL Wurm, LKA.

of Pohl's and defendant from the same Nuremberg trial, Case 4.[64] These sixteen men were referred to as the "red jackets" owing to the distinctive red jacket the condemned men wore while awaiting execution. McCloy was responsible for reviewing the cases of individuals tried at Nuremberg and not those convicted in the army's Dachau trials. Therefore all sixteen "red jackets" were under his jurisdiction whereas General Thomas Handy had sole responsibility for the army's cases whose number of death-row inmates was significantly higher.

McCloy's attitude toward the war criminals issue differed significantly from that of his predecessor who had adopted an unwaveringly hard-line. Like many in Washington, the new High Commissioner believed that a strong Germany and improved German-American relations could act as a bulwark to the expanding Soviet Union.[65] McCloy was under a tremendous amount of political pressure. Along with the endless stream of requests for clemency, German officials also pressured him to grant amnesty to war criminals including all those arrested, tried and convicted under CCL10, in other words, all the Nuremberg convicted.[66] Amnesty, German officials stated, should extend to those who were fifty-six or older or twenty-one or younger, those in poor health, those who were sentenced to ten years in prison or less, and for anyone convicted under *ex post facto* law.[67] Finally, they asked McCloy to establish a clemency board to review all sentences. In effect, the Germans wanted nothing less then the amnesty of all war criminals. These measures, the Germans concluded, would not only go a long way in improving relations between the two nations, but more importantly amnesty would have an important and lasting "moral effect... among the [German] population" who uniformly rejected the American judicial process as it applied to its citizens in the immediate post-war period.[68]

Like Clay before him and because no appellate court existed, McCloy had the "discretionary power and authority at any time to mitigate, reduce or otherwise alter the sentences (including death sentences) imposed by the Nuremberg Military Tribunals," but not the guilt or innocence of any defendant which was considered final.[69] According to High Commission policy, under no circumstance were issues of "amnesty, pardon, clemency,

[64] Cable from HICOG Frankfurt to US Secretary of State, October 5, 1949, in NARA RG 466, Office of the Executive Director, Security Segregated GR 1949–1955, box 28, 321.6 War Criminals folder.

[65] Schwartz, "McCloy and the Landsberg Cases," 436.

[66] Letter, German Federal Government to the High Commissioner, undated circa July–September 1949, B305/141/36–40 Deutsche Kriegsverurteilte im Landsberg 1949–1952, BA.

[67] *Ibid.*

[68] *Ibid.*

[69] Memorandum, Mortimer Kollender to McCloy, October 11, 1949, in NARA RG 466, GR 1949–1952, box 3, D(49) 271–292 folder.

parole, or release . . . [to] be delegated to the German authorities."[70] From the very beginning of his tenure, McCloy was not inclined to carry out the death sentences of the sixteen condemned men in Landsberg, but nor was he inclined to grant amnesty to any or all war criminals.[71] That said, he did realize that some solution to the war criminals problem was necessary, especially because such a broad spectrum of Germans, including the clergy, professionals, and officials of the Federal Republic, demanded amnesty.[72] Many Germans were of the opinion that even if justice had been served at Nuremberg, it was inhuman to make the condemned men wait any longer to have their sentences carried out.[73] As Bishop Wurm stressed to McCloy, "none of the prisoners knows whether or not today is the last day of his life" and, thus, "the severity of the death sentence is increased to an unheard of degree and is at variance with all feelings of decency."[74] McCloy vehemently disagreed with Wurm's interpretation of suffering, but, nonetheless, was persuaded that some course of action was necessary if relations between the former enemies were to improve. Thus, he instituted a system of time credits for good conduct for the Nuremberg convicted. The system allowed time off of a convicted man's sentence for good behavior at the rate of five days per month. The new formula led to the immediate release from prison of six of the Nuremberg convicted (almost all from the trials of the economic leaders). Their release gave the appearance that McCloy was particularly lenient toward the German economic elite.[75] Although McCloy's initiative of good time credits was no different than that granted to American citizens, it was the beginning of a slippery slope to freedom for the *Einsatzgruppen* defendants.

In the early months of McCloy's tenure, he thought a lot about a solution to the war criminals problem. One option was to "piggyback" on the

[70] Policy Directive for US High Commissioner, November 17, 1949, in NARA RG 466, GR 1949–1952, box 4, November D(49) 383–392 folder.

[71] McCloy told Neuhäusler, "I have not committed the United States to a program of wholesale commutation of sentences of war criminals." Letter, McCloy to Neuhäusler, January 16, 1951, D1/295, NL Wurm, LKA.

[72] Letter, Gebhard Müller to Adenauer, October 21, 1949, B120/395 Nürnbergerprozesse, BA.

[73] In early 1950, Konrad Adenauer wrote McCloy that "the death penalty in the Federal Republic of Germany was abolished. . . . Under these circumstances it would be felt by the German people as particularly harsh, if nearly five years after the end of the war executions were still carried out on German soil by the American occupation powers." Letter, Adenauer to McCloy, February 28, 1950, B305/142/14–15 Deutsche Kriegsverurteilte im Landsberg 1949–1952, BA.

[74] Letter, Wurm to McCloy, January 27, 1950, D1/295, NL Wurm, LKA.

[75] Press Release, HICOG, December 19, 1949, in *ibid.*, box 5. D(49) 461–493 folder, and memorandum, Handy, December 1949, NARA RG 238, Advisory Board on Clemency, Office of HICOG 1947–1950, Correspondence 1950, box 1, Indexes folder; and, Schwartz, "McCloy and the Landsberg Cases," 438–439.

army's new clemency program. In November 1949, the army had created the War Crimes Modification Board to review clemency requests for the Dachau cases. McCloy wrote to General Handy who was in charge of the Modification Board, indicating his desire to expand the jurisdiction of the War Crimes Board to include the Nuremberg defendants under his jurisdiction.[76] When the State Department learned of McCloy's plan, Dean Acheson strenuously opposed it, not wanting the State Department to be involved in or tainted by the controversial Malmédy trial. He also worried that to include the Nuremberg defendants in the army's clemency program, would only undermine the "legal basis and procedure" of the Pohl and Ohlendorf cases. He asked McCloy to reconsider.[77] McCloy acquiesced, but he insisted he be allowed to establish his own clemency commission to review Nuremberg cases. Obviously he had been giving the issue thought for quite sometime since he had told Cardinal Frings as early as December 1949, that "important lawyers would come from America to Germany, who would have the order to study the whole complex question [of war criminals] and prepare a practical solution."[78] The High Commissioner had explained that the "thorny" war criminals problem could not be resolved without an impartial review process, besides he told Acheson, "my own conscience is involved and though I am quite prepared to make ultimate decision and accept ultimate responsibility I require the help of such a group."[79] Acheson accepted McCloy's demands and in February 1950, McCloy established a board of final review for all the convictions and death sentences handed out by tribunals in the Subsequent Nuremberg Proceedings.[80]

The Advisory Board on Clemency or "Peck Panel," as it was called, consisted of three impartial individuals: David W. Peck the chairman of the panel and the Presiding Judge of the New York Supreme Court's Appellate Division, Conrad Snow, an assistant legal advisor in the State Department and Frederick A. Moran, the Chairman of the New York State Board of

[76] List and synopsis of correspondence between McCloy, Handy, and Colonel Gunn, undated, in NARA RG 338, JAD, WCB, Post-Trial Activities 1945–1949, box 15, Clippings and Correspondence re Review of Sentences folder.
[77] Telegram, Acheson to McCloy, February 8, 1950, RG 12.000, Drawer 24 WCT, box 2 folder A, John J. McCloy file, BBF, USHMM. See also, Schwartz, "McCloy and the Landsberg Cases," 439–440.
[78] Bericht, Bundesminister der Justiz, January 30, 1950, B305/141/203 Deutsche Kriegsverurteilte im Landsberg, 1949–1952, BA and Vermerk, February 14, 1950, B305/142/1-2 in *ibid.*
[79] Memorandum, McCloy to Acheson, February 17, 1950 in *ibid.*
[80] Memorandum, Acheson to McCloy, February 22, 1950, in NARA RG 466, Office of the Executive Director, Security Segregated GR 1949–1955, box 28, 321.6 War Criminals folder. The creation of the HICOG Advisory Board on Clemency caused great tensions among Landsberg inmates. Internal Route Slip, Headquarters European Command, July 25, 1950, in NARA RG 338, JAD, WCB, Records Relating to Landsberg, box 6, Lbg. 201 1950 folder.

Parole.[81] The three men were considered impartial in that none of them had any relationship whatsoever to the Nuremberg trials, nor had any of them publicly expressed any opinion about Nuremberg. The Peck Panel was a compromise solution, not intended to function as an appellate court, despite Peck's job as an appellate court judge in the United States. Rather, the panel's principal task was to make recommendations for sentence reductions, clemency, and commutations of death sentences for the Nuremberg convicted and thereby, McCloy hoped, "solve" the war criminals problem that now stood in the way of healthy German-American relations.[82] To make recommendations, the Panel had to review the judgments of the twelve trials, interview the war criminals personally, review their psychological profiles and family situations, and then find reasons for mitigating sentences. McCloy made it clear to the Panel that final decisions were his. He would use their recommendations as a basis for sentence modifications, but he had no obligation to abide by their recommendations.

The Advisory Board on Clemency began its work in the spring of 1950, when Frederick Moran went to Germany to carryout legwork for the panel, including reviewing the case files of some of the convicted war criminals.[83] While there, he personally interviewed all of the Nuremberg-Landsberg prisoners, investigated their personal histories, character, and backgrounds. Once this work was complete he returned to the U.S. to brief his colleagues on his findings. All three Board members returned to Germany in June to review cases. They officially began their work on July 11 in Munich.[84] For six weeks, the Board speedily, some might say carelessly, reviewed all petitions submitted by the war criminals, and there were a lot of them – Eduard Strauch alone submitted twenty-two petitions – reviewed all of the judgments of the twelve Nuremberg tribunals (nearly 3,300 pages), interviewed 105 of the petitioners personally, and heard oral arguments from as many as ninety attorneys.[85] The Panel was mandated to consider sentence disparities

[81] Memorandum, John Bross to Gerald Fowlie, May 18, 1950, in NARA RG 238, Advisory Board on Clemency, HICOG, Correspondence, box 2, Clemency Committee General folder; "Clemency Board Member Completes Preliminary Survey," Press Release No. 312, May 2, 1950 in *ibid* RG 466, John J. McCloy, Classified GR 1949–1952, box 13, D(50) 1273–1318 folder; and Besprechung, Bowie mit Aschenauer, April 1, 1950, B305/142/25, Deutsche Kriegsverurteilte im Landsberg 1949–1952, BA.

[82] Memorandum, Moran to Gerald Fowlie, Re:Neuro-psychiatric examinations, July 12, 1950, in NARA RG 238, Advisory Board on Clemency, HICOG, Correspondence and Other Records 1950, box 2, Clemency Committee-General folder.

[83] Report, Advisory Board on Clemency to McCloy, August 28, 1950, in RG 12.000, Einsatzgruppen Trial, Darmstadt, Clippings file, BBF, USHMM.

[84] *Ibid* and memorandum, Bross to Wolfe, May 16, 1950, in NARA RG 466, Security Classified Records, Arrest–German Criminal Code, box 6, Clemency Advisory Board General folder. See also, Schwartz, "McCloy and the Landsberg Cases," 442–443.

[85] Letter, Fowlie to Peck, Snow and Moran, July 24, 1950, in NARA RG 238 (WCR), Advisory Board on Clemency, HICOG, Correspondence and Other Records 1950, box 1, Research

among the convicted as well as the physical condition and family situation of defendants, in deciding who should and should not receive sentence reductions, clemency, and commutations of death sentences. What the group was not allowed to do was question the jurisdiction of the tribunals, matters of fact or of law, nor were any provisions made for involving former prosecutors in the review process, despite Benjamin Ferencz's offer to do so.[86] Rather their entire task was limited to issues of mitigation.[87]

Although the Board was limited in its scope of inquiry, it did give weight to the issues of the defense of superior orders and "situations analogous to combat conditions" as mitigating factors when considering those sentenced to death. But it simply refused to consider the issue of the long periods spent in confinement under sentence of death, the issue that most Germans were now routinely pointing to as a valid reason for pardon.[88] Even before the Advisory Board completed its review, Peck recommended that good conduct time should be increased from five to ten days per month. This was applied immediately and an additional eight convicted war criminals were released from prison including Frederick Flick, the head of the Flick Corporation, and the director of the IG Farben group, two important symbols of the Nuremberg proceedings.[89] On August 28, 1950, after six weeks of work, an admittedly short period of time to review 105 cases, the Peck Panel submitted its recommendations to McCloy.[90]

The Peck Panel's report strongly supported the Nuremberg principles of individual responsibility and justice, but it also recognized that the convicted

---

for the Board folder. Of the 105 petitioners, Rudolf Aschenauer represented five from the *Einsatzgruppen* case (Ohlendorf, Braune, Schubert, Ott, and Klingelhöfer). After sentencing, Strauch was transferred to Belgian authorities to stand trial for crimes he committed there. He was eventually returned to Landsberg to serve the remainder of his sentence. File note Case No. 9, August 3, 1949, RG 238, OCCWC, Correspondence 1947–1949, miscellaneous files, box 2, NM 70, Case 9 folder.

[86] In appellate courts prosecutors participate in the process. Ferencz was one of the only prosecutors still in Germany and had volunteered his services to the Peck Panel who turned him down. Staff Announcement No. 117, Establishment of Advisory Board on Clemency, July 18, 1950, in NARA RG 466, John J. McCloy, Classified GR 1949–1950, box 17, July 1950 DC50 1789–1812 folder. See also, Letter, Ferencz to Moran, August 1, 1950 and Letter, Gerald Fowlie to Ferencz, August 7, 1950 in *ibid*, box 2, Correspondence E213, August 1–September 20, 1950 folder.

[87] Letter, Fowlie to Peck, Snow and Moran, July 20, 1950 in *ibid*.

[88] Internal Route Slip, Headquarters, European Command, August 4, 1950, in NARA RG 338, JAD, WCB, Post Trial Activities 1945–1957, box 2, Clemency Files 1950 folder.

[89] Untitled article, *Die Neue Zeitung*, August 17, 1950, in *ibid* RG 238, Advisory Board on Clemency, Correspondence, box 1, Clipping File on Committee folder.

[90] Report, Advisory Board on Clemency to McCloy, August 28, 1950, 1, in RG 12, Einsatzgruppen Trial, Darmstadt, Clippings folder, BBF, USHMM. Unfortunately, no written record of the Board's work exists as no minutes were kept. Rules of Procedure in Clemency Board Hearings, July 22, 1950, in NARA RG 466, Prisons Division, GR, box 36, War Crimes Clemency Board Operational History folder.

TABLE 9. *Recommendations of the Advisory Board on Clemency (Peck Panel), August 28, 1950**

Defendant	Original Sentence	Recommendation
Blobel, Paul	Death	Death
Biberstein, Ernst	Death	15 years
Blume, Walter	Death	20 years
Braune, Werner	Death	Death
Haensch, Walter	Death	15 years
Klingelhöfer, Waldemar	Death	Death
Naumann, Erich	Death	Death
Ohlendorf, Otto	Death	Death
Ott, Adolf	Death	Death
Sandberger, Martin	Death	Death
Schubert, Heinz	Death	Time Served
Seibert, Willy	Death	Time Served
Steimle, Eugen	Death	15 years
Jost, Heinz	Life	10 years
Nosske, Gustav	Life	10 years
Radetzky, Waldemar von	20 years	Time served
Schulz, Erwin	20 years	10 years
Six, Franz	20 years	Time served
Fendler, Lothar	10 years	Time served
Rühl, Felix	10 years	Time served

* Report, Advisory Board on Clemency to McCloy, August 28, 1950, in RG 12, *Einsatzgruppen* Trial, Darmstadt, Clippings folder, BBF, USHMM. NB: Strauch had been delivered to the Belgians on June 24, 1948 to be tried for war crimes. He was found guilty and sentenced to death. Letter to Ferencz, June 17, 1949, RG 12.002.02.04 BBF, USHMM.

men were part of a larger Nazi "program" of criminality; and, each of the twelve trials represented a "segment" of this criminal and inhuman system.[91] The Panel expressed its dismay when it discovered that "the majority of the defendants still seem to feel that what they did was right." Too much charity toward the perpetrators, the report warned, "would be a mistake as it would undo what Nuremberg has accomplished."[92] Yet, in spite of their own warnings, the panel nonetheless found many reasons to recommend sentence reductions. Their mandate was, after all, to temper justice with "charity and generosity."[93] As such, they took into consideration every possible "mitigating circumstance," and what resulted were some

[91] *Ibid.*
[92] Peck Panel quoted in Bower, *Blind Eye*, 421.
[93] McCloy instructed them to be as charitable as possible. Rules of Procedure in Clemency Board Hearings, July 22, 1950, in NARA RG 466, Prisons Division, GR, box 36, War Crimes Clemency Board Operational History folder.

incredible recommendations for sentence reductions.[94] For instance, of the twenty *Einsatzgruppen* leaders sentenced to prison terms or death, the Peck Panel recommended sentence reductions for all, except seven, in some cases drastically.

The Advisory Board's recommendations to reduce and commute sentences of the *Einsatzgruppen* leadership was based on a number of factors, but the issue of "superior orders," which was continually promoted as a mitigating factor, was not one of them. The Board found that in the case of the *Einsatzgruppen* there was no credence to the claim that their tasks were military in nature. Just as the tribunal had found that their principal assignment was to execute the "political policy of genocide," so too did the Board and, therefore, superior orders could not be considered in mitigation in these cases.[95] Thus, the Board had to find other, more disingenuous reasons for mitigating the sentences of these men and to do so, in some cases; they extended their authority beyond its scope by considering the facts of the trial, even though they admittedly had no knowledge of them. For instance, in the case of Franz Six, the Board found that "the guilt of the defendant was not proved beyond a reasonable doubt," and that he was convicted based solely on the issue of his membership in a criminal organization, this despite the fact that they neither reviewed the trial transcript nor any of the evidence submitted by the prosecution in reaching their decision. The Board was impressed with Six's personality; they found he made a "very favorable impression" in their discussions with him (it will be recalled that Six was a university professor). He was well spoken and prison officials believed if he were to be released from Landsberg he would make an "excellent" citizen.[96] On this basis, and without probing very deeply into the case, the Board recommended that Six's sentence of twenty years, be reduced to time served.[97] The Board was willing to use just about any reason for mitigation as seen in the case of Gustav Nosske. They found that, although he was certainly involved in a large number of murders, he had taken personal risk when he refused to execute *Mishlinge* in Dusseldorf upon his return from the Soviet Union in 1943. Therefore, they concluded that his sentence of life imprisonment should be reduced to ten years as he had demonstrated courage, at least once, against the Reich's murderous policies.[98] The recommendation

[94] *Ibid.*

[95] Report, Peck Panel, Case No. 9, circa September 1950, in NARA RG 466, Prisons Division, War Criminal Case Files, box 4, Case 9 folder.

[96] Recommendations for Six, Advisory Board on Clemency part II, September 1, 1950, in NARA RG 466, Prison Division, box 6, Report of the HICOG Advisory Board on Clemency Part II folder.

[97] *Ibid.*

[98] Recommendations for Nosske, Advisory Board on Clemency, Einsatzgruppen, July 1950, in NARA RG 466, Administration of Justice Division, Classified Records 1947–1954, box 1, War Criminals folder.

that Walter Blume's sentence of death be commuted to twenty years shows clearly how ridiculous the grounds were for mitigation. In deciding Braune's case the Board noted that they "simply" took the convicted war criminal's word as fact instead of investigating his case further. When Braune told the Board members that he had always objected to the *Führerbefehl*, but had to carry it out, they believed him. In their view, unlike in the view of the tribunal that convicted him, a thought was enough of a mitigating factor to recommend sparing his life, illustrating just how far removed from the war the Americans had become.[99]

Although the Advisory Board submitted its report to McCloy in late August 1950, the High Commissioner did not make any decision regarding their recommendations until January 1951. The Korean War had broken out in June and McCloy was duly convinced that now, more than ever, the U.S. needed Germany as an ally against the bourgeoning communist threat.[100] German opposition groups also took advantage of the changing political situation using the war criminals issue as a *quid pro quo* for the rearmament of Germany as protection against communism in Europe.[101] In fact, by late 1950 most Germans, even those who had been victims of Nazism, viewed the American war crimes trials as an attack on German sovereignty and many Germans wrote the High Commissioner demanding clemency for those convicted by U.S. tribunals and still incarcerated. Even Konrad Adenauer, the new German chancellor, personally requested that McCloy commute all pending death sentences.[102] It was under tremendous pressure, including threats of death and political upheaval, that McCloy considered the Advisory Board's recommendations. Not wanting to execute anyone over the Christmas holiday, McCloy waited until January 31, 1951, to announce his decisions regarding sentence modifications.

By all accounts, the Advisory Board's recommendations were incredibly merciful, perhaps even too much so. McCloy's closest legal advisor, Robert Bowie, expressed grave concerns about the "excessive" nature of forty-six of the ninety-three sentence recommendations worrying that they simply were not warranted, especially since the Peck Panel had not consulted any of the evidence used to convict these men when coming to their decisions.[103] McCloy was under a tremendous amount of pressure to resolve the irresolvable and "make a decision that would satisfy the sense of justice among nations with very different understandings and experiences of World

---

[99] Recommendations for Blume, *ibid.*

[100] Schwartz, "McCloy and the Landsberg Cases," 444–445.

[101] *Ibid.*

[102] *Ibid.*

[103] Memorandum, Bowie to McCloy, October 31, 1950, in NARA RG 466, Office of the Executive Director, Security Segregated GR 1949–1955, box 28, 321.6 War Criminals folder.

War II."[104] Weighing his options carefully, McCloy opted for leniency, taking "into account every factor which could justify clemency . . . in favor of the convicted" men.[105] What resulted was the commutation of eleven of the sixteen death sentences and the reduction of sentences of nearly all of those convicted and sentenced to prison terms in the Nuremberg trials. Only five men did not have their death sentences commuted, four from the *Einsatzgruppen* trial including Ohlendorf, Blobel, Braune, and Naumann as well as Oswald Pohl. Their crimes were judged to be so heinous, even the High Commissioner admitted in his press release on the subject, that "clemency [was] out of reason."[106] As far as McCloy was concerned, he had to be fair, not only to the defendants, but to the "concepts of law and justice," and therefore these five men must "discharge their debt to society," with their lives.[107] When Ohlendorf learned of McCloy's decision to carry out his death sentence, he was outraged. As far as the former leader of *Einsatzgruppe* D was concerned, McCloy's decision was an injustice. Echoing future complaints by war criminals, Ohlendorf reasoned that thousands of members of the *Einsatzgruppen* had contributed to the murders in the occupied Soviet Union, not just the fourteen who were sentenced to death. More important for his own future, he and three of his colleagues were to be the only ones to pay for the crimes of the *Einsatzgruppen* with their lives. Ohlendorf believed that McCloy's decision would make him a "martyr."[108] He was wrong. As Table 10 shows, McCloy showed greater leniency than the Peck Panel for the *Einsatzgruppen* leaders. Overall, the High Commissioner was satisfied with the results of the commutations, but whether or not his actions were the result of political expediency or a moral position was a matter of debate among the participants.[109] Benjamin Ferencz believed the latter pointing to a letter McCloy had sent him years after the fact. In it, McCloy seemed to indicate some misgivings about his decisions, writing that "if I had all the facts I now have, I might have reached a more just result," in the commutation of sentences for war criminals.[110] Telford Taylor was much less forgiving, noting that McCloy's decisions were "the embodiment of political expediency."[111] Whether or not he was motivated by politics, from today's perspective, McCloy's decisions seem remarkably lenient.

---

[104] Schwartz, "McCloy and the Landsberg Cases," 452.
[105] Statements Regarding John McCloy's Final Decisions on Requests for Clemency for War Criminals Convicted at Nuremberg, January 31, 1951, Paris Storey File, box 179, Subject file, Foreign Affairs, HST.
[106] *Ibid.*
[107] Letter, McCloy to Wurm, February 14, 1951, D1/295, NL Wurm, LKA.
[108] Ohlendorf cited in Hilberg, *Destruction*, 1079–1080 and Bower, *Blind Eye*, 422.
[109] Bloxham, *Genocide on Trial*, 162–163.
[110] Letter, McCloy to Ferencz, April 10, 1980, RG 12, John J. McCloy File, Drawer 24, box 2, BBF, USHMM.
[111] Taylor quoted in Bloxham, *Genocide on Trial*, 162.

TABLE 10. *Recommendations of the Advisory Board on Clemency and John McCloy's Decisions**

Defendant	Original Sentence	Advisory Board	McCloy
Blobel, Paul	Death	Death	Death
Biberstein, Ernst	Death	15 years	Life
Blume, Walter	Death	20 years	25 years
Braune, Werner	Death	Death	Death
Haensch, Walter	Death	15 years	15 years
Klingelhöfer, Waldemar	Death	Death	Life
Naumann, Erich	Death	Death	Death
Ohlendorf, Otto	Death	Death	Death
Ott, Adolf	Death	Death	Life
Sandberger, Martin	Death	Death	Life
Schubert, Heinz	Death	Time served	10 years
Seibert, Willy	Death	Time served	15 years
Steimle, Eugen	Death	15 years	20 years
Jost, Heinz	Life	10 years	10 years
Nosske, Gustav	Life	10 years	10 years
Radetzky, Waldemar von	20 years	Time served	Time served
Schulz, Erwin	20 years	10 years	15 years
Six, Franz	20 years	Time served	10 years
Fendler, Lothar	10 years	Time served	8 years
Rühl, Felix	10 years	Time served	Time served

* Series C, Final Decisions Regarding Requests for Clemency, undated, NARA R6 466, Classified GR 1949–1952, box 24, D(51) 126 War Crimes folder.

Reaction to Sentence Revisions

Contemporary reactions to McCloy's sentence reductions were mixed. Former Nuremberg participants heavily criticized the High Commissioner for his "sweeping" clemency program, claiming the decisions were not only misguided, but also overly generous. Many found them simply incomprehensible given the nature of the crimes.[112] Whereas most Germans, not surprisingly, reacted favorably to his decisions, especially Konrad Adenauer who praised the High Commissioner's even handedness and "objective" decisions in this matter.[113] But, as had been the case earlier, it was not long before German

[112] For example, Taylor, "The Nazis Go Free. Justice and Mercy or Misguided Expediency?" *The Nation*, February 24, 1951, in NARA RG 466, GR 1949–1952, box 12, 321.6 folder; Letter, Hans Weigert to McCloy, March 5, 1951 in *ibid*; and Letter from Hans Frohlich, March 2, 1951 in *ibid*.
[113] Summary of German editorials, February 1, 1951, in NARA RG 466, GR 1949–1952, box 24, D(51) 94–134 folder; Letter from Karl Hartenstein, Council of the Evangelical Church of Germany, February 2, 1951; Letter, McCloy to Peck, February 5, 1951; memorandum, Saliger to Settel, re: Press Reaction to Publication of Landsberg Decisions,

nationalists renewed their public and vociferous lobbying for the commutation of death sentences for the remaining five Landsberg red jackets.[114] Between January 31 (when the sentence reductions were announced) and March 9, 1951, the High Commissioner received more than 1,000 letters on the issue. Most of the writers complained that further sentence reductions were necessary and demanded that the five remaining red jackets be pardoned.[115] Propaganda directed at the Americans also proliferated. One pamphlet referred to the case of Oswald Pohl as "Germany's 'Dreyfus Affair,'" and Pohl himself wrote an open letter titled, "I Accuse!"[116] Even McCloy's children and wife were threatened by an unidentified individual should he carry out the remaining death sentences.[117]

In spite of all the pressure and opposition, and sincerely hoping to end the war criminals issue once and for all, McCloy announced that the five remaining red jackets would be executed on February 16, 1951.[118] Germans opposed to McCloy's decision knew time was running out for the condemned men. In order to have the executions stayed as soon as possible, the Office for the Legal Protection of War Criminals or *Zentrale Rechtsschutzstelle* (founded in 1949 as part of the Federal Republic's Justice Department and headed by Hans Gawlik the former attorney for Erich Naumann) hired an American attorney, Warren Magee, paid for by the Bonn government, to work in the U.S. on behalf of the five condemned men. Magee was not a random choice. As one of only two Americans to serve as defense counsel at the NMT – he was Ernst von Weizsäcker's attorney in the Ministries case – he knew the issues intimately. He immediately filed for writs of habeas corpus with the U.S. Supreme Court on February 14, 1951, only

February 5, 1951, all in *ibid*. The only German newspaper to attack the Landsberg decisions was *Christ und Welt*, whose editors had been extremely active in reporting favorable attitudes toward the Landsberg prisoners. Public reaction was not nearly so favorable in the United States, where many Americans viewed McCloy's clemency program as nothing more than "political expediency." McCloy's sentence reductions particularly angered those who had participated in the Nuremberg trials. See Memorandum, Secretary of State to McCloy, February 6, 1951, in *ibid*, box 24, D(51) 55-93B folder and John J. McCloy interview with Ferencz, April 24, 1984, USHMM, RG 12 BBF, Drawer 24, WCT, box 2, McCloy Interview folder.

[114] For example, see the letter from Wurm to McCloy, February 10, 1951, in NARA RG 466, GR 1949–1952, box 24, D(51) 126 War Crimes folder; Letter, Wurm to McCloy, February 12, 1951, D1/295, NL Wurm, LKA; Letter, Amtsstelles des Evangelical Anstaltspfarrers, Landsberg, to Landesbischof Meiser, February 5, 1951, in *ibid*; and, Letter, Wurm to Neuhäusler, in *ibid*.

[115] Analysis of Letters on the Landsberg Decisions, March 9, 1951, in NARA RG 466, GR 1949–1952, box 24, 126 War Crimes folder.

[116] "Germany's 'Dreyfus Affair'" and "I Accuse!" February 23, 1951 in *ibid*, WCB, General Administration Records, box 4, War Crimes 201 folder.

[117] Telegram, McCloy to Department of State, March 5, 1951, in *ibid*, Classified GR 1949–1952, box 25, D(51) 275- D(51) 296 folder.

[118] Letter, McCloy to Handy, February 13, 1951, in *ibid*, box 25, D(51) 178-D(51) 224a folder.

two days before the five men were to be executed; a common practice in the United States when all avenues of appeal have been exhausted.[119] Appeals to the U.S. Supreme Court almost always come with a stay of execution, but McCloy refused to issue one, despite an eleventh hour appeal from Konrad Adenauer who personally asked the High Commissioner to wait until all of the legal issues had been resolved before executing the five convicted war criminals.[120] Having agonized over his decisions he was determined not to renege on his goal of resolving the war criminals problem once and for all, even if it flew in the face of standard operating procedure. To execute these five men, he believed, would put the matter to rest. But, hours before the red jackets were to be hanged, a message arrived from Secretary of State Dean Acheson warning that he "should not proceed with executions until further advised."[121] Acheson's decision to stay the executions set in motion a renewed and intense campaign to free the condemned men.

After Acheson's announcement, the atmosphere surrounding the pending execution of the condemned war criminals became incredibly charged, causing a frenzy of activity by both the Germans and Americans.[122] The tension can easily be compared to that of a contemporary high-profile (American) death-row case, where a legal team uses every means at its disposal to fight for an inmate's life. As the date of execution approaches, the tension mounted. On the legal front Warren Magee, the American attorney hired to help the condemned Landsberg prisoners, filed petitions with the Supreme Court less than forty-eight hours before their scheduled execution. The petitions were turned down for lack of jurisdiction, but Magee immediately appealed the decision. The American lawyer soon realized he had an up-hill battle when, much to his surprise, the U.S. Solicitor General, the Assistant Solicitor General, the Judge Advocate General of the Army, and legal counsel for the State Department all showed up at the Court of Appeals to oppose his motion.[123] Such high profile figures made it clear to Magee that the Americans were prepared to carry out the executions of the condemned men

[119] According to the Geneva Convention of August 12, 1949, prisoners of war who are sentenced to death are automatically entitled to writs of habeas corpus. Aschenauer tried to apply this to the Landsberg condemned. Letter, Aschenauer to Magee, February 20, 1951, B305/137, Deutsche Kriegsverurteilte im Landsberg 1951–1952, BA, and Letter, Frederick Wiehl to Krekeller, German General Consul, February 1951, in *ibid.*

[120] Letter, Adenauer to McCloy, February 13, 1951, B305/147 Deutsche Kriegsverurteilte im Landsberg, Einzelfälle, 1949–1950, BA.

[121] Memorandum, Acheson to McCloy, February 15, 1951, in NARA RG 466, GR 1949–1952, box 25, D(51) 178-D(51) 224a folder.

[122] On February 16, members of the Württemberg-Baden Landtag got into a heated row over the issue, when Heinz Burneleit of the DVP stood up and asserted that to execute the Landsberg prisoners would constitute "legalized murder." The SPD and CDU members stormed out in protest. Memorandum, Jim Kind to McCloy, February 16, 1951, in *ibid*, box 24, D(51) 126 War Crimes folder.

[123] Letter, Magee to Hellmut Becker, March 1, 1951, B305/137, Deutsche Kriegsverurteilte im Landsberg 1951–1952, BA.

and it seemed, the sooner the better. Germans opposed to the executions were equally as determined not to allow this to happen.

Letters requesting clemency and stays of execution for the condemned men began to pour into McCloy's office.[124] Interestingly, most of the letters he received dealt with Oswald Pohl's case. A lesser number concerned the cases of Werner Braune and Erich Naumann. Ohlendorf had some support, although appeals in his behalf were based mostly on his personality and not the general "unfairness" of McCloy's clemency decision. Oddly, no one petitioned the High Commissioner on behalf of Paul Blobel who American officials surmised was "friendless."[125] The majority of the letters received by the High Commissioner's office were "strikingly similar" in content and tone, leading American officials to conclude that while it was "commendable" that Germans were "taking advantage of the democratic privilege of expressing their views on controversial issues," they were not representative of the German population at large, but rather reflected the opinion of a certain segment of the population – the right and far right who persisted in believing that "the Landsberg inmates [were] victims of persecution and not criminals."[126] Despite a tremendous amount of pressure, McCloy refused to budge on the five remaining death cases. He firmly believed that to commute these death sentences would not only "further undermine the moral and legal principles established at the Nuremberg Trials," but that to do so would also "strike another blow at the prospects for a democratic Germany, provide the communists with a powerful propaganda weapon to use against us and make a mockery of American standards of justice and law."[127]

Those who supported the condemned men still held out hope that they could persuade the Americans to grant pardons, clemency, or reduce sentences. To this end, Magee filed appeal after appeal in courts in the U.S. hoping for a retrial for the condemned men. Many letters were written to the High Commissioner, including a petition for a blanket pardon signed by nearly 610,000 people.[128] Rudolf Aschenauer, still working for the Landsberg prisoners, filed several additional requests for clemency for Ohlendorf,

---

[124] Summary of Clemency Requests, February 20, 1951, in NARA RG 338, JAD, Post-Trial Activities, box 3, General Clemency folder. See also telegram, to Klaus Kuntze, "Bitte um Hinrichtungsstop Landsberg," unnamed sender, "Hinrichtungsbegruendung bodenlos," and telegram from unnamed sender, "Gerechtigkeit wird zum mord," all sent February 15, 1951, in *ibid*, WCB, Records Relating to Landsberg, box 6, Landsberg 201 folder.

[125] Letter, B. Rintels, Chief, Administration of Justice Division, to John Raymond, March 16, 1951, in *ibid* RG 466, GR 1949–1952, box 12, 321.6 folder.

[126] Analysis of Letters on the Landsberg Decisions, March 19, 1951 in *ibid*, Office of the Executive Director, Security Segregated GR 1949–1955, box 28, 321.6 folder.

[127] Telegram, McCloy to Secretary of State, March 22, 1951, in *ibid*, box 12, 321.6 folder.

[128] Letter, Libby to Princess Isenburg, June 9, 1951, D1/303, NL Wurm, LKA, and Letter to the editor of the *Washington Post* from Libby, June 4, 1951, in *ibid*.

Braune, Naumann, and Blobel.[129] With each failure the atmosphere surrounding the executions became more charged and the efforts of those involved more desperate. When the U.S. Supreme Court denied Magee's request for certiorari on May 22 and McCloy lifted the stay of execution ordering the commander of Landsberg prison to carry out the death sentences on May 25, hope quickly faded.[130]

Magee acted quickly. On May 23, he sought a "declaratory judgment" on the Bonn constitutional provision that prohibited capital punishment in Germany, as well as requesting a permanent injunction against executions.[131] Another stay of execution was granted when a sympathetic Washington judge agreed to hear arguments. The condemned men had a five-day reprieve to convince the American judge of the merits of their appeal.[132] On May 28, the day before the executions were to take place, Federal District Court Judge Walter M. Bastian extended the stay until 4 A.M., June 5, to give counsel for the condemned men time to file an appeal if one should prove necessary.[133] On May 29, Bastian dismissed Magee's motions noting that American courts were not the right place to consider issues of jurisdiction and German law.[134] Magee appealed immediately but for naught. On June 4, the United States Court of Appeal denied any further extension of the stay, affirming the lower court's decision.[135] The final blow to the defense came later that day, when the Chief Justice of the Supreme Court, Fred Vinson, denied a further stay of execution thereby shutting down the possibility of all future appeals, and assuring that the executions would take place.[136] With their legal channels exhausted, and virtually no possibility of an additional stay, time had run

---

[129] For example see Letter, Magee to Gawlik, April 6, 1951 and Letter, Gawlik to Magee, April 12, 1951, B305/137, Deutsche Kriegsverurteilte im Landsberg 1951–1952, BA and memorandum, Rintels to Bowie, May 11, 1951, in NARA RG 466, Prisons Division, Petitions for Clemency for War Criminals, box 24, Ohlendorf folder.

[130] Letter, McCloy to Handy, May 22, 1951 in *ibid* RG 338, JAD, WCB, Post Trial Activities 1945–1957, box 13, Executions of War Criminals June 1951 folder.

[131] Memorandum, Acheson to McCloy, May 23, 1951 in *ibid*, Security Segregated Records 1945–1957, box 10, War Criminals Trials 1951 folder.

[132] "DC Judge Save 7 Nazis," *Times Herald*, May 25, 1951, in *ibid*; record of conversation between Colonel Raymond and Mr. Hulse, HICOG, May 24, 1951, in *ibid*, Classified GR 1949–1952, box 24, D(51) 126 War Crimes folder; and, memorandum for the Record, by Handy, May 25, 1951, in *ibid* RG 338, JAD, WCB, Post-trial Activities 1945–1957, box 13, Executions of War Criminals June 1951 folder.

[133] Letter, Magee to Gawlik, May 28, 1951, B305/137, Deutsche Kriegsverurteilte im Landsberg 1951–1952, BA, and Letter, Magee to Gawlik, May 29, 1951, in *ibid*.

[134] Bastian quoted in "Court Rejects Plea for Nazis," *Stars and Stripes*, May 30, 1951, in NARA RG 338, JAD, WCB, Post-Trial Activities 1945–1957, box 15, Clippings folder.

[135] Telegraph, Acheson to McCloy, June 4, 1951, in *ibid* RG 466, GR 1949–1952, box 24, D(51) 126, War Crimes folder.

[136] Telegram, Magee to Gawlik, June 5 highlights the futility of the situation, B305/138, Deutsche Kriegsverurteilte im Landsberg, BA. See also Letter, Magee to Gawlik, June 8, 1951, in which he explains in detail the events from May 29 to June 7, B305/137, *ibid*.

out for the condemned men. Even Magee said he "did not know what more he could do to keep . . . [the five Landsberg prisoners] from the gallows."[137] On June 5, under the advice of Acheson, McCloy ordered that the death sentences of the five Landsberg prisoners be carried out expeditiously.[138] This time the five red jackets would not escape the hangman. At McCloy's request, preparations were made at Landsberg prison for the executions, which would take place within forty-eight hours.[139]

The night before the five men were to be hanged, their wives visited them for the last time.[140] According to the prison records, the condemned men were calm and appeared resigned to their fate, a truly ironic observation for men who had said the same of their victims years earlier.[141] After they had said their goodbyes to their wives, the five condemned men were hanged in the courtyard at Landsberg prison, in alphabetical order by last name, between midnight and 1:43 A.M. on June 7, 1951.[142] Blobel was executed first, just after midnight, followed twenty minutes later by Braune, then Naumann, Ohlendorf, and Pohl.[143] Blobel and Braune went to their deaths proclaiming their innocence, whereas Ohlendorf called for the reconciliation of his people, and a change in direction for Germany.[144] Naumann simply said, the "time will come in which it will be shown whether (sic) my execution has been justified or not. Into Your hands, Lord, I deliver my soul."[145] Reportedly, his wife suffered a heart attack after his execution.[146] The men were buried immediately in unmarked graves so as to prevent any show of martyrdom in the future, although at some point later, Ohlendorf's remains were moved to his family grave.

Needless to say, reactions to the Landsberg executions were mixed. Some Germans called the four year wait the prisoners endured "a crime against

---

[137] Magee quoted in transcription of telephone conversation between McCloy and Handy, June 5, 1951, in NARA RG 338, JAD, WCB, Post-Trial Activities 1945–1957, box 13, Executions of War Criminals June 1951 folder.

[138] Letter, McCloy to Handy, June 5, 1951, in *ibid* RG 466, Prisons Division, Security Segregated Records 1945–1957, box 12, WCT Landsberg and Dachau Cases B-13 folder and cable from Acheson to McCloy, June 4–5, 1951, in *ibid*, box 11, Landsberg Prison Cables folder.

[139] Report of Dr. Spengler, Landsberg Prison, June 6–7, 1951, B305/137, Deutsche Kriegsverurteilte im Landsberg 1951–1952, BA.

[140] *Ibid.*

[141] Reportedly Naumann said, "Ich bin zu sterben bereit (I am ready to die)." Braune expressed concern for his wife and Ohlendorf was typically philosophical about his fate. There is no record of Blobel's last hours. *Ibid.*

[142] Report of Execution of War Criminals, June 8, 1951, in NARA RG 466, Administration of Justice Division, Execution of War Criminals on June 8, 1951, box 1, F-133 folder.

[143] *Ibid.*

[144] Last words of Ohlendorf, Braune, Naumann and Blobel, June 7, 1951, in *ibid.*

[145] Last words of Erich Naumann, June 7, 1951, in *ibid.*

[146] "7 Nazi War Criminals Hanged," untitled newspaper clipping, June 8, 1951, in RG 12.000, Einsatzgruppen Trial, Darmsstadt, Clippings, BBF, USHMM.

TABLE 11. *Sentence Modifications of the Einsatzgruppen Leaders between 1948 and 1958**

Name	Original Sentence	January 31, 1951 Sentence	Subsequent Actions
Biberstein, Ernst	Death	Life	Paroled February 1958
Blobel, Paul	Death	Death	Hanged June 7, 1951
Blume, Walter	Death	25 years	Paroled March 1955
Braune, Werner	Death	Death	Hanged June 7, 1951
Fendler, Lothar	10 years	8 years	Time served, released March 1951
Haensch, Walter	Death	15 years	Time served, released August 1955
Jost, Heinz	Life	10 years	Paroled January 1952
Klingelhöfer, W.	Death	Life	Paroled December 1956
Naumann, Erich	Death	Death	Hanged June 7, 1951
Nosske, Gustav	Life	10 years	Sentence commuted December 1951
Ohlendorf, Otto	Death	Death	Hanged June 7, 1951
Ott, Adolf	Death	Life	Paroled, May 1958
Radetzky, W. von	20 years	Time served	Released January 1951
Rühl, Felix	10 years	Time served	Released January 1951
Sandberger, Martin	Death	Life	Paroled February 1958
Schubert, Heinz	Death	10 years	Sentence commuted December 1951
Schulz, Erwin	20 years	15 years	Paroled January 1954
Seibert, Willy	Death	15 years	Paroled May 1954
Six, Alfred	20 years	10 years	Time served, released October 1952
Steimle, Eugene	Death	20 years	Paroled June 1954

* See, Prison Records of the convicted men. NARA RG 466, Prisons Division, Administration and Medical Records; Good Conduct Time Release Order of Walter Haensch, August 26, 1955, in *ibid*, box 4, Haensch folder; Telegram from McCloy, January 11, 1952 in *ibid*, Security Segregated Records 1949–1955, box 28, 321.6 War Criminals folder; Parole Supervisor Reports, April 22–25, 1955, in *ibid*, RG 338, JAD, WCB, Post-Trial Activities 1945–1957, box 6, U.S. Parole Officer Summaries folder; Letter, Deforest Barton, Parole Supervisor, to the Chairman of the Mixed Board, July 17, 1957, B305/808, Eugen Steimle, BA; Supplemental Information, Sandberger, undated 1958, B305/785, Martin Sandberger, BA; Personenliche Beobactungen, Haensch, undated, B305/716, Walter Haensch, BA; and, Application for Parole and Clemency of Klingelhöfer, December 13, 1956, B305/837, Sitzungen des Ausschusses 1956, BA.

humanity" and others acknowledged that McCloy did everything humanly possible to temper justice with mercy.[147] With the execution of the Landsberg prisoners, the issue of sustained punishment lost much of its force, except with the most committed German nationalists who remained hopeful that one day the Americans would pardon all of the remaining war

[147] For initial reactions to the executions, see "First German Press Comments on Landsberg Executions," June 8, 1951, in NARA RG 466, GR 1949–1952, box 12, 321.6 folder. For an analysis of British, French, and American reactions, see Schwartz, "McCloy and the Landsberg Cases," 449–452.

criminals at Landsberg prison. McCloy had never intended the war criminals issue to become political, but this is precisely what occurred in the years that followed. His clemency program, as one historian has noted, "set in motion a process" whereby between June 7, 1951, and May 9, 1958, all of the remaining Landsberg prisoners were released, including the remainder of the *Einsatzgruppen* leaders, to "appease Germany" and maintain good relations.[148]

1951–1958

Although McCloy did not grant clemency to the *Einsatzgruppen* leaders or any other Landsberg prisoners after January 31, 1951, he did implement a Christmas amnesty program in December 1951 and again in 1952 in which Gustav Nosske and Heinz Schubert, among others, were released after having their sentences commuted to time served.[149] After McCloy left Germany, the new High Commissioner James B. Conant, further appeased the Germans. In accordance with Article 6 of the *Grundgesetz* and its agreements concerning a solution to the war criminals problem, on August 31, 1953, Conant approved the creation of an Interim Mixed Parole and Clemency Board.[150] The Interim Board included one representative each from Britain, France, and the United States and two representatives from Germany.[151] While the Interim Board was forbidden from questioning the fairness of the Nuremberg tribunals that had tried the Landsberg prisoners, they could consider age, health, employment opportunities, and the condition of the prisoners family when determining issues of clemency and parole, a fairly good indication that the Americans were no longer serious about punishing former Nazis for their crimes.[152] Between 1953 and 1955, the Interim Board granted parole or clemency to twenty-four Nuremberg defendants including four from the *Einsatzgruppen* case, Erwin Schulz, Willy Seibert, and Eugen

[148] Schwartz, "McCloy and the Landsberg Cases," 453. Mendelsohn, "War Crimes and Clemency," 253 agrees.

[149] Letter, Ferencz to Taylor, December 17, 1951, RG 12, Drawer 11, Biographical Material, box 1, Correspondence 1945–1955 folder, BBF, USHMM; and, memorandum, re: Terms of 1951 Christmas Clemency, to Hagan, October 28, 1952, in NARA RG 466, Prison Division, box 6.

[150] Letter, Gawlik to Heckel, July 2, 1955, B305/134, Deutsche Kriegsverurteilte im Landsberg, BA.

[151] Edwin Plitt was the U.S. member and later Spencer Phenix, Gustave Laroque was the French member, and Edward Jackson the British member. Hellmuth von Weber, Emil Lersch and Gottfried Kuhnt were the German members. The mixed Board began its work on August 11, 1955. See Vermerk, B305/758, Adolf Ott, BA; and, Vermerk, "Kriegsverurteilte in der Bundesrepublik," B305/53, Bereinigung des Kriegsgefangenenproblems – Gemischte deutsche – alliierte Ausschusse zu Überprüfung der Urteile, BA.

[152] Mendelsohn, "War Crimes and Clemency," 253.

Steimle released in 1954, and Walter Blume who was paroled in March 1955.[153]

When Germany gained full sovereignty in 1955, the Interim Board became a permanent fixture and was renamed the Mixed Clemency and Parole Board or Mixed Board for short.[154] The new body reviewed the clemency and parole applications of the remaining Landsberg prisoners, of which there were only seven from the Nuremberg trials left in prison.[155] Like its predecessors, the Mixed Board found a variety of reasons to release prisoners.[156] Between 1955 and 1958, the Mixed Board emptied Landsberg prison, one by one, of the remaining war criminals.[157] May 9, 1958, marked the end of the war criminals "problem" in Germany. That day, the three remaining *Einsatzgruppen* defendants, Ernst Biberstein, Adolf Ott, and Martin Sandberger, were released back into German society to live out their lives in relative peace and security.[158] It would now be up to Germans to plan and organize their own reckoning with their past.[159]

[153] *Ibid.*, 253–254.

[154] Foreign Service Despatch, U.S. Embassy Bonn, re: Composition of Mixed Board on War Criminals in Western Allied Custody, September 16, 1955, in NARA RG 466, Office of the Executive Director, Security Segregated GR 1949–1955, box 164, 321.6 folder.

[155] Mendelsohn, "War Crimes and Clemency," 252–254.

[156] Letter, Gawlik to Heckel, July 2, 1955, B305/134, Deutsche Kriegsverurteilte im Landsberg, BA; and, Schwartz, "McCloy and the Landsberg Cases," 453.

[157] Letter, Adenauer to August Fischer, Präsidenten des Heimkehrer, May 23, 1957, B305/134, Deutsche Kriegsverurteilte im Landsberg, BA and Aufzeichnung (report number 204/515-12/1957), June 28, 1957, B305/53, Bereinigung des Kriegsgefangenenproblems – Germischte deutsche – alliierte Ausschusse zu Überprüfung der Urteile, BA.

[158] The German Foreign Office filed Ott, Biberstein and Sandberger's requests for parole in 1958. Letter, Hardy Lee, Legal Officer American Embassy, Bonn, to the mixed Board, February 20, 1958, B305/758, Ott, BA, and Letter, Deforest Barton, Parole Officer, to Mixed Board, February 12, 1958, in *ibid.*

[159] For instance, Steimle lived in Württemberg and worked in an Protestant boys' school as a teacher of modern languages from 1955 until he retired. Statement of Heinrich Gutbrod, Sponsor of Steimle, May 13, 1957, B305/808, Eugen Steimle, BA and Letter, Steimle to Paul Gernert, March 19, 1955, in *ibid.* According to Klee, *Persilscheine und falsche passe*, 8, Steimle also taught history. Steimle died October 9, 1987, in Wilhelmsdorf. Blume worked as a lawyer for a real estate firm and was very bitter about his treatment as a war criminal. Report of Parole Officer on Blume, April 22, 1955, in NARA RG 338, JAD, WCB, Post-Trial Activities 1945–1957, box 6, US Parole Officers summaries folder. Seibert worked at a brokerage firm in Bremen. Report of Parole Officer on Seibert, April 25, 1955 in *ibid.*

Conclusion

The trial of Otto Ohlendorf and twenty-one other leaders of the *Einsatzgruppen* at Nuremberg, in 1947, has been described as "the biggest murder trial in history." Although apt, this assessment was perhaps an understatement, not in the sense of the number of victims or defendants, but rather in terms of the significance of the trial. The systematic slaughter of more than 1 million human beings represented a crime of such unprecedented brutality, that even the presiding judge had trouble comprehending its magnitude. In some ways, the *Einsatzgruppen* trial was itself nearly as novel as the crime with which the defendants were charged. One year earlier, Hermann Göring, Rudolf Hess, and the other former leaders of the Nazi regime had occupied the very same dock charged with war crimes, but never before had defendants been called to answer for crimes associated with genocide, an offense so abhorrent that the term "genocide" had only been coined three years earlier to describe it.[1] The significance of the *Einsatzgruppen* trial has been lost on subsequent generations numbed to the phenomenon of mass murder by genocides in Cambodia, Rwanda, Bosnia, and now Darfur. But, at the time the trial was held, the world was shocked and simply horrified by the crimes these men committed. Those who would find fault with the way the case was handled, however, would do well to remember that like so many of the other Subsequent Nuremberg Proceedings, the prosecutors and judges alike had entered uncharted legal territory, the traversing of which presented manifold problems, some of which were overcome, some of which were not. It is with shedding light on these difficulties, then, as well as with explaining the legal complexities, the personalities of the participants, and the historical significance of the *Einsatzgruppen* trial, that this study has been concerned.

---

[1] In his the opening statement, John Glancy said, "the Einsatzgruppen trial deals mainly with the crime of genocide," *Trial*, roll 1, 3.

One of the greatest accomplishments of the Nuremberg trials generally was in laying bare the crimes of the Third Reich. The *Einsatzgruppen* trial has contributed to the historical record as it was here that the perpetrators first spoke of their experiences and in doing so have left a vast repository of testimony, interrogations, affidavits and other documents for scholars to utilize. The documentary evidence generated by the *Einsatzgruppen* trial allows us to build on our ever-growing understanding of the Nazi perpetrator and the record shows that this group of perpetrators believed in the principles of National Socialism so much that they made its ideology the very basis of their behavior. Their testimony at Nuremberg illustrates that like other perpetrator groups who worked in the field and face to face with their victims, they were not born with an eliminationist-type antisemitism, but rather as a group they adopted a form of national chauvinism that germinated in the aftermath of Germany's defeat in the First World War. If Ohlendorf is typical of this group as I have argued he is, the *Einsatzgruppen* leaders convinced themselves that the road to German rehabilitation was through racial, cultural, and ideological purity and their murderous actions in the Soviet Union were thus right and justified: important attitudes to recognize when contemplating the motivation and behavior of this particular group of perpetrators.[2]

The trial's legal legacy is more ambiguous than its documentary record, this is in part due to the unprecedented nature of the crimes and in part due to bad timing. The *Einsatzgruppen* trial took place at the exact moment when the international community was debating and finalizing the definition of genocide. In 1944, Raphael Lemkin sought to give legal meaning to the systematic murder of Europe's Jews by coining the new word. While Lemkin was in Nuremberg during the formulation of the indictment against the leaders of the *Einsatzgruppen*, the prosecutors of this trial did not yet possess a clear legal definition of the crime. To be sure, the Americans knew that Jews were special targets of Nazi policy, but mass murder was not genocide. The truth was that the *Einsatzgruppen* trial took place at a transitional moment in history, a time when the international community was on the cusp of constructing a larger framework for prosecuting the crimes of the Nazis. That the term genocide was yet to be officially defined meant that the prosecutors and judges in the trial lacked the necessary structure to bring together all the threads of criminality and give legal meaning to the newly identified crime of genocide. What emerged at trial, instead, was a more traditional prosecution of murder, an approach that by necessity overlooked the complexities of genocide and the role of other important paramilitary and party organizations in the murder of Soviet Jewry, but one that nonetheless ensured that the individual leaders of the *Einsatzgruppen* would be found

---

[2] For example, Orth, *ibid.*, 322–323 highlights internal justifications, such as notions of "decency" among the concentration SS.

guilty of crimes against humanity as laid out in the indictment. Had the case against the *Einsatzgruppen* leaders gone to trial today, the court would demand substantive proof of their intentions to destroy the group in order to prove genocide, but in 1947, no such demands were placed on the prosecutors whose ample documentary evidence was enough to prove the guilt of the defendants.

To be sure, the main aim of the planners of the Subsequent Nuremberg Trials was to render justice. But justice is a difficult concept to define. It means different things to different peoples and cultures and is probably best understood as a reflection of the society from which it emanates. In the case of Nazi Germany, justice would have meant summary execution, but in terms of the Anglo-American ideals upon which the Nuremberg proceedings were based, it meant utilizing an impartial judiciary to determine the innocence or guilt of individuals while employing the notion of innocent until proven guilty: a principle inherent in western democratic legal systems. In the context of the post-war world, the trial of the *Einsatzgruppen* leaders as one of the twelve Subsequent Proceedings must be seen as the closest way of approximating justice that American authorities had at their disposal. If justice is a reflection of the society from which it comes, in the early post-war years, a time of chaos and uncertainty, it is remarkable that the Americans were able to employ any system of justice at all, let alone such a complicated and comprehensive program as Nuremberg became. Trying one individual, let alone 185, is no small feat and doing so after a major conflagration and under pressure from every nation not to, is a testament to the strength of the American commitment. That said, American justice did not translate fully to foreign soil in the immediate postwar period. In their haste, the Nuremberg planners did not always afford suspects and defendants the same legal rights as they would an American in the United States. Sometimes rights were denied because the planners wanted to circumvent American laws they themselves did not like or, more often, the denial of rights were the result of poor planning and haste as was the case with appellate courts which were not provided as an automatic recourse for the convicted as they are in the United States. Unfortunately, this has become a pattern of behavior for which Americans justice is known of late; beginning at Nuremberg, and continuing today, justice away from American soil has become suspect. For transitional justice to work, it has to be free of the taint of bias. That the fundamental tenets of American justice were not always employed at Nuremberg may have blemished these trials. Unfortunately, this trend persists. Later American efforts such as the trial of Sadam Hussein have also been influenced by expediency and some would argue, politics.

In his book, *The American War Crimes Trial Program in Germany*, Frank Buscher remarked that he was inspired to investigate the U.S. war crimes trial program after looking at the original sentences of the *Einsatzgruppen* leaders and comparing those sentences to their release dates from prison.[3] In his view, the massive sentence reductions and early releases were proof that the American war crimes trial program, in general, was a failure.[4] But what constitutes a successful war crimes trial? Is success or failure determined solely by the longevity of a sentence or does other criteria matter, such as the scope and quality of the prosecution and the advancement of law? Perhaps Buscher's definition is too restrictive; to measure success by lengthy prison terms alone is to put success in the realm of the political, ignoring the other, positive aspects of law. The *Einsatzgruppen* trial was both a success and a failure. The trial itself was as fair a hearing as these men would ever receive, and certainly no one would dispute that their treatment by the Americans was better than the Nazis ever gave their own enemies. Admittedly, there were some procedural problems with this trial, as there were with all the Nuremberg trials. Perhaps the worst outrage, that which initially inspired Buscher's investigation, was that the men who were found guilty of murdering 1 million people were prematurely released from prison and allowed to live out their lives as ordinary Germans. Certainly this is a great disappointment, even a failure, but the failure was not that of the planners of the trial, nor the prosecutors or judges, but rather a political failure born out of the perceived necessities of the cold war. Had sentence enforcement been left to the participants of the trial, prison terms would have been carried out to their fullest. That they were not highlights the link between political will and a sustained and complete judicial reckoning with war criminals. For the *Einsatzgruppen* trial to have been completely successful, indeed, for any war crimes trial to be successful, it takes sustained political will. Unfortunately, political will is more often than not ephemeral. The exception might be the IMT trial in which all of the defendants fulfilled their sentences, even Rudolf Hess, who was sentenced to life, served his full sentence because of the political will of the Soviets who refused an early release for Hess even though the Americans and British were willing to do so.[5] In the case of the *Einsatzgruppen* defendants, American officials lost their political resolve at the height of the cold war, the exact same moment at Germany regained a position of importance on the international stage. As a result, compromises were made and war criminals were released. What Buscher sees as a judicial failure was in fact a change in context and political climate. In a world divided, war criminals weighed as less important than the military and strategic alliance of west Germany and in an odd twist, the Germans too must take responsibility for the failure. The lesson of Nuremberg is that international cooperation, sustained political will, and compliance by the perpetrating nation are the only way to carry out justice fully. This was

[3] Buscher, *US War Crimes Trial Program in Germany*, 3–4.
[4] *Ibid.*, 2.
[5] Norman Goda, *Tales from Spandau: Nazi Criminals and the Cold War* (New York, 2007), 221–264.

the case with the IMT, the Subsequent Nuremberg Proceedings and for all other post-war judicial processes, and it remains true today.

Important in its own right, the *Einsatzgruppen* trial must also be seen as part of a larger legal development. The trial of *Einsatzgruppen* personnel was part of a longer process of identifying, prosecuting, and punishing war criminals that began after the war, and which continues today. The later trials in German courts of other *Einsatzgruppen* members make it clear that the twenty-two men convicted at Nuremberg represented but a fraction of all those who had participated in the genocide of the Jews. Continuing the process begun in 1945, the Germans in their own war crimes trials tried many of those who were not tried by the Allies. It was when the Allies terminated their involvement in the identification and punishment of Nazi war criminals that they paved the way for Germany to come to terms with its own past, and bring to justice those Nazis who had escaped punishment in allied courts. Germans had been trying Nazi war criminals on their own since 1945, when allied authorities re-enacted the 1871 German penal code and CCL10, which allowed the trial of Germans for crimes committed against Germans, provided that the trials were "authorized by the occupying authorities."[6] Both the British and the French permitted German trials to take place in their zones of occupation, whereas the Americans were far less willing to do so.[7] Between 1945 and 1957, German courts prosecuted approximately 800 defendants under these laws, until 1958 when the Federal Republic put in place a central coordinating authority for the punishment of Nazi war criminals.[8]

That year, the states of the German Federal Republic established the Central Office of the State Judicial Authorities for the Investigation of National Socialist Crimes or *Zentrale Stelle der Landesjustizverwaltungen zur Aufklärung nationalsozialistischer Verbrechen* headed by Erwin Schüle.[9] The head office of the *Zentrale Stelle* was located in Ludwigsburg, near Stuttgart in southwestern Germany. Here, legal authorities coordinated the investigations of non-military crimes committed by Germans against

[6] Henry Friedlander, "The Deportation of the German Jews: Post-War German Trials of Nazi Criminals," *Leo Baeck Institute Year Book* 29 (1984), 202–203; Control Council Law No. 10, *TWC*, vol. 4, xviii–xxi.

[7] Adalbert Rückerl, *The Investigation of Nazi Crimes 1945–1978* (Heidelberg, 1979), 34.

[8] On this issue, see Rückerl, *Investigation of Nazi Crimes*, 32–39. See also, "Schwerpunkte der Strafverfolgung in Westdeutschland 1945–1997," in C.F. Rüter and D.W. de Mildt (eds.) *Justiz und NS-Verbrechen. Sammlung Deutscher Strafurteile Wegen Nationalsozialistischer Tötungsverbrechen 1945–1966*, http://www.jur.uva.nl/junsv/. The complete collection of National Socialist trial summaries is available under the same title, 22 volumes, Amsterdam (1968–present).

[9] Müller, *Hitler's Justice*, 215; Hilberg, *Destruction*, 1087–1088, and Rückerl, *Investigation of Nazi Crimes*, 48–49. Rückerl took over the directorship of the organization in 1966.

civilians during World War II, of which murder and manslaughter were the most frequently investigated crimes.[10] Unlike at Nuremberg, those targeted for investigation were lower-ranking men from the units of the *Einsatzgruppen*, *Ordnungspolizei*, and other police units of the SS, SD, and RSHA. German authorities investigated approximately 1,770 members of the *Einsatzgruppen* yet only indicted 136, of which eight were sentenced to life and fifty-three to sentences greater than four years.[11] None of the *Einsatzgruppen* leaders who had been indicted, tried, and sentenced at Nuremberg in 1947 and 1948 were investigated in these later German trials, despite their premature release from prison, due to a law against double jeopardy.[12] This fact had, as historian Jeffrey Herf has noted, "a profoundly negative impact on later trials in German courts because higher-ranking officials who had been amnestied in 1951 offered testimony in trials in the 1960s against lower-ranking officials who bore less guilt."[13] The distinction lies in the German penal code that sees a difference between an accomplice and a perpetrator. The former is less culpable because presumably he lacks an independent will.[14] The practice of trying the so-called accomplices caused great resentment among low- ranking Nazis who believed they were treated more harshly than their former superiors had been, and indeed it made the job of prosecution more difficult for the Germans. But complicity ran deep into the ranks of the Nazi regime, and as the defendants at Nuremberg learned themselves, the *tu quoque* argument is not legally binding. In the end, what was begun at Nuremberg in 1947 – the trial of the *Einsatzgruppen* leadership – was partially completed in German courts with the rank-and-file members.

Seen from a still broader perspective, the legal proceedings at Nuremberg provided a legal foundation for the trial of war criminals in the future. We see the fruits of this process today at The Hague, and even more in the

---

[10] *Ibid.*, 49.

[11] Helmut Langerbein, "Profiles of Mass Murder: The Einsatzgruppen Officers," unpublished Ph.D. dissertation, University of California, Santa Cruz, 2000, 1.

[12] The Transition Agreement of August 5, 1955, signed by the United States, Britain, France, and the Federal Republic of Germany, prohibited the Germans from trying any individual already investigated and tried by the occupying authorities. This included all those tried by Military Tribunal II in the *Einsatzgruppen* trial. *Ibid.*, 46–47.

[13] Jeffrey Herf, *Divided Memory: The Nazi Past in the Two Germanys* (Cambridge, 1997), 206. Several of the defendants from the *Einsatzgruppen* trial were interrogated by German officials for cases they were preparing against other *Einsatzgruppen* personnel. For instance, Walter Blume and Martin Sandberger were both interrogated by German officials in an investigation against Bruno Streckenbach, "Protokoll in der gerichtlichen Voruntersuchung gegen Bruno Streckenbach," May 1971 and November 1972, 201 AR-Z 76/59, vols. 8 and 18, 9ff and 8667ff, Zentrale Stelle der Landesjustizverwaltungen zur Aufklärung nationalsozialistischer Verbrechen.

[14] Langerbein, "Profiles of Mass Murder," 6.

creation of the permanent international court of justice. In many ways, through their successes as well as their failures, the Nuremberg trials contributed to the development of international law and set new standards for just retribution. In spite of their imperfections, therefore, the Subsequent Nuremberg Proceedings set a precedent. They contributed to defining new international standards for the behavior of belligerents in times of war; they led to the United Nations' definition of, and convention on, genocide in 1948; they went some way toward eliminating national boundaries as insulation from punishment; and most importantly, they introduced the idea of universal jurisdiction for crimes against humanity, although not the practice.[15] The Subsequent Nuremberg Trials contributed fundamentally to international law by advancing the notion that individuals, and not abstract entities called states, were responsible for their criminal actions.

The American planners of the Nuremberg proceedings hoped to educate Germans about democratic justice, and in so doing, provide an historical record of the criminal policies enacted by Hitler's Third Reich. Today, Germany stands as a centerpiece of democracy in Europe. Whether or not the war crimes trials in general or the *Einsatzgruppen* trial in particular, had anything to do with that success is difficult to determine. What is certain, however, is that the Subsequent Nuremberg Proceedings, including the *Einsatzgruppen* trial, exposed the insidiousness of National Socialism to the entire world. The inner workings of the twentieth century's worst genocide were laid bare for all to see, and this result alone gives the trials at Nuremberg immense historical significance. Each trial has its legacy and the *Einsatzgruppen* process is no different. However, in addition to the beneficial legal legacy, the trial of Otto Ohlendorf and his comrades also left the world with a troubling sense of the cruelty of which human beings are capable. Looking into the eyes of the arrogant Ohlendorf, the cold and callous Erich Naumann, or the distraught and psychologically crippled Paul Blobel, one recognizes the spark of human intelligence. These men were responsible for the deaths of untold numbers of innocent people; in a sense they pulled the trigger. The killers offered reasons and explanations for their behavior during the trial, reasons that we might find ludicrous and unacceptable. But in the context of the Third Reich and its ideology, we now know we cannot be so assuming. With the hindsight of more than six decades, the ultimate irony of the *Einsatzgruppen* trial is that the monstrous criminals were given a human face, they were exposed as ordinary people alive in extraordinary times, and most of them did indeed, as it turns out, believe in the regime and its ideology for which they acted. Human beings, not monsters, as the *Einsatzgruppen* trial so aptly showed, committed genocide.

[15] Bassiouni, "The History of Universal Jurisdiction," 39–63.

In the end, although the trial of the *Einsatzgruppen* leaders did not mete out perfect justice, it was important. As Michael Musmanno aptly concluded, Nuremberg may have been the home of the Nazi party, but it was also "its grave." Discrediting Nazism forever, Nuremberg provided an important and fitting closure to the criminal Nazi regime.[16]

---

[16] Musmanno, *Eichmann Kommandos*, 16.

Bibliography

Archives

United States

NATIONAL ARCHIVES AND RECORDS ADMINISTRATION, COLLEGE
PARK, MARYLAND (NARA)

Record Group 94: The Adjutant General's Office
The Adjutant General's Office, World War II. Operation Reports
Record Group 153: Records of the Judge Advocate General (Army)
War Crimes Branch
Nuremberg Administrative Files 1944–1949.
Record Group 238, Records of World War II War Crimes
US Military Tribunal I-VI B
Central Secretariat
Official Court Files (Originals)
Office of Chief of Counsel For War Crimes (OCCWC)
Interrogation and Other Records Received From Various Allied Military
Agencies
Office File, 1945–1949
Interrogation Summaries
Correspondence and Other Records
Correspondence and Lists
Memoranda, and Other Records
Office File, SS Division
Correspondence, Memoranda, Reports, and Other Records
Correspondence, Reports, and Other Records, 1948–1949
Internee Personnel Records (201 files)
Correspondence, Memoranda, and Other Records
Memoranda, Reports, and Lists, SS Division
Correspondence, Reports, Petitions For Clemency, and Other Records
Relating to Defendants in Subsequent Proceedings (HICOG)

Correspondence and Other Records
Schutzstaffel (SS) Series
Record Group 260, Records of United States Occupation Headquarters, World
War II
  Records of the United States Group Control Council (Germany) USGCC
  Records Related to the Basic Preliminary Plan for Allied Control and
      Occupation of Germany 1944–1945
    Daily Journal May–October 1945
    Staff Studies, 1944–1945
  Records of the Office of Military Government, US Zone (OMGUS)
  Records of the Office of the Adjutant General
    Military Government Ordinances and Related Records, 1945–1949
  Records Relating to the Allied Control Council Laws, 1945–1948
    Allied Control Council Directives and Related Records, 1945–1949
  Records of the Office of the Chief of Counsel for War Crimes (OCCWC)
  General Records of the Office of Chief Counsel for War Crimes
  Records of the Administrative Division
  Records Relating to Defendants and Internal Administration 1946–1949
  Records of the Evidence Division
    Staff Evidence Analyses and Interrogation Summaries 1946–1948
  Records of the Special Projects Division
  Records Relating to Witnesses, Defendants, and Documents, 1947–1949
  Records of the Publications Division
  Records Relating to the Publication of Proceedings of US Military Tribunals at
      Nuernberg, 1948–1949
  Records of the Language Division
    Daily Trial Reports, 1947–1948; Language Tests 1947–1948
  Records of the Central Secretariat of the Nuernberg Military Tribunals
  General Records of the Office of the Secretary General
  General Records, 1946–1949
  Daily Trial Summaries, 1947–1948; Motions and Requests ("Case files"),
      1947–1949
    Clemency Pleas and Petitions, 1947–1949
  Records of the Marshal's Office
  Records Pertaining to Defendants and Witnesses, 1947–1948.
  Records of the Defense Center
    Administrative Records, 1946–1949
  Records Relating to Witnesses and Documents, 1946–1949
  Records of the Office of the Director of Printing
  Records Relating to Publication and Distribution of Official Trial Records,
      1945–1949
  Records of the US Element of Inter-Allied Organizations
  Records of the Control Council
    General Records 1945–1948
  Records of the Coordinating Committee
    General Records 1945–1948
  Records of the Legal Directorate
    General Records 1945–1948
Record Group 319: Records of the Army Staff
  Records of the Office of the Assistant Chief of Staff, G-2, Security Classified

Intelligence and Investigative Dossiers of the CIC (Counter Intelligence
     Corps)
Record Group 338: The United States Army in World War II (HG USAREUR).
     Judge Advocate Division
     War Crimes Branch
     Records relating to post-trial Activities 1945–57
     General Administrative Records, 1945–57
     Records Relating to War Criminal Prison No. 1, Landsberg
     Parolee Records; Executed Prisoner Records
     Released Inmates Records
Record Group 466: Records of the Office of the US High Commissioner for
     Germany
     Prisons Division: Security-Segregated Records of the Prisons Division
        Petition for Clemency or Parole and Related Records on Persons Convicted by
           the US Military Tribunals at Nuremberg, 1947–1957
        Administrative and Medical Records of Landsberg Prisoners, 1946–1957
     HICOG Clemency Panels, 1950–1955
        Clemency Panels, 1950–1955
     US Secretariat, Allied High Commission: Criminal Case Files, 1949–1955
     Records Relating to the Central Registry of War Crimes Suspects, (Crosscass)
        Administration of War Crimes Trials, 1945–1949

UNITED STATES HOLOCAUST MEMORIAL MUSEUM, WASHINGTON, D.C. (USHMM)

Record Group 12.000, Benjamin B. Ferencz Collection 1919–1994 (BBF)
Record Group 06.002 War Crimes Investigation and Prosecution: Joseph Maier
     Collection, 1945–1976, Otto Ohlendorf Testimony, October 4, 1945
RG 06.002.05*01 Records Relating to International Military Tribunal; "An
     Approach to the Preparation of the Prosecution Against Axis Criminality"
     Telford Taylor Memo
RG 06.002.02*01 Records Relating to US Investigations and Prosecution:
     OCCWC Nuremberg, Germany. Preliminary Briefs of the Economic
     Division. Vol. 1
RG 2005.347 Rolf and Hannah Wartenberg Collection

LIBRARY OF CONGRESS, MANUSCRIPT DIVISION, WASHINGTON, D.C. (LC)

The Papers of Justice Robert H. Jackson (RHJ)

GUMBERG LIBRARY, DUQUESNE UNIVERSITY, PITTSBURGH, PENNSYLVANIA

The Papers of Justice Michael A. Musmanno.

*NB much of this collection is not arranged or indexed and the majority of the files are as
Musmanno left them in his original file system. Other documents found in this collection
bear no identifying box or file and hence will be cited as loose documents. (MMP)

Files:

955	FDR
1120	Albert Speer
1138	Lucius Clay
1170	Telford Taylor
1186	General William Glassford
1277	Nuremberg Sentences (missing)
1302	War Crimes Tribunal
1315	Nuremberg Opinions (missing)
1376	Hitler Documentary Film
1412	Hitler's Death
1437	Nuremberg: Biggest Murder Trial in History
1445	Nuremberg Correspondence
1477	Capital Punishment
1485	Eichmann Trial
1470	Truman
1553	War Crimes (missing)
1683	Superior Orders defense
1691	Einsatzgruppen
1812	Mark Clark
1825	Eichmann Kommandos
1904	War Criminal Trials
1905	Hannah Arendt
2124	Eichmann Kommandos, reviews of
2150	Nuremberg Clippings
2292	Dachau
2340	Navy
2977	Fascists
2953	Goebbels

TRUMAN PRESIDENTIAL LIBRARY, INDEPENDENCE, MISSOURI (HST)

The Papers of Harry S Truman, White House Files:
Official File (OF)
President's Personal File (PPF)
Confidential File (CF)
President's Secretary's Files (PSF)
White House General File (GF)
Alvin Rockwell Papers
Eleanor Bontecou Papers
John C. Young Papers
George Elsey File
Catherine Fite Lincoln Papers
Charles C. Ross Papers
J. Anthony Panuch Papers
Samuel I. Rosenman Papers
Samuel I. Rosenman Oral History

Tom C. Clark Papers
Konrad Adenauer Oral History
Josiah E. Dubois Oral History
Lucius D. Clay Oral History

COLUMBIA UNIVERSITY, DIAMOND LAW LIBRARY, NEW YORK, NY

Telford Taylor Papers (1908–1998) (TTP)
   Series 4: International Military Tribunal (IMT)
   Series 5: Nuremberg Military Trials (NMT)
   Series 14: Correspondence
   Series 15: Photographs
   Series 19: Newspaper Clippings
   Series 20: Research Materials

THE NEW YORK PUBLIC LIBRARY HUMANITIES AND SOCIAL SCIENCES
LIBRARY, MANUSCRIPTS AND ARCHIVES DIVISION

Andy Logan Papers, 1923–2000

MANUSCRIPTS DEPARTMENT, LIBRARY OF THE UNIVERSITY
OF NORTH CAROLINA AT CHAPEL HILL,
SOUTHERN HISTORICAL COLLECTION

RG 3567, Richard Dillard Dixon Records of Nuremberg War Crimes Trials,
1947–1948

Germany

ZENTRALE STELLE DER LANDESJUSTIZVERWALTUNGEN
AUFKLÄRUNG VON NS-VERBRECHEN. LUDWIGSBURG

415 AR 1310/63-E32 volume XLV
201 AR-Z 76/59 volumes. 2, 5, 6, 8, 9, 13, 16, 18
201 AR-Z 76/59 Sonderband I
201 AR-Z 74/59, volume 6

BUNDESARCHIV, KOBLENZ (BA)

Bestand 305, Bundesministerium. Records of the Zentrale Rechtsschutzstelle
Files: 1–89; 92–102; 119–120; 125–148; 395–396; 547–549; 662–665; 800; 830;
835–859

B305/681   Walter Blume
B305/716   Walter Haensch
B305/717   Walter Blume
B305/736   Waldemar Klingelhöfer

B305/758	Adolf Ott
B305/785	Martin Sandberger
B305/789	Willy Seibert
B305/800	Erwin Schulz
B305/808	Eugen Steimle
3790/50	Walter Haensch
4138/50	Gustav Nosske
3041/50	Adolf Ott
4135/50	Heinz Jost
3103/50	Werner Braune
2381/50	Paul Blobel
2417/50	Ernst Biberstein
3155/50	Waldemar Klingelhöfer
3574/50	Erich Naumann
3051/50	Franz Six
2413/50	Otto Ohlendorf
2450/50	Felix Rühl
2399/50	Willy Seibert
2488/50	Erwin Schulz
2560/50	Martin Sandberger

Nachlaß Kleine Erwerbungen 66 Otto Ohlendorf
Nachlaß 120 Friedrich Grimm 1888–1959
  Files: 18, 22, 37, 78, 109, 114, 120, 124–125
R58 Reichssicherheitshauptamt (RSHA)
  Files: 214–221; 218–221; 241, 272, 486, 544, 565, 574, 612, 623, 826, 830, 956, 982, 984, 991, 996

BUNDESARCHIV-MILITÄRARCHIV, FREIBURG (BA-MA)

Bestand N 642 Nachlaß des Rechtsanwaltes Dr. Rudolf Aschenauer
  Boxes 1–6, 11, 15, 29, 44, 46–47, 53, 55–57, 62, 65, 73

LANDESKIRCHLICHES ARCHIV, STUTTGART (LKA)

Bestand D-Nachlässe und Sammlungen: Bestand D1 Nachlaß Landesbischof D.
  Theophil Wurm
  Files: 272, 278–279, 284–336

AUSWÄRTIGES AMT, POLITISCHES ARCHIV, BONN (AA-AP)

Bestand 2, Büro Staatssekretäre, 1949–1967
Bestand 10, Politische Abteilung 2, 1949 and 1951–1958
  Files: 2087–2107, 2114, 2118, 2209, 2214–2219, 2224

MICROFILM COLLECTIONS

Merritt Collection on Public Opinion: Reports of the OMGUS Surveys, Germany
  1945–1949. Urbana: University of Illinois, 1980.

Merritt Collection on Public Opinion: Reports of the HICOG Surveys, Germany 1949–1955. Urbana: University of Illinois, 1980.

National Archives Microfilm Publication M895, Records of the Untied States Nuremberg War Crimes Trials, United States of America v. Otto Ohlendorf et al. (Case 9), 38 rolls.

National Archives Microfilm Publication M1019, Records of the United States Nuremberg War Crimes Trials Interrogations, 1946–1949, 91 rolls.

National Archives Microfilm Publication M1270, Interrogation Records Prepared for War Crimes Proceedings at Nuremberg 1945–1947, OCCPAC Interrogations, 31 rolls.

INTERVIEWS

Benjamin Ferencz, April 24 and June 24, 1997
A. E. Lawson, November 2001
Henry Lea, June 2006

Published Primary Sources

Aschenauer, Rudolf. *Zur Frage einer Revision der Kriegsverbrecherprozess.* Nuremberg, 1949.
_____. *Landsberg.* Munich, 1951.
Arad, Yitzhak, Shmuel Krakowski, and Shmuel Spector, eds. *The Einsatzgruppen Reports. Selections from the Dispatches of the Nazi Death Squads' Campaign against the Jews in Occupied Territories of the Soviet Union, July 1941–January 1943.* New York: Holocaust Library, 1989.
Cargas, Harry James, ed. *Voices from the Holocaust.* Lexington: University Press of Kentucky, 1993.
Daniell, Raymond. "'So What?' Say the Germans of Nuremberg." *The New York Times Magazine* (December 2, 1945): 5–6.
de Mildt, D.W. and C.F. Rüter-Ehlermann, eds. *Justiz und NS-Verbrechen: Sammlung deutscher Strafurteile wegen nationalsozialistischer Tötungsverbrechen 1945–1966.* 22 volumes. Amsterdam: University Press of Amsterdam, 1968–present.
Gellately, Robert, ed. *The Nuremberg Interviews conducted by Leon Goldensohn: an American Psychiatrist's Conversations with the Defendants and Witnesses.* New York: Alfred A. Knopf, 2004.
Gilbert, Gilbert M. *Nuremberg Diary.* New York: DA Capo Press, 1995 <1947>.
Jackson, Robert. "Final Report to the President from Supreme Court Justice Robert H. Jackson." *United States Department of State Bulletin* 382:15 (1946): 771–776.
Kersten, Felix. *The Kersten Memoirs, 1940–1945.* Trans. Constantine Fitzgibbon and James Oliver. New York: The Macmillan Company, 1957 <1956>.
Klee, Ernst, Willie Dreßen, and Volker Riess, eds. *"The Good Old Days" The Holocaust as Seen by the Perpetrators and Bystanders.* New York: Free Press, 1988.
Kogon, Eugen, Langbein, Hermann and Rückerl, Adalbert, eds. *Nazi Mass Murder: A Documentary History of the Use of Poison Gas.* Trans. Mary Scott and Caroline Lloyd-Morris. New Haven: Yale University Press, 1993 <1983>.

312

Bibliography

Marrus, Michael, ed. *The Nuremberg War Crimes Trial, 1945–1946. A Documentary History*. New York: Bedford Books, 1997.
McCloy, John. *The Challenge to American Foreign Policy*. Cambridge, MA: Harvard University Press, 1953.
Mendelsohn, John, ed. *Punishing the Perpetrators of the Holocaust: The Brandt, Pohl and Ohlendorf Cases*. Volume 17. New York: Garland, 1982.
———, ed. *Punishing the Perpetrators of the Holocaust: The Ohlendorf and Von Weizsäcker Cases*. Volume 18. New York: Garland, 1982.
———. *Trial by Document: The Use of Seized Records in the US Proceedings at Nuremberg*. New York: Garland, 1988.
———. *Nuernberg. War Crimes Trials Records of Case 9: United States of America v. Otto Ohlendorf et al*. Washington: Government Printing Office, 1978 (Special List 42).
Merritt, Anna J., and Richard L. Merritt. *Public Opinion in Occupied Germany*. Urbana: University of Illinois Press, 1970.
———. *Public Opinion in Semi-Sovereign Germany. The HICOG Surveys, 1949–1955*. Urbana: University of Illinois Press, 1980.
Musmanno, Michael A. *The Eichmann Kommandos*. London: Peter Davies, 1962 <1961>.
———. *Verdict! The Adventures of the Young Lawyer in the Brown Suit*. New York: MacFadden Books, 1963 <1958>.
———. *Ten Days to Die*. London: Peter Davies, 1951.
———. *Black Fury*. New York: Fountainhead Publishers, 1966.
———. *Columbus Was First*. New York: Fountainhead Publishers, 1966.
———. *Across the Street from the Courthouse*. Philadelphia: Dorrance and Company, 1954.
Noelle, Elisabeth and Erich Peter Neumann, eds. *The Germans: Public Opinion Polls, 1947–1966*. Bonn: Allansbach, 1967.
OMGUS. *Official Gazette of the Control Council for Germany*. Berlin: Allied Secretariat, 1945–1948.
Report of the Military Governor. *Denazification*. Cumulative Review. Washington: Government Printing Office, 1948.
Report of the Subcommittee of the Committee on Armed Services, U.S. Senate, 81st Congress, 1st session, October 13, 1945.
Stave, Bruce M. and Michele Palmer, eds. *Witnesses to Nuremberg. An Oral History of American Participants at the War Crimes Trials*. New York: Twayne Publishers, 1998.
Taylor, Telford. *Final Report to the Secretary of the Army on the Nuremberg War Crimes Trial under Control Council Law No. 10*. Washington: United States Government Printing Office, 1949.
———. *The Anatomy of the Nuremberg Trials: A Personal Memoir*. Toronto: Little, Brown and Company, 1992.
Trials of War Criminals before the Nuernberg Military Tribunals under Control Council Law No. 10. 15 volumes. Washington: United States Government Printing Office, 1951.
The German Press in the US Occupied Area, 1945–1948. Special Report of the Military Governor, November 1946.

United Nations War Crimes Commission. *History of the United Nations War Crimes Commission and the Development of the Laws of War.* 1948.
US Office of Military Government for Germany. *Military Government Information Bulletin.* Berlin: 1945–49.

Secondary

Allen, William Sheridan. "Farewell to Class Analysis in the Rise of Nazism: Comment." *Central European History* 17 (1984): 54–62.
Ancel, Jean, "The German-Romanian Relationship and the Final Solution," in *Holocaust and Genocide Studies*, vol. 19, no. 2 (Fall 2005): 252–275.
Anderson, Kenneth. "Nuremberg Sensibility: Telford Taylor's Memoir of the Nuremberg Trials." *Harvard Human Rights Journal* 7 (Spring 1994): 281–295.
Angrick, Andrej. *Besatzungspolitik und Massenmord. Die Einsatzgruppe D in der südlichen Sowjetunion 1941–1943.* Hamburg: Hamburger Edition HIS Verlagsges mbH, 2003.
_____. "Otto Ohlendorf und die SD-Tätigkeit der Einsatzgruppe D." In Michael Wildt, ed. *Nachrichtendienst, politische Elite, Mordeinheit. Der Sicherheitsdienst des Reichsführers SS*, 267–302. Hamburger: HIS Verlagsges. mbH, 2003.
_____. "Die Einsatzgruppe D. Struktur und Tätigkeiten einer mobilen Einheit Der Sicherheitspolizei und des SD In der deutsch besetzten Sowjetunion." 2 volumes. Ph.D., Berlin: Technical University of Berlin, 1999.
Angrick, Andrej et al. "'Da hätte man schon ein Tagebuch führen müssen.' Das Polizeibatallion 322 und die Judenmorde am Bereich der Heeresgruppe Mitte während des Sommers und Herbstes 1941." In Helge Grabitz et al., eds. *Die Normalität des Verbrechens: Festschrift für Wolfgang Scheffler*, 325–385. Berlin: Edition Hentrich, 1994.
Arendt, Hannah. *Eichmann in Jerusalem: A Report on the Banality of Evil.* New York: Viking, 1963.
Aronson, Shlomo. *Reinhard Heydrich und die Frühgeschichte von Gestapo und SD.* Stuttgart: Verlag-Anstalt, 1971.
Banach, Jens. *Heydrichs Elite: Das Führerkorps der Sicherheitspolizei und des SD 1936–1945.* Paderborn: Ferdinand Schöning, 1998.
Bassiouni, M. Cherif. *Crimes against Humanity in International Criminal Law*, 2nd revised edition. The Hague and London: Kluwer Law International, 1999.
_____. "The History of Universal Jurisdiction and Its Place in International Law." In Stephen Macedo, ed. *Universal Jurisdiction. National Courts and the Prosecution of Serious Crimes under International Law*, 39–63. Philadelphia: University of Pennsylvania Press, 2004.
Benton, Wilbourn E. and Georg Grimm eds. *Nuremberg: German Views of the War Trials.* Dallas: Southern Methodist University Press, 1955.
Biddis, Michael. "Victors' Justice? The Nuremberg Tribunal." *History Today* 49 (October 1993): 40–46.
Birn, Ruth Bettina. *Die Höheren SS-und Polizeiführer: Himmlers vertreter im Reich und den besetzten Gebieten.* Düsseldorf: Droste Verlag, 1986.
_____. "Guilty Conscience, Antisemitism and the Personal Development of Some SS Leaders." *Remembering for the Future: Working Papers and Addenda*

vol. II: The Impact of the Holocaust on the Contemporary World, 2083–2092. New York: Pergamon Press, 1989.

———. "Revising the Holocaust." *Historical Journal* 40 (1997): 195–215.

Black, Peter. *Ernst Kaltenbrunner: Ideological Soldier of the Third Reich*. Princeton: Princeton University Press, 1984.

Bloxham, Donald. *Genocide on Trial. War Crimes Trials and the Formation of Holocaust History and Memory*. Oxford: Oxford University Press, 2001.

———. "From Streicher to Sawoniuk: the Holocaust in the Courtroom." In Dan Stone, ed. *The Historiography of the Holocaust*, 397–419. New York: Palgrave Macmillan, 2004.

———. "'The Trial that Never Was': Why there was no Second International Trial of Major War Criminals at Nuremberg." *History* 87 (2002): 41–60.

Boehling, Rebecca. *A Question of Priorities: Democratic Reform and Economic Recovery in Postwar Germany*. Providence, RI: Berghahn Books, 1996.

Boehnert, Gunnar C. "The Third Reich and the Problem of 'Social Revolution': German Officers and the SS." In Volker R. Berghahn and Martin Kitchen, eds. *Germany in the Age of Total War*, 203–217. Totowa, NJ: Barnes and Noble Books, 1981.

———. "The Jurists in the SS-Führerkorps, 1925–1939." In Gerhard Hirschfeld and Lothar Kettenacker, eds. *Der "Führerstaat": Mythos und Realität: Studien zur Struktur und Politik des Dritten Reiches*, 361–373. Stuttgart: Klett-Cotta, 1981.

———. "An Analysis of the Age and Education of the SS Führerkorps, 1925–1939." *Historical and Social Research* 12 (1979): 4–17.

Bower, Tom. *Blind Eye to Murder. Britain, America and the Purging of Nazi Germany: A Pledge Betrayed*. London: Andre Deutsch, 1981.

Bracher, Karl Dietrich. *The German Dictatorship. The Origins, Structure and Effects of National Socialism*. Trans. Jean Steinberg. New York: Praeger Publishers, 1970.

Breitman, Richard. *The Architect of Genocide: Himmler and the Final Solution*. New York: Alfred A. Knopf, 1991.

———. *Official Secrets: What the Nazis Planned, What the British and Americans Knew*. New York: Hill and Wang, 1998.

———. "Himmler's Police Auxiliaries in the Occupied Soviet Territories." *Simon Wiesenthal Center Annual* 7 (1994): 23–39.

———. "Himmler and the Terrible Secret among the Executioners." In Yehuda Reinharz and George Mosse, eds. *The Impact of Western Nationalism: Essays Dedicated to Walter Laqueur on the Occasion of his 70th Birthday*, 77–97. London: Sage Publications, 1991–1992.

———. "Intelligence and the Holocaust." In David Bankier, ed. *Secret Intelligence and the Holocaust*, 17–47. Jerusalem and New York: Enigma Books, 2006.

Broszat, Martin et al. *Anatomy of the SS State*. Trans. Dorothy Long and Marian Jackson. New York: Walker, 1968 <1965>.

Brow, Peter. "Nuremberg Remembered." *Contemporary Review* 267 (November, 1995): 257–260.

Browder, George. *Hitler's Enforcers: The Gestapo and the SS Security Service in the Nazi Revolution*. New York: Oxford University Press, 1997.

———. *Foundations of the Nazi Police State: The Formation of Sipo and SD*. Lexington: University Press of Kentucky, 1990.

_____. "The SD: The Significance of Organization and Image." In George L. Mosse, ed. *Police Forces in History*, 205–229. Beverly Hills, CA: Sage Publications, 1977 <1975>.

_____. "The Numerical Strength of the Sicherheitsdienst des RFSS." *Historical Social Research* 28 (1983): 30–41.

_____. "Perpetrator Character and Motivation: An Emerging Consensus." *Holocaust and Genocide Studies* 17: 3 (Winter, 2003): 480–497.

Browning, Christopher. *Ordinary Men: Reserve Police Battalion 101 and the Final Solution in Poland*. New York: Harper Collins, 1992.

_____. *The Origins of the Final Solution: The Evolution of Nazi Jewish Policy, September 1939–March 1942*. Lincoln: University of Nebraska Press, 2004.

_____. *Fateful Months: Essays on the Emergence of the Final Solution*. New York: Holmes and Meier, 1985.

_____. *The Path to Genocide: Essays on Launching the Final Solution*. Cambridge: Cambridge University Press, 1992.

_____. *Nazi Policy, Jewish Workers, German Killers*. Cambridge: Cambridge University Press, 2000.

_____. *Collected Memories. Holocaust History and Postwar Testimony*. Madison: University of Wisconsin Press, 2003.

_____. "A Reply to Martin Brozat Regarding the Origins of the Final Solution." *Simon Wiesenthal Center Annual* (1984):113–132.

_____. "German Memory, Judicial Interrogation, and Historical Reconstruction: Writing Perpetrator History from Postwar Testimony." In Saul Friedlander, ed. *Probing the Limits of Representation: Nazism and the 'Final Solution,'* 22–36. Cambridge: Harvard University Press, 1992.

_____. "Daniel Goldhagen's Willing Executioners." *History and Memory: Studies in Representation of the Past* 1:8 (Spring/Summer, 1996): 88–108.

Büchler, Yehoshua. "Kommandostab Reichsführer-SS: Himmler's Personal Murder Brigades in 1941." *Holocaust and Genocide Studies* 1 (1986): 11–25.

Burrin, Philippe. *Hitler and the Jews. The Genesis of the Holocaust*. London: Edward Arnold, 1994.

Burstein, William. *The Logic of Evil. The Social Origins of the Nazi Party, 1925–1933*. New Haven: Yale University Press, 1996.

Buscher, Frank M.. *The United States War Crimes Trial Program in Germany, 1946–1955*. New York: Greenwood Press, 1989.

_____. "German Catholic Bishops and the Holocaust, 1940–1952." in *German Studies Review* 3:11 (October 1988): 463–486.

Campbell, Bruce. *The SA Generals and the Rise of Nazism*. Lexington: University Press of Kentucky, 1998.

Cassel, Douglas W., Jr. "Judgment at Nuremberg: A half-century Appraisal." *The Christian Century* 112 (December 6, 1995): 1180–1183.

Caute, David. *The Great Fear. The Anti-Communist Purge under Truman and Eisenhower*. New York: Simon and Schuster, 1978.

Childers, Thomas. *The Nazi Voter: The Social Foundations of Fascism in Germany, 1919–1933*. Chapel Hill: University of North Carolina Press, 1983.

_____. "Who, Indeed, Did Vote for Hitler?" *Central European History* 17 (1984): 45–53.

Clifford, Brian R. "The Relevance of Psychological Investigation to Legal Issues in Testimony and Identification." *The Criminal Law Review* (1979): 153–163.

Conot, Robert. *Justice at Nuremberg*. New York: Harper and Row, 1983.

Cooper, Belinda, ed. *War Crimes: The Legacy of Nuremberg*. New York: TV Books, 1999.

Dalleck, Robert. *Franklin D. Roosevelt and American Foreign Policy, 1932–1945*. New York: Oxford University Press, 1979.

Davidson, Eugene. *The Trial of the Germans: An Account of the 22 Defendants before the International Military Tribunal at Nuremberg*. New York: Macmillan, 1966.

Dawidowicz, Lucy S. *The War against the Jews, 1933–1945*. New York: Bantam Books, 1978.

de Mildt, Dick. *In the Name of the People: Perpetrators of Genocide in the Reflection of their Post-War Prosecution in West Germany*. The Hague: Martinus Nijhoff Publishers, 1996.

Dimsdale, Joel E., ed. *Survivors, Victims and Perpetrators: Essays on the Nazi Holocaust*. Washington: Hemisphere Publishing Corporation, 1980.

Dinstein, Yoram. *The Defense of 'Obedience to Superior Orders' in International Law*. Leyden: A.W.Sijthof, 1965.

Doeneke, Justus D. "Protest over Malmédy: A Case of Clemency." *Peace and Change* 2: 4 (1977): 28–33.

Donson, Andrew. "Why did German youth become fascists? Nationalist males born 1900 to 1908 in war and revolution." *Social History* 31, 3 (August, 2006): 337–358.

Douglas, Lawrence. *The Memory of Judgment. Making Law and History in the Trials of the Holocaust*. New Haven: Yale University Press, 2001.

———. "Film as Witness: Screening Nazi Concentration Camps Before the Nuremberg Tribunal." *The Yale Law Journal* 2:105 (November 1995): 449–480.

———. "Wartime Lies. Securing the Holocaust in Law and Literature." In F. C. Decoste and Bernard Schwartz, eds. *The Holocaust's Ghost: Writings on Art, Politics, Law and Education*, 15–25. Edmonton: University of Alberta Press, 2000.

Drumbl, Mark A. *Atrocity, Punishment, and International Law*. New York: Cambridge University Press, 2007.

Earl, Hilary. "Biographical Method and Historical Analysis: Explaining Perpetrators' 'Route to Crime' using War Crimes Trial Documentation." Simone Lässig and Volker Berghahn, eds. *Biography between Structure and Agency: Approaches to German History*, 162–181. New York: Berghahn Books and Oxford University Press, 2008.

———. "Confessions of Wrong-doing or How to Save Yourself from the Hangman? An Analysis of British and American Intelligence Reports of the Activities of Otto Ohlendorf, May–December 1945." David Bankier, ed. *Secret Intelligence and the Holocaust*, 301–326. New York and Jerusalem: Yad Vashem and Enigma Books, 2006.

———. "Scales of Justice: History, Testimony and the Einsatzgruppen Trial." Jeffry Diefendorf, ed. *Lessons and Legacies VI. New Currents in Holocaust Research*, 325–351. Northwestern University Press: Evanston, Illinois, September 2004.

Eser, Albin. "Defenses in War Crimes Trials." In Yoram Dinstein and Mala Tabory, eds. *War Crimes in International Law*, 251–274. The Hague: Martinus Nijhoff Publishers, 1996.

Eser, Albin and George P. Fletcher, eds. *Justification and Excuse: Comparative Perspectives I*. The Max-Planck-Institute for foreign and International Criminal Law: Freiburg, 1987.

Fahy, Charles. "Legal Problems of German Occupation." *Michigan Law Review* 47 (November 1948): 11–22.

Ferencz, Benjamin. *Less than Slaves: Jewish Forced Labor and the Quest for Compensation*. Cambridge: Harvard University Press, 1979.

_____. "Nürnberg Trial Procedure and the Rights of the Accused." *Journal of Criminal Law, Criminology and Police Science* 39 (July-August 1948): 144–151.

_____. "From Nuremberg to Rome: A Personal Account." In Mark Lattimer and Philippe Sands, eds. *Justice for Crimes against Humanity*, 31–46. Oxford: Hart Publishing, 2003.

Feuerlicht, Roberta Strauss. *Justice Crucified. The Story of Sacco and Vanzetti*. New York: McGraw-Hill, 1977.

Fischer, Conan. "The Occupational Background of the SA's Rank and File Membership During the Depression Years, 1929 to Mid-1934." In Peter D. Stachura ed. *The Shaping of the Nazi State*, 131–159. New York: Barnes and Noble Books, 1978.

Fletcher, George P. *Basic Concepts of Criminal Law*. New York: Oxford University Press, 1998.

Förster, Jürgen. "The Wehrmacht and the War of Extermination Against the Soviet Union." *Yad Vashem Studies* 14 (1981): 413–447.

Fox, John P. "The Final Solution: Intended or Contingent?" *Patterns of Prejudice* 3:18 (1984): 27–39.

Fratcher, William Franklin. "American Organization for Prosecution of German War Criminals." *Missouri Law Review* 13 (1948): 45–75.

Freedman, Abraham E. "The Dissenting Opinions of Justice Musmanno." *Temple Law Quarterly* 30 (1957): 250–262.

Frei, Norbert. "'Vergangenheitsbewältigung' or 'Renazification?'" The American Perspective on Germany's Confrontation with the Nazi Past in the Early Years of the Adenauer Era." In Michael Ermarth, ed. *America and the Shaping of German Society, 1945–1955*, 47–59. Providence: Berg Publishers, 1993.

Friedlander, Henry. *The Origins of Nazi Genocide: From Euthanasia to the Final Solution*. Chapel Hill: University of North Carolina Press, 1995.

_____. "The Deportations of the German Jews: Post-War Trials of Nazi Criminals." *Leo Baeck Institute Year Book* (1984): 201–206.

Friedrich, Jorg. *Die kälte Amnestie: NS-Täter in der Bundesrepublik*. Frankfurt: Fischer, 1984.

Fromm, Erich. *Escape from Freedom*. New York: Avon Books, 1969.

Gardner, Lloyd C. "America and the German 'Problem,' 1945–49." In *The Politics and Policies of the Truman Administration*, 113–149. Barton J. Bernstein, ed. Chicago: Quadrangle, 1970.

Gaskin, Hilary, ed. *Eyewitnesses at Nuremberg*. London: Arms and Armour, 1991.

Gerlach, Christian. *Krieg, Ernährung, Völkermord: Forschungen zur deutschen Vernichtungspolitik im Zweiten Weltkrieg.* Hamburg: Hamburger Edition, 1998.

———. "The Wannsee Conference, the fate of German Jews, and Hitler's decision in Principle to exterminate all European Jews." In Omer Bartov, ed. *The Holocaust: Origins, Implementation, Aftermath,* 106–161. New York: Routledge, 2000.

———. "The Eichmann Interrogations in Holocaust Historiography." *Holocaust and Genocide Studies* 15:3 (Winter 2001): 428–452.

Geus, Elmar. *Mörder, Diebe, Räuber: Historische Betrachtung des deutschen Strafrechts von der Carolina bis zum Reichsstrafgesetzbuch.* Berlin: scrîpvaz-Verlag Christof Krauskopf, 2002.

Gilbert, Gustav M. "The Mentality of SS Murderous Robots." *Yad Vashem Studies on the European Jewish Catastrophe and Resistance* 5 (1963): 35–41.

Giles, Geoffrey. "National Socialism and the Educated Elite in the Weimar Republic." In Peter D. Stachura ed. *The Nazi Machtergreifung* , 49–67. London: Allen and Unwin, 1983.

———. *Students and National Socialism in Germany.* Princeton: Princeton University Press, 1985.

Ginsburgs, George and V.N. Kudriavtsev eds. *The Nuremberg Trial and International Law.* Dordrecht, Netherlands: Martinus Nijhoff Publishers, 1990.

Glees, Anthony. *Reinventing Germany: German Political Development Since 1945.*Washington: Berg, 1996.

Glueck, Sheldon. *The Nuremberg Trial and Aggressive War.* New York: Alfred A. Knopf, 1946.

Goda, Norman J.W. *Tales from Spandau: Nazi Criminals and the Cold War.* New York: Cambridge University Press, 2007.

Goldhagen, Daniel Jonah. *Hitler's Willing Executioners: Ordinary Germans and the Holocaust.* New York: Alfred Knopf, 1996.

———. "The 'Humanist' as a Mass Murderer: The Mind and Deeds of SS General Otto Ohlendorf." Unpublished Honours Thesis, Cambridge: Harvard University, 1982.

Grabitz, Helge. *NS-Prozesse: Psychogramme der Beteiligten.* Heidelberg: F. Müller, 1985.

———. *Für Führer, Volk, und Vaterland-: Hamburger Justiz im Nationalsozialismus.* Hamburg: Ergebnisse, 1992.

———. "NS-Prozesse heute." *Zeitschrift für Rechtspolitik* 15 (1982): 14–16.

———. "Problems of Nazi Trials in the Federal Republic of Germany." *Holocaust and Genocide Studies* 3 (1988): 209–222.

Grosman, Brian A. "Testing Witness Reliability." *The Criminal Law Quarterly* 5 (1962–1963): 318–327.

Haberer, Erich. "History and Justice: Paradigms of the Prosecution of Nazi Crimes." *Holocaust and Genocide Studies* 19:3 (Winter, 2005): 487–519.

Hachmeister, Lutz. *Der Gegnerforscher: Die Karriere des SS-Führers Franz Alfred Six.* Munich: Verlag C.H. Beck, 1998.

Hamilton, Richard. *Who Voted For Hitler?* Princeton, NJ: Princeton University Press, 1982.

Harris, Whitney. *Tyranny on Trial: The Evidence at Nuremberg.* New York: Barnes and Noble Books, 1995 <1954>.

_____. "Justice Jackson at Nuremberg." *The International Lawyer* 3:20 (Summer 1986): 867–896.

Headland, Ronald. *Messages of Murder: A Study of the Reports of the Einsatz-gruppen of the Security Police and the Security Service, 1941–1943.* Toronto: Associated University Presses, 1992.

_____. "The Einsatzgruppen: The Question of Their Initial Operations." *Holocaust and Genocide Studies* 4:4 (1989): 401–412.

Hébert, Valerie. *Hitler's Soldiers on Trial: the Nuremberg High Command case and the politics of punishment, 1947–1958.* Lawrence: University Press of Kansas, 2009.

Heer, Hannes and Klaus Naumann, eds. *Vernichtungskrieg: Verbrechen der Wehrmacht 1941–1944.* Hamburg: HIS Verlags, 1995.

Heinemann, Isabel. "'Another Type of Perpetrator': The SS Racial Experts and Forced Population Movements in Occupied Regions." *Holocaust and Genocide Studies* 3:12 (Winter, 2001): 387–411.

Hellendall, F. "Nazi Crime before German Courts: The Immediate Post-War Era." *The Wiener Library Bulletin* 3:24 (1970): 14–20.

Herbert, Ulrich. *Best. Biographische Studien über Radikalismus, Weltanschauung und Vernunft, 1903–1989.* Bonn: J. H. W. Dietz, 1996.

_____. "Rückkehr in die Bürgerlichkeit? NS-Eliten in der Bundesrepublik." In Bernd Weisbrod, ed. *Rechtsradikalismus in der politischen Kultur der Nachkriegszeit: Die verzögerte Normalisierung in Niedersachsen,* 157–173. Hanover: Hahn, 1995.

Herbst, Ludolf. *Der Totale Krieg und die Ordnung der Wirtschaft.* Stuttgart: Deutsche Verlags-Anstalt, 1982.

Herf, Jeffrey. *Divided Memory: The Nazi Past in the Two Germanys.* Cambridge: Harvard University Press, 1997.

Heydecker, Joe, and Leeb, Johannes. *Der Nürnberger Prozeß: Bilanz der Tausend Jahre.* Cologne: Kiepenheuer and Witsch, 1959 <1958>.

Hilberg, Raul. *The Destruction of the European Jews,* revised and definitive edition. 3 volumes. New York: Holmes and Meier, 1985.

_____. *Perpetrators Victims Bystanders: The Jewish Catastrophe, 1933–1945.* New York: Harper Collins Publishers, 1992.

_____. "Sources and Their Usage." In Michael Berenbaum and Abraham J. Peck, eds. *The Holocaust and History: The Known, the Unknown, the Disputed, and the Reexamined,* 5–11. Bloomington: Indiana University Press, 1998.

Hilger, Andreas, Ute Schmidt, and Günther Wagenlehner (eds.). *Sowjetische Militärtribunale. Band 1: Die Verurteilung Deutscher Kriegsgefangener 1941–1953.* Köln: Böhlau Verlag, 2001.

Hilger, Andreas. *Deutsche Kriegsgefangene in der Sowjetunion 1941–1956. Kriegsgefangenenpolitik, Lageralltag und Erinnerung.* Essen: Klartext Verlag, 2000.

Hirsch, Francine. "The Soviets at Nuremberg: International Law, Propaganda, and the Making of the Postwar Order." *American Historical Review* 113 (June, 2008): 701–730.

Hockett, Jeffrey D. "Justice Robert A. Jackson, The Supreme Court, and the Nuremberg Trial." *The Supreme Court Review* (1990): 257–299.

Höhne, Heinz. *The Order of the Death's Head: the Story of Hitler's SS.* Trans. Richard Barry. New York: Ballantine Books, 1972 <1966>.

Horowitz, Irving. *Genocide: State Power and Mass Murder.* New Brunswick, NJ: Transaction Books, 1976.

Housden, Martyn. *Hans Frank, Lebensraum and the Holocaust.* New York: Palgrave Macmillan, 2003.

Jamin, Mathilde. *Zwischen den Klassen: Zur Sozialstruktur der SA-Führerschaft.* Wuppertal: P. Hammer Verlag, 1984.

Janowitz, Morris. "German Reactions to Nazi Atrocities." *The American Journal of Sociology* 52 (1946): 141–146.

Jones, Priscillia Dale. "British Policy towards German Crimes against the Jews, 1939–1945." *Leo Baeck Institute Year Book* 36 (1991): 339–366.

Joughin, Georg Louis and Edmund M. Morgan. *The Legacy of Sacco and Vanzetti.* Chicago: Quadrangle, 1964 <1948>.

Kahn, Leo. "Achievement and Failure at Nuremberg." *Weiner Library Bulletin* 3–4: 25 (1972): 21–29.

Kater, Michael. *The Nazi Party: A Social Profile of Members and Leaders, 1919–1945.* Cambridge: Harvard University Press, 1983.

———. "Problems of Political Reeducation in West Germany, 1945–1960." *Simon Wiesenthal Center Annual* 4 (1987): 99–105.

———. "The New Nazi Rulers: Who Were They?:" In Charles S. Maier, Stanley Hoffmann, and Andrew Gould, eds. *The Rise of the Nazi Regime: Historical Reassessments*, 41–44. Boulder, CO: Westview, 1986.

Kempner, Robert M.W. "Cross Examining War Criminals." *Yad Vashem Studies on the European Catastrophe and Resistance* 5 (1963): 43–68.

———. *SS im Kreuzverhör. Die Elite, die Europa in Scherben brach.* Hamburg: F. Greno, 1987 <1964>.

———. *Das Dritte Reich im Kreuzverhör. Aus den unveröffentlichen Vernehmungsprotokollen des Anklägers Robert M.W. Kempner.* Munich: Bechtle, 1969.

Kitterman, David H. "Those who Said No: Germans who Refused to Execute Civilians During World War II." *German Studies Review* 2:11 (May 1988): 241–254.

———"Otto Ohlendorf: Gralshüter des Nationalsozialismus." In Ronald Smelser and Enrico Syring, eds. *Die SS: Elite under dem Totenkopf*, 379–393. Paderborn: F. Schöningh, 2000.

Klee, Ernst. *Persilscheine und falsche Pässe. Wie die Kirchen den Nazis halfen.* Frankfurt: Fischer Taschenbuch Verlag, 1992.

Klee, Ernst and Willi Dreßen, eds. *"Gott mit uns" Der deutsche Vernichtungskrieg im Osten 1939–1945.* Frankfurt: Fischer Verlag, 1989.

Klein, Peter, ed. *Die Einsatzgruppen in der besetzten Sowjetunion, 1941/42: die Tätigkeits- und Lageberichte des Chefs der Sicherheitspolizei und des SD.* Berlin: Edition Hentrich, 1997.

Kochavi, Arieh J. *Prelude to Nuremberg: Allied War Crimes Policy and the Question of Punishment.* Chapel Hill, NC: University of North Carolina Press, 1998.

Koehl, Robert. *The Black Corps: The Structure and Power Struggles of the SS.* Madison: University of Wisconsin Press, 1983.

Kogen, Eugen, Langbein, Hermann and Rückerl, Adalbert, eds. *Nazi Mass Murder: A Documentary History of the Use of Poison Gas.* Trans. Mary Scott and Caroline Lloyd-Morris. New Haven: Yale University Press, 1993.

Koonz, Claudia. *The Nazi Conscience*. Cambridge, MA: Harvard University Press, 2003.

Kramer, Helmut. "Kriegsverbrechen, deutsche Justiz und das Verjährungsproblem – Amnestie durch die legislative Hintertür." In Wolfram Wette and Gerd R. Ueberschär, eds. *Kriegsverbrechen im 20. Jahrhundert*, 493–506. Darmstadt: Primus, 2001.

Kramer, Jorg D. *Das Verhaltnis der politischen Parteien zur Entnazifizierung in Nordhein-Westfalen*. Frankfurt: P. Lang, 2001.

Kranzbuhler, Otto. "Nuremberg Eighteen Years Afterwards." *DePaul Law Review* 16 (1964–1965): 333–347.

Krausnick, Helmut and Hans-Heinrich Wilhelm. *Die Truppe des Weltanschauungskrieges: Die Einsatzgruppen der Sicherheitspolizei und des SD, 1938–1942*. Stuttgart: Deutsche Verlags-Anstalt, 1981.

Krausnick, Helmut and Jürgen Förster. "The Wehrmacht and the War of Extermination against the Soviet Union." *Yad Vashem Studies* 14 (1981): 7–34.

Kwiet, Konrad. "Auftakt zum Holocaust: Ein Polizeibatallion im Osteinsatz." In Wolfgang Benz et al., eds. *Der Nationalsozialismus: Studien zur Ideologie und Herrschaft*, 191–208. Frankfurt: Peter Lang, 1993.

Landsman, Stephan. *The Adversary System: A Description and Defense*. Washington and London: American Enterprise Institute for Public Policy Research, 1984.

_____. *Readings on Adversarial Justice: The American Approach to Adjudication*. St. Paul, MN: West Publishing, 1988.

_____. *Crimes of the Holocaust: The Law Confronts Hard Cases*. Philadelphia: University of Pennsylvania Press, 2005.

Langerbein, Helmut. "Profiles of Mass Murder: The Einsatzgruppen Officers." PhD Dissertation, University of California, Santa Cruz, 2000.

Lemkin, Raphael. *Axis Rule in Occupied Europe: Laws of Occupation, Analysis of Government, Proposals for Redress*. Washington: Carnegie Endowment for International Peace, 1944.

_____. "Genocide." *American Scholar* 2:15 (1946): 227–270.

Lichtenstein, Heiner. *Himmlers grüne Helfer: Die Schutzpolizei und Ordnungspolizei in "Dritten Reich."* Cologne: Bund Verlag, 1990.

Lippman, Matthew. "The Other Nuremberg: American Prosecutions of Nazi War Criminals in Occupied Germany." *Indiana International and Comparative Law Review* 1: 3 (Fall 1992): 1–100.

Lipset, Seymour. *Political Man: The Social Bases of Politics*. Expanded and updated ed. Baltimore: Johns Hopkins University, 1981 <1960>.

Lloyd-Bostock, Sally M.A. and Brian R. Clifford, eds. *Evaluating Witness Evidence. Recent Psychological Research and New Perspectives*. Toronto: Toronto University Press, 1983.

Longerich, Peter. *Politik der Vernichtung: Eine Gesamtdarstellung der nationalsozialistischen Judenverfolgung*. Munich: Piper, 1998.

_____. *The Unwritten Order: Hitler's Role in the Final Solution* (Port Stroud: Tempus, 2001).

_____. "Vom Massenmord zur 'Endlösung'. Die Erschißungen von jüdischen Zivilisten in den ersten Monaten des Ostfeldzuges im Kontext des nationalsozialistischen Judenmords." In Bernd Wegner, ed. *Zwei Wege nach Moskau. Vom Hitler-Stalin-Pakt zum 'Unternehmen Barbarossa,'* 249–260. Munich: Piper, 1991.

_____. "Policy of Destruction: Nazi-Anti-Jewish Policy and the Genesis of the 'Final Solution'." Joseph and Rebecca Meyerhoff Annual Lecture, 1–30. Washington: United States Holocaust Memorial Museum, 2001.

Lowenberg, Peter. "The Psychohistorical Origins of the Nazi Youth Cohort." *American Historical Review* 76 (1971): 1457–1502.

Lozowick, Yaacov. "Rollbahn Mord: The Early Activities of Einsatzgruppe C." *Holocaust and Genocide Studies* 2:2 (1987): 221–241.

Luban, David. "The Legacies of Nuremberg." *Social Research* 54 (Winter, 1987): 779–829.

MacLean, French L. *The Field Men: The SS Officers Who Led the Einsatzkommandos of the Nazi Mobile Killing Units* Atglen, PA: Schiffer, 1999.

Madden, Paul. "Some Social Characteristics of Early Nazi Party Members, 1919–1923." *Central European History* 1:15 (1982): 34–56.

_____. "Generational Aspects of German National Socialism, 1919–1933." *Social Science Quarterly* 63 (1982): 445–464.

Maguire, Peter. "Nuremberg: A Cold War Conflict of Interest." PhD dissertation. New York: Columbia University, 1995.

_____. *Law and War: An American Story.* New York: Columbia University Press, 2000.

Mallmann, Klaus-Michael. "Die Türöffner der 'Endlösung'." In Gerhard Paul and Klaus-Michael Mallmann, eds. *Die Gestapo im Zweiten Weltkrieg*, 437–463. Darmstadt: Primus, 2000.

Mann, Michael. "Were the Perpetrators of Genocide 'Ordinary Men' or 'Real Nazis'? Results from Fifteen Hundred Biographies." *Holocaust and Genocide Studies* 3:14 (Winter, 2000): 331–366.

Marrus, Michael R. "History and the Holocaust in the Courtroom." In Gary Smith and Florent Brayard, eds. *Vom Prozeß zur Geschichte: Die juristische und historische Aufarbeitung der Shoa in Frankreich und Deutschland*, 1–35. Berlin: 2002.

_____. "The Nuremberg Trial: Fifty Year After." *The American Scholar* 66 (Autumn 1997): 563–570.

_____. "The History of the Holocaust: A Survey of Recent Literature." *Journal of Modern History* 59 (March, 1987): 114–160.

_____. "The Holocaust at Nuremberg." Paper originally presented at conference "Political Justice in Europe in the Aftermath of World War Two." Institut für Wissenshcaften vom Menschen. Vienna: November, 1995, revised February 1996.

_____. "The Nuremberg Doctors' Trial in Historical Context." *History and Medicine* 73 (1999): 107–123.

Maser, Werner. *Nuremberg: A Nation on Trial.* New York: Charles Scribner's Sons, 1977.

Mätthaus, Jürgen. "What about the 'Ordinary Men'? The German Order Police and the Holocaust in the Occupied Soviet Union." *Holocaust and Genocide Studies* 2:10 (Fall, 1996): 134–150.

_____. "A Case of Myth-Making: The 'Führer Order' During the Einsatzgruppen Trial, 1947–1948." Unpublished article, United States Holocaust Memorial Museum, Center for Advanced Holocaust Studies, 1–20.

_____. "Historiography and the Perpetrators of the Holocaust." In Dan Stone, ed. *The Historiography of the Holocaust*, 197–215. New York: Palgrave Macmillan, 2005.

Mendelsohn, John. "Trial by Document: The Problem of due Process for War Criminals at Nuernberg." *Prologue* 4:2 (Winter, 1975): 227–34.

_____. "War Crimes Trials and Clemency in Germany and Japan." In Robert Wolfe, ed. *Americans as Proconsuls: United States Military Government in Germany and Japan*, 226–259. Carbondale: Southern Illinois University Press, 1984.

Merritt, Richard L. *Democracy Imposed: U.S. Occupation Policy and the German Public, 1945–1949*. New Haven: Yale University Press, 1995.

Melis, Damien van. *Entnazifizierung in Mecklenberg-Vorpoommern: Herrschaft und Verwaltung 1945–1948*. Munich: R. Oldenbourg, 1999.

Meyrowitz, Henri. *La Répression par les Tribunaux allemands des Crimes contre l'Humanité et de l'Apparttenance á une Organisation criminelle en application de la Loi No. 10 du Conseil de Contrôle Allié*. Paris: Librairie Générale de Droit et de Jurisprudence, 1960.

Miale, Florence R. and Selzer, Michael. *The Nuremberg Mind. The Psychology of the Nazi Leaders*. New York: Quadrangle Books, 1975.

Milgram, Stanley. *Obedience to Orders*. New York: Harper and Row, 1974.

Miquel, Marc von. "Explanation, Dissociation, Apologia. The Debate over the Criminal Prosecution of Nazi Crimes in the 1960s." In Philipp Gassert and Alan E. Steinweis, eds. *Coping with the Nazi Past. West German Debates on Nazism and Generational Conflict, 1955–1975*, 50–63. New York: Berghahn Books, 2006.

Moses, A. Dirk. "The Holocaust and Genocide." In Dan Stone, ed. *The Historiography of the Holocaust*, 533–555. New York: Palgrave MacMillan, 2005.

Mosse, George. *The Crisis of German Ideology. The Intellectual Origins of the Third Reich*. London: Grosset and Dunlap, 1964.

Müller-Hill, Benno. "The Idea of the Final Solution and the Role of Experts." In David Cesarani, ed. *The Final Solution: Origins and Implementation*, 62–72. New York: Routledge, 1996 <1994>.

Müller, Ingo. *Hitler's Justice: The Courts of the Third Reich*. Trans. Deborah Lucas Schneider. Cambridge: Harvard University Press, 1991.

O'Brien, Edward J. "The Nuremberg Principles, Command Responsibility, and the Defense of Captain Rockwood." *Military Law Review* 149 (Summer 1995): 275–291.

Ogorreck, Ralf. *Die Einsatzgruppen und die Genesis der Endlösung*. Berlin: Metropol, 1997.

Okroy, Michael. "Vor 50 Jahren in Nürnberg: Der Einsatzgruppenprozess und Paul Blobel." *Tribüne, Zeitschrift zum Verständnis des Judentums* 142 (2. Quartal, 1997): 21–32.

Olick, Jeffrey K. *In the House of the Hangman: The Agonies of German Defeat, 1943–1949*. Chicago: The University of Chicago Press, 2005.

Orth, Karin. *Die Konzentrationslager-SS. Sozialstrukturelle Analysen und biograhische Studien*. Göttingen: Wallstein Verlag, 2000.

_____. "Rudolf Höss und die 'Endlösung der Judenfrage.'" *Werkstattgeschichte* 18 (1997): 45–57.

———. "The Concentration Camp SS as a Functional Elite." In Ulrich Herbert, ed. *National Socialist Extermination Policies: Contemporary German Perspectives and Controversies*, 306–336. New York and Oxford: Berghahn Books, 2000.

Overy, Richard. *Interrogations: The Nazi Elite in Allied Hands, 1945.* New York: Viking, 2001.

Pendas, Devin O. *The Frankfurt Auschwitz Trial, 1963–1965. Genocide, History and the Limits of the Law.* London and New York: Cambridge University Press, 2006.

Peskett, John S. "Forty Years On – Looking Back at Nuremberg." *History* 72 (February, 1987): 62–68.

Phayer, Michael. *The Catholic Church and the Holocaust, 1930–1965.* Bloomington: Indiana University Press, 2000.

———. "The German Catholic Church After the Holocaust." *Holocaust and Genocide Studies* 2:10 (Fall, 1996): 151–167.

Podgers, James. "Remembering Nuremberg." *American Bar Association Journal* 79 (October, 1993): 88–92.

Reitlinger, Gerald. *The SS. Alibi of a Nation 1922–1945.* New York: The Viking Press, 1989 <1957>.

Robinson, Jacob. "The International Military Tribunal and the Holocaust: Some Legal Reflections." *Israel Law Review* 1:7 (Winter, 1972): 1–13.

Robinson, Jacob and Henry Sachs. *The Holocaust: The Nuremberg Evidence.* Jerusalem: Yad Vashem, 1976.

Robinson, Paul H. "Causing the Conditions of One's Own Defense: A Study in the Limits of Theory in Criminal Law Doctrine." In Albin Eser and George P. Fletcher, eds. *Justification and Excuse: Comparative Perspectives,* 659–743. New York: Transnational Juris Publications, Inc., 1987.

Rossino, Alexander. *Hitler Strikes Poland: Blitzkrieg, Ideology, and Atrocity.* Lawrence: University Press of Kansas, 2003.

———. "Nazi Anti-Jewish Policy During the Polish Campaign: The Case of the Einsatzgruppe von Woyrsch." *German Studies Review* 24:1 (February, 2001): 35–54.

Rubenstein, Joshua and Ilya Altman, eds. *The Unknown Black Book: The Holocaust in the German-Occupied Soviet Territories.* Bloomington: Indiana University Press, 2008.

Rückerl, Adalbert. *The Investigation of Nazi Crimes 1945–1978: A Documentation.* Trans. Derek Rutter. Heidelberg: C. F. Müller, 1979.

———. *NS-Verbrechen vor Gericht: Versuch einer Vergangenheitsbewältigung.* Heidelberg: C. F. Miller, 1982.

Russell, Francis. *Tragedy in Dedham: The Story of the Sacco-Vanzetti Case.* New York: Harper and Row, 1971.

———. *Sacco and Vanzetti: The Case Resolved.* New York: Harper and Row, 1986.

Sacher, Abram. "The Nuremberg Trials and the Trials that Came After." *The Redemption of the Unwanted,* 115–144. New York: St. Martins' Press, 1983.

Schabas, William A. *Genocide in International Law: The Crimes of Crimes.* Cambridge: Cambridge University Press, 2000.

Schulzinger, Robert D. *American Diplomacy in the Twentieth Century.* 2nd edition. New York: Oxford University Press, 1990 <1984>.

Schwartz, Thomas Alan. *America's Germany: John J. McCloy and the Federal Republic of Germany*. Cambridge: Harvard University Press, 1991.

———. "John J. McCloy and the Landsberg Cases." In *American Policy and the Reconstruction of West Germany, 1945–1955*, 433–455. Washington: Cambridge University Press, 1995.

———. "Reeducation and Democracy: The Policies of the United States High Commission in Germany." In *America and the Shaping of German Society, 1945–1955*, 443–454. Oxford: Berg Publishers, 1993.

Sereny, Gitta. *Albert Speer: His Battle with Truth*. New York: Vintage Books, 1995.

Smith, Arthur. "Life in Wartime Germany. Colonel Ohlendorf's Opinion Service." *The Public Opinion Quarterly* 36 (Spring, 1972): 7–23.

Smith, Bradley. *Reaching Judgment at Nuremberg*. New York: Basic Books, 1977.

———. *The Road to Nuremberg*. New York: Basic Books, 1981.

Smith, Jean Edward. *Lucius D. Clay: An American Life*. New York: Henry Holt and Company, 1990.

Sydnor, Jr., Charles W. "On the Historiography of the SS." *Simon Wiesenthal Center Annual* 6 (1989): 249–262.

Sowade, Hanno. "Otto Ohlendorf: Non-Conformist, SS leader, and Economic Functionary." In Ronald Smelser and Rainer Zitelmann, eds. *The Nazi Elite*, 155–164. New York: New York University Press, 1993.

Spector, Steven B. "Judicial Activism in Prose: A Librarian's Guide to the opinions of Justice M.A. Musmanno." *Law Library Journal* 86 (Spring 1994): 311–321.

Spotts, Frederic. *The Churches and Politics in Postwar Germany*. Middleton: Weslyn University Press, 1973.

Stachura, Peter D. "Who Were the Nazis? A Socio-Political Analysis of the National Socialist Machtübernahme." *European Studies Review* 11 (1981): 293–324.

Stark, Jared. "The Task of Testimony: On 'No Common Place': The Holocaust Testimony of Alina Bacall-Zwirn." *History and Memory* (1999): 37–61.

Steigmann-Gall, Richard. *The Holy Reich. Nazi Conceptions of Christianity, 1919–1945*. New York: Cambridge University Press, 2003.

Stokes, Lawrence. "Otto Ohlendorf, the Sicherheitsdienst and Public Opinion in Nazi Germany." In George L. Mosse, ed. *Police Forces in History*, 231–261. Beverly Hills: Sage Publications, 1977.

Stollhof, Alexander, "SS-Gruppenführer und Generalleutnant der Polizei Otto Ohlendorf – eine biographische Skizze." Unpublished Ph.D. dissertation: University of Vienna, 1993.

Straub, Ervin. *The Roots of Evil*. New York: Cambridge University Press, 1989.

Streim, Alfred. *Die Behandlung Sowjetischer Kriegsgefangener im "Fall Barbarossa": Eine Dokumentation*. Heidelberg: C.F. Müller, 1981.

———. "Zur Eröffnung des allgemeinen Judenvernichtungsbefehls gegenüber den Einsatzgruppen." In Eberhard Jäckel and Jürgen Rohwer, eds. *Der Mord an den Juden im zweiten Weltkrieg: Entschlussbildung und Verwirklichung*, 107–119. Stuttgart: Deutsche Verlags-Anstalt, 1985.

———. "Zum Beispiel: Die Verbrechen der Einsatzgruppen in der Sowjetunion." In Adalbert Rückerl, ed. *NS-Prozesse Nach 25 Jahren Strafverfolgung: Möglichkeiten-Grenzen-Ergebnisse*, 65–106. Karlsruhe: C. F. Müller, 1971.

———. "The Tasks of the Einsatzgruppen." *Simon Wiesenthal Center Annual* 4 (1987): 309–328.

Streim, Alfred and Helmut Krausnick. "Helmut Krausnick to Alfred Streim and Alfred Streim Replies to Helmut Krausnick." *Simon Wiesenthal Center Annual* 6 (1989): 311–347.

Steiner, John M. "The SS Yesterday and Today: A Sociopsychological View." In Joel E. Dimsdale, ed. *Survivors, Victims and Perpetrators: Essays on the Nazi Holocaust*, 405–442. Washington: Hemisphere Publishing, 1980.

Streit, Christian. *Keine Kameraden. Die Wehrmacht und die sowjetischen Kriegsgefangenen, 1941–1945*. Bonn: Verlag J.H.W. Dietz, 1991 <1978>.

———. "*Wehrmacht, Einsatzgruppen*, Soviet POWs and Anti-Bolshevism in the Emergence of the Final Solution." In David Cesarani, ed. *The Final Solution: Origins and Implementation*, 103–118. New York: Routledge, 1996 <1994>.

Sydnor, Charles W. Jr. "On the Historiography of the SS." *Simon Wiesenthal Center Annual* 6 (1989): 249–262.

Trankell, Arne. *Reliability of Witness Evidence: Methods for Analysing and Assessing Witness Statements*. Stockholm: Rotobeckman AB, 1972.

Tusa, Ann and John Tusa. *The Nuremberg Trial*. New York: Atheneum, 1983.

Überschar, Gerd R., ed. *Der Nationalsozialismus vor Gericht: die alliierten Prozesse gegen Kriegsverbrecher und Soldaten*. Frankfurt: Peter Lang, 1999.

Vollnhals, Clemens. *Evangelische Kirche und Entnazifizierung 1945–1949. Die Last der nationalsozialistischen Vergangenheit*. Munich: R. Oldenbourg, 1989.

Waite, Robert G.L. *Vanguard of Nazism: The Free Corps Movement in Postwar Germany 1918–1923*. Cambridge: Harvard University Press, 1952.

Waller, James. Becoming Evil. *How Ordinary People Commit Genocide and Mass Killing*. 2nd Edition. New York: Oxford University Press, 2007.

———. "Perpetrators of the Holocaust: Divided and Unitary Self Conceptions of Evildoing." *Holocaust and Genocide Studies* 1:10 (Spring, 1996): 11–33.

Wechsler, Herbert. "The Issues of the Nuremberg Trial." *Principles, Politics, and Fundamental Law*. Cambridge: Harvard University Press, 1961.

Weindling, Paul. *Nazi Medicine and the Nuremberg Trials: From Medical War Crimes to Informed Consent*. New York: Palgrave MacMillan, 2004.

———. "From International to Zonal Trials: The Origins of the Nuremberg Medical Trial." *Holocaust and Genocide Studies* 3:14 (Winter, 2000): 367–389.

Wieviorka, Annette. *The Era of the Witness*. Translated from the French by Jaret Stark. Ithaca and London: Cornell University Press, 2006.

West, Rebecca. *A Train of Powder*. New York: Viking Press, 1965.

Westermann, Edward R. *Hitler's Police Battalions. Enforcing Racial War in the East*. Lawrence: University Press of Kansas, 2005.

———. "'Ordinary Men' or 'Ideological Soldiers'? Police Battalion 310 in Russia, 1942." *German Studies Review* 1:21 (February, 1998): 41–68.

Wildt, Michael. *Generation des Unbedingten. Das Führungskorps des Reichssicherheitshauptamtes*. Hamburg: Hamburger Edition HIS Verlagsges mbH, 2003.

———. "The Spirit of the Reich Security Main Office (RSHA)." *Totalitarian Movements and Political Religions* 6:3 (December, 2005): 333–349.

———, ed. *Nachrichtendienst, Politische Elite und Mordeinheit: Der Sicherheitsdienst des des Reichsführers SS*. Hamburg: Hamburger Edition, 2003.

_____. "Differierende Wahrheiten. Historiker und Staatsanwälte als Ermittler von NS-Verbrechen." In Norbert Frei, Dirk van Laak and Michael Stolleis, eds. *Geschichte vor Gericht. Historiker, Richter und die Suche nach Gerechtigkeit,* 46–59. München: Verlag C.H. Beck, 2000.

Willis, James F. *Prologue to Nuremberg: The Politics and Diplomacy of Punishing War Criminals of the First World War.* Westport: Greenwood Press, 1986.

Wittmann, Rebecca. *Beyond Justice: The Auschwitz Trial.* Cambridge, MA: Harvard University Press, 2005.

Woetzel, Robert K. *The Nuremberg Trials in International Law.* New York: Praeger, 1960.

Wohl, Robert. *The Generation of 1914.* Cambridge: Harvard University Press, 1979.

Wolfe, Robert, ed. *Americans As Proconsuls United States Military Government in Germany and Japan, 1944–1952.* Carbondale, IL: Southern Illinois University Press, 1984.

_____. "Putative Threat to National Security as a Nuremberg Defense for Genocide." *Annals of the American Academy of Political and Social Science* 450 (1980): 46–67.

_____. "Flaws in the Nuremberg Legacy: An Impediment to International War Crimes Tribunals' Prosecution of Crimes against Humanity." *Holocaust and Genocide Studies* 3:12 (Winter, 1998): 434–453.

Wright, Quincy. "The Law of the Nuremberg Trial." *American Journal of International Law* 41 (1947): 38–72.

_____. "War Criminals." *American Journal of International Law* 39 (1945): 257–285.

Zeck, William Alan. "Nuremberg: Proceedings Subsequent to Goering et al." *North Carolina Law Review* 26 (1948): 350–389.

Ziegler, Herbert. *Nazi Germany's New Aristocracy. The SS Leadership 1925–1939.* Princeton: Princeton University Press, 1989.

Ziller, Eric A., Harrower, Molly, Ritzler, Barry A., Archer, Robert P. *The Quest for the Nazi Personality. A Psychological Investigation of Nazi War Criminals.* Hillsdale, NJ: Lawrence Erlbaum Associates, 1995.

Zukier, Henri. "The 'Mindless Years'? A Reconsideration of the Psychological Dimensions of the Holocaust, 1938–1945." *Holocaust and Genocide Studies* 2:11 (Fall 1997): 190–212.

Index

Made in the USA
Middletown, DE
26 June 2015